Wordpress for Beginners & SEO

Learn to create Wordpress sites from scratch, and master the art of Wordpress SEO.

DISCLAIMER AND TERMS OF USE AGREEMENT

Contents

Book 1 :: Wordpress for Beginners

Book 2 :: Wordpress SEO

WordPress for Beginners

A Visual Step-by-Step Guide to Creating your
Own WordPress Site in Record Time, Starting from Zero!

Dr. Andy Williams

http://ezseonews.com

Updated 12th May 2014

What people are saying about this book:

"I work in the education department at one of the top academic institutions in the U.S. and if I could hire Dr. Williams to write all of my online training, I wouldn't hesitate." **Laura**

"Another fine book from Dr. Andy. " **Mr. Bearly**

"Wow! I am not new to WordPress but I love this book." **Albert J**

"Fantastic WordPress Guide! I highly recommend this guide to anyone - new or experienced - because he points out the little things that make a WordPress site fun and rewarding!" **Dawn Carter**

"This screenshot-based book makes it drop-dead simple to create a site. Screenshots allow you to make sure your screen looks like the one in the book." **James E. Hunter**

"I've only gotten partway through this book and had to stop to say how impressed I am! If I had this a few weeks ago I'm sure I would have had my site up & running by now. I love how Mr. Williams uses screen shots and guides you through the process step by step. His explanations are easy to understand & his instructions are easy to follow. I can't believe how much more I understand about WordPress & setting up a site now than I did just a few hours ago. I would highly recommend this book to anyone whose using WordPress for the first time (or even the second, third or fourth time!!). It will save you hours of time and frustration and make the whole process so much easier." **gail87821**

"Another Masterpiece from Doc Andy!" **David Harvey**

"..Then I found WordPress for Beginners and WOW - my progress took off. Having a visual guide with extensive photos really helps those of us who are visual learners. But the best thing to me is that Williams not only describes what to do and how to do it, he explains why you should do it. I'm not a professional tech person and this book is

exactly what I needed. I suspect I will continue to refer to it in the future. Highly recommended." **SamanthaSSJ**

"If you want to have a website but don't know how, this book by Dr. Andy Williams will take you by the hand and walk you through the process of setting up your own blog correctly. He tells you not only exactly how to do it, but also explains the why you are taking the steps he walks you through. The instructions and visuals are clear and easy for anyone to follow." **J. Tanner**

"Dr. Andy Williams released another winner friends! Knowing Andy is a trusted teacher and internet expert I jumped on the opportunity to learn, study and apply WordPress for Beginners. It amazes me how much hype, bogus information and garbage there is on the market today about WordPress - but where do you go to get the real deal? This is exactly what you get with Andy's work - the real deal." **Chris Cobb**

Who am I & why should you listen to me?

My name is Andy Williams and I am a teacher. In 2001 I gave up teaching in schools where I had been a Science teacher working with students from 11 to 18 years of age. I needed a new challenge and most of all I wanted to spend more time with my family.

Since then my work (and my hobby), has been to study the search engines and build websites for profit. It's been a long journey and a large number of people have followed me on that passage by reading my free weekly newsletter published over at ezSEONews.com. My newsletter has covered a wide range of topics relevant to webmasters - that's people who own and build their own website(s). If you are interested, you can sign up to receive my free newsletter too.

In the early days, websites were hand-built using a code called Hyper Text Markup Language, or HTML for short. To create good-looking websites you needed to be something of a geek. Tools like Macromedia Dreamweaver (now owned by Adobe), and Microsoft Front Page (discontinued in 2006), were developed to reduce the coding learning curve associated with building a website in HTML, but these tools were expensive.

Then in May 2003, Matt Mullenweg & Mike Little, released a tool that would change the face of website building forever. They called it WordPress.

I have to admit to being a little reluctant to give up my copy of Dreamweaver, but in 2004 I started to experiment with the WordPress platform. At that time, WordPress was just starting to get interesting with the introduction of "plugins". Don't worry, we'll look at those later in the book, but for now just understand that plugins are an easy and pain-free ways of adding great new functionality to your website.

Fast-forward to today and WordPress is now the site-building tool of choice for many professionals and enthusiasts alike. For example; home businesses run by moms & dads, school kids running blogs about their favorite bands, large corporations, and everyone in between, have all turned to WordPress. It's extremely powerful, flexible, produces very professional looking websites or blogs, is relatively easy to use, and perhaps best of all, it's totally free.

Sure, there is a learning curve, but that is where I come in.

With years of experience teaching technical stuff in an easy to understand manner, I am going to take you by the hand and guide you as you construct your very own professional looking website or blog, even if you know absolutely nothing about how to go about this. The only thing you need to know is how to use a web browser. So if you have ever searched Google for something, then you already have the skills necessary to follow this book.

I have made this book a step-by-step, visual guide to creating your website. Just follow along with the exercises, and in no time at all you'll be using WordPress like a pro as you build a website you can be proud to show your family and friends. In fact, they will probably start asking YOU to help them build their own projects.

Excited?

OK, let's get on with it.

How to Use this Book

I have written this book as a hands-on tutorial. To get the most out of it, I recommend that you sit at your computer, following the steps outlined in its pages. Whenever I do something on my demo site, you then do it on your own site. Don't be afraid of making mistakes; just have fun and experiment with WordPress. Mistakes can easily be undone or deleted, and anyway, most of us learn better by making a few blunders along the way.

By the end of this book you will have a solid understanding of how WordPress works and how you can get it to do what YOU want it to do. If you then decide to take your WordPress knowledge to the next level, you'll have an excellent foundation from which to build upon.

What is WordPress?

WordPress is a Content Management System (CMS). That just means it is a piece of software that can help you manage and organize your content into an impressive and coherent website.

Initially WordPress was created as a blogging tool, but over the years it has become so much more than that. Today, many WordPress driven sites look nothing like blogs (unless that's what the user wants). This is down to the flexibility of this amazing tool.

WordPress powers simple blogs, corporate websites and everything in between. Companies like Sony, the Wall Street Journal, Samsung, New York Times, Wired, CNN, Forbes, Reuters and many others, all use WordPress as part of their online presence.

WordPress is 'open source', meaning that all of its code is free to use and customize. This is one of the powers of WordPress, since programmers the world over have created their own additions to this powerful publishing platform; from website templates to plugins that extend the functionality of this amazing site building tool.

Some of the features that make WordPress great

• Template system for site design means that changing the look and feel of your site is as simple as installing a new theme. There's a plethora of free and quality WordPress themes available.

• Plugins are pieces of code that you can download into your WordPress site to add new features and functions. There are literally thousands of plugins available and many are totally free.

• Once it is set up, you can concentrate on adding great content to your site. You simply type it into a text editor within the WordPress Dashboard, hit publish, and WordPress takes care of the rest.

• WordPress also has a feature called Widgets that allows the user to drag and drop "features" and place them in, for example, the sidebar. You may have a widget that allows you to display a poll to your visitors – for example. You can place that poll in the sidebar of your site by dragging the poll widget to the appropriate place. Widgets are typically used in the sidebars, but some templates allow widgets to be placed in the site footer as well as on the homepage. We will look at widgets in much more detail later on in this book.

• WordPress can help you with the SEO (Search Engine Optimization), of your site, so that it has the potential to rank better in search engines like Google and BING.

WordPress.com v WordPress.org

There are actually two "flavours" of WordPress. Firstly there is WordPress from WordPress.com. The second one is WordPress from WordPress.org.

It is vital that you understand the difference between these two.

WordPress.com

WordPress.com allows anyone to sign up for a free WordPress site that WordPress will host on *their* servers. All you need to provide is the content for the site.

Example: Say you wanted to create a website on "educational toys for kids". You could set up a website called educationaltoysforkids.wordpress.com (assuming no one else has taken that address (name), already).

Your website address (URL) would be:

educationaltoysforkids.wordpress.com

.. and by visiting that address in your web browser, you'd see the homepage of your site.

What you actually have is a sub-domain on the wordpress.com domain.

The problem with this is that you do not own the site, Wordpress.com do. One day you might go to look at your site and find that it's no longer there.

There is also a number of restrictions onWordPress.com. For example, there are some plugins you won't be able to install and you'll also have a limited choice of themes/templates.

For these reasons, I do not recommend you create your site on WordPress.com. This book will assume you are going to use the other WordPress - the one from WordPress.org.

WordPress.org

WordPress.org is a site where you can download your own copy of WordPress for free. You can then upload that copy of WordPress to any web server you like and start building a site that YOU own. You will also be able to choose whatever domain name you like, so you could call your site educationaltoysforkids.com (if it's available). Doesn't that look more professional than the options on WordPress.com?

Think of the difference between WordPress.com and WordPress.org as being similar to renting or owning a house. When you rent a house, there are limits to what you can do to it. You can be thrown out at any time. When you own the building outright, you can do whatever you want with it and no one can tell you how to design, decorate, or renovate *your* home.

The only disadvantages of using WordPress from WordPress.com are the costs involved. These costs are minimal though, so let's look at them now.

The costs of owning your own site

So how much is a website going to cost you? As you build your site there will be optional costs - things like a website theme, autoresponder or mailing list, but these are totally optional since most things can be done for free. However, there are two costs that you cannot avoid.

The website domain

The website domain is your site's address on the internet. **Google.com** is the website domain of our favourite search engine. **CNN.com** is the domain of a popular international news service.

You will need to buy a domain for your website. We'll look at this later, but for now, let's just consider the price. Typically a domain name will cost around $10 per year. You can sometimes get the first year for free when you buy web hosting, but once that first year is up, you'll be paying the $10 per year to keep your domain name live.

Your domain name will be registered with a company called a registrar. It is this registrar that will collect the $10 payment every year. The registrar can actually be the same company that you use for your web hosting, or a different company. We'll look at the pros and cons of both options.

Website hosting

Your website needs to be on a computer somewhere that is attached to the internet 24/7 so that people can find it. We call these computers "web servers" and companies that lease, rent or buy them are called web hosts. Their job is to make sure the servers are up, running, and well maintained at all times. You therefore need to rent some disk space on one of these servers to hold your website. We rent server space from a web hosting company. This is a monthly fee of around $5 per month (although it does vary greatly between web hosts).

As mentioned earlier, some web hosts offer a free domain name (for the first year). They can offer a free domain name because you are paying them a monthly fee for the web hosting; therefore they get their investment back over time. In order to take advantage of the free domain offers, you will need to use your web host as the registrar for your domain.

The total essential costs of running your own website are therefore around $70 per year.

Registrar & web hosts

When you sign up with a web host, you have the choice to let them be the registrar for your website as well. The advantage of this is that all payments you need to make are to the same company, meaning you only have to deal with ONE outfit.

There are disadvantages to this arrangement though, and a lot of people (including myself), prefer to keep host and registrar separate.

Potential problem: If for any reason your web host decides your website is causing them problems (i.e. they get spam complaints, or your website is using up too many system resources), they can take your site down without any warning. What happens next?

Let's look at what happens if you use your web host as registrar.

1. Your site goes down.
2. You contact your host and they tell you that they received spam complaints from your domain.
3. They refuse to put your site back up.
4. You need to move your site to a new host, but your existing host is the registrar and can make that difficult.
5. Your site remains down for a long period of time while you sort things out, and eventually move the site to a new host and registrar.

OK, let's look at what happens if your registrar is separate from your host.

1. Your site goes down.
2. You contact your host and they tell you that they received spam complaints from your domain.
3. They refuse to put your site back up.
4. You order hosting at a new host, and copy your site to the new host.
5. You login to your registrar account and change the name servers (don't worry about this, we'll look at it later), to the new host. This takes seconds to do.
6. Your site is back up within 24 hours or sooner.

This is one scenario where using a separate host and registrar is important.

Another scenario, which doesn't bear thinking about, is if your hosting company goes out of business (it does happen sometimes). So what becomes of your site? Well, you probably lose it AND your domain name if your hosting company is also your registrar.

If your registrar and host are with two separate companies, and this happened, you'd simply get hosting somewhere else and change the name servers at your registrar. With this arrangement, your site would only be down for 24 hours or less.

Another situation that I have heard about is when a hosting company locks you out of your control panel (a login area where you can administer your domain(s)), because of a dispute over something. That means you cannot possibly move the domain to a new host, because you must have access to that control panel to do it. Consequently your domain will be down for as long as the dispute takes to resolve.

A final word of caution! I have heard horror stories of people not being able to transfer their domain out from a bad webhost. Even worse than that, the domain they registered at the hosting company was not registered in their name, but in the name of the hosting company. I therefore recommend that when you are ready to buy hosting, you consider the web host and registrar that I personally use.

I also recommend that you use a separate registrar and ignore those "free for the first year" offers. However, if you just want the easy option of using one company, use the web host I recommend. I have used them for years (sometimes as a combined host and registrar on a few sites), and never had a problem.

Recommended registrars & webhosts

Since the details (prices, features, etc.), of web hosts in particular, can change so much, I have created a page on my website that list the currently recommended web hosts and registrars.

On that page you'll find out about the features and prices.

Check out my recommended web host and domain registrar:

http://ezseonews.com/dwh

While you are there, you might like to sign up for my free weekly newsletter.

Tasks to complete

1. Sign up for web hosting. If you are going to use a separate registrar, sign up for the registrar first and buy the domain name. Once that is cleared, go and sign up for web hosting and point the domain at your new web server by changing the DNS. Instructions to do this are given on the webpage I mentioned above.

Installing WordPress

For this, you need to login to the cPanel of your hosting. The URL, username and password were all in the welcome email the host sent you when you signed up.

Once you are logged in, scroll down to the **Software/Services** section, and click on **Softaculous**.

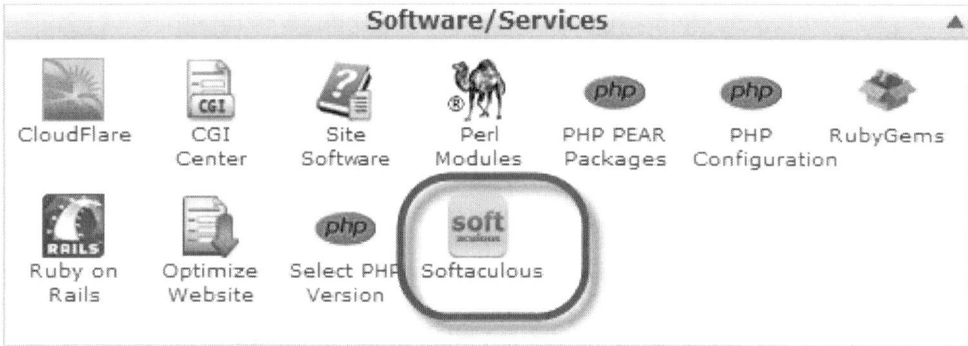

On the next screen, you'll see a box containing the Wordpress logo. Move your mouse over it, and an **Install** button will appear:

Click the **Install** button.

At the top of the next screen, you'll see this:

In the **"Choose Domain"** box, select your domain.

In the **"In Directory"** box, delete the pre-filled value, leaving this empty.

Under "**Database Name**", you can leave this as the default value. I personally change it a little, so I know which database in my account belongs to which website, but that is because I have a number of sites in my hosting package.

Next we have these settings:

You can leave the table prefix as it is. I always change mine, just to make it more difficult for hackers that might be trying to hack my site. wp_ is the default value, and hackers know this. If you want, change it to a different 2 or 3 letters, followed by an underscore.

Enter a name & description for your site. You can change these later, so don't worry too much about it.

Leave Enable Multisite (WPMU) unchecked.

Next we have the Admin account settings:

Don't use admin as your username. Again, this is the default and makes it easier for hackers. Change your admin username to something else. Also add a strong password. This username and password combination will be used to login to your Wordpress Dashboard, so make a note of what you enter here. The "Admin email" box will set the admin email in your Wordpress dashboard, and this will be used to notify you of events, like people leaving comments. This can be changed later.

By default, the language will be set to English, but change this if you need to.

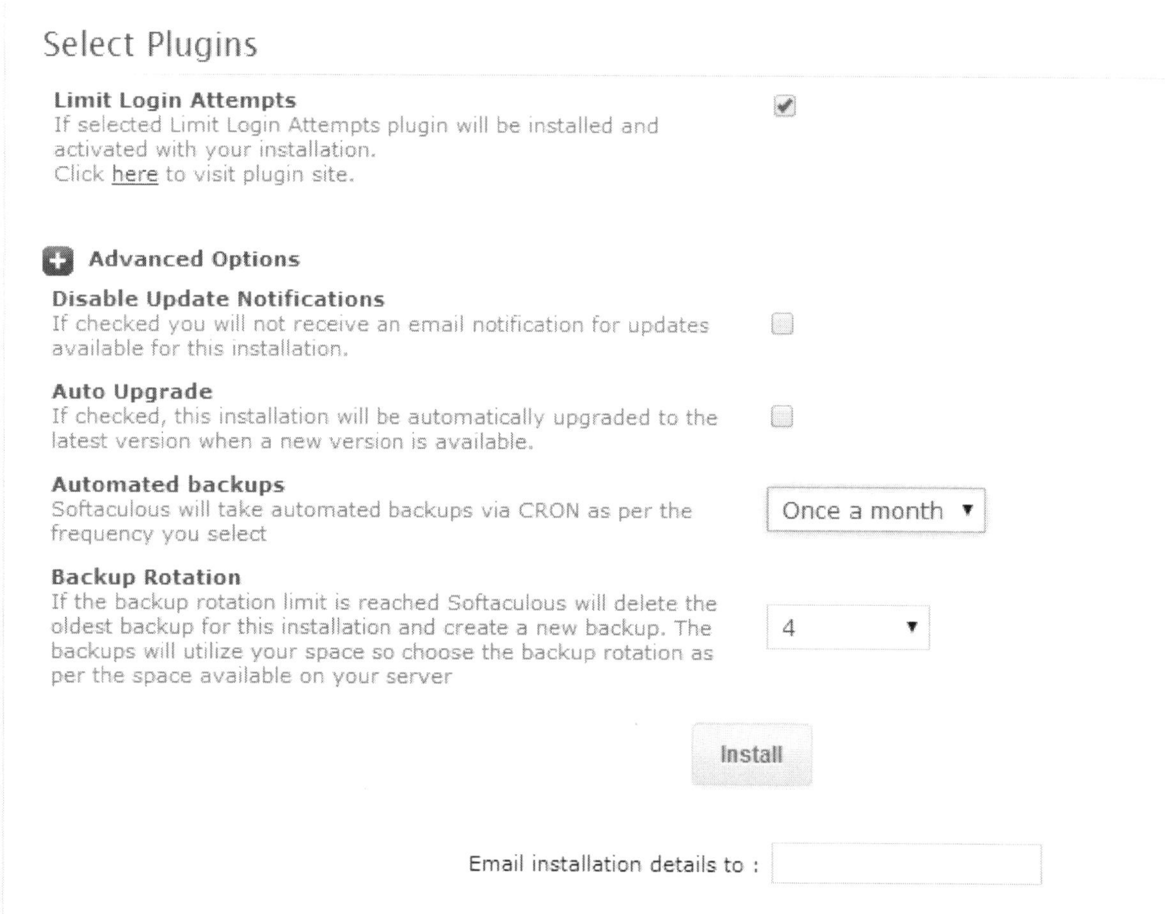

Check the box next to **"Limit Login Attempts"**. This is another layer of protection against hackers.

Under the "**Advanced Options**", select "**Once a Month**" for automated backups (or more frequently if you will be adding content on a daily basis).

The "Backup Rotation" is the number of backups the host will keep for you. Once that number of backups has been created, the oldest will be deleted to make room for the new backup. On a monthly backup schedule, 4 is about right. If you are backing up more frequently, choose a larger number of backups.

Finally, enter your email address at the bottom before clicking the install button. You Wordpress login details will be emailed to you at this address when Wordpress is installed.

OK, once the installation has finished, you'll be shown something like this:

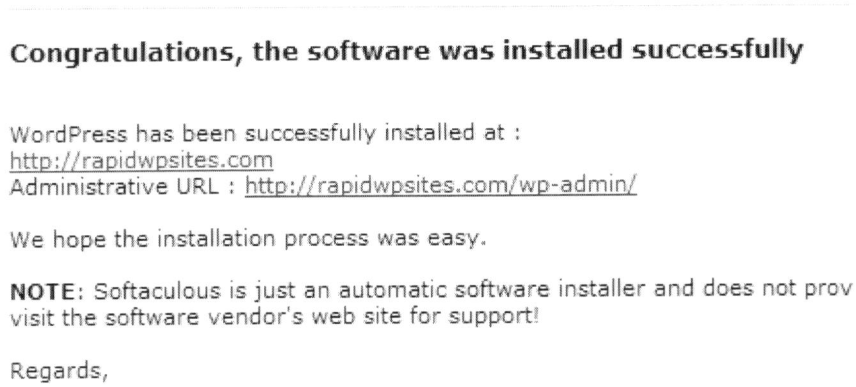

Congratulations, the software was installed successfully

WordPress has been successfully installed at :
http://rapidwpsites.com
Administrative URL : http://rapidwpsites.com/wp-admin/

We hope the installation process was easy.

NOTE: Softaculous is just an automatic software installer and does not prov
visit the software vendor's web site for support!

Regards,

The first link will load your website (currently a skeleton site created by Wordpress). Here is mine:

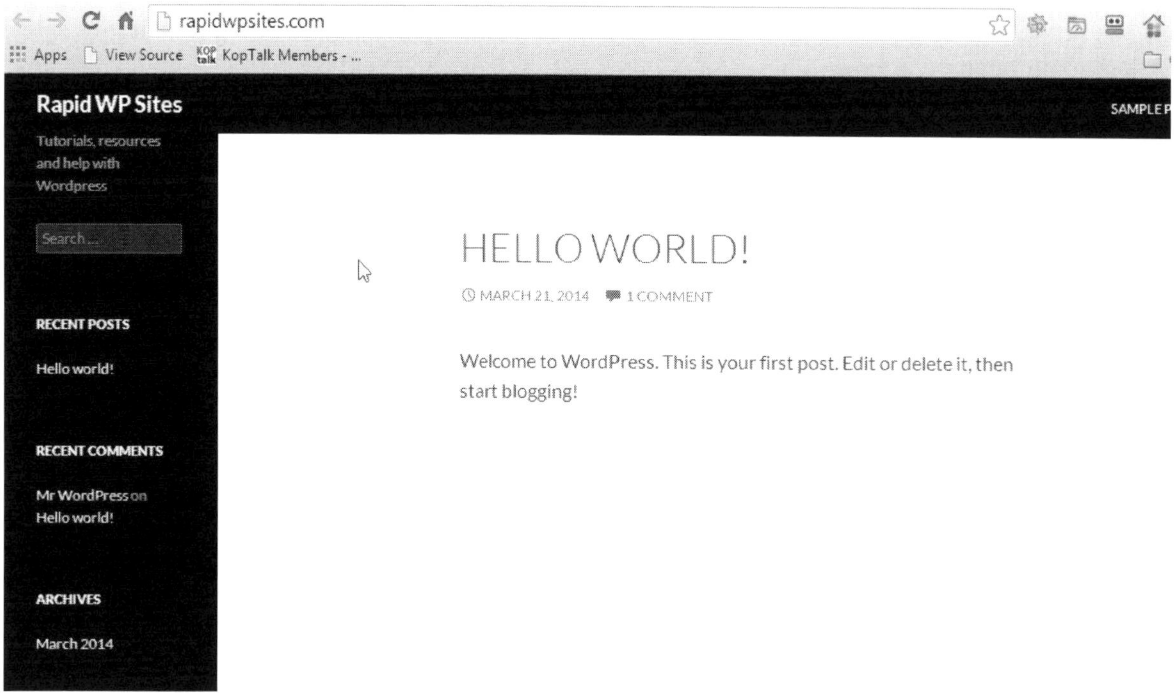

Yours will probably look very similar.

The second URL listed is the Administrative URL. You can click that link to login to the Wordpress Dashboard for your site. The username and password are those that you used when filling in the Admin Details a few minutes ago.

Go check out your site

Go and look at your website in a web browser by typing in the domain URL into the address bar.

You should see your WordPress site up and running. Of course, it won't have any of your content yet and it does come pre-installed with a few pages you'll need to delete, but you should see the homepage displaying a "Hello World!" post.

Before we start learning how to configure the site, let's just login, and then logout again, so we know how.

You should have made a note of the login URL, but if not, just add **/wp-login.php** to the end of your domain name (you can also access the site by adding **/wp-admin** to the end of the URL), e.g.

http://mydomain.com/wp-login.php

or

http://mydomain.com/wp-admin

You'll be taken to the login screen:

Enter the username and password you chose when you were installing WordPress then click the "Log In" button.

I also recommend you check the "Remember Me" box so that your username and password will be automatically entered next time you come to login to your Dashboard.

NOTE: If you ever forget your password, you can click the link under the login boxes to get the password resent to your admin email address (that's the one you entered when installing WordPress).

After logging in, you will now find yourself inside your Dashboard. You can have a look around but don't go changing anything just yet. Don't worry if it looks a little daunting in there. We'll take a tour of the Dashboard and I'll show you step-by-step, with screenshots, how to set it all up so you can have a great looking website.

NOTE: You will more than likely have notifications that there are some plugins (and even WordPress itself), that need updating. We'll do that in a moment. For now, let's log out so you are clear on how to do that.

Move your mouse over the top right where it says “Howdy Yourname”. A menu will appear:

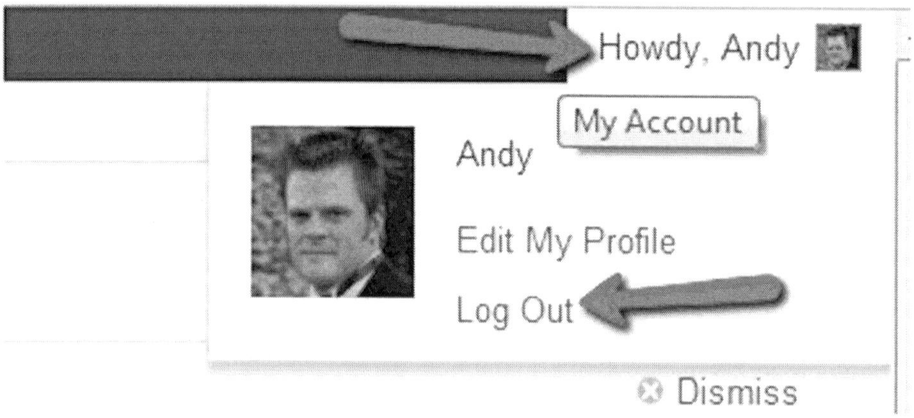

Click the “Log Out” link and you’ll be logged out and taken back to the login screen.

Great, WordPress is installed and you now know how to login and logout of your Dashboard.

In the next section we’ll take a tour of the Dashboard so you can get your bearings.

Tasks to complete

1. Install WordPress.
2. Login, have a quick look around the Dashboard, then logout again.

Installing the Twenty Eleven Theme

Every year or so, Wordpress releases a new default theme. Currently that theme is Twenty Fourteen. However, to get you up and running, I am going to stick to Twenty Eleven in this book. Although it is a few years old, it is easy to handle and ideal for Wordpress beginners. Once you have gone through this book, working with Twenty Eleven, you can switch your site over to the latest default Wordpress template (or any other template you want to use), and start having fun making your site look the way YOU want it to look.

Chances are, you won't have Twenty Eleven installed in your Wordpress Dashboard, so that is the first thing we are going to do.

Before you do though, go and look at your site homepage. Once we have installed and activated the Twenty Eleven theme, the appearance will change. You are about to see how easy it is to change the look and feel of your site, just by installing a new theme.

First thing to do is click on the **Themes** menu inside the **Appearance** menu:

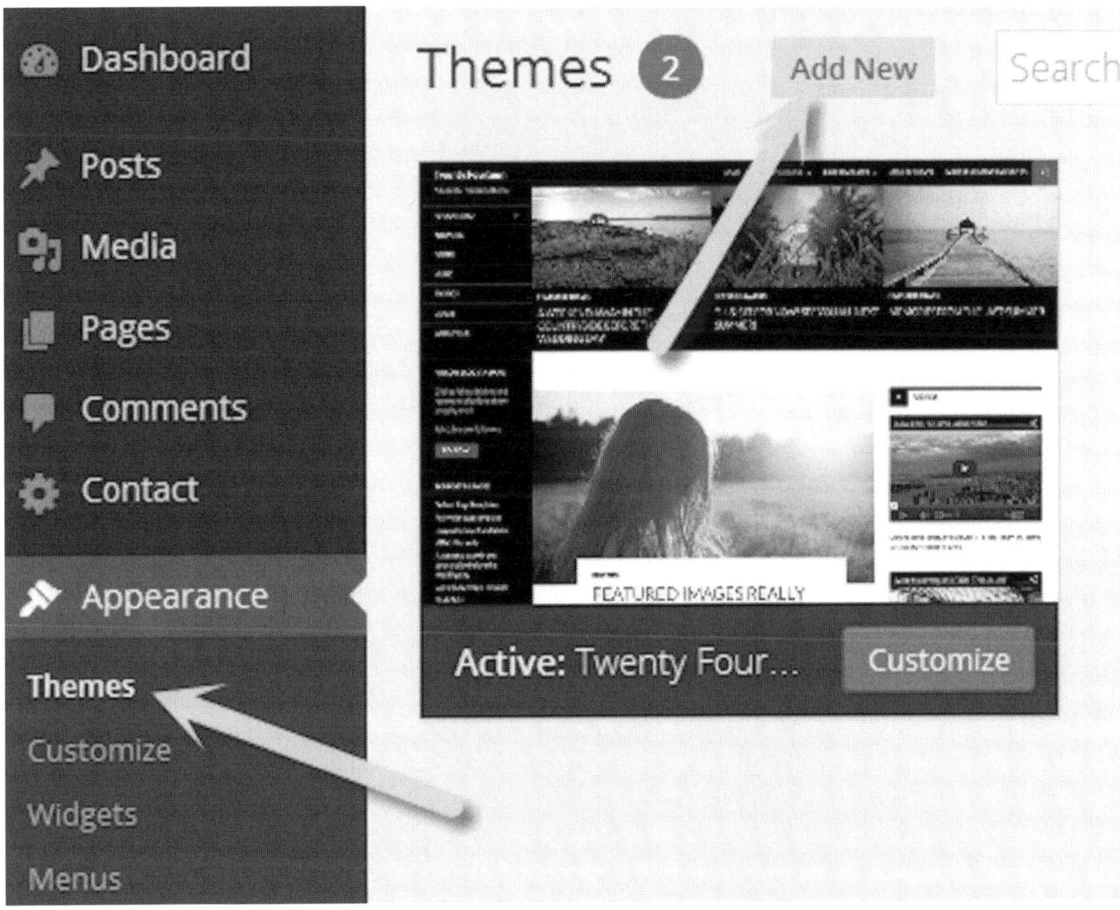

You will see an **Add New** button at the top. Click it.

You can now enter the theme name into the search box, and click the Search button. Search for **Twenty Eleven**.

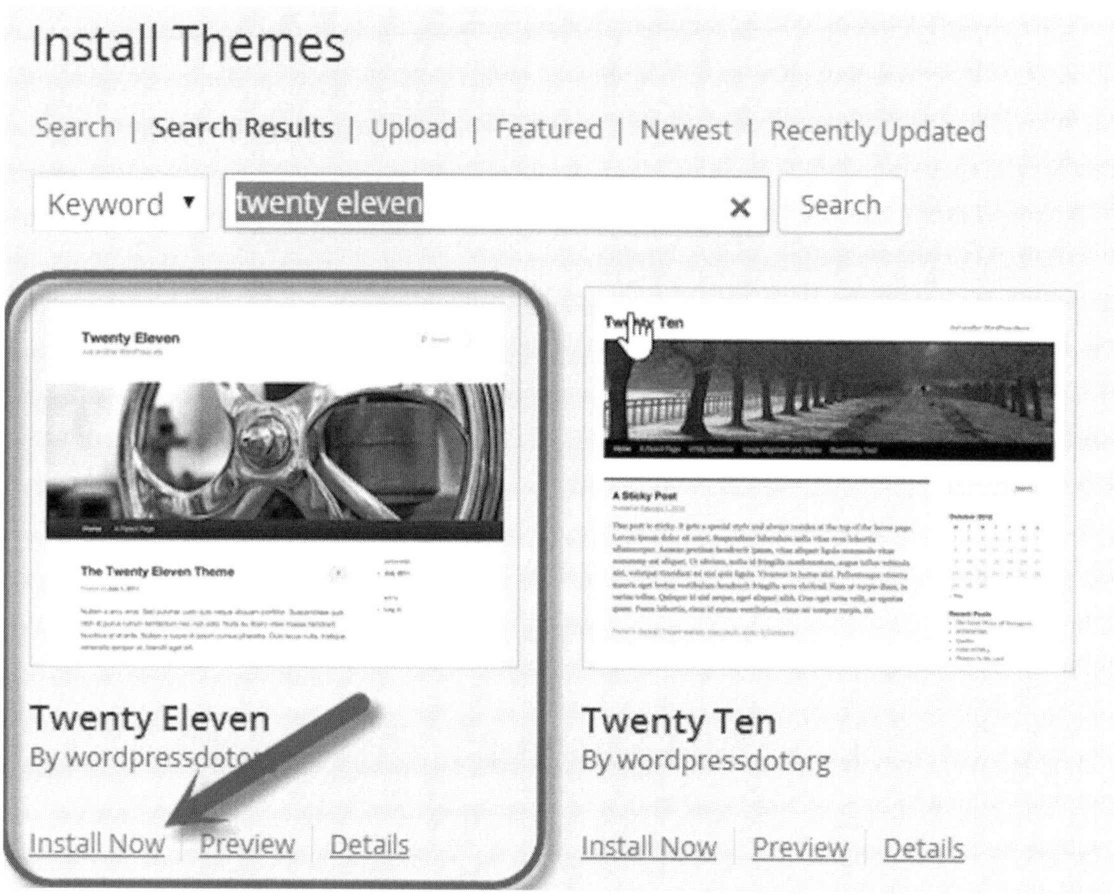

You will see the Twenty Eleven theme in the search results. Click the **Install Now** link.

The theme will install. Once done, there will be a link to **Activate** the theme. Click the activate link.

If you now visit your site homepage, you will see the Twenty Eleven theme installed on your site.

That is how easy it is to change the look and feel of your site. OK, now the theme is installed, let's get on.

An overview of the Dashboard

When you login to WordPress, you are presented with the Dashboard. This is what it looks like:

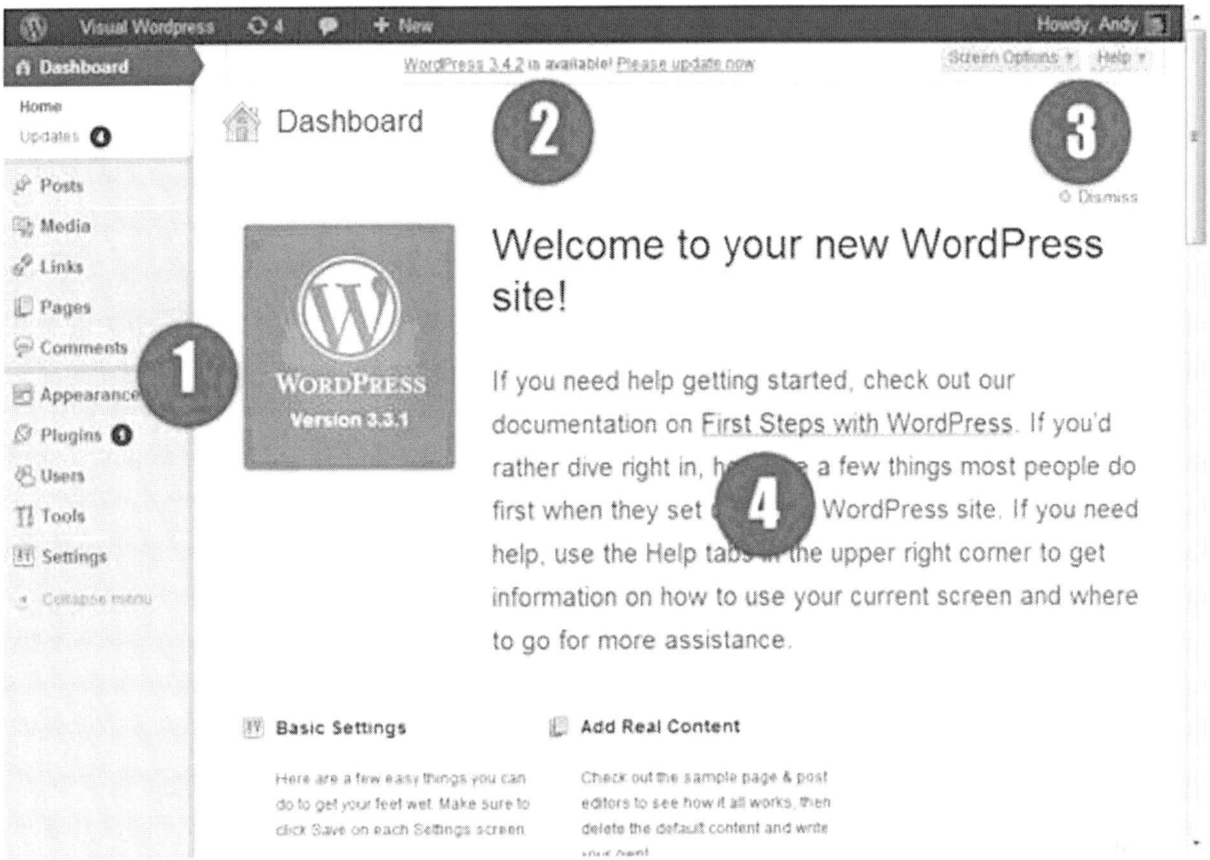

1. The Sidebar
2. Update Notification
3. Screen Options, Help, Profile & Logout
4. The Main screen

Let's look at each of these in turn.

The sidebar

The sidebar is the main navigation system of your Dashboard. From the sidebar, you can set up your website to look and behave as you want it to. This is where you can add/edit content on your site, upload images, moderate comments, change your site theme, add/remove plugins, and everything else you will need to do as a website owner. We'll look at all of these features in detail later in the tutorial.

Update notification

Occasionally you'll see a notification in this area to tell you that there is an update to WordPress. Whenever you see an update notification, it is a good idea to update your installation (we'll see how to do that later). This will ensure your site has the latest bug fixes and enhancements that the new version of WordPress brings. Be aware that hackers can take advantage of vulnerabilities in the WordPress security, and as WordPress finds out about these vulnerabilities, they fix them and release an update. Therefore, always update whenever you see the notification.

Screen options, help, profile & logout

Screen Options is a drop down menu that allows you decide what is shown on the various screens within the Dashboard. If you click the Screen Options link you'll see something like this:

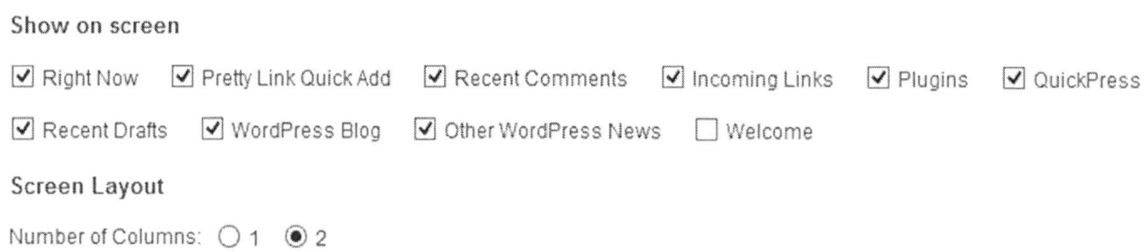

What you see will depend on where you are in the dashboard (and what version of Wordpress you are using), because the options that are shown are relevant to the current page you are viewing. For example, if you are in section for moderating comments, the screen options you will see will be relevant to commenting.

By checking the boxes in the screen options, you display those sections on the page. If you don't want to see something you simply uncheck it. For example, to hide "WordPress News",

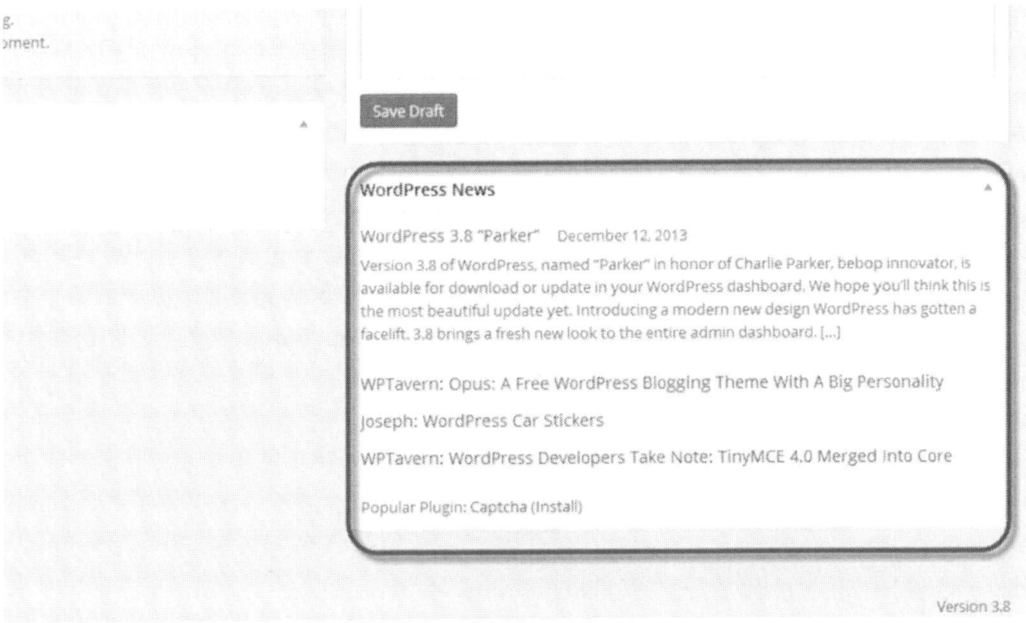

just uncheck it in the Screen Options, and that section of the page will disappear.

If you find that something is missing from the screen in a certain part of the dashboard, go in and check the screen options to ensure that it's enabled. We will be popping into the screen options a few times during this book.

To the right of the Screen options button is a button to access WordPress help. Clicking it opens up a help panel:

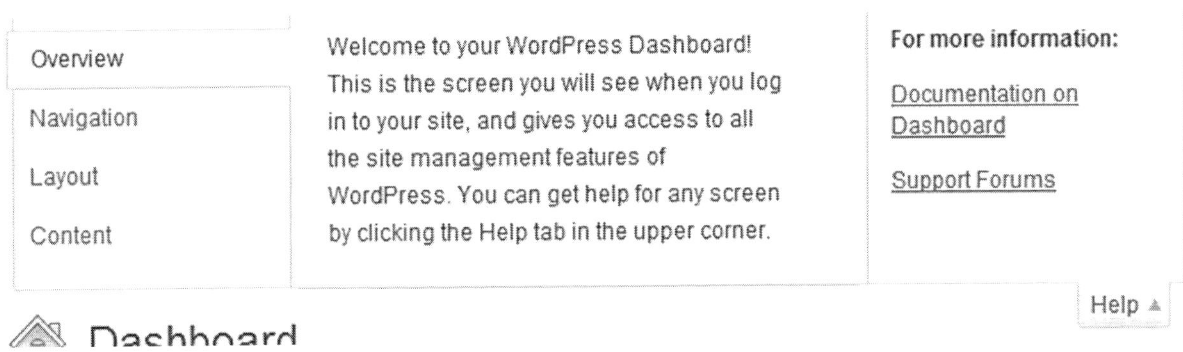

The left side of this help panel is tabbed, offering you help sections on various aspects of the Dashboard like navigation & layout. If you need more detailed help, there are links on the right side which point to the WordPress support forums and more Dashboard documentation.

Finally in this area of the Dashboard screen, if you place your mouse over the "Howdy Yourname" top right, a panel opens up:

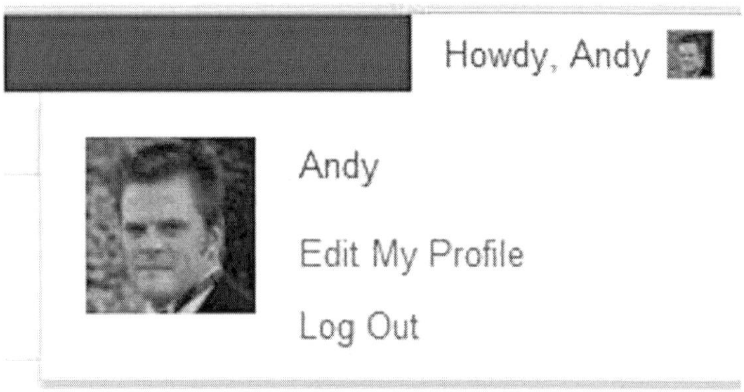

NOTE: Mine shows a photo of myself. I'll show you how & why later when we look at Gravatars in the User Profile section of the book.

This section of the Dashboard gives you a direct link to your profile (which we will fill out later), and a link to logout of your WordPress Dashboard. Whenever you finish a session in the WordPress Dashboard, it's always a good idea to log out.

The main screen

This is where all of the work takes place. What you see in the main screen area will depend on where you are in the Dashboard. For example, if you are in the comments section, the main screen area will list all the comments people have made on your site. If you are in the appearance section of your Dashboard, the main screen section will show you the theme/template of your site. If you are adding or editing a post, the main screen area will have everything you need to add/edit a post.

Tasks to complete

1. Go in and explore the Dashboard to familiarize yourself with the system.
2. Click on a few of the menu items in the left navigation column and then open the screen options to see what it contains. See how the options are related to the page you are viewing in the Dashboard?
3. Have a look at the help options - the forum and the other WordPress documentation. You won't need any of that now, but it is a good idea to be familiar with these options just in case you get stuck in the future.

Cleaning out the preinstalled stuff

When you install WordPress, it installs a few default items like the "Hello World" post you saw on the homepage earlier. In addition to that post, there is a "Sample page", a comment, and some widgets. WordPress also pre-installs a "blogroll" (which we'll discuss later), that we need to get rid of.

NOTE: WordPress allows you to create two types of content - posts and pages. Don't worry about the differences between these just yet as we'll look at them later.

OK, let's clean out the preinstalled stuff.

Deleting the "Hello World" post

This is the first thing we need to delete. If you visit your site homepage right now - before deleting it - you'll see that the "Hello World" post is displayed front and centre.

To delete the post, we need to open the "Posts" menu from the left hand sidebar navigation:

To do this you can either click the word "posts", or just hover your mouse over it. With the menu open, click the "All Posts" link.

This will open up a table of all posts on your site:

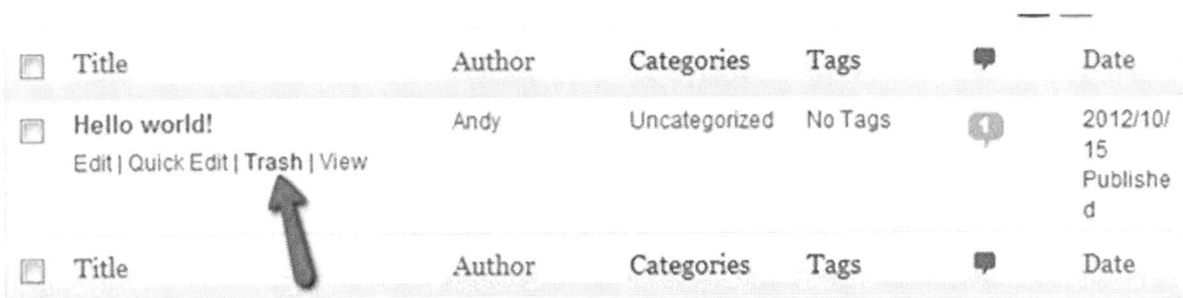

Under "Title" you'll see the "Hello World!" post. Move your mouse over the title and a menu appears underneath the title.

This menu allows you to:

1. Edit the post
2. Quick Edit - which allows you to edit title, category, etc., but not the content of the post.
3. Move the post to Trash (i.e. delete it).
4. View the post - which will open the post in the current browser window.

We want to delete the post, so click on the “Trash” link. The screen will refresh and the post will be gone.

NOTE: I am going to keep the “Hello World!” post on my site so that I can use it later in the book. If you want to keep it for now as well, you can. When you need to delete it, you know how.

If you delete a post by accident, don’t worry. At the top of the screen, you’ll see a link to the Trash.

In the screenshot above, you’ll see that there is a (1) next to the Trash link. That means there is one item in the trash. If you click on the Trash link, you’ll be taken to the trash bin where you can see all of the posts that were sent to there.

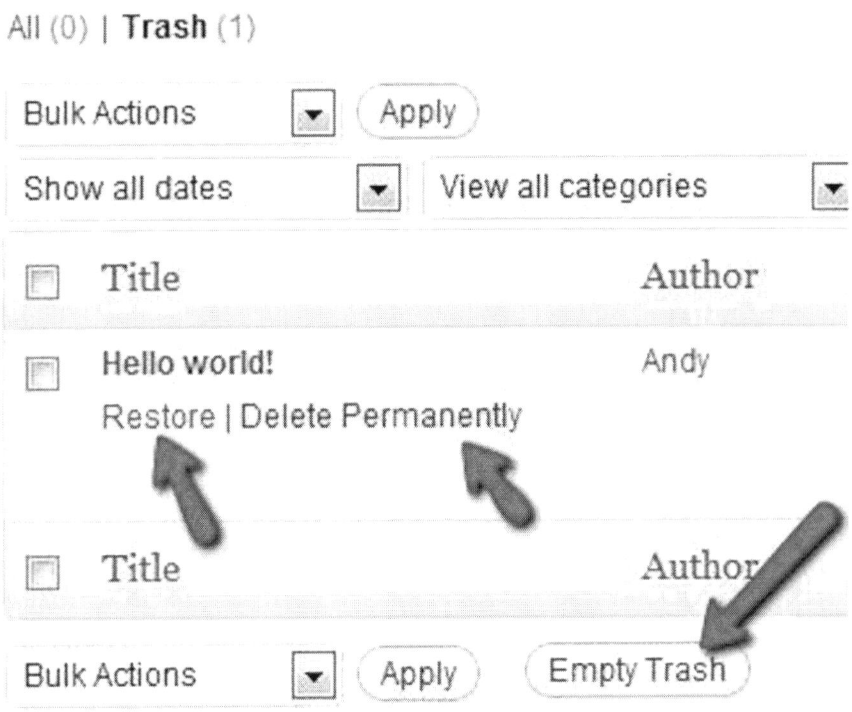

If you mouse-over the post title, you'll get another popup menu. This one allows you to restore the post (i.e. undelete it), or delete it permanently.

If you have a lot of posts in the trash and you want to delete them all, click the "Empty Trash" button at the bottom.

When WordPress created the "Hello World!" post, it also added a comment to it. When you deleted the post, the comment was also deleted because it belonged to that post.

OK, that's the Hello World post gone. Let's now get onto that sample page.

Deleting the sample page

In the sidebar navigation of your Dashboard, click on the Pages link. Again, you can click directly on the link, or mouse-over to open the menu. Click on "All Pages".

Like the posts section, this will bring up a list of all pages on the site. Mouse over the Sample page title, and click the Trash link underneath it.

Deleting the blogroll

NOTE: WordPress 3.5 removed the blogroll by default, so you won't have this section if you are using WordPress version 3.5 or above. Therefore, just skip this section.

A "blog roll" is simply a list of websites that can be displayed in the sidebar of your website. When you installed WordPress, it installed a list of sites into the blogroll.

Blogrolls have been popular in the past, with websites owners swapping links in each other's blogroll in an attempt to gain higher rankings in Google. However, Google does not look at this type of link favourably anymore, and might actually penalize you or the sites you link to, so I would recommend you do not use a blogroll at all. So let's get rid of it now.

In the sidebar navigation menu, click on Links:

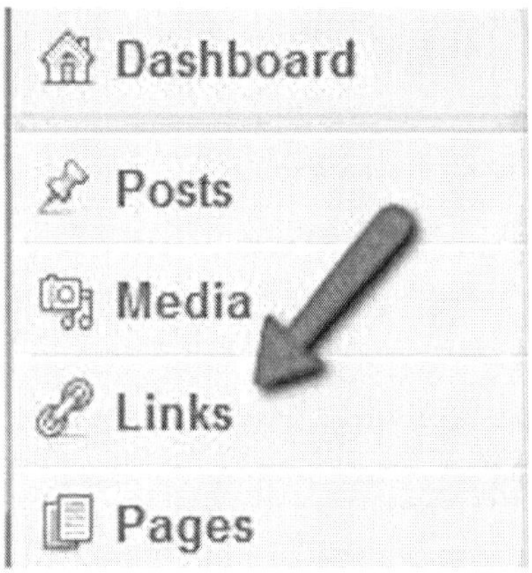

NOTE: By now you should be familiar with the menus that sometimes open when you hover over the sidebar menu items. The Links section also has a sub-menu allowing you to view all links, add new links or work with link categories.

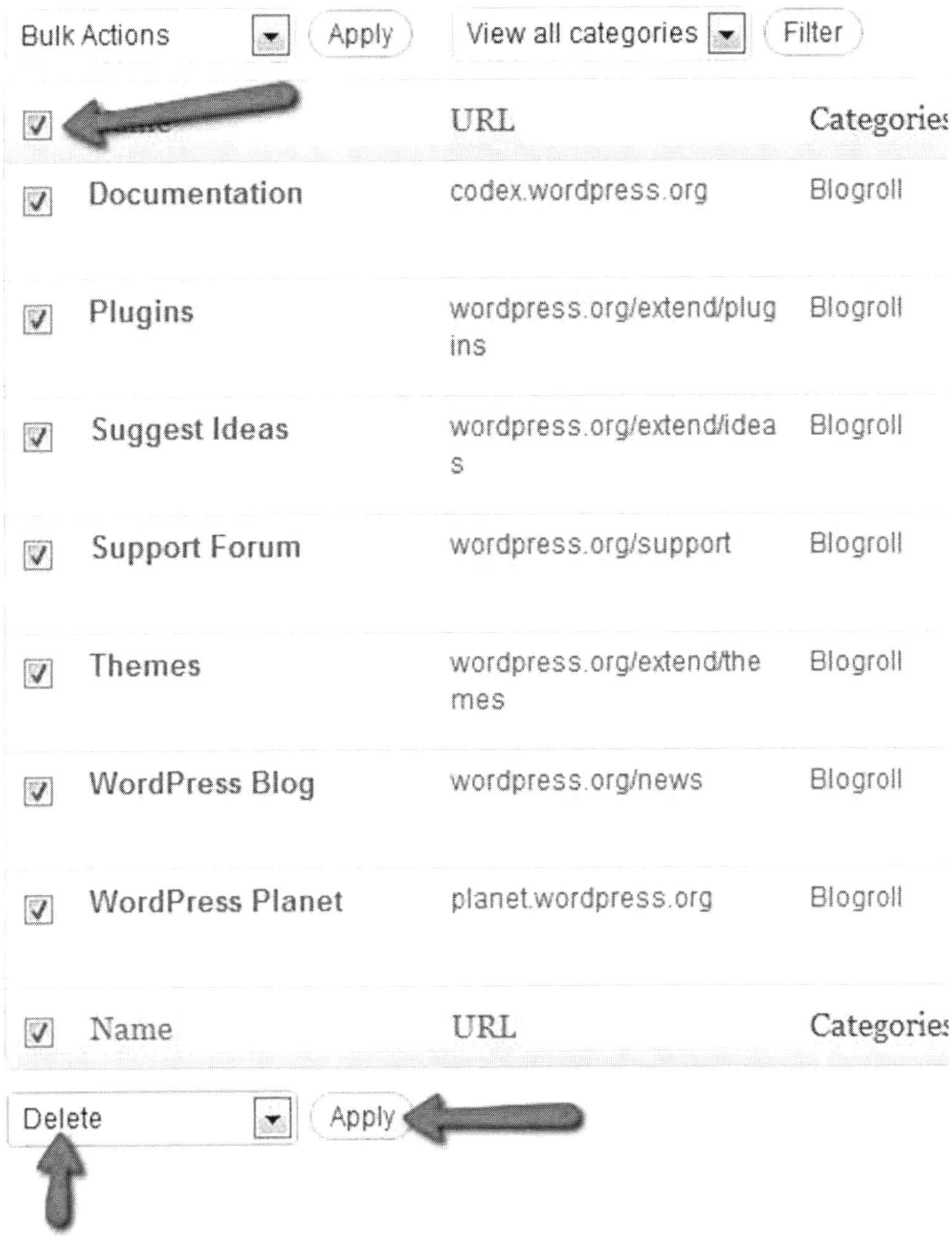

On the Links screen, click the box at the very top on the left. This will put a check mark next to every item in the table.

Now select Delete from the drop down box at the bottom. Click Apply. This will delete all of the links in the "blogroll".

Deleting widgets

WordPress pre-configured your website with a number of widgets in the sidebar of your website. You can see them if you look at your website:

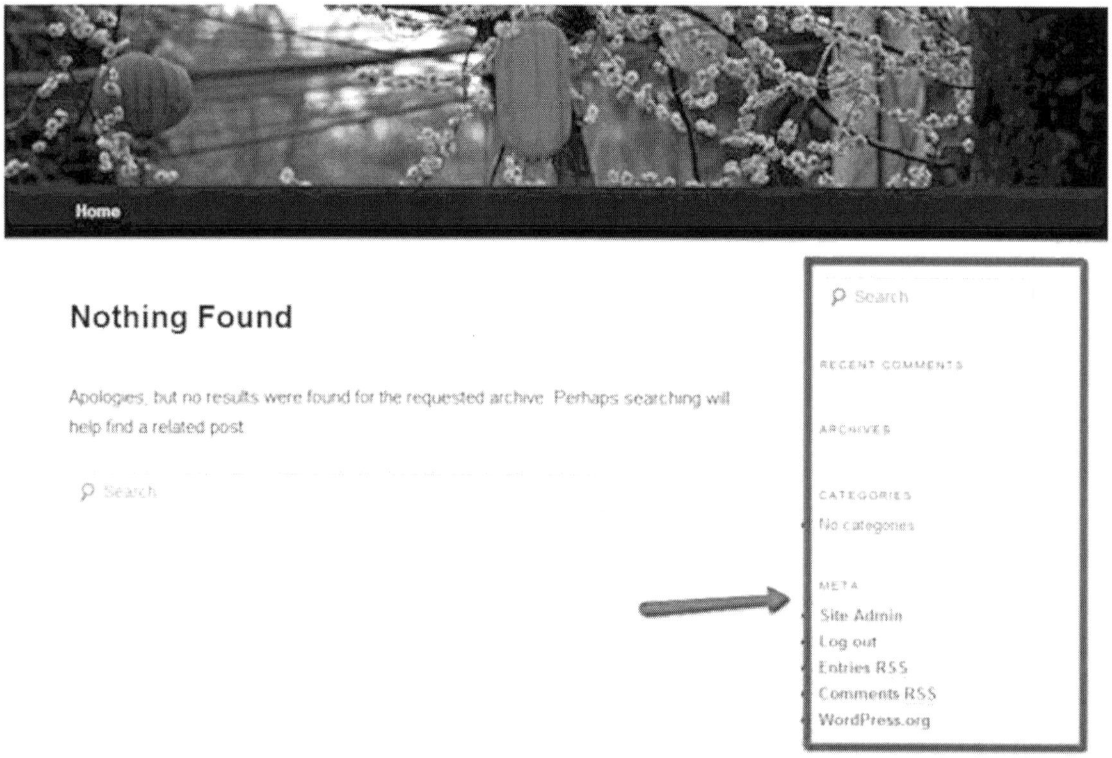

Those are widgets on the right. Let’s delete them.

In your Dashboard, move your mouse over the Appearance menu, and click on Widgets:

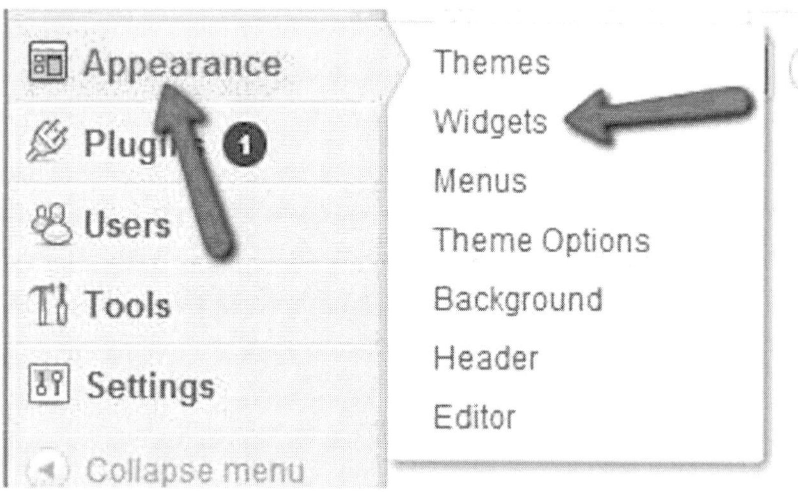

This will take you to the widget screen:

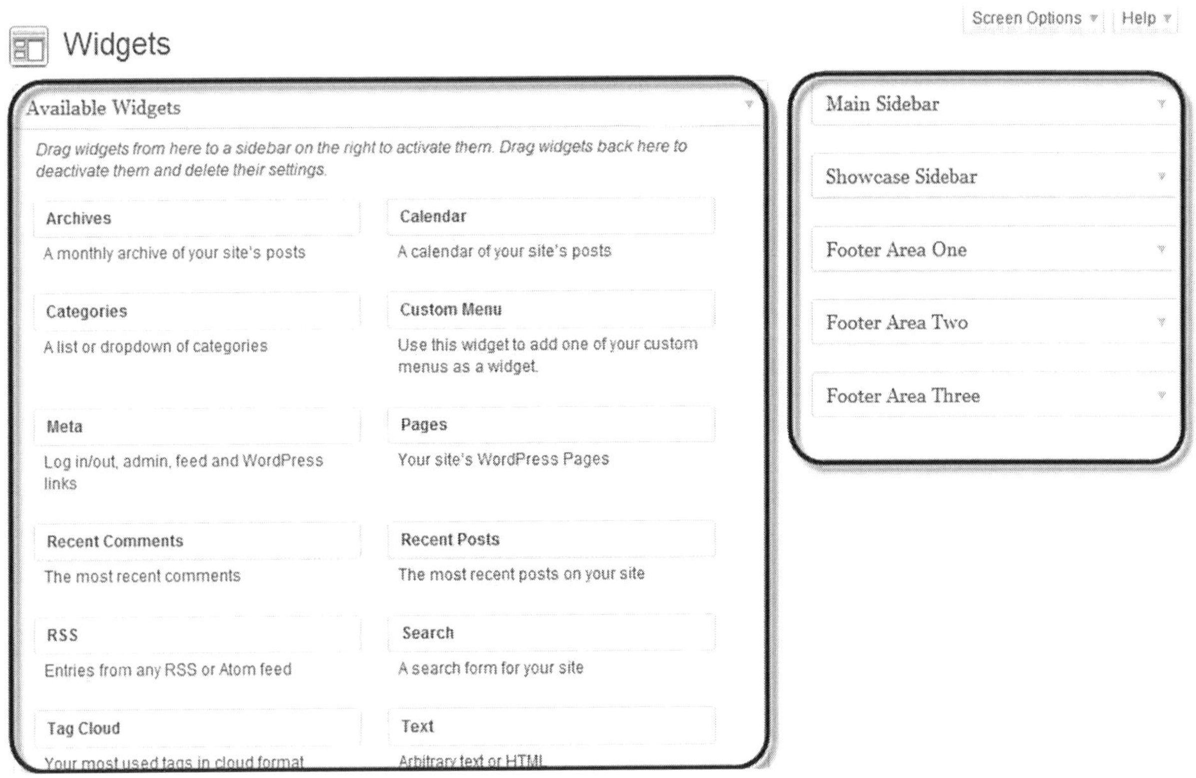

The screen is split into two sections. On the left you'll see the "available widgets". You can insert these into the sidebar of your site by dragging and dropping them onto a widgetized area listed on the right. Be aware that different templates have different widgetized areas, so if you are not using the Twenty Eleven theme from Wordpress, you will be seeing something a little different on the right hand side.

So what is a widgetized area?

It's simply a section of your website template that allows widgets to be used. E.g. your site sidebar is a widgetized area that allows you to add any widgets you like. When you installed WordPress, there were several widgets added here by default.

You will also notice on the right that there are widgetized areas called "Footer Area One", "Footer Area Two" and "Footer Area Three". This means you can add widgets to the footer (left, middle and right side of the footer), with this particular WordPress template/theme.

NOTE: All WordPress templates/themes are different. Not all templates will allow you to place widgets in the footer and some templates will allow widgets in areas that this default template doesn't. The best way to find out where each widgetized area is on the website is to consult the documentation that came with your theme or just add a widget and see where it appears.

WordPress installed several widgets into the "Main Sidebar" area of your site.

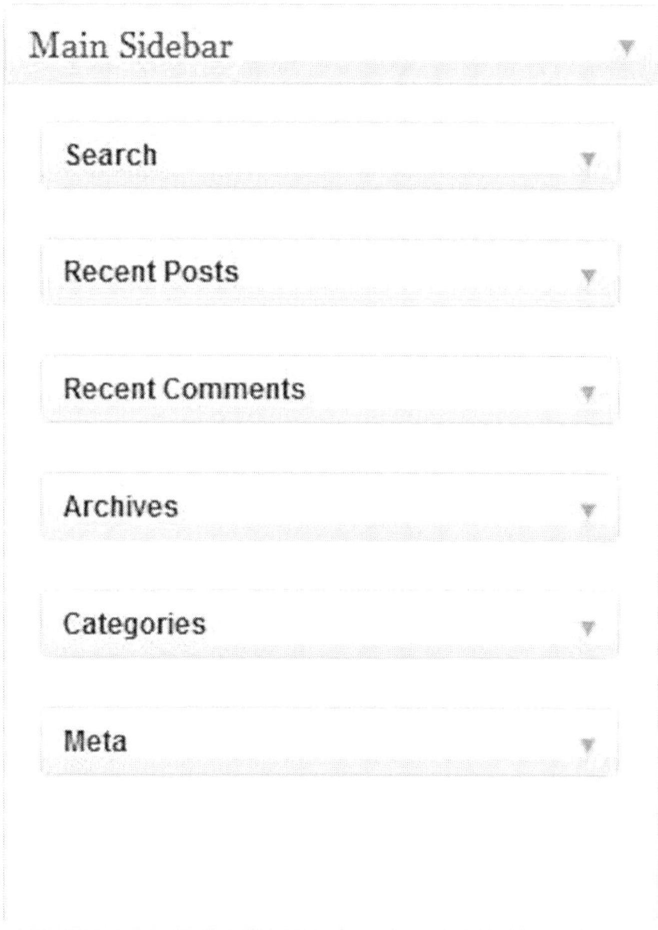

The widgets you see above are: Search, recent posts, recent comments, archives, categories and Meta.

Each installed Widget has a small downward-pointing arrow next to it on the right. Click this arrow to open up the settings for that particular widget:

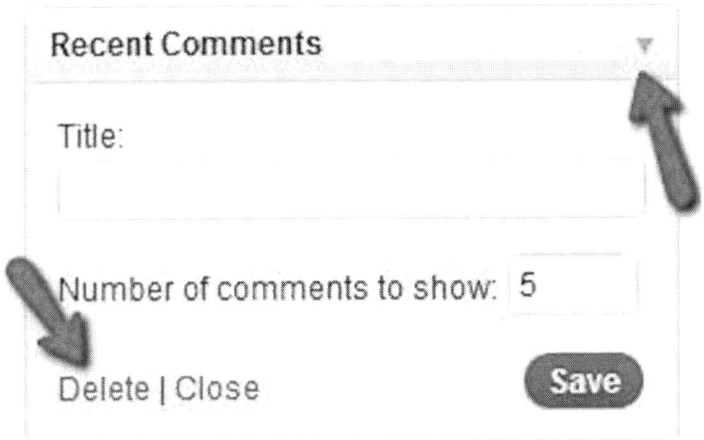

You'll see that there are a couple of options available for this "Recent Comments" widget. You can enter a title (leaving this blank will use the default title for the widget, in this case "Recent Comments"). You can also specify how many comments to show. This one is set to 5.

To delete the widget, click the Delete link bottom left.

The widget will disappear from the Main Sidebar area. Repeat to delete all of the other widgets. The only one I am leaving in my install for now is the Meta widget. This gives me an easy link to login to my site from the homepage, so I'll keep it there for now. You can do the same if you wish.

OK, we are done cleaning out WordPress.

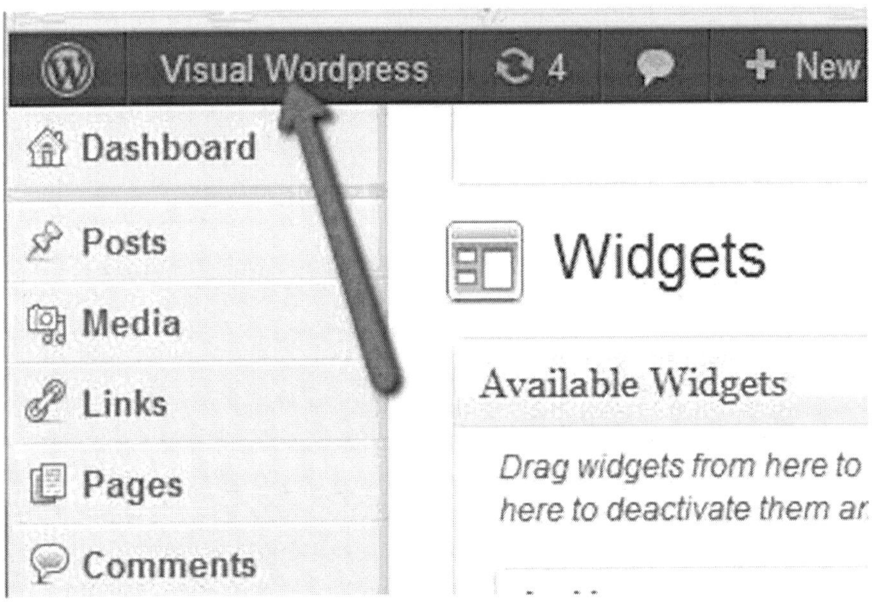

Click the link to your homepage (top left of the dashboard) to see what your site now looks like:

The site will be bare. The homepage will read: "Nothing Found". In my screenshot you can still see the Meta widget I left in the right sidebar.

Before we start configuring WordPress and creating a website, we should take care of any updates that are required.

Tasks to complete

1. Delete the pre-installed Page, Post, Widgets and Comment.

Dashboard updates

WordPress makes it easy for us to know when there are updates. At the top of the screen, you'll see the notification area whenever there is a new update to WordPress itself.

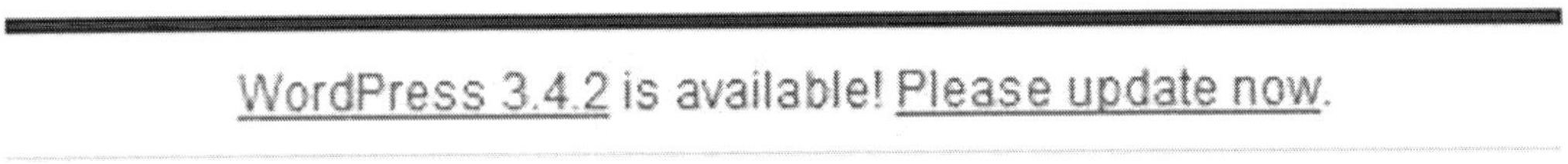

...

This area doesn't show us when there are updates to plugins but WordPress does have a way to tell us that as well. Whenever there is a plugin to update, WordPress will display a circle with a number inside, right next to the Plugins menu in the sidebar navigation.

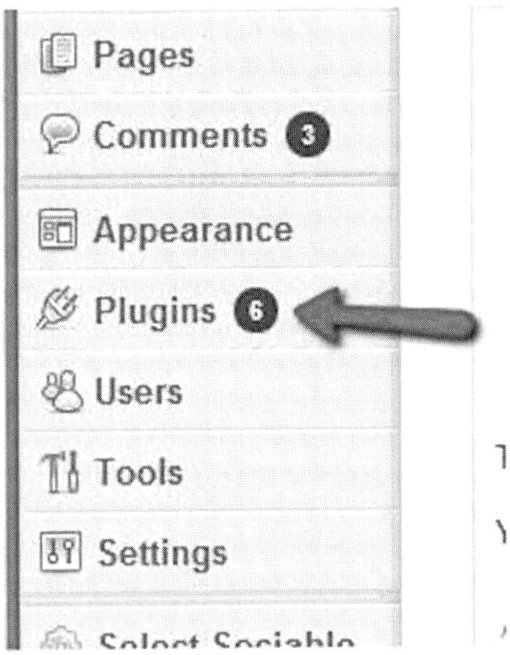

NOTE: You'll also see in that screenshot that there are 3 comments waiting to be approved.

In addition to these notification areas, we can find all available updates in the "Updates" section:

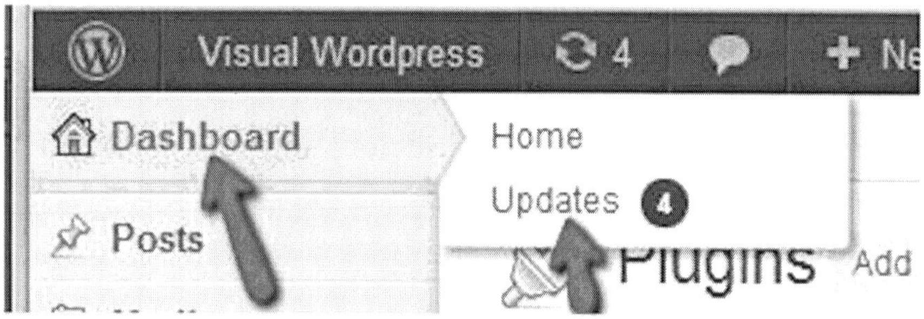

In the above screenshot there are 4 updates I need to take care of.

Click on the Updates menu item to go to the updates screen.

At the top of that screen, there will be a section for WordPress updates (if there is one available):

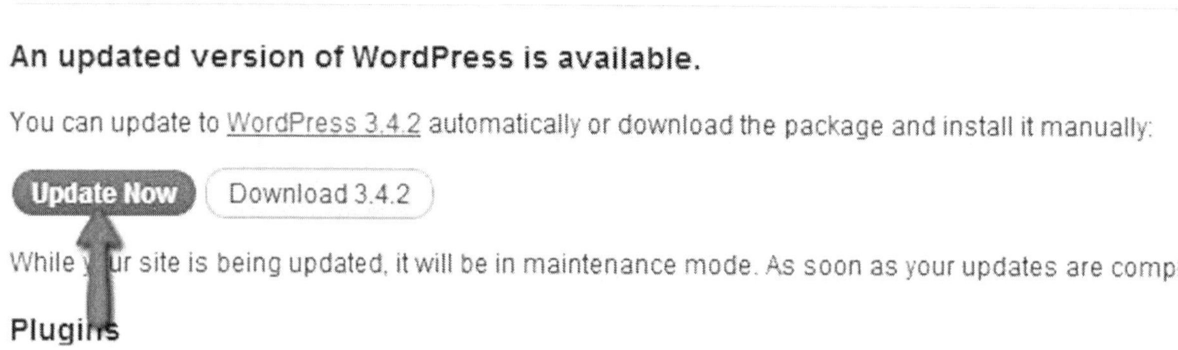

To update WordPress to the latest version, simply click the “Update Now” button and follow the onscreen instructions.

Occasionally these WordPress updates will require you to click a button or two, but on this occasion with mine, it went ahead and completed the update all on its own.

After the update, I was taken back to the main Dashboard screen with news of the update and what it fixed/added. However, I need to go back to the updates screen to continue with the other 3 updates.

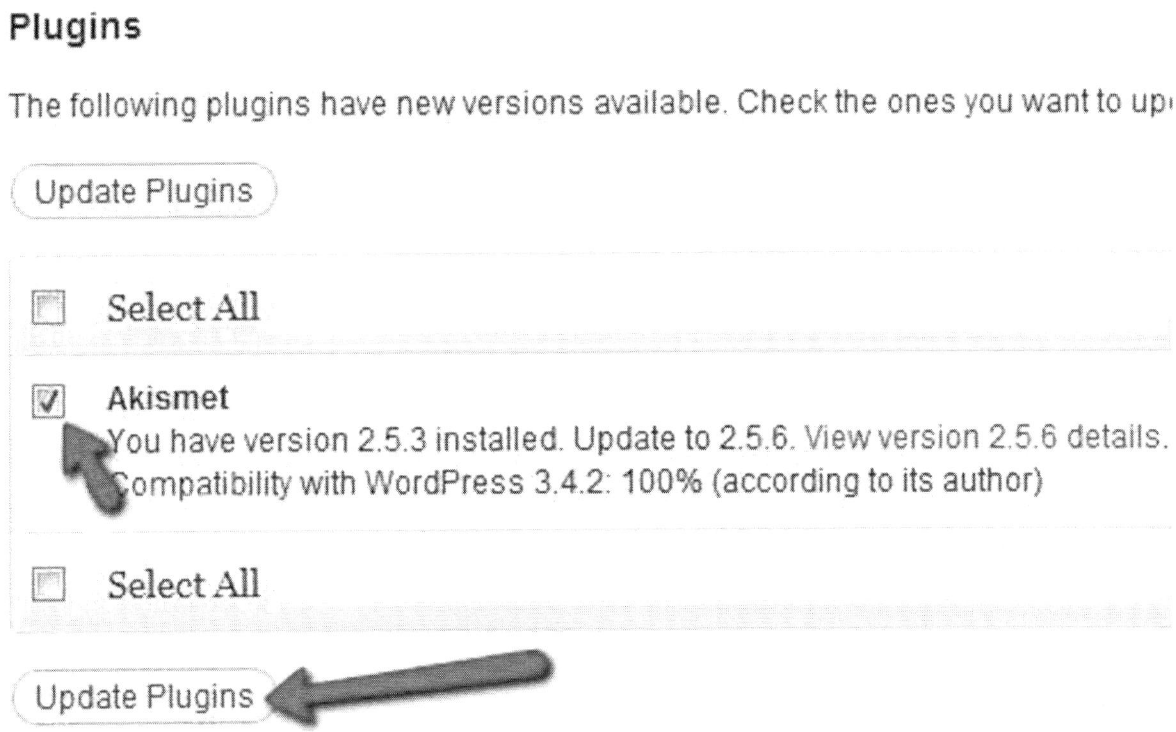

Simply place a check mark next to all plugins in the list (only one in my screenshot), and click the "Update Plugins" button.

NOTE: If there are multiple plugins to update, click the check box next to the "Select All" text and that will check each one for you and update those that have updates pending.

Once the plugin updates have been completed, WordPress will ask you where you want to go next:

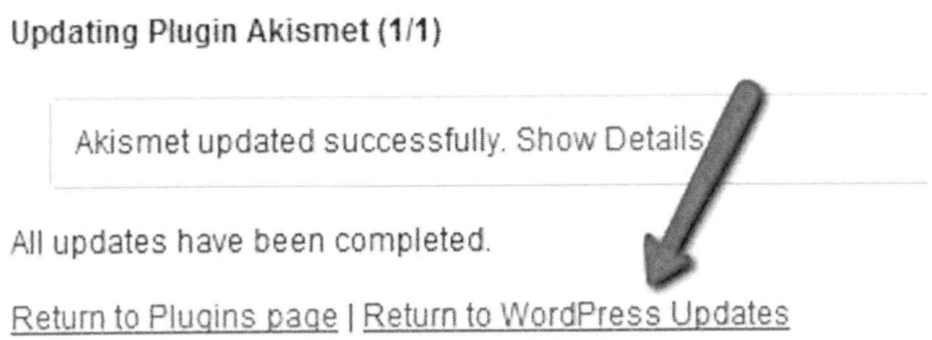

If there are still updates to perform, click the link to return to WordPress updates.

The last updates we need to do are for the preinstalled WordPress themes:

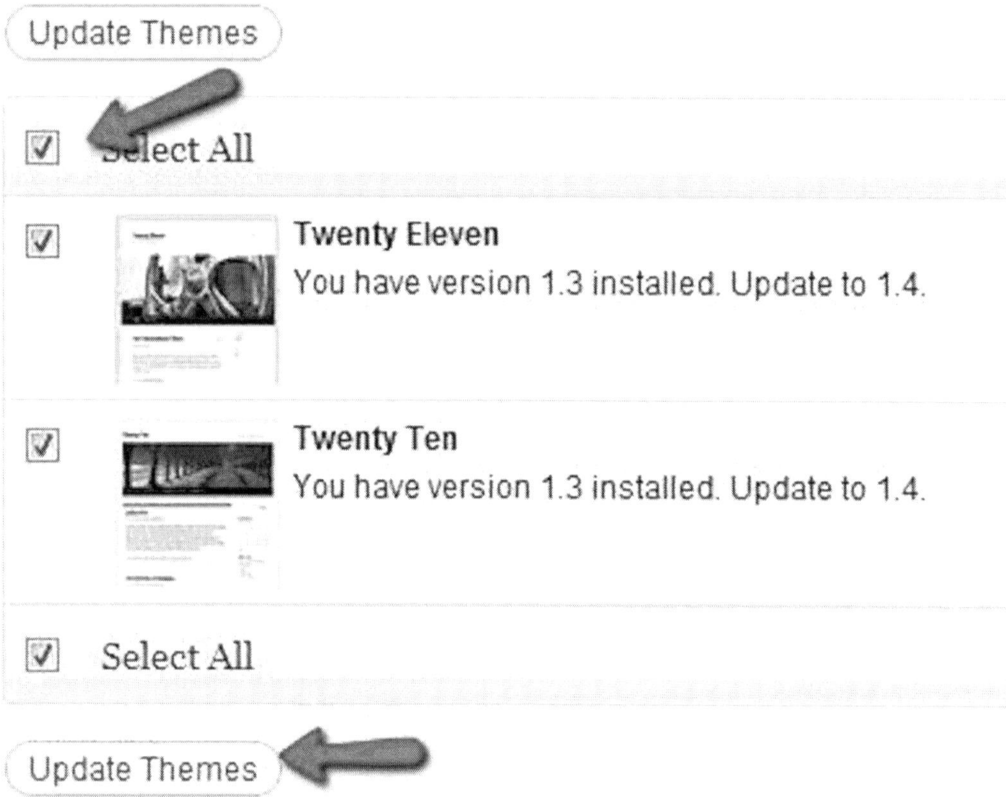

NOTE: We may decide we don't want to use one or both of these themes later on. If that is the case we can delete them now. However, for the moment, let's just update them.

Check the boxes next to both and then click the "Update Themes" button.

The update will proceed and WordPress will again ask you where you want to go when it is finished updating. With all updates now complete, we can actually go anywhere we want by clicking the relevant option in the Dashboard's navigation sidebar.

OK, let's configure WordPress so that it is ready for our content.

Tasks to complete

1. Update WordPress if necessary and any plugins that are out of date.

WordPress Settings

In the sidebar navigation of your Dashboard, you'll see an item labeled "Settings".

Once again, hovering your mouse over the "Settings" will open a menu.

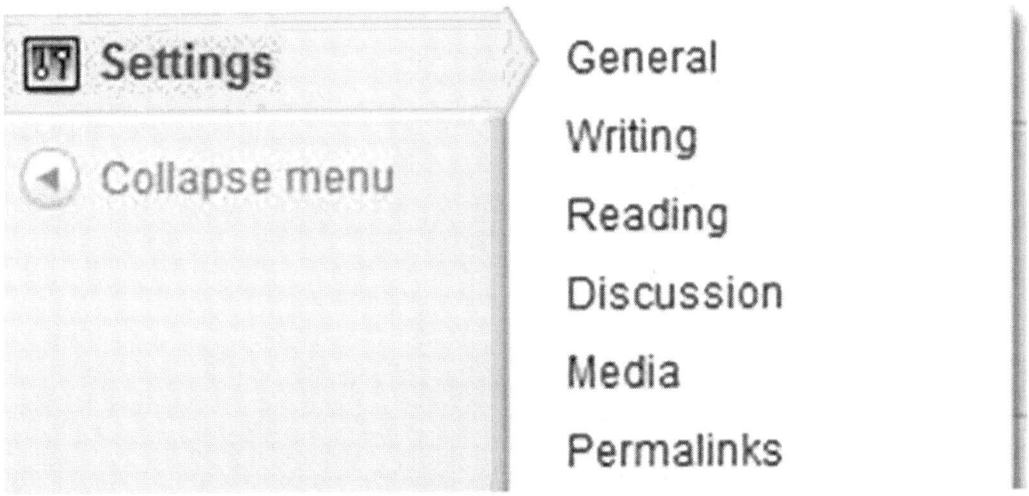

This "floating" menu is only visible when you move your mouse over the Settings link. If you click directly on the "Settings" link in the sidebar (instead of just hovering the mouse over it), the Settings menu will be expanded directly in the sidebar so all items are visible:

NOTE: If after clicking any top level link in the Dashboard's navigation menu, that top item will open its respective page within a few seconds unless you select one of the other options from the expanded menu before that happens.

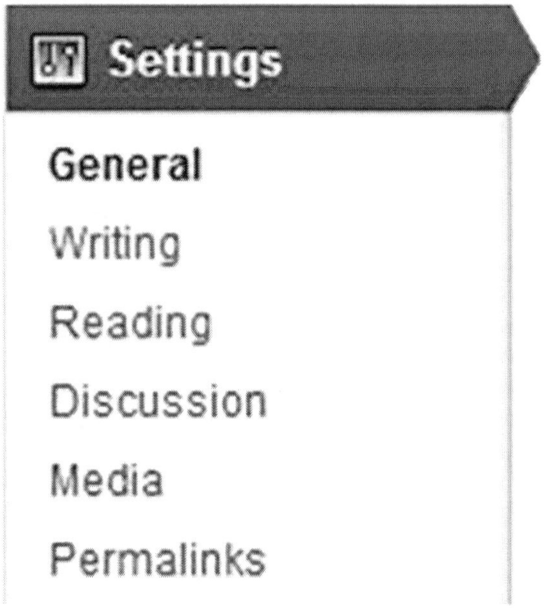

You can actually do this with any item in the navigation sidebar that has a sub-menu. Just click the main term to expand the menu directly within the sidebar.

Within Settings we have a number of items. Let's look at each one in turn and configure things as we go through.

General Settings

The General settings page defines some of the basic website settings.

At the top of the screen, the first few settings look like this:

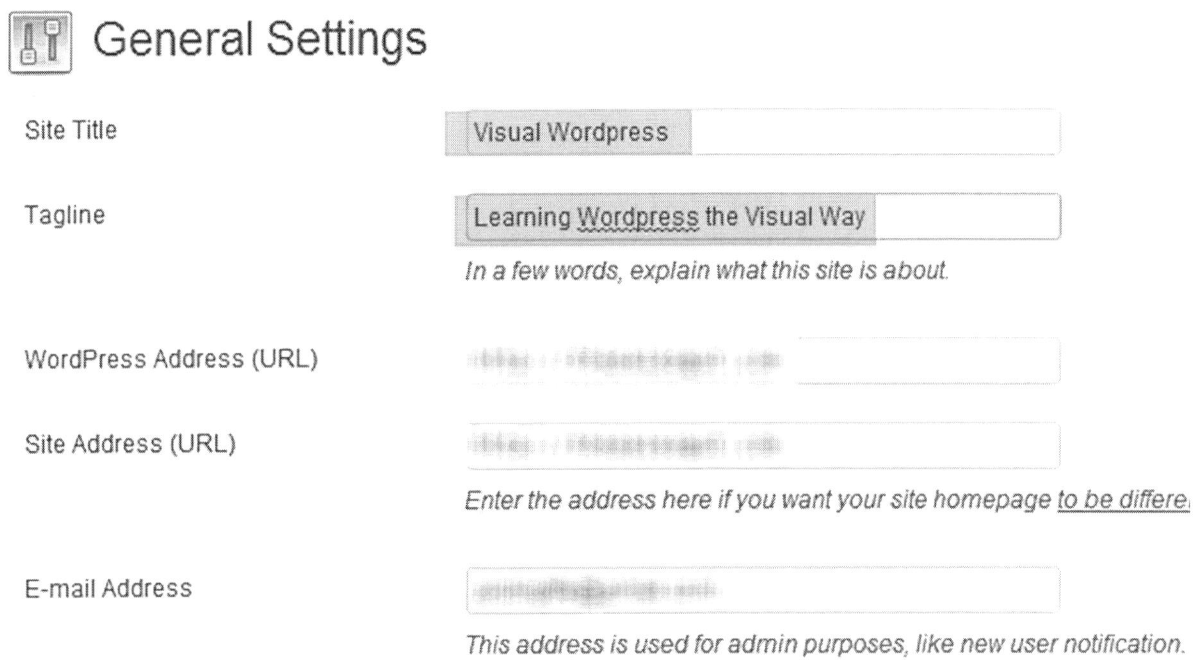

The information on the General Settings page was filled in when you installed WordPress, and there is probably no reason to change anything.

Right at the top is the Site Title. This is usually the same as the domain name.

Under the title is the Tagline. On some themes the tagline is displayed in the site header right under the site name. You typically use the tagline to give your visitors a little bit more information about your website. A tagline may be your website's "catch phrase", slogan, mission statement, or just a very brief, one sentence description.

You can see the tagline on the default WordPress theme under the title:

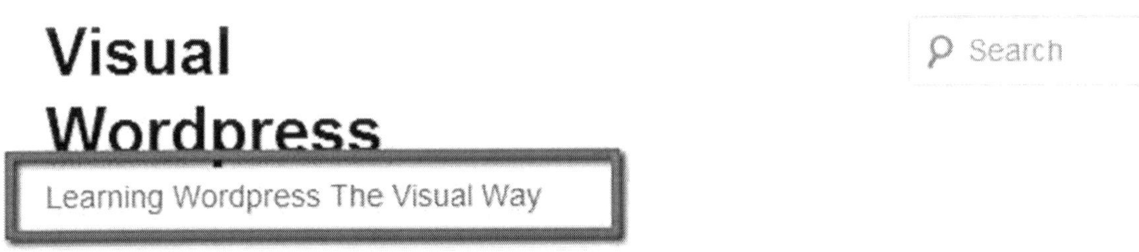

The next two fields on this settings page are the **WordPress Address (URL)** and the **Site Address (URL)**. The WordPress Address is the URL where WordPress is installed. Since we installed it in the root folder of this site, the WordPress Address is identical to the Website Address.

NOTE: Advanced users might want to install WordPress in a folder on their site, yet still have the WordPress site appear as if it were in the root folder. They can achieve this by using the WordPress Address (URL) field. Confused? Don't be. You won't be doing this.

Next on this setting page is the email address. This is very important as you'll get all notifications sent to this email address. Make sure you use a valid email that you actually check frequently. Later in the book we'll assign a Gravatar to this email address and set up a backup system that sends you an email backup of your WordPress database at set intervals.

Lower down this General Setting page are some more options:

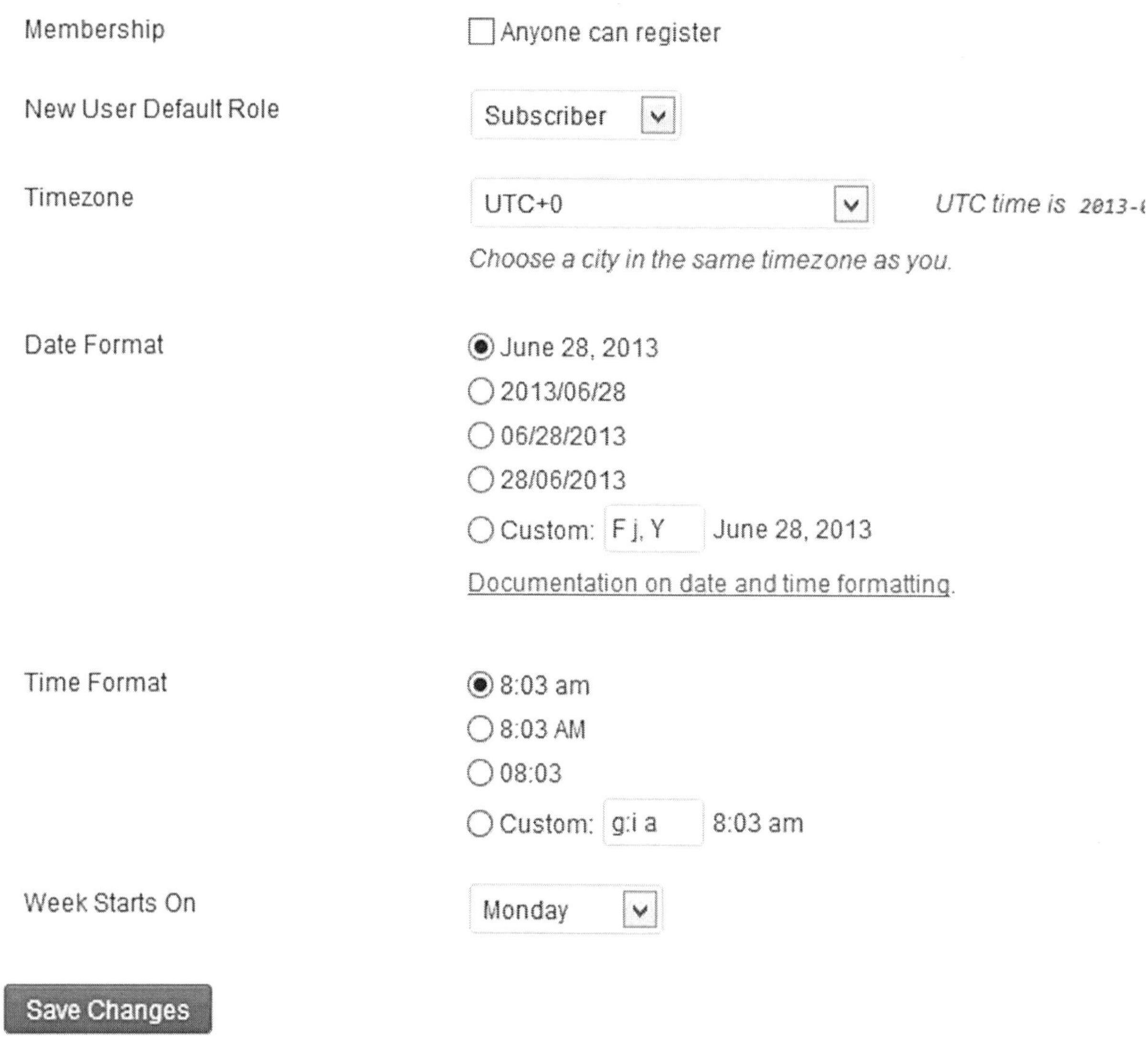

We can ignore the **Membership** and **New User Default Role** since we are not setting up a site where visitors can register and contribute content.

The rest of the settings on this page allow you to set your time zone, date and time formats.

The time zone is used to correctly timestamp posts on your site. Since we'll look at how you can also schedule your posts into the future, the correct time zone will ensure your posts are going out at the intended dates and times.

Select the date and time format you use.

You can also set the day you use for the start of the week. This will be used if you use a calendar widget in your sidebar (more on widgets later). If you choose Monday as the start of the week, then Monday will be the first column in the calendar.

If you make any changes to the settings on the General Settings tab, make sure you save the changes when you are finished.

Writing

The writing settings control the user interface you see when you are adding/editing posts. Let's look at the options.

Here are the first few:

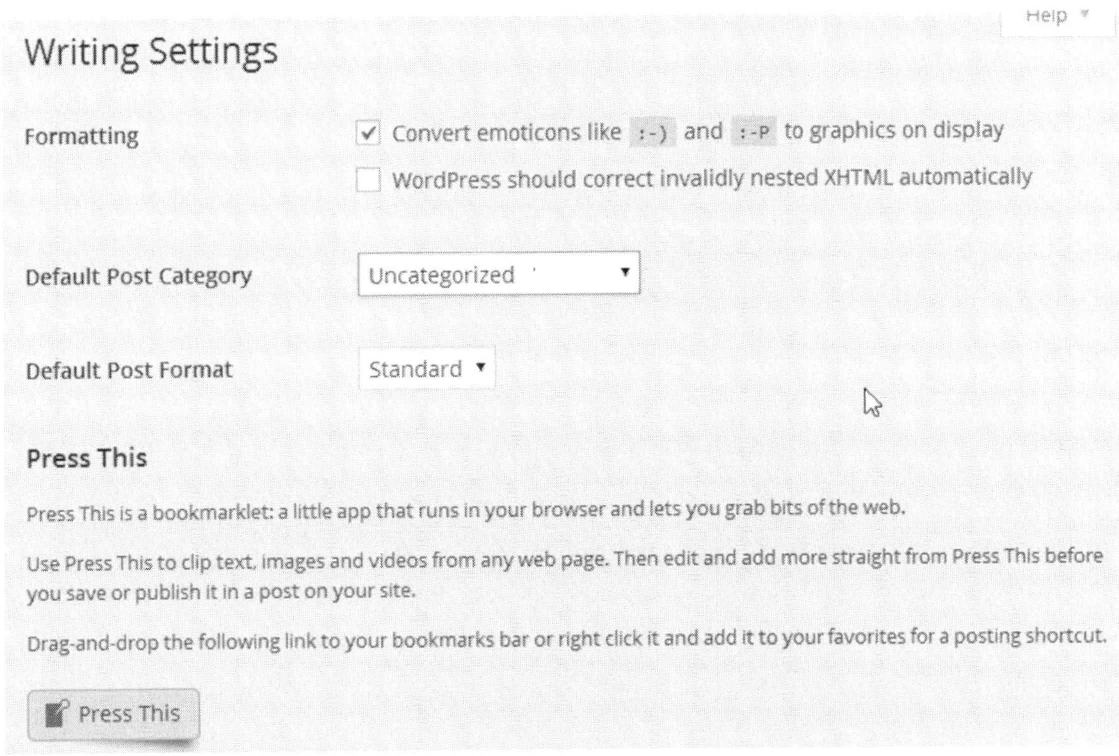

Formatting has two options. The first one will automatically convert text based emoticons (keyboard characters used to represent facial expressions), to graphic versions. The second option will try to correct any badly nested XHML. I'd leave these set at the defaults.

The final option, **Default Post Format**, is the default appearance of the posts you add to your site. This is controlled by the template you are using, with different templates having different options. Here are some of those options:

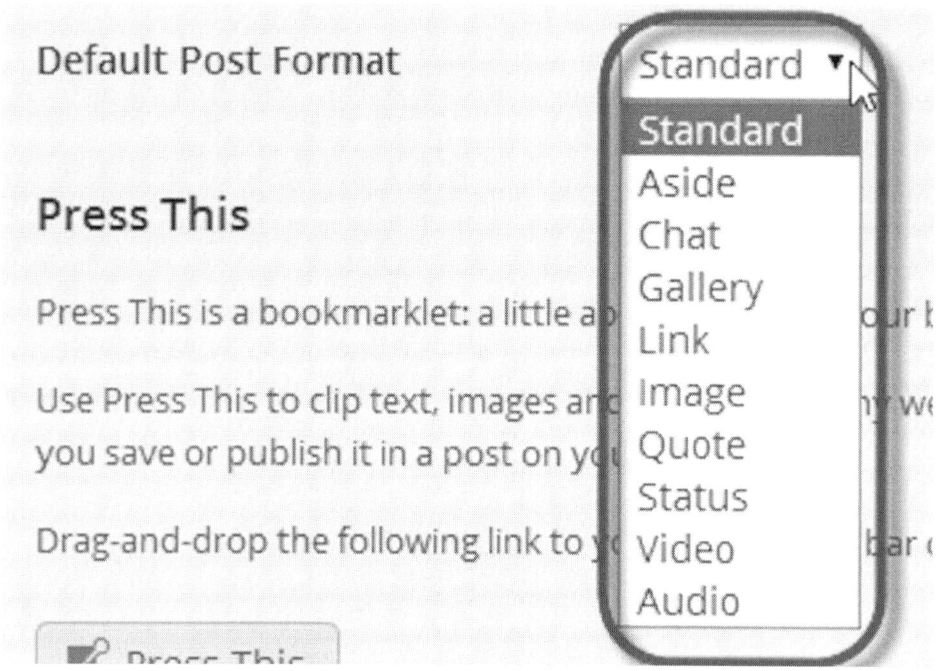

Each of these will modify how the posts look, so I recommend you use the Standard option for the default value, and then change the format on a post by post basis if needed. We'll see how to do that later.

"**Press This**" is something that most people don't use. However, I will show you how it works and what it is for.

Essentially this is an easy way to add content to your site. Imagine you are on another website, reading a fantastic article and you decide you'd like to mention this article on your own site. The "PressThis bookmarklet" gives us a quick way of doing that.

To use the Bookmarklet, click and drag the Press This button in your WordPress Dashboard up to the bookmarks bar of your web browser and drop it there. Here it is in my own browser:

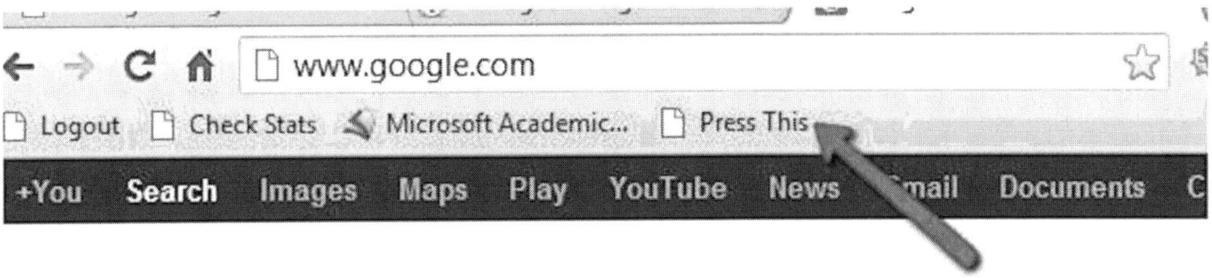

Let's see what happens when I am on a site that I want to talk about on my own site.

After navigating to a site that I found very interesting, I clicked the Press This button in my bookmark bar:

A window opens with the title of the post already filled in (using the title of the page I want to talk about), plus a link to the post in the main post editor. I can add my own commentary to the post and the link will credit the source of the information.

When you have finished adding your own commentary about why you found the page so interesting, or why your visitors should go and read it, click the **Publish** button to add the post to your own site.

Here are the next few settings:

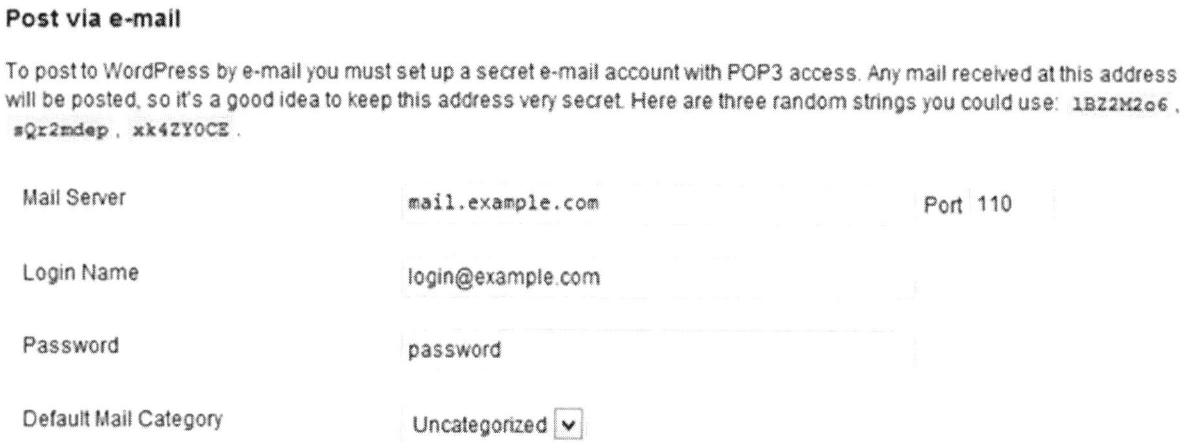

The Post via e-mail can be set up so that you can post content to your site by sending it in an email. This is beyond the scope of this book.

The final setting on this page IS important. It's the update services:

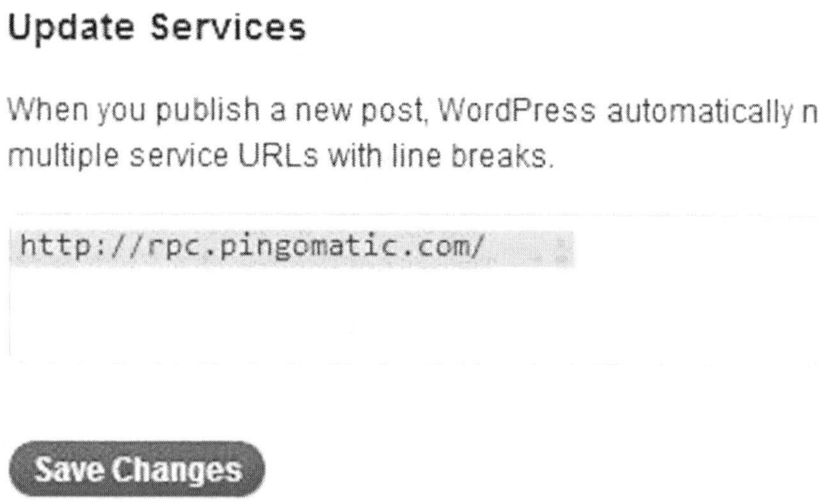

Basically, every time you post new content to your site, a message is sent to any service in this list (currently just one). This helps get your content noticed by, and included in, the search engines a lot faster. WordPress installs just one service, but I recommend you add more.

Do a search of Google for "WordPress Ping List" and you'll find people have created lists of services you can add. Just find a list and paste it into the box. Save your changes before moving to the next settings page.

Reading

The reading settings define how your visitors will see certain aspects of your site.

There are only a few settings here, but they are important.

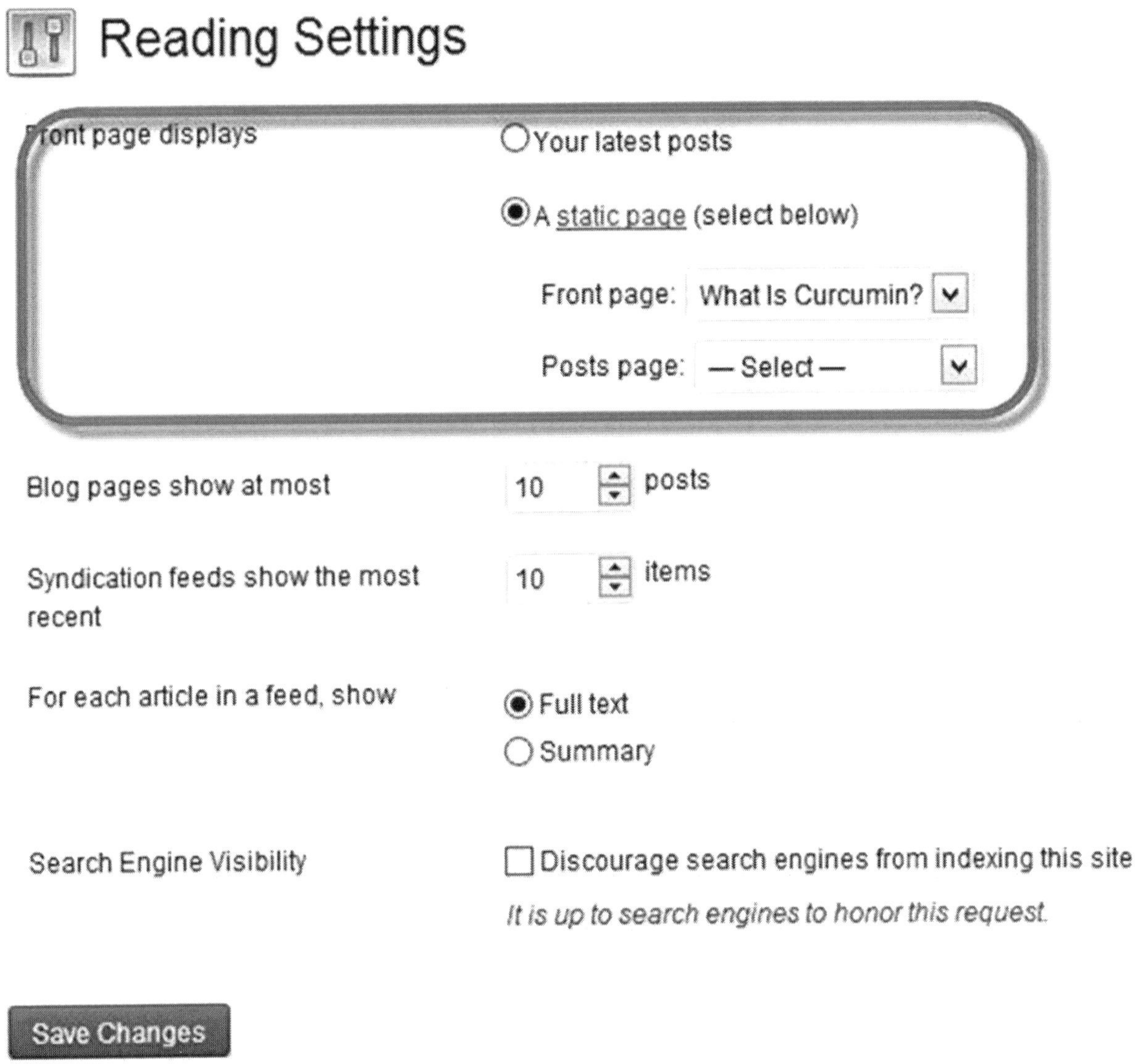

NOTE: The options surrounded by the red box will only appear if you have a WordPress Page created. Since we deleted the sample page, you won't see this yet. However, this option is very important because it defines what content appears on your website homepage. We'll look at this again later.

The default setting is **Your Latest Post**. This will display the most recent posts on your homepage. The number of posts displayed on your homepage is determined by whatever you have the **Blog pages show at most** set to. Since the default is 10, that means your last 10 posts will appear on your homepage.

However, it is possible to set up the homepage like a more traditional website, with a single article forming the basis of the homepage content. You can do this in WordPress by creating a WordPress PAGE that contains your homepage article. You then select **A Static Page** from the options and choose the page from the **Front Page** drop down list. We'll do this later.

Blog pages show at most, defines how many posts appear on a page. We mentioned this above in relation to the homepage.

This setting will make more sense when you start adding content to your site. You'll then be able to see what WordPress does with that content as you add it. It's not just the homepage that this setting affects.

If you have a category on your site called "types of roses", then WordPress will create a category page called "Types of Roses" that lists all of the articles in that category. If you have 15 articles, each describing a different rose, then WordPress will create two category pages to hold those articles. The first category page will have links to the first 10, and the second will list the remaining 5.

There are other cases where WordPress collects articles together to display on a page, but we'll look at those later in the book. For now though, just realize that this setting defines how many articles WordPress puts onto a single page. I recommend you leave the setting at the default 10.

Syndication feeds show the most recent, refers to your website's RSS feed. Every WordPress site has an RSS feed (in fact it has many RSS feeds). An RSS feed is just a list of the most recent articles with a link and a description for each post. This particular setting allows you to define how many of your most recent posts appear in the feed. Again, I recommend 10. We'll look at RSS feeds in more detail later on.

For each article in a feed, show, defines what content is shown in the feed. If you select "Full Text", then the complete articles are included in the feed. This can make your feed very long, but also give spammers a chance to steal your content with tools designed to scrape RSS feeds and post the content to their own sites.

I recommend you change this setting to Summary. That way only a short summary of each post will be displayed in the feed, which is far less appealing to spammers and easier on the eye for those who genuinely follow your active RSS feeds.

Search Engine Visibility allows you to effectively turn off the site from the search engines. If you are working on a site that you don't yet want the search engines to spider and index, you can check this box.

I actually allow search engines to visit and index my site from day 1. Yes, the search engines will find content that is not finished, but that's OK because they'll come back and check the site periodically to pick up changes.

Whether you block the search engines now or not is up to you. Just remember that if you do, your site won't start appearing in the search engines until you unblock them.

I recommend you leave this setting unchecked.

Discussion

The discussion settings are related to comments that visitors may leave at the end of your posts. There are a few settings we need to change from the default.

Here are the first few settings in the discussion options:

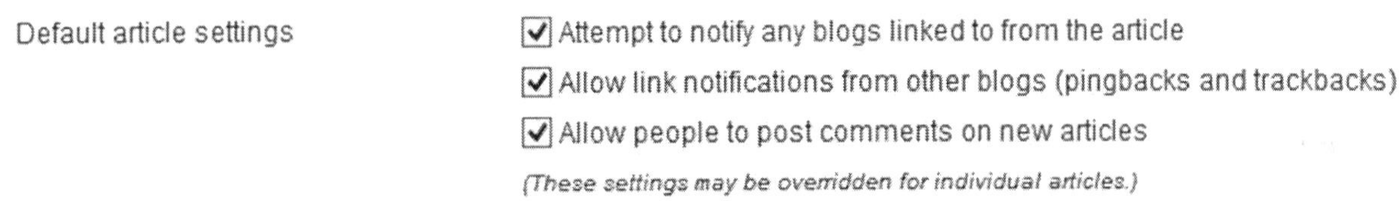

Attempt to notify any blogs linked to from the article should be left checked. Whenever you write an article and link to another site, WordPress will try to notify that site that you have linked to them. WordPress does this by sending what is called a Ping. Pings will show up in the comment system of the receiving blog and can be approved like a comment. If it is approved, that Pingback will appear near the comments section on that blog, giving you a link back to your site.

NOTE: Any website can turn pingbacks off. If a ping is sent to a site where pingbacks are OFF, then it won't appear in their comment system.

Here are some example pingbacks published on a web page:

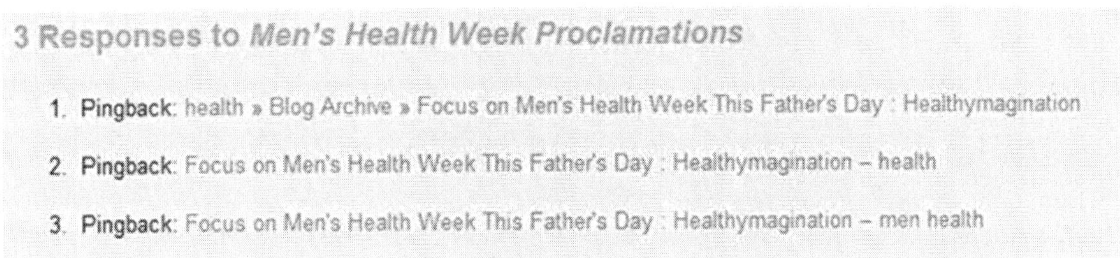

Each pingback is a link back to a website that has linked to this webpage.

The next option - **Allow link notifications from other blogs (pingbacks and trackbacks)** allows you to turn pingbacks and trackbacks (trackbacks are very similar to pingbacks) off. If you uncheck this, you will not receive pingbacks or trackbacks.

Should you check it or not?

Well, it's always nice to see when a site is linking to your content. However, there is a technique used by spammers to send fake trackbacks & pingbacks to your site. They are trying to get you to approve their trackback so that your site will then link to theirs.

Personally I leave this options checked (so I can see any new links to my site), but I never approve a trackback or pingback.

Allow people to post comments on new articles should remain checked. It is important that you let your visitors comment on your site's content. A lot of people disable this because they think moderating comments it too much work. However, we'll look at a plugin later that will cut back on spam, which helps a lot with this. Besides, the benefits of having a dialog with your visitors far outweigh the negatives.

The next section of options is shown below:

Leave all of these at their default value (shown above).

The options are fairly self-explanatory.

The second item should remain unchecked, because we do not allow visitors to register and login to our site. We do want *all* visitors to have the option of leaving a comment though.

The third option allows you to close the comment sections on posts after a certain number of days. I like to leave comments open indefinitely as you never know when someone will find your article and want to have their say.

Nested comments should be enabled. This allows people to engage in discussions within the comments section, with replies to previous comments appearing "nested" underneath the comment they are replying to. Here is an example showing how nested comments appear on my site:

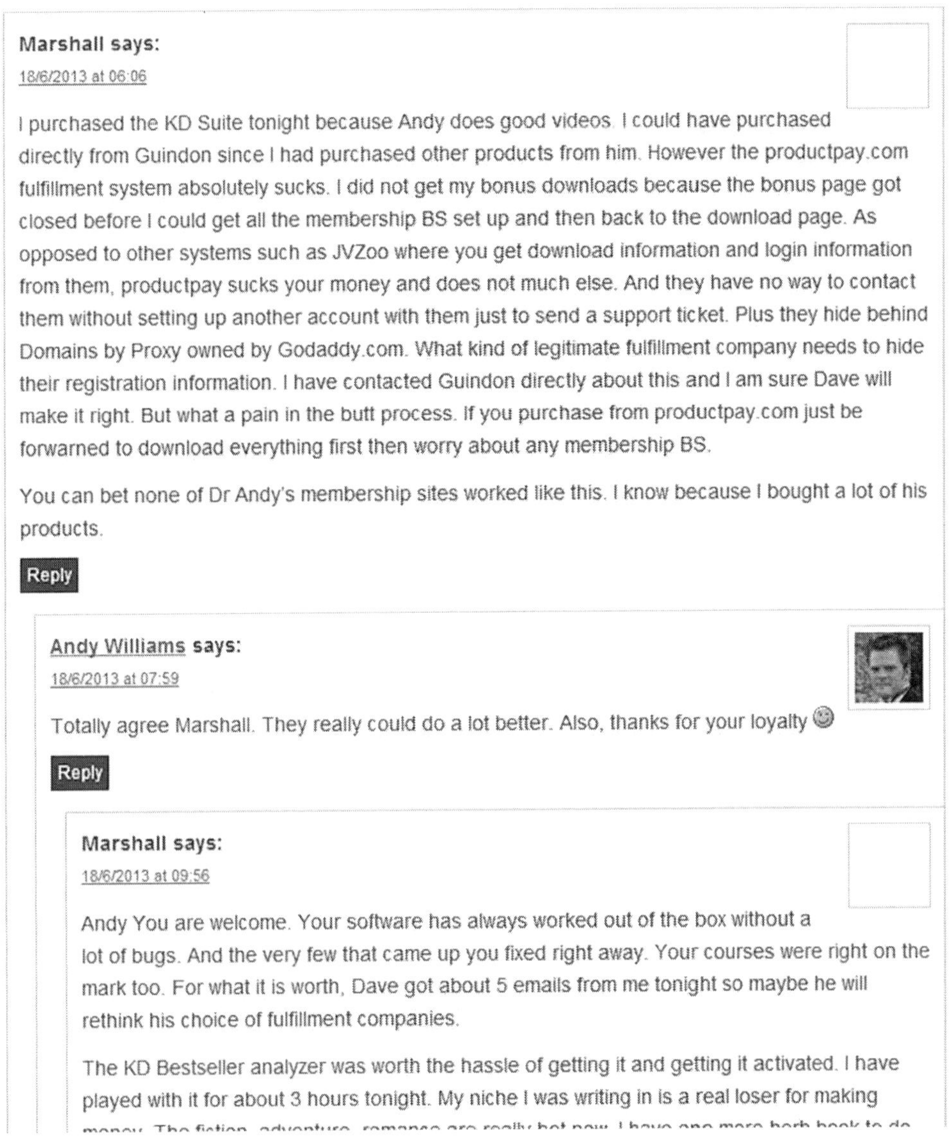
Marshall says:
18/6/2013 at 06:06

I purchased the KD Suite tonight because Andy does good videos. I could have purchased directly from Guindon since I had purchased other products from him. However the productpay.com fulfillment system absolutely sucks. I did not get my bonus downloads because the bonus page got closed before I could get all the membership BS set up and then back to the download page. As opposed to other systems such as JVZoo where you get download information and login information from them, productpay sucks your money and does not much else. And they have no way to contact them without setting up another account with them just to send a support ticket. Plus they hide behind Domains by Proxy owned by Godaddy.com. What kind of legitimate fulfillment company needs to hide their registration information. I have contacted Guindon directly about this and I am sure Dave will make it right. But what a pain in the butt process. If you purchase from productpay.com just be forwarned to download everything first then worry about any membership BS.

You can bet none of Dr Andy's membership sites worked like this. I know because I bought a lot of his products.

Reply

Andy Williams says:
18/6/2013 at 07:59

Totally agree Marshall. They really could do a lot better. Also, thanks for your loyalty :)

Reply

Marshall says:
18/6/2013 at 09:56

Andy You are welcome. Your software has always worked out of the box without a lot of bugs. And the very few that came up you fixed right away. Your courses were right on the mark too. For what it is worth, Dave got about 5 emails from me tonight so maybe he will rethink his choice of fulfillment companies.

The KD Bestseller analyzer was worth the hassle of getting it and getting it activated. I have played with it for about 3 hours tonight. My niche I was writing in is a real loser for making

You can see that replies to the previous comment are nested underneath them, making it clear that the comments are part of a conversation.

The last two options in this section relate to how comments are displayed on the page. If you want, comments can be spread across multiple pages, with say 50 comments per page (default). However, I leave this option unchecked so that all comments for an article appear on the same page. If you find that you get hundreds of comments per article, you might like to enable this option just so pages load a lot quicker.

The final option in this section allows you to show older or newer comments at the top of the comments section.

I prefer to have comments listed in the order in which they are submitted as that makes more sense. Therefore leave the setting as "older".

The next section of these settings is shown below:

The first two options will send you an email whenever someone posts a comment, and when a comment is held for moderation. We'll actually set up comments so that ALL comments must be moderated so the second option is less important.

Leave both of the first two options checked so that you know when someone leaves a comment. When you get an email notification, you can then login to your Dashboard and either approve the comment (so it goes live on your site), or send it to trash if it's blatant spam.

The second two options shown above relate to when a comment can appear on the site. Check the box next to **An administrator must always approve the comment.** This will mean ALL comments must be moderated. We don't want spammy comments appearing on the site and since they'll only appear when we approve them, we have 100% control.

Since we are now moderating all comments, the **Comment author must have a previously approved comment** becomes less important. What this setting can do is auto-approve comments for any author that has a previously approved comment on the site. For this to work, the previous option should remain unchecked. However, I don't advise this. Set up your settings as I have them in the screenshot above.

The next setting is not important to us since all our comments are moderated.

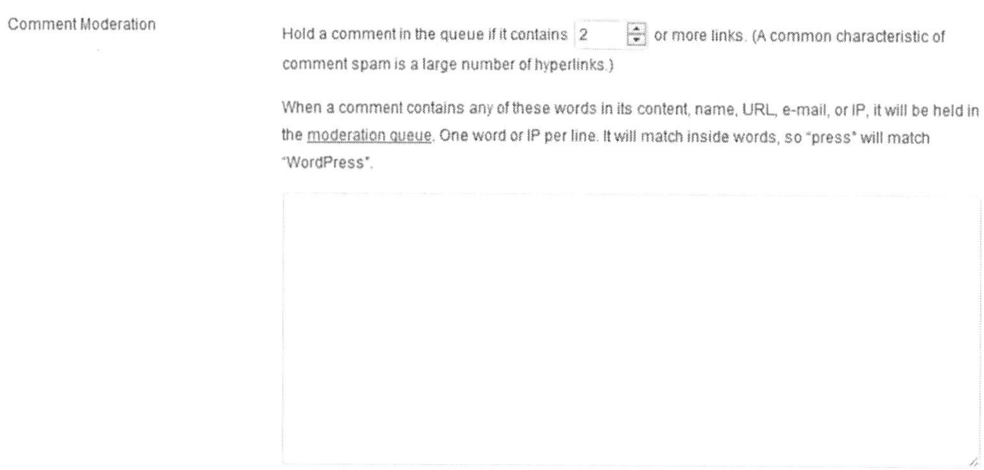

If you do not have it set up to moderate all comments, you can use this setting to automatically add comments to the moderation queue IF it has a certain number of links in it (default is 2), OR the comment contains a word that is listed in the big box.

Since all of our comments are moderated anyway, we can leave this section as it is.

The Comment Blacklist box allows you to set up a blacklist to automatically reject comments that meet the criteria listed here.

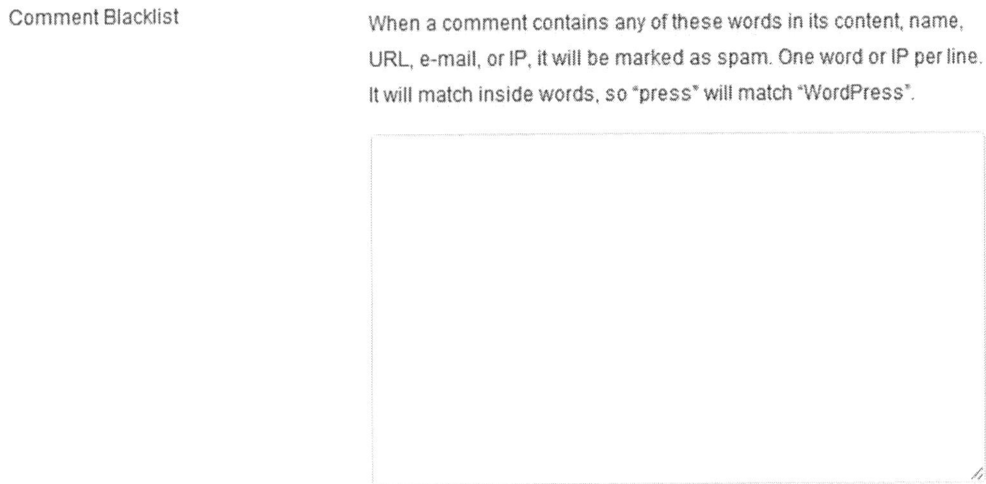

Essentially any comment that contains a word listed in this box, contains a URL listed in this box, comes from an email address listed in this box, or comes from an IP address listed in this box, will automatically be sent to the comment spam folder.

That means you can set up your blacklist with "unsavory" words, email addresses, URLs or IP addresses of known spammers, and you'll never see those comments in your moderation queue. The comment blacklist can significantly cut down on your comment moderation, so I suggest you do a search on Google for **WordPress comment blacklist**, and use a list that someone else has already put together (you'll find a few). Just copy and paste their list into the box and save the settings.

The final section of the discussion options is related to Avatars:

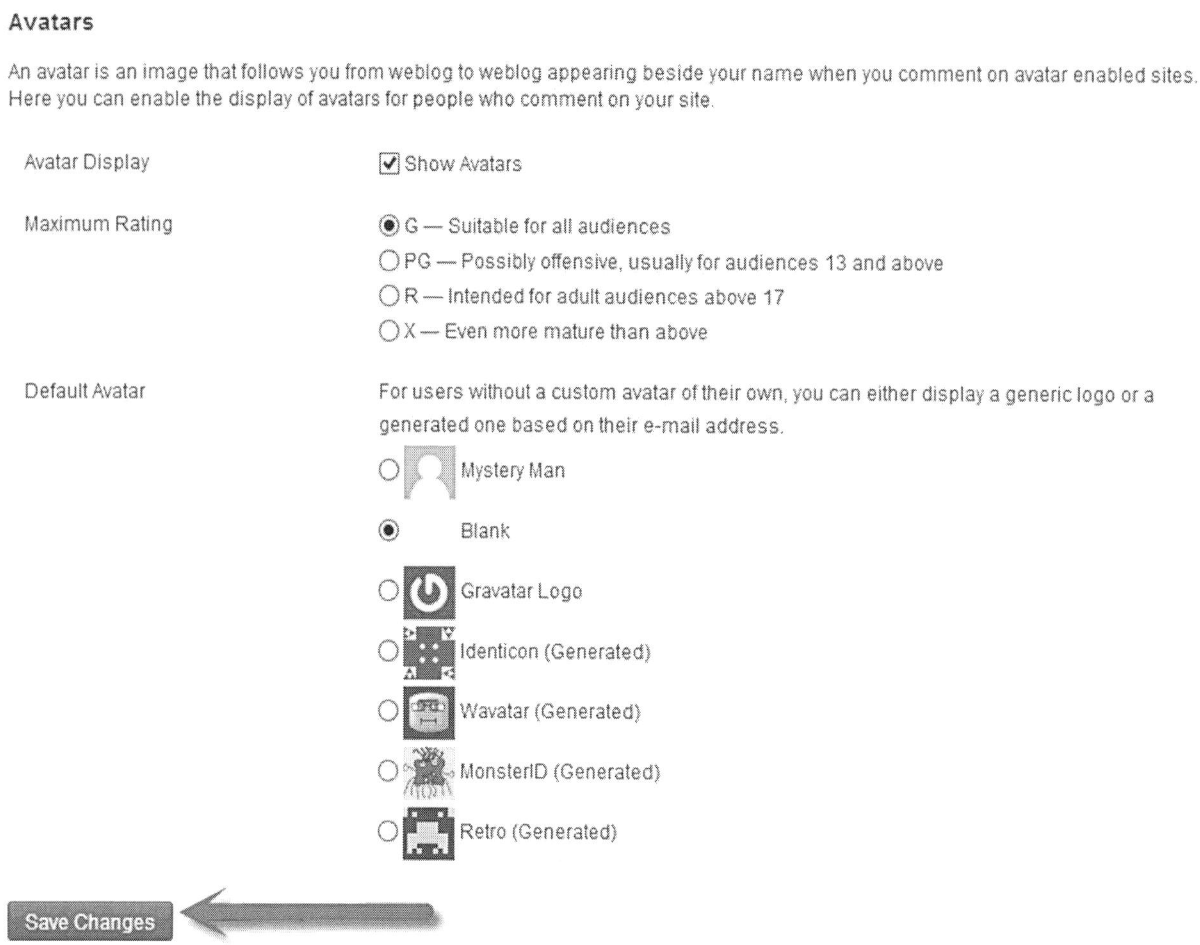

An Avatar is a little graphic that appears next to the commenter's name.

I think it is nice to see who is leaving comments, so I recommend you leave Avatars on (first setting).

For most websites you should have the maximum rating set to G. Avatars are assigned ratings when you create them over at Gravatar.com, so this ratings system is only as good as the honesty of the person creating the avatar.

The final setting allows you to define the default action if someone does not have an Avatar set up for their email address. In the screenshot above, I still have it set to **Mystery Man** but I recommend you select **Blank** so that no avatar is shown. This is because Avatar images need to load with the page. Any page with a lot of comments will have a lot of Avatars to load and this slows down the load speed of the page. Why slow it further with "Mystery Man" avatars when the commenter doesn't have an avatar set up?

When you have finished with these settings, save the changes you made.

Media

The media settings relate to images and other media that you might insert into your site.

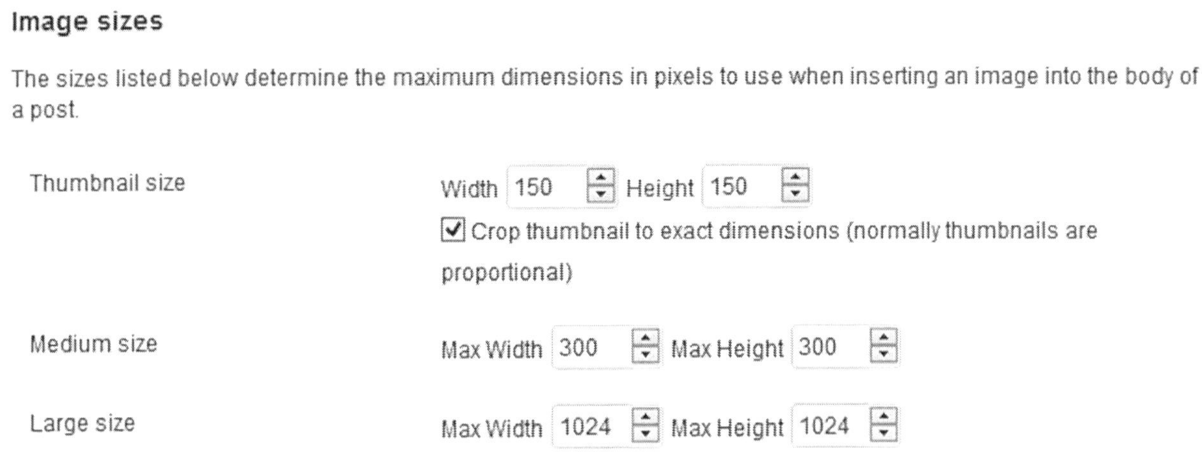

These first few settings allow you define the maximum dimensions for thumbnail, medium and large images. You can leave these are the default setting.

The final option asks whether you want your images organized into month and year based folders.

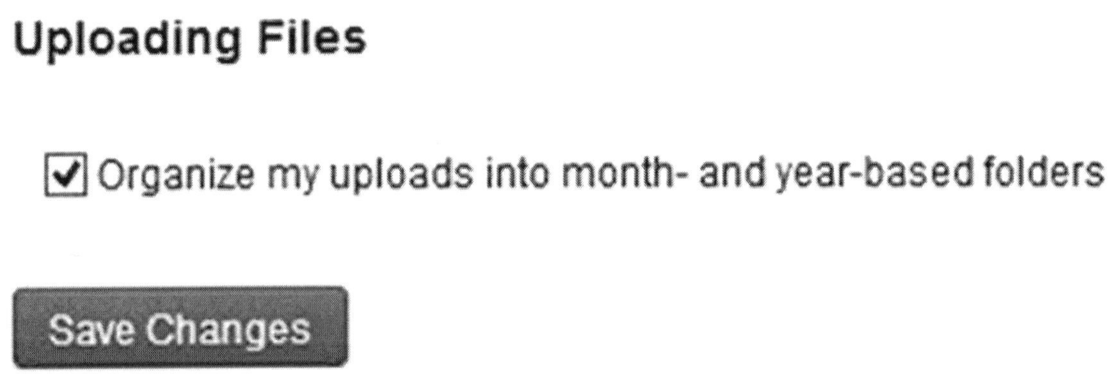

I'd recommend you leave this checked, just so your images are organized into dates on your server. It can help you find the images later if you need to.

Permalinks

The final settings are the permalinks. Basically these define how the URLs (web address), are constructed for content on your site. This needs to be changed from the default value.

We want the URLs on our site to help visitors and search engines, so we'll add in the post's category and name to the URL:

Select the **Custom Structure** radio button at the bottom of the list, and enter the following into the box:

/%category%/%postname%/

Save the changes.

The URLs on your site will now look like this:

http://mydomain/category/post-name

The last two options on this settings page are shown below:

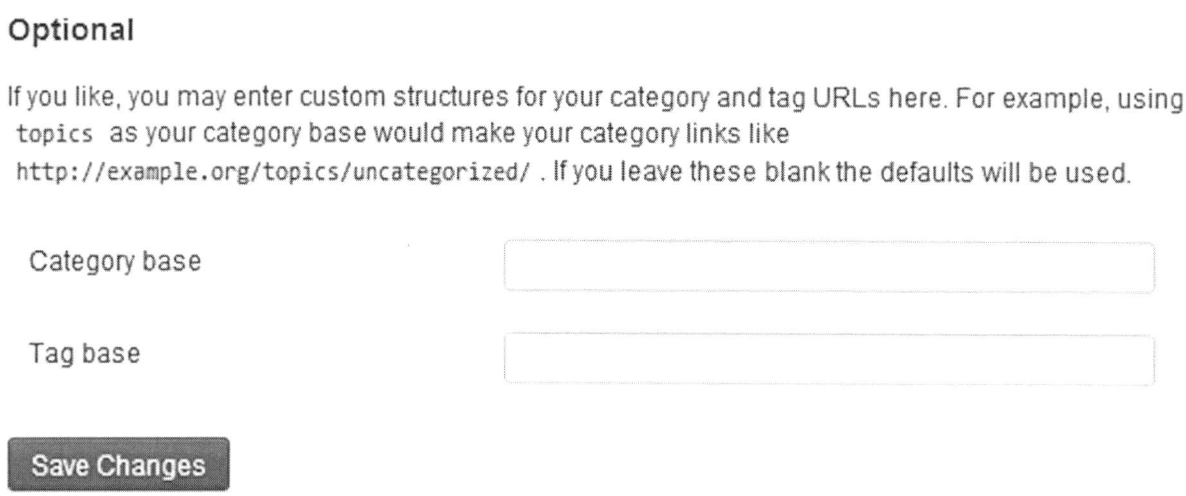

I would leave these two boxes empty.

When WordPress creates a category page or a tag page, the URL will include the word "category" or "tag".

For example:

http://mydomain.com/**category**/roses/

.. might be the URL of a category page listing my posts on Roses, and

http://mydomain.com/**tag**/red

.. might be a tag page listing all posts on my site that were tagged with the word "red".

If you enter a word into the category base or tag base, when the URLs are constructed, they'll contain the category base or tag base you specified, rather than the default words, "category" or "tag".

Having keywords in your URL can be helpful, BUT, with Google on the warpath of web spammers, I would not even consider entering a category base or tag base. Leave those boxes empty.

Congratulations, you have now set up your main WordPress Settings.

Tasks to complete

1. Go through each of the menus inside the settings menu and make the changes described in this chapter.

RSS feeds

We mentioned RSS feeds earlier when setting up the Reading options.

RSS feeds are an important part of your WordPress website, so I wanted to spend a little more time on this.

RSS stands for **R**eally **S**imple **S**yndication (or **R**ich **S**ite **S**ummary). An RSS feed lists information about the most recent posts on your site. This information is typically the title of the post (which links to the article on your website), and a description of it, which can be short or the entire piece.

The RSS feed is an XML document that would be difficult to read without special software, but XML is the perfect "language" to store this particular type of information.

Most web browsers can read RSS feeds and show its content as readable text. Here is an RSS feed from a websites on "juicing", as displayed in Google Chrome:

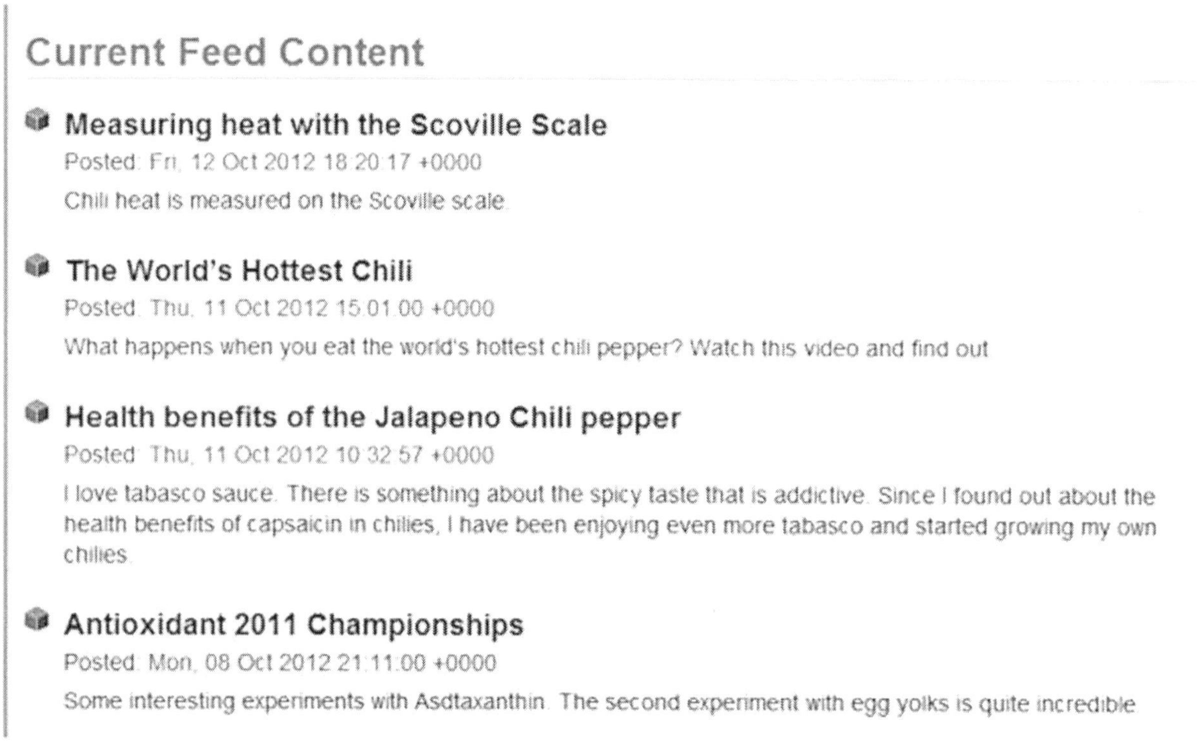

You can see the summaries of the last 4 posts on my site.

Each entry has the title of the post which is hyperlinked to the article on my site. Under the title is the date and time of the post and then a short description under that.

This is much easier for humans to read than the raw XML code. Here is the raw XML for just the first item in that RSS feed:

```
<feedburner:feedburnerHostname xmlns:feedburner="
http://rssnamespace.org/feedburner/ext/1.0">http://feedburner.google.com
</feedburner:feedburnerHostname>
<item>
    <title>Anti-inflammatory juice</title>
    <link>http://juicingtherainbow.com/2380/recipes/anti-inflammatory-juice/</link>
    <comments>
    http://juicingtherainbow.com/2380/recipes/anti-inflammatory-juice/#comments
    </comments>
    <pubDate>Fri, 14 Jun 2013 09:42:46 +0000</pubDate>
    <dc:creator>Andy Williams</dc:creator>
    <category><![CDATA[Recipes]]></category>
    <guid isPermaLink="false">http://juicingtherainbow.com/?p=2380</guid>
    <description><![CDATA[Inflammation is one of the main causes of disease, and a
    lot of the foods we eat contribute to the inflammation.  With chronic
    inflammation comes disease.  This juice is a powerful anti-inflammatory drink,
    and it's tasty too.]]></description>
    <wfw:commentRss>
    http://juicingtherainbow.com/2380/recipes/anti-inflammatory-juice/feed/
    </wfw:commentRss>
    <slash:comments>0</slash:comments>
</item>
<item>
    <title>Carrot pulp salad</title>
    <link>http://juicingtherainbow.com/2320/recipes/carrot-pulp-salad/</link>
    <comments>http://juicingtherainbow.com/2320/recipes/carrot-pulp-salad/#comments
```

Every post in the RSS feed has an entry like this.

RSS feeds provide an easy way for people to follow information they are interested in.

For example, if someone was interested in juicing, they could take the RSS feed from their favorite juicing websites and then add them to an RSS reader, like the free Feedly.com for example.

Using a tool like Feedly, you can follow dozens of RSS feeds of interest. RSS used this way allows you to scan hundreds of articles by title and description, and only click through to read the ones that you are really interested in.

That is why we have RSS feeds on our site.

WordPress has multiple RSS feeds

WordPress has a main RSS feed at **mydomain.com/feed**. Type that into your web browser substituting mydomain.com for your real domain name, and you'll see yours. However, WordPress also creates a lot of other RSS feeds.

For example, an RSS feed is created for each category of posts on your site. If you have a category called "roses", then there will be an RSS feed showing just the posts in the roses category.

To find the URL of any feed, simply go to the category page on the site and add **feed** to the end of it, like this:

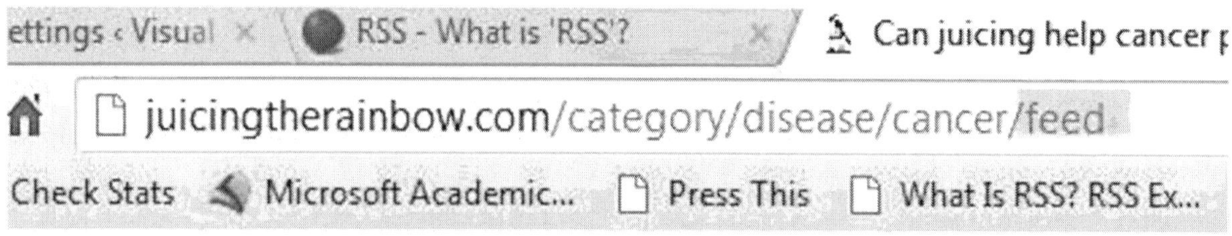

.. and it will display the feed for that category:

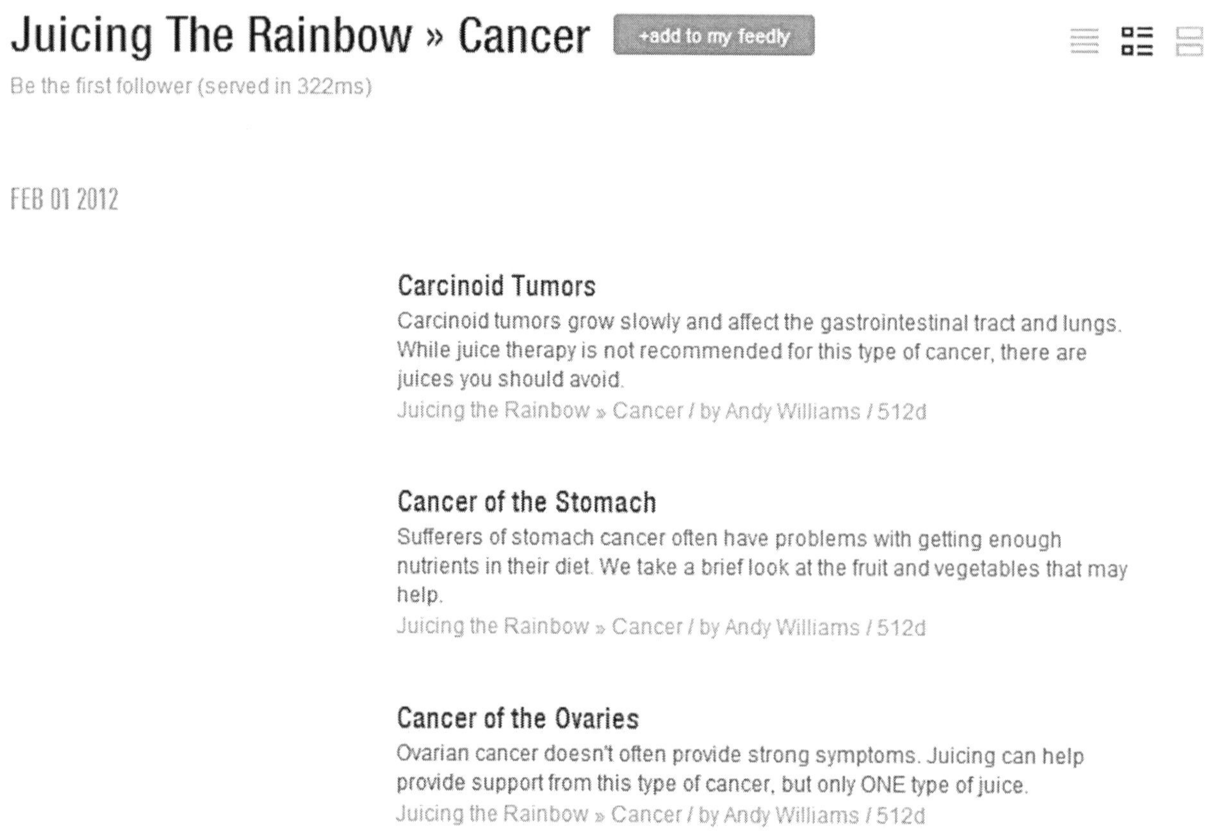

NOTE: The feed in the screenshot above is being displayed by a Google Chrome plugin called Feedly News Reader. If you use Google Chrome, you can find this plugin in the Chrome web store (it's totally free):

http://goo.gl/7xUUQ

Other RSS feeds created by WordPress include RSS feeds for tag pages, author pages, comments, search results, and so on. You can read more about WordPress RSS feeds here if you're interested:

http://goo.gl/CBX40

RSS feeds can help our pages get indexed

Since RSS feeds link back to our website, we can get some backlinks to our pages, which in turn help them get found by the search engines. The backlinks you get from these RSS feeds are very low quality, so they won't affect your search engine rankings much, but they do help get content indexed quickly, so it is worth submitting your main site feed to an RSS Directory like Feedagg.com.

Search Google for **RSS feed submission** and you'll find more sites you can submit your main feed to. I recommend only submitting it to 3 or 4 of the top RSS feed directories though.

When you next post a new article to your site, the feeds on your site are updated, which in turn updates the feed on Feedagg, which now includes a link back to your new article. The search engines monitor sites like this to find new content, so your new article is found very quickly.

Tasks to complete

1. Go and have a look at Google Reader. If necessary create an account but you can just login with a gmail address if you have one.
2. Subscribe to some feeds that are of interest and look through them to find articles that appeal to you. This will give you a good idea of how feeds can be helpful.
3. At the moment, because you have no content on your site, you won't have any meaningful feeds. However, as soon as you start adding content to your site, find the feed URLs where that content appears (main feed, category feed, tag feed, author feed & search feed).

User Profile

When someone comes to your website, they often want to see who is behind the information. Your user profile in WordPress allows you to tell your visitors a little bit about yourself.

In the Dashboard, hover your mouse over the **Users** link in the navigation menu and then select **Your Profile**.

Your user profile should then load. If you see a list of users instead of the profile, it means you clicked the **Users** link, so just click on your username to get to your profile.

At the top of the Profile screen you'll see a couple of settings:

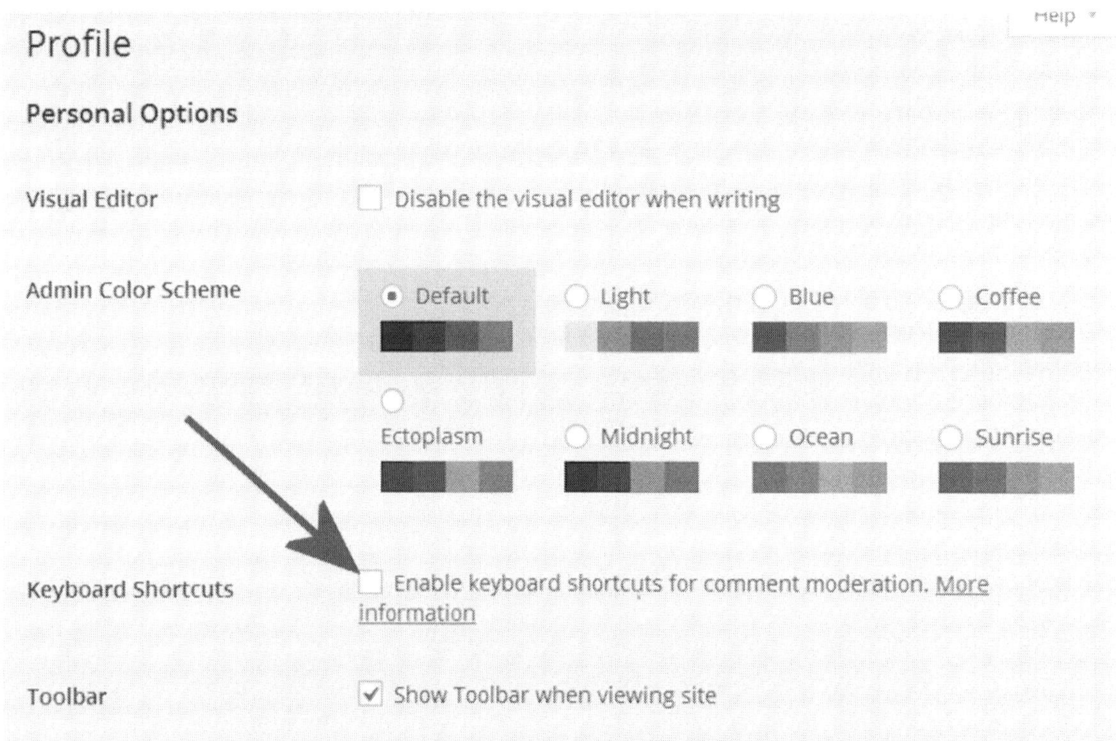

The top box should be left unchecked as we want the visual editor to be displayed when we are writing content. We'll cover that later in the book.

The Admin color scheme – choose whichever you prefer. As you check an option, your Dashboard color scheme will change to reflect your choice. You may be spending a lot of time in your Dashboard, so choose a color scheme you like.

I don't use keyboard shortcuts for comment moderation, but if you are not a mouse person, then you might like to enable this and follow the "more Information" link to learn how to use it.

What is important on this screen is the **Show Toolbar when viewing site**. We will look at that later, but for now, make sure it is checked.

The next set of Profile options are for your name:

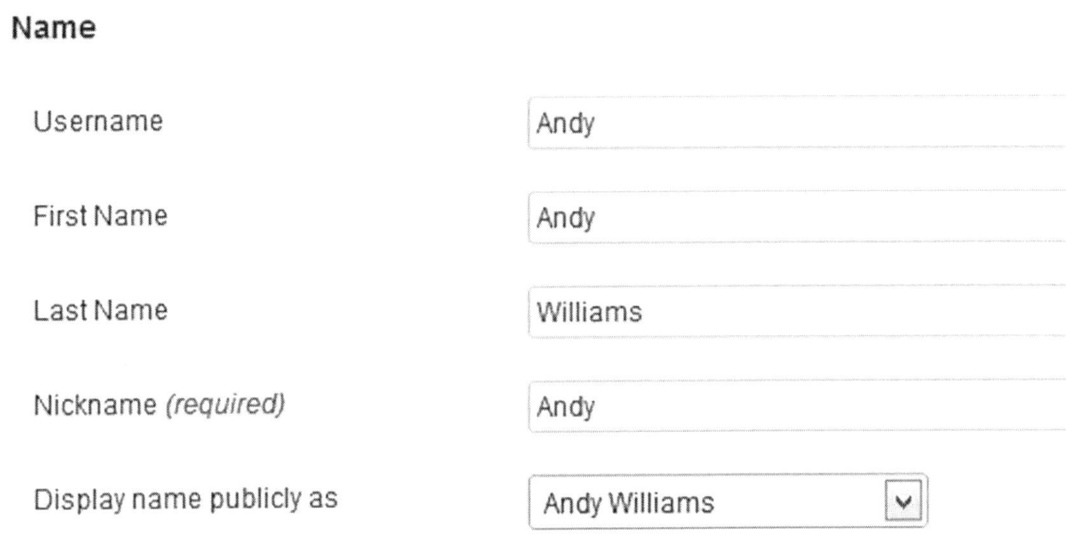

Your username cannot be changed. It will be whatever you chose when you installed WordPress.

Enter your real first and last name (or your persona name if you are working with a pen name).

Under nickname you can write anything. I typically use my first name.

The **Display name publicly as** field will be the name used on each page of your web site telling the visitors who wrote the article. Here it is on one of my sites:

NOTE: If you have a Google Plus account and want to link your content to your Google plus profile, use the same name as your Google plus profile for your display name. Linking your site to your Google plus account is beyond the scope of this book.

The next few options are contact information.

The only one that is required here is the email address and we have talked earlier about how important that is. If you want to fill out the website field, you can, but this is more useful if you have multiple authors on your site, each with their own personal website.

The last bit of information in your profile is your "bio".

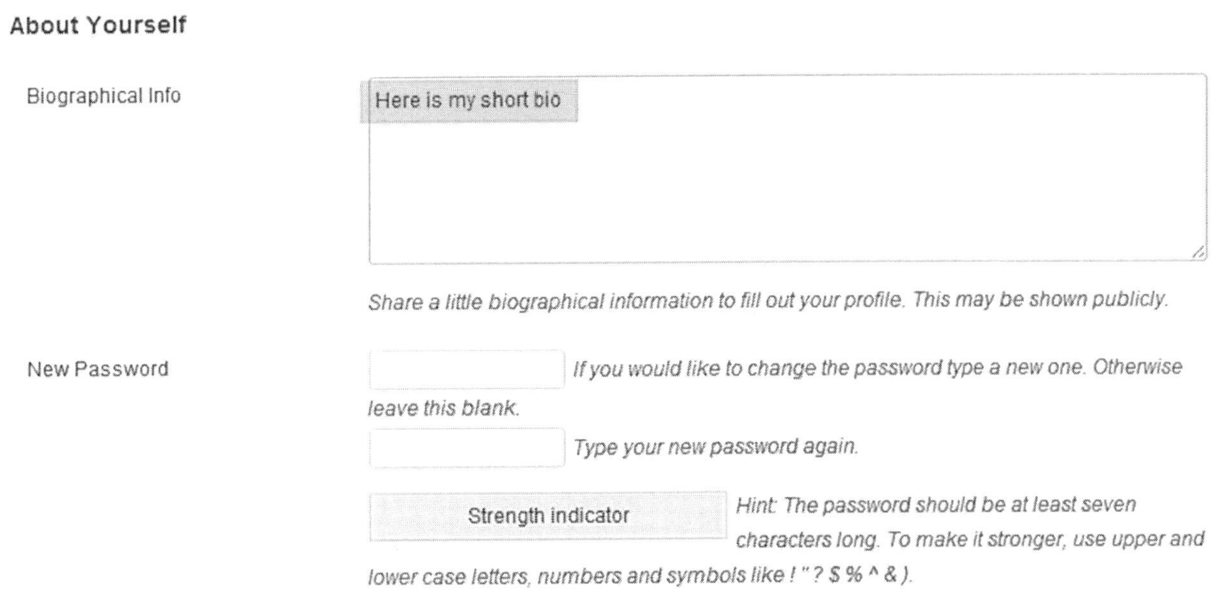

I recommend you fill in a short biography as some themes will show this on the author page. Here is the author page on my demo website. It will list all posts I have made on the website:

See how it has pulled in the Bio from my profile page?

Also, note how my photo is included? Let's see how to do that now.

Gravatars

A Gravatar is simply a photograph or image that you can connect to your email address.

Sites that use Gravatar information, like WordPress, will show that image whenever possible, if you contribute something.

For example, your photo will show on your author page. It will also show on any WordPress site where you leave a comment (assuming you use that email address when leaving the comment). Some themes can even show your photo after each post along with your author's bio.

Go over to Gravatar.com.

Fill in your email address in the form and click **Get Your Gravatar**.

You'll be taken to another screen to sign up. Just enter your email again.

Gravatar.com will send an email to your email address. You need to open it and click the confirmation link to activate your new Gravatar account.

On clicking that link, you'll be taken back to a signup screen that asks you for a username and password (twice). Fill these in to create your Gravatar account.

NOTE: You may need to try several usernames as you obviously cannot use one that someone else has taken. If your desired username is taken, then try adding the year of your birth to the end. That usually works for me.

After submitting your registration information, you will then be taken to a screen that allows you to assign a photo to your email address:

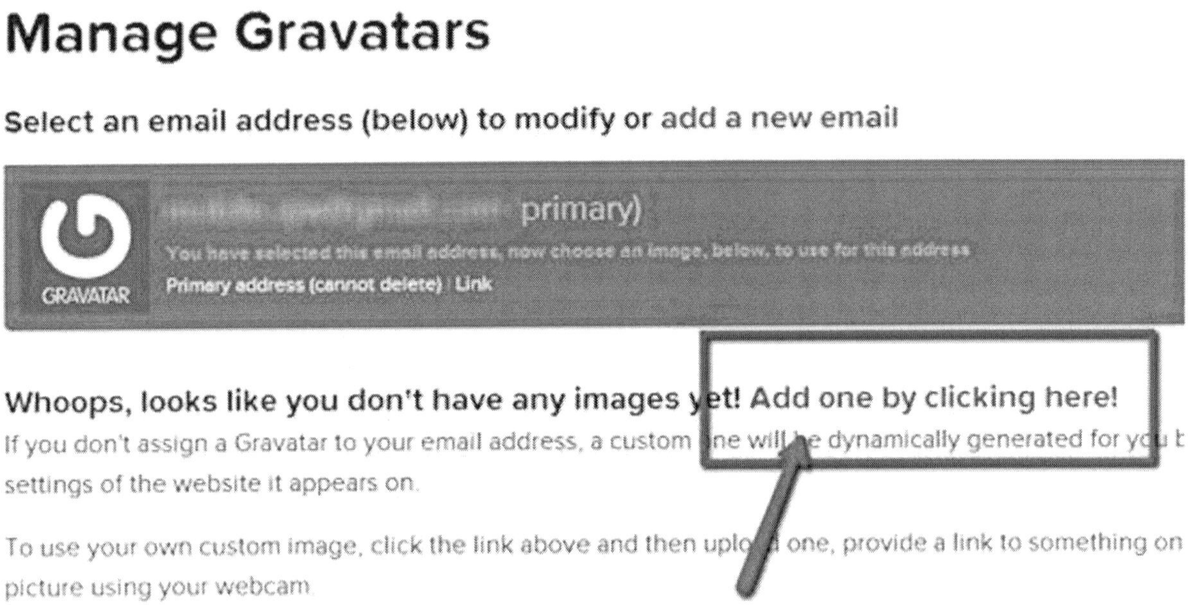

Just click the link and you'll be able to choose an image from a number of different places, including images stored on your hard disk. You'll get an option to crop the image, so don't worry if there is other stuff in the photo that you don't want included. Just crop it out when given the chance.

You now need to rate your image (remember, we mentioned Gravatar ratings earlier when setting up WordPress):

Just click the appropriate button.

That's it. Your Gravatar should now be attached to your site's email address. Now, whenever you leave comments on a WordPress site, use that email address and your image will show up along with your comment (assuming they haven't turned Avatars off).

OK, in the next section we'll start to improve the visual aspects of our website by looking at themes, headers and much more.

Tasks to complete

1. Go and claim your Gravatar.
2. Go in and complete you user profile.
3. Find a WordPress site in your niche, and go leave a relevant comment. Watch as your image appears next to your comment.

Tools

The Tools menu has three options:

The Available tools screen offers you "Press This", which we saw earlier in the book. There is also another tool called **Categories and Tag Converter**. This helps make categories into tags and vice versa. This functionality needs to be installed separately as a WordPress plugin. Clicking on the Import link will take you to the Import screen which has a link to that tool's download page. If you want to use it, I suggest you read the instructions on the Plugin's download page.

The Import and Export features allow you to move content from one blog to another. I have used it when I wanted to merge two or more websites into one larger website. Simply export from one WordPress site, and import its data into the one you want to add the content to.

Again, Importing content requires a plugin that you'll get from the Import screen.

To Export Content, click the Export menu:

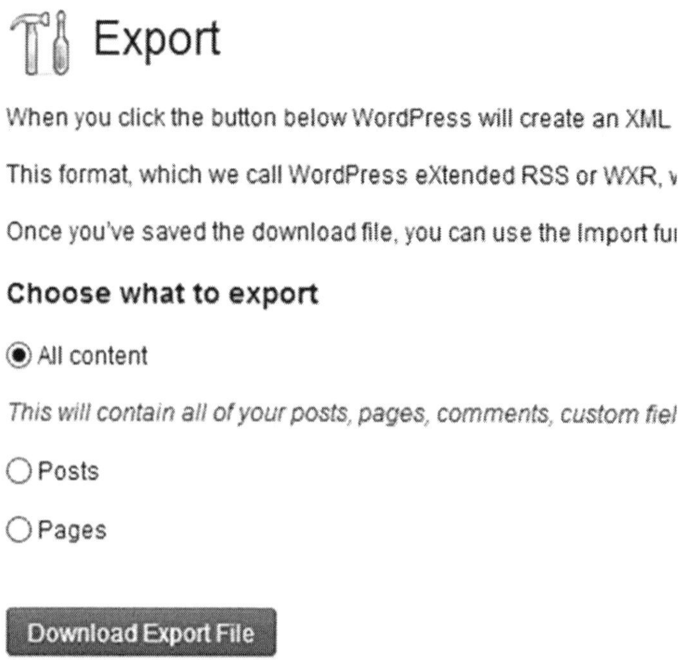

You can then choose what to export. All content, or choose between posts or pages. If you select posts (or pages), you will be given more options including categories to export, export by author, date range or status (published, scheduled, draft, etc).

You will then click the export button to download the export file to your computer.

To Import, install the Import plugin that is linked to from the Import screen:

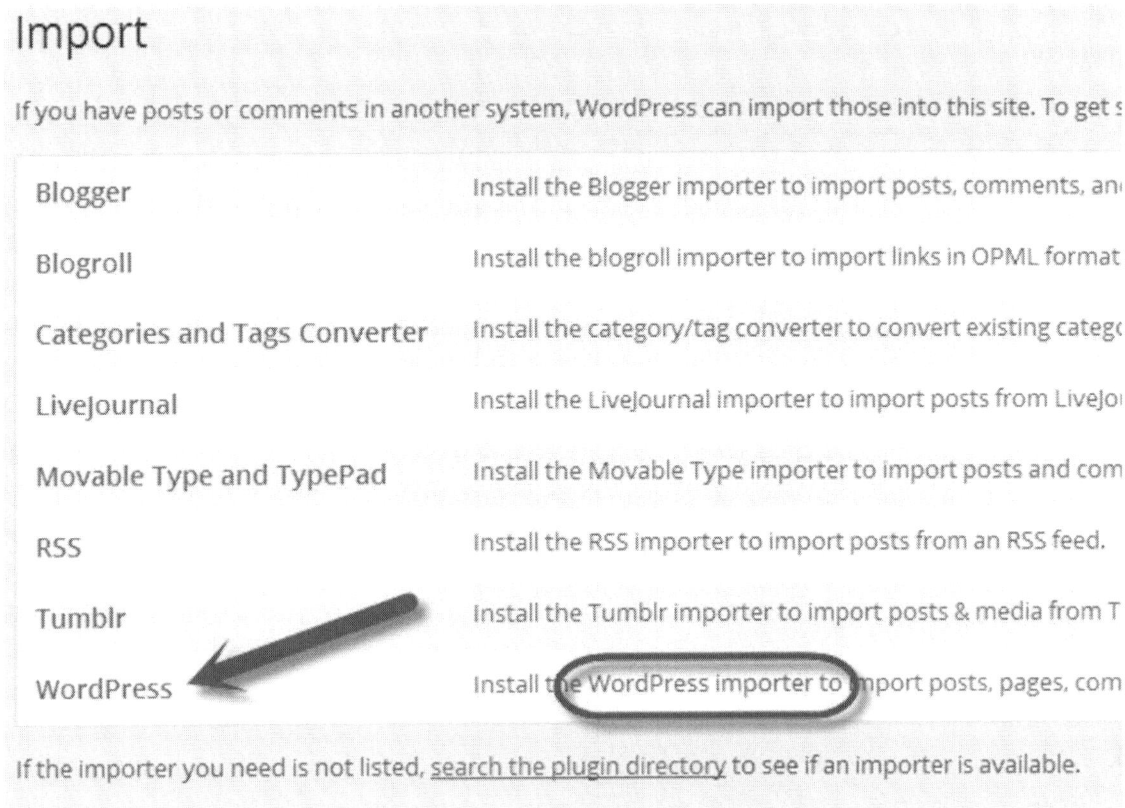

Then make sure you activate it. You can now import the file that was previously exported. Just go to the Import screen again, click the link to the WordPress plugin, and you'll see the following screen:

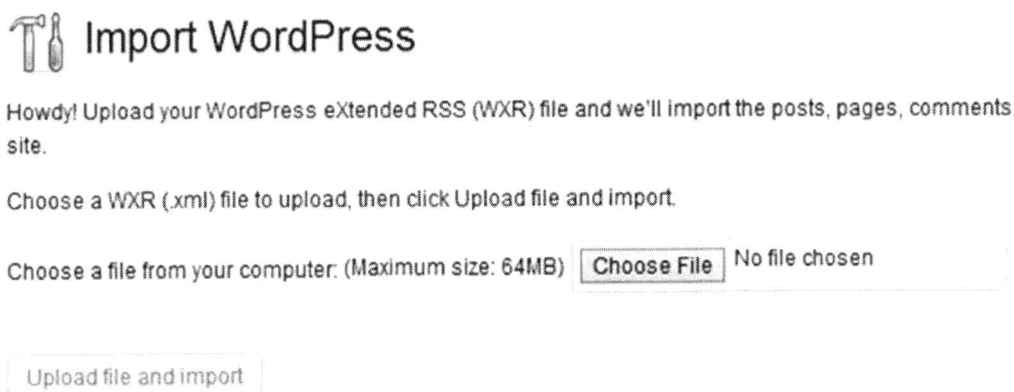

Choose the file and upload.

Appearance menu

If you click on the Appearance link in the Dashboard Navigation sidebar, it will open up to expose you more menu items:

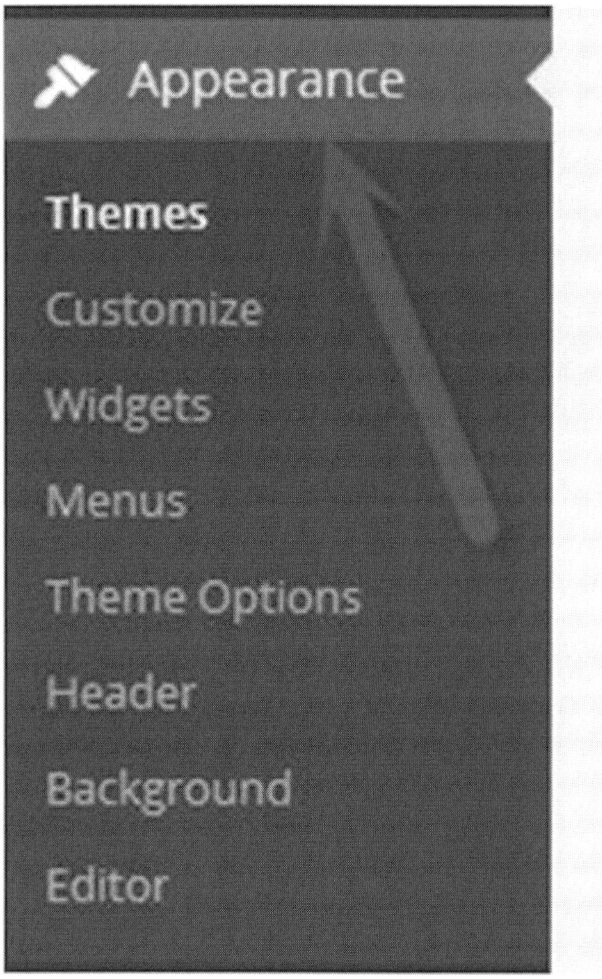

This menu gives you access to settings that control how your website looks. It specifically relates to the template or theme you are using.

Clicking on the Appearance menu actually opens up the themes setting page.

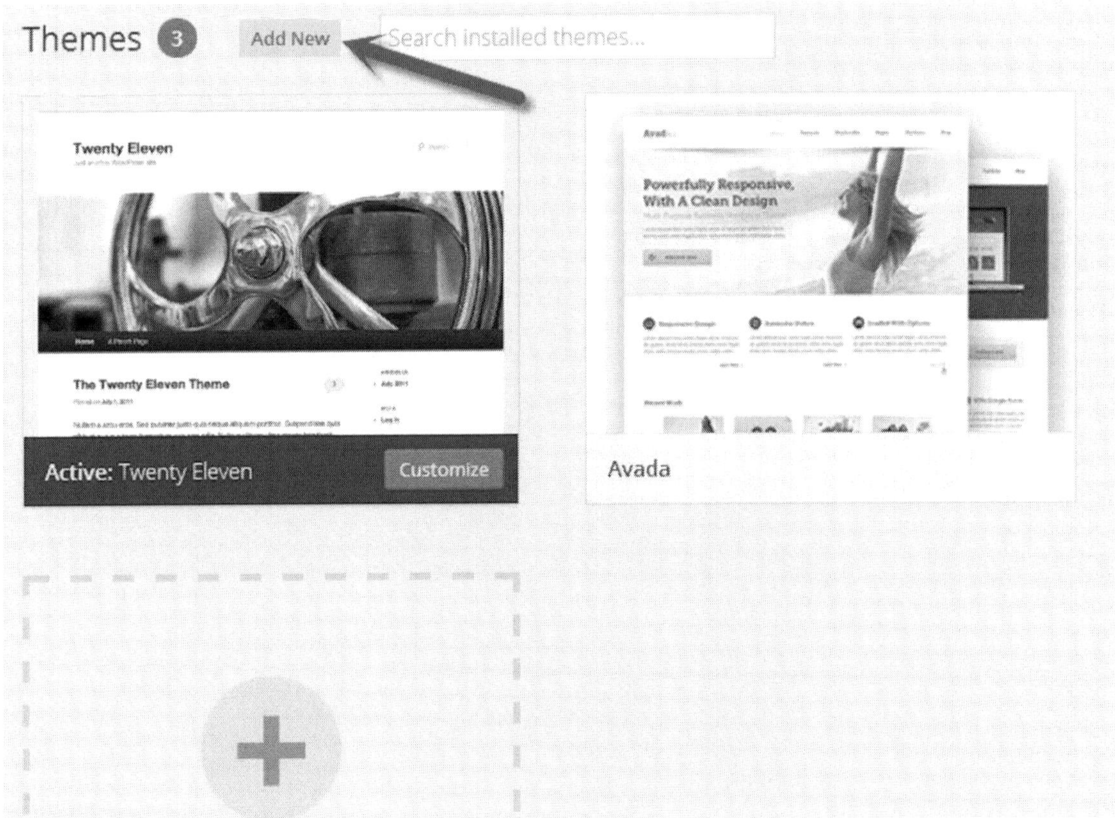

At the top of the themes screen, you have the option of searching for an installed theme (you will only have a couple of installed themes and you can see thumbnails of them all below this top bar) or **Add New** theme, which will search Wordpress approved themes on the internet.

NOTE: You will often hear people referring to WordPress themes as templates. While the two things are not totally the same thing, people often use the words interchangeably to mean the same. So for the purpose of this book, templates and themes are the same thing.

The currently selected theme is shown in the first position, with a **Customize** button next to the text **Active: Twenty Eleven** (or whatever your active theme is called).

The customize button will take you to a WYSIWYG editor allowing you to make some design changes to the appearance of your site.

In this book, we will work with the Twenty Eleven theme to get the look and feel we want for our site.

Click on the customize button to open the editor:

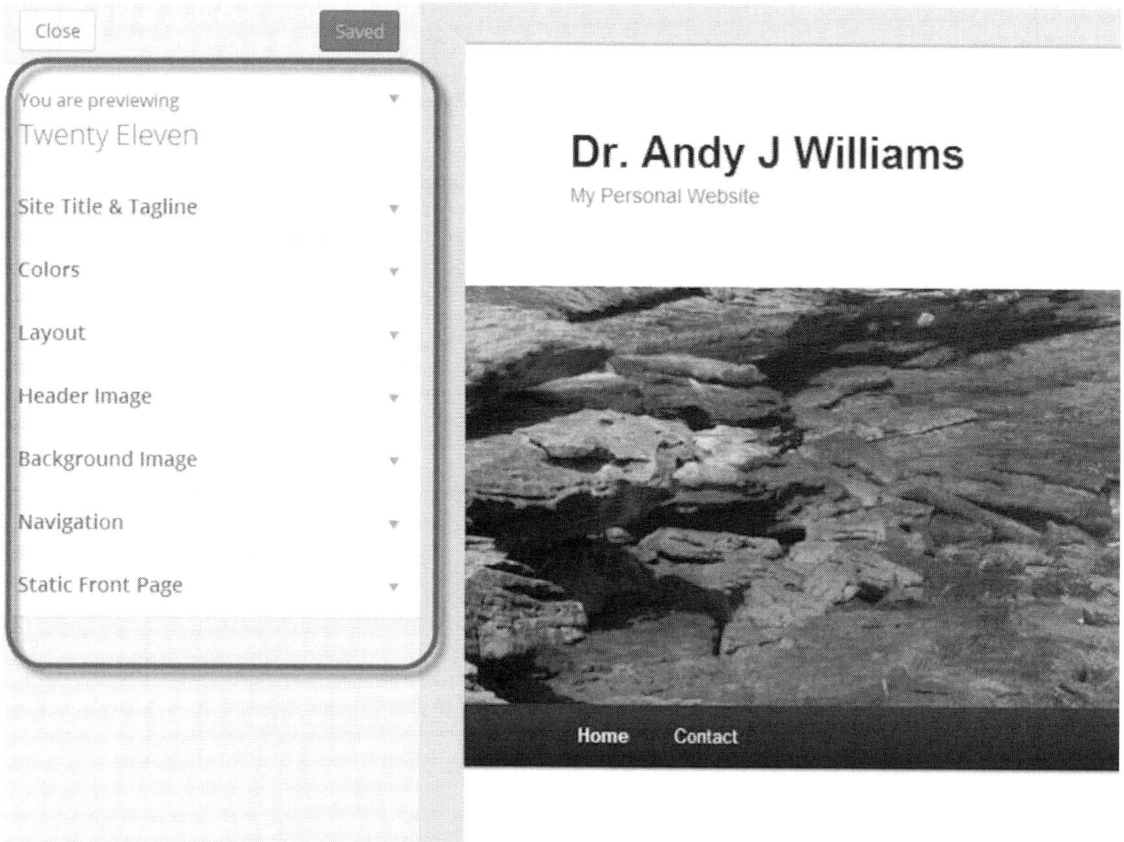

On the left is a menu that gives you access to certain configuration settings. On the right, the large window shows a preview of how your site will appear with the currently selected settings. Make changes and watch the preview update as you design how your site will look and feel.

At the top of the menu is Site Title & Tagline. These options can also be changed in the General Settings we saw earlier (with the exception of one setting).

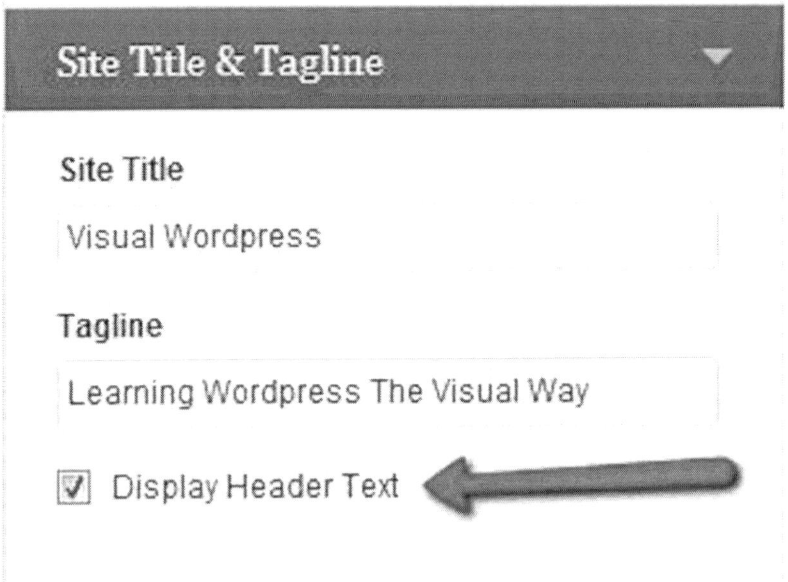

You can type in the title and tagline and watch the preview display on the right side update with the new settings.

The one setting that is new here is the **Display Header Text** checkbox. If you uncheck this, see what happens to the preview. The Site name and tagline disappear. The search box is also moved from this area down to the black menu bar. Try it.

Why might you want to remove the Site title and tagline?

You might decide to include the title and tagline within the header image instead. By combining the two, you can save space at the top of your theme (which currently shows this information as two separate sections). We'll look later at how you can easily create a custom header graphic containing the Site Title and tagline. You can then come back here and remove the header text from your site by unchecking this box.

The next menu is the colours menu:

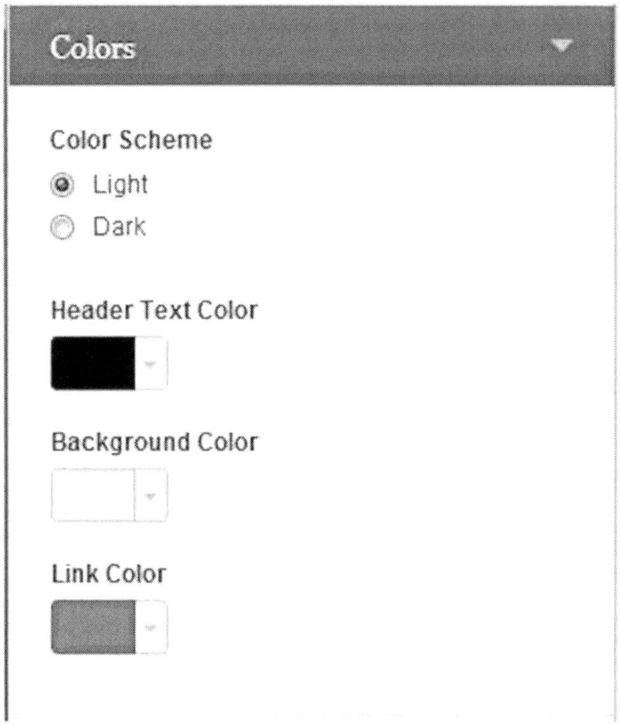

At the top you'll see a couple of radio buttons that allow you to switch between two readymade schemes - light and dark. The light scheme is basically dark text on a white background, and the dark scheme is light text on black background. Play around by selecting each one to see how they display in the preview screen.

You can manually change the colours of the header text, background colour, and link colour. I suggest you actually leave these alone because too many colours can ruin a design. Simple is better. If you do want to experiment, click the box under the setting that you wish to change. You can click directly inside the coloured box to open the colour selector.

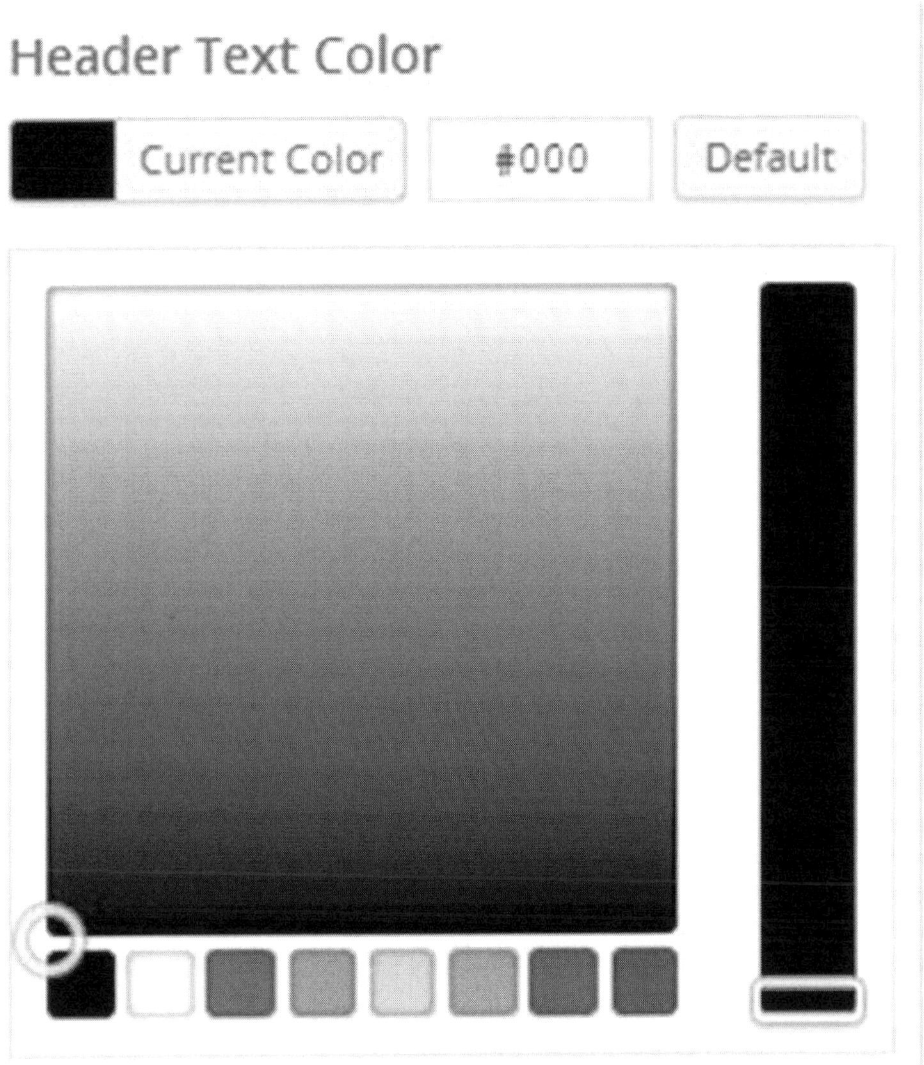

From here, you can select a basic colour from the color boxes along the bottom, and then choose the tone of that colour using the large central square. You can also lighten or darken your selected color using the vertical bar on the right.

The next menu is the layout menu.

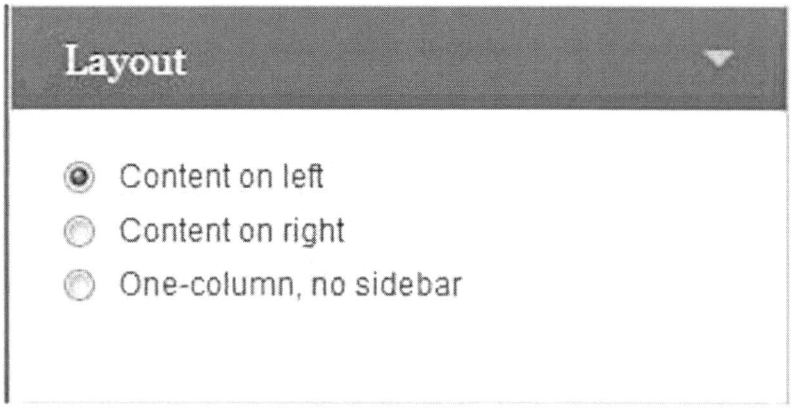

This allows you to select which side of your webpage the menu is located. If you select **Content on left**, the menu will be on the right. **Content on right** leaves the menu on the left. You can also choose to have no sidebar if that's what you want. I don't recommend a **one-column, no sidebar** layout for a multipage site though, as the sidebar is an important area for adding navigation, monetization, promotional stuff, and so on.

The settings you choose will be your personal preference. I prefer my sidebar on the right (content left).

The next menu is the header image.

I have cut out part of the middle section as it just lists lots of default header images. If you like one, select it and see how the preview changes. Later in the book we will replace this header with our own unique custom image.

At the bottom, there is also a link to **Remove Image**. This will take the image off your site and just leave the Title and Tagline in the header area. Try it! You can easily add it back if you want to by clicking on one of the images.

The next option is the Background image.

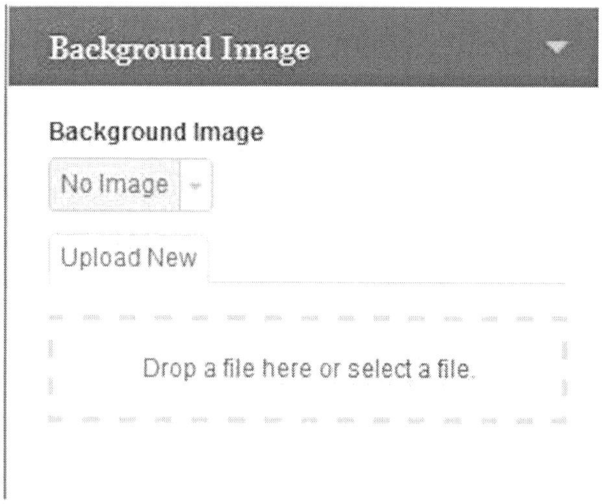

You can drag and drop an image from your computer into the dashed box above and it will upload to your site as a background image. Go ahead and try it now.

When the image is uploaded, more options become available to you:

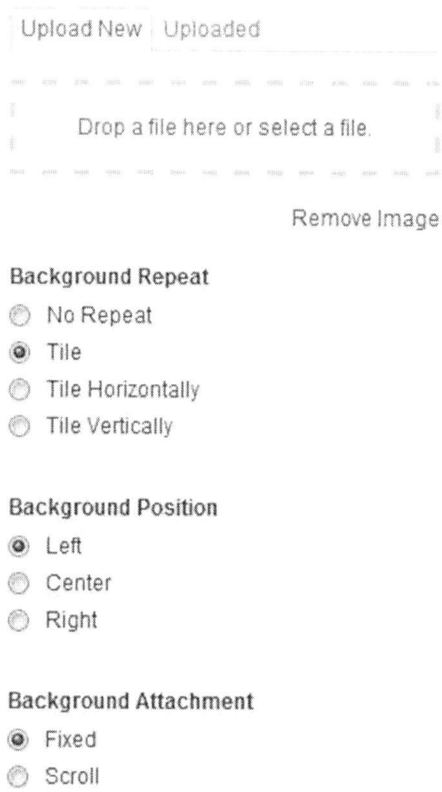

Background repeat allows you to repeat the image over the entire background by tiling over the whole background (along both the x and y axis), tiling horizontally (only a single layer of the image on the x axis) or tiling vertically (single layer of the image along the y axis).

The next option down is to position the background in a certain place - left, centre or right. This will determine where the image is positioned before any tiling takes place. For example, if you choose right, and have chosen to tile vertically in the repeat options, then the image will be repeated in a single column down the right side of your webpage.

The final options are to either have the background image fixed, which means it stays where it is when you scroll through the content, or scroll, which means the background image scrolls (moves), with the content.

NOTE: If you choose to have the image fixed, it may not display as fixed in the actual preview pane. Therefore, save the changes and then go to your homepage URL. Here you will be able to see the fixed image effect.

I don't recommend using a background image at all. Simply colour is better as images often look messy and unprofessional. However, I do recommend you upload an image and play around with the settings to see what they do. When you have finished, click the remove image to get rid of it.

The next option is the Navigation options, which allow you to select menus to use on your site. Menus are built in another area of the dashboard, and you have total control over the contents of these menus. We will look at this later.

The final options in the customize screen are for a Static Front Page.

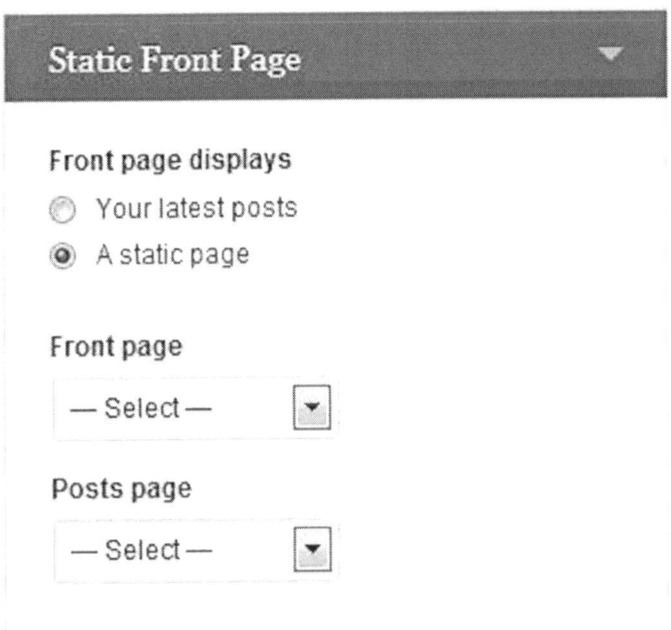

These options are identical to the ones we saw earlier in the Reading Settings.

We will look at this later.

NOTE: If you haven't created a WordPress PAGE, then you won't be able to set your front page (home page), to show a page instead of posts.

OK, when you have finished playing with the customize settings, either save and publish your changes or cancel to undo your experimentation.

Let's now go back and see how we can install new themes to completely change the look of our website.

Finding Wordpress Themes, Installing and Selecting them

We installed the Twenty Eleven theme earlier, so there is nothing to worry about here.

Click on the **Themes** link under the **Appearance** menu if it is not already selected.

Click on the **Add** New button at the top of the themes screen.

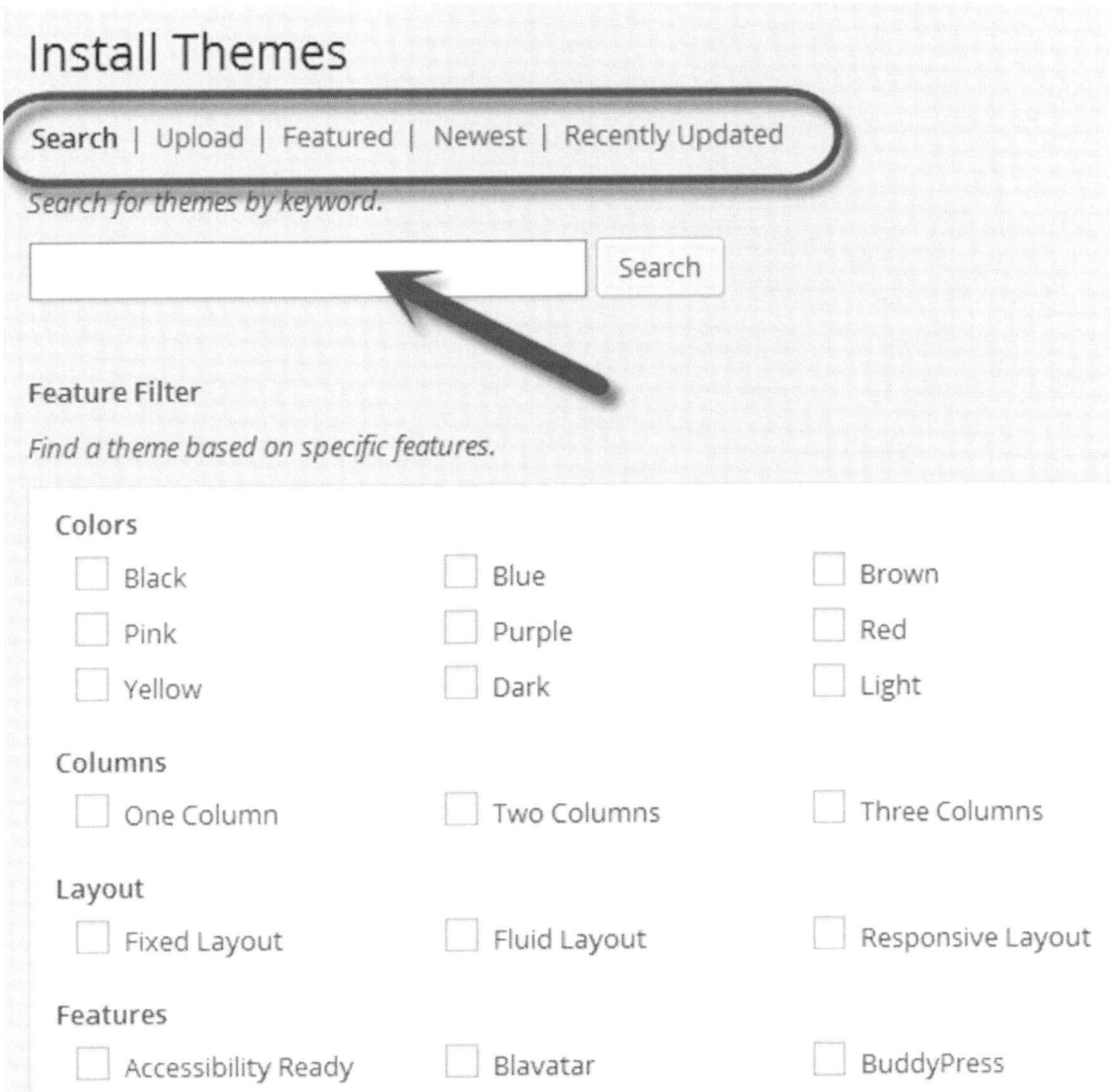

Across the top is a menu that allows you to search for themes by:

Upload - This allows you to upload a zipped theme file that you bought or downloaded elsewhere. It needs to be uploaded in a zip file format, so **do not** unzip it.

Featured - These are some of the more popular themes that WordPress thinks are good.

Newest - These are the newest themes that have been accepted into the WordPress Theme library.

Recently Updated - These are the themes that have been recently updated. Updated themes are more likely to work with latest versions of WordPress, so this is a good place to start.

You can also do a search using the **Feature Filter** check boxes in the bottom section of the screen.

If you want a light, two-column theme with fixed width, you might select these options and hit the search button.

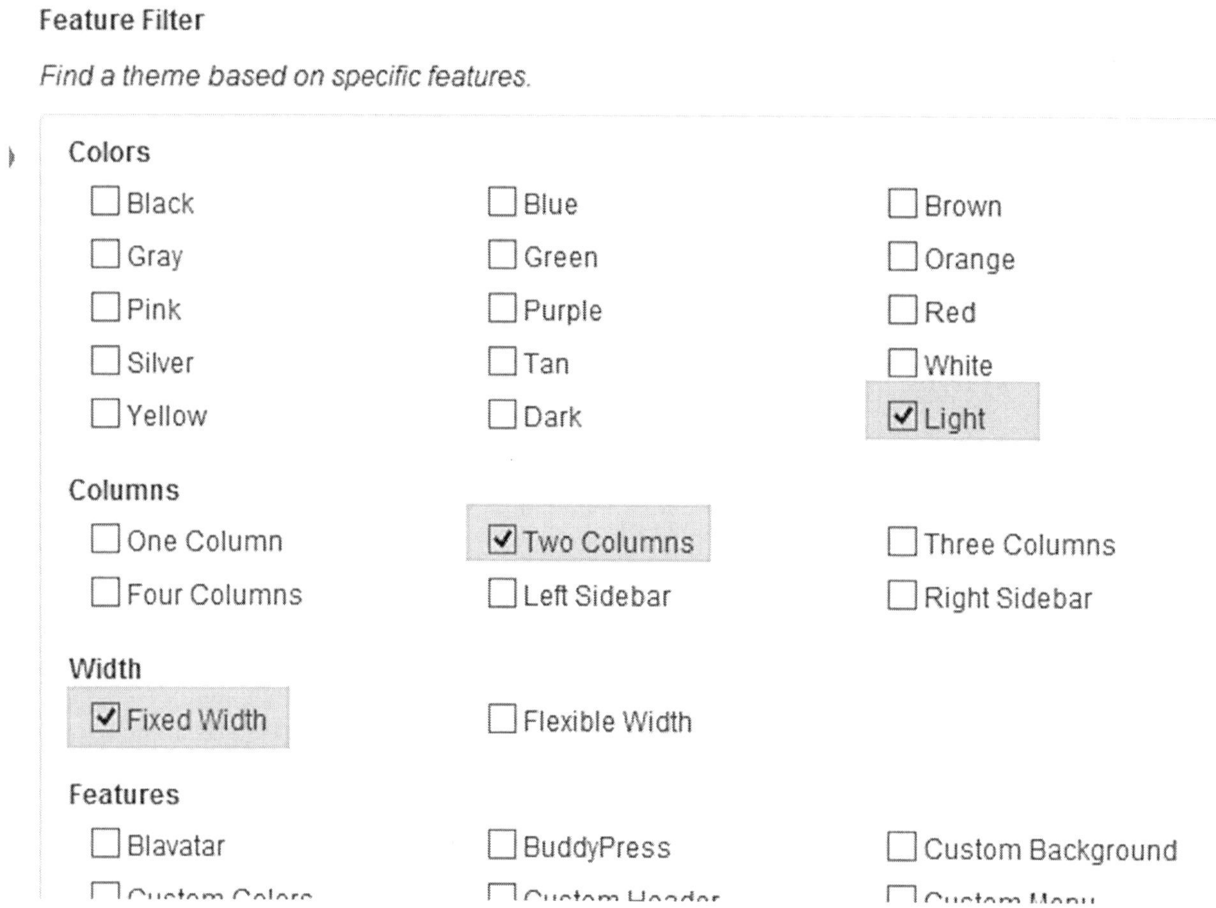

WordPress will go away and find the themes that match the features you have selected.

When you do a search (with the exception of the Upload feature which requires you to navigate to the zip file on your computer), you are presented with previews of the themes relevant to your search:

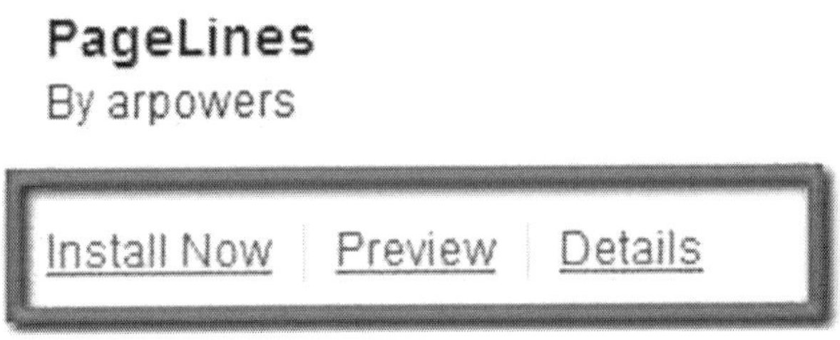

Under the thumbnail image of each theme is a menu. This menu lets you install the theme, preview it before installing, and see more details of that theme.

The details link opens up a description of the theme.

The preview link is well worth clicking before installing any new theme. A window opens to show you a preview of the theme, with headers, fonts, bullets etc., so you know exactly what the various aspects of your pages can look like.

If you like a particular theme, you can simply install it. If not, move onto the next one. Feel free to install a few themes. If you don't like them you can always uninstall them easily enough.

When you install a theme, you'll get presented with a menu asking what you want to do:

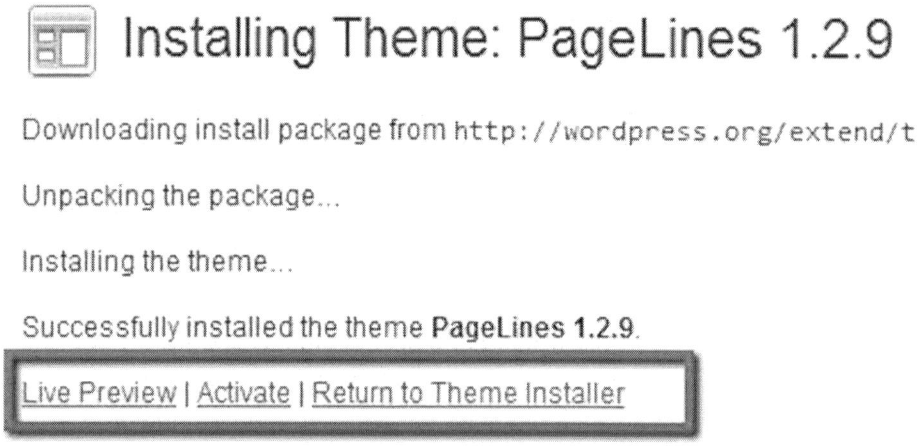

I recommend you click Live Preview first to see what the theme looks like using the existing content on your site. This will show you exactly how YOUR site will look with this theme. However, you will need content on your site in order to get a good idea of how things will look.

NOTE: For some themes, the live preview will not work and you'll be forced to activate it to see how it appears and functions. If you find a theme like this, don't worry. It's easy to switch back to a previous one if you don't fancy the new design.

To switch between installed themes, go to the Themes page inside the Appearance menu. You will see the familiar current theme in the first position, and all of the other installed themes appear after as thumbnails.

If you move your mouse over the thumbnails of installed, inactive themes, you'll see the thumbnail change to include a menu:

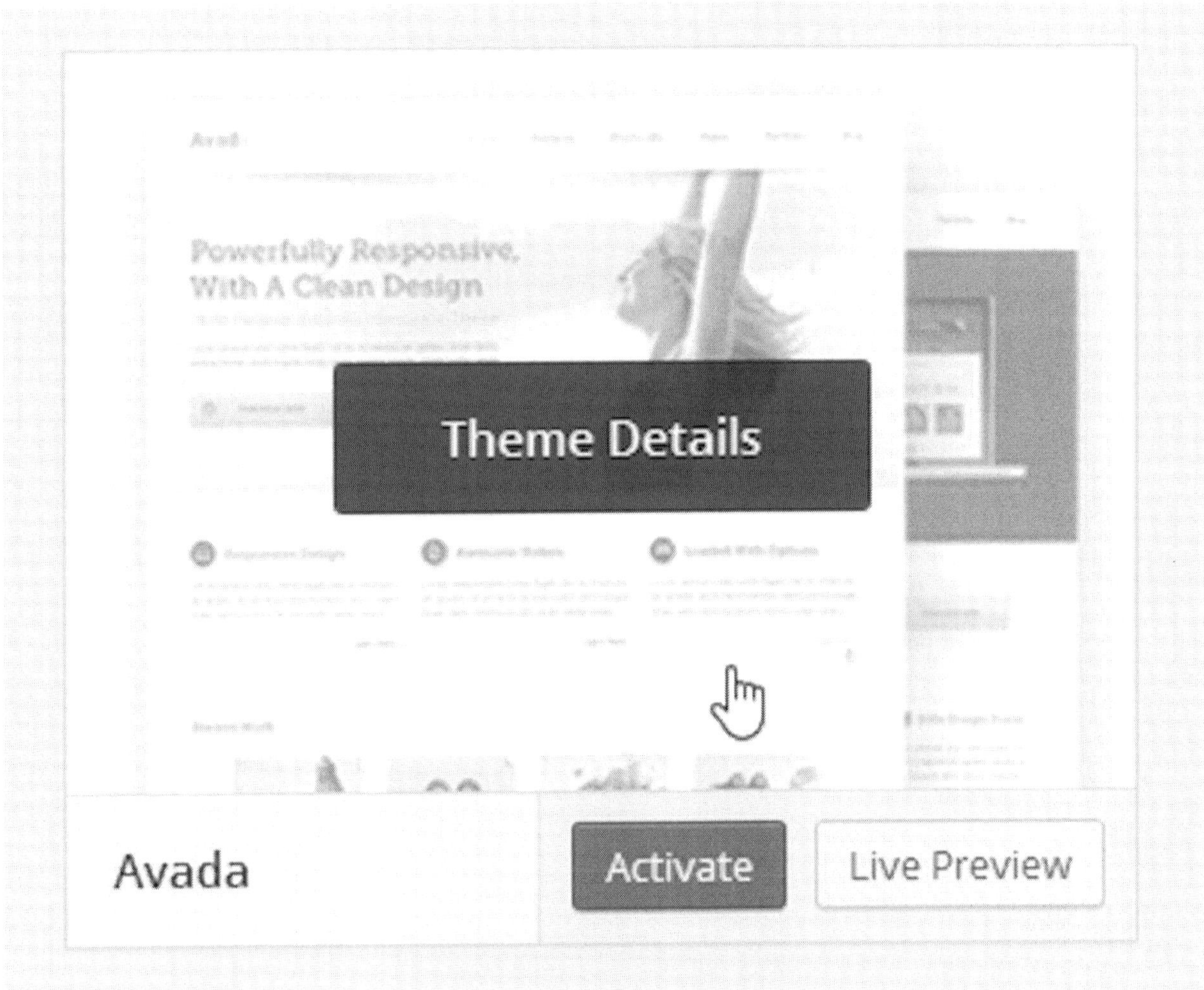

You have an option called **Live Preview** that allows you to see what the theme will look like on your site. The Live Preview opens in the same theme customize screen we saw earlier. If you want to activate one of the installed themes, simply click the **Activate** button.

The other option you have on this thumbnail is **Theme Details**. Clicking this will bring up more details on the theme. How much more detail? Well that depends on the author of the theme, and how much detail they included with the theme.

NOTE: As a matter of security, I don't recommend you keep themes that you do not use. Once you have decided which theme you want to use for your site, delete all other themes using the delete link under that theme in the Themes page.

We are going to continue working with the Twenty Eleven theme in this book, so I'll activate it and delete the other themes that are installed.

Adding a custom graphic header to your site

OK, click on the **Header** link in the **Appearance** menu.

There is a setting here that we need to explore. Essentially it allows you to upload your own graphic for the header of your website. I always create a header image for my sites that includes the Site Title and tagline.

The only thing you need to get right is to use the correct width & height for the header image. The dimensions differ depending on the theme. This screen will tell you what dimensions you need for your chosen theme.

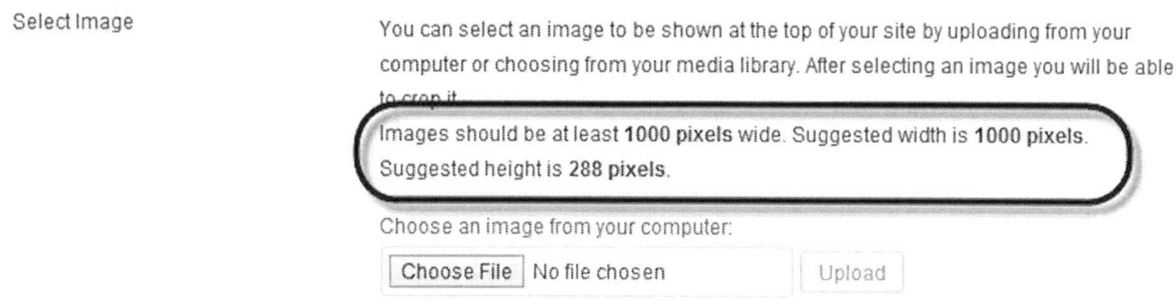

For the Twenty Eleven theme, the image needs to be 1000 pixels wide and 288 pixels high. Any image that is not the correct size will look distorted on the site, so do stick to the suggested image dimensions.

I have created a quick header image with just my Site Title and tagline. Let's add it to the site.

Click the **Choose File** button and select the header image from your computer. Then click the upload button to upload it to your website.

You'll then be taken to a screen showing your header and asking if you want to crop it:

Since my image is exactly 1000 x 288 pixels, I don't need to crop it. I can simply click the **Skip Cropping, Publish Image as Is** button.

If I now look at my homepage, there is a problem:

You can see that the site Title & Tagline are still showing.

We can remove this on the header setting screen. Scroll to the bottom and you'll see the checkbox:

Uncheck the box and then click the Save Changes button.

After reloading my homepage I can now see that everything looks fine:

If you are not particularly good with graphics software, you can hire someone to create a logo for you on Fiverr.com. It'll only cost you $5! However, there is also a free software tool you can use to create a header that looks OK (and usually better than those you can get on Fiverr.com). It's called XHeader and you can watch a short video I created on using the software here:

http://goo.gl/P1eg5

The theme Editor menu

The bottom item in the Appearance menu is the Editor. This allows you to edit the theme template files. We won't be covering this in the book, as it is an advanced topic requiring programming skills.

OK, the last two options in the appearance menu are very important - Widgets and Menus. However, they'll actually make a lot more sense once we have some content on the site, so let's leave those until a little later on in the book.

Tasks to complete

1. Choose a theme you want to use. For your first site I recommend you stick with Twenty Eleven (you can always change it later), as we'll use it throughout this book as our reference theme.
2. Modify your theme.
3. Add a header graphic if you want a unique one.

Plugins

In this section, I want to explain what plugins are, where you can get them, and how to install them, etc. I'll also walk you through the installation and configuration of a few plugins as we go through this section. We will install more plugins later when there is something specific that we need on our site, but for now, let's concentrate on those that I feel are essential to all WordPress sites.

NOTE: from time to time, plugins get updated. Sometimes this is for feature enhancements, and other times it's so that the plugin remains compatible with an updated version of WordPress. Either or, there may be times where you could see different interfaces and perhaps some options removed (or added), from those illustrated in this book. Most modifications though, should be easy enough to figure out.

In the Dashboard Navigation bar, you'll see the Plugins menu:

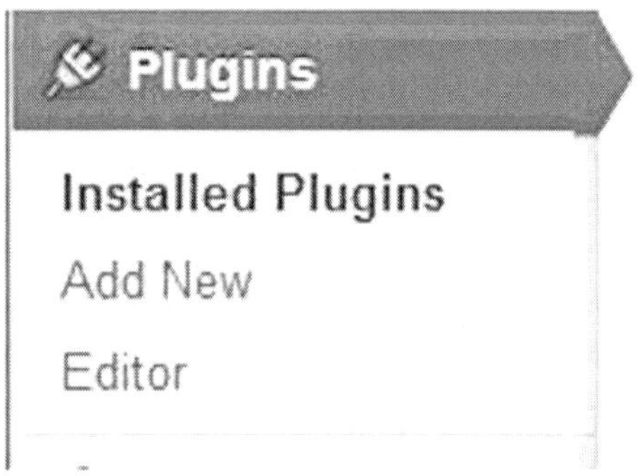

The menu has three options:

Installed Plugins - To view the current list of installed plugins.

Add New - For when you want to add a new plugin.

Editor - This is a text editor that allows you to modify the code of the plugins. We won't be looking at this advanced aspect.

Click on the installed plugins menu.

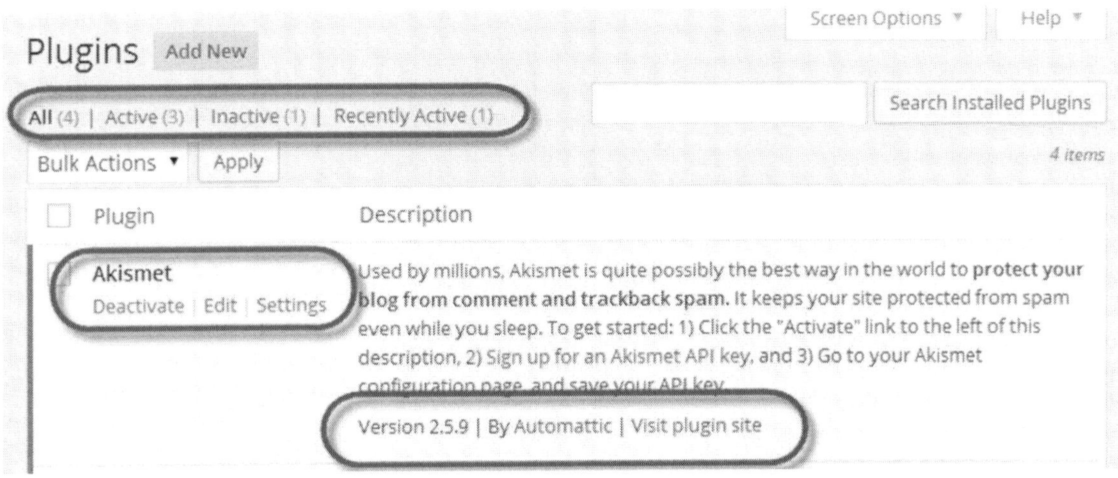

At the very top left of this screenshot you'll see where it says:

All(4) | Active (3) | Inactive (1) | Recently Active (1)

This refers to the plugins you have installed. The numbers in brackets next to each of these items tells you how many plugins are in that group. Therefore we have a total of 4 plugins installed on this site, and 1 is inactive.

To activate a plugin is easy. Just click the Activate link underneath the name of the plugin.

NOTE: You may also have a menu item at the top labelled Drop-ins. These are special types of plugins that alter core Wordpress functionality.

The menu at the top will change to reflect the new activated plugin. At the moment, the **All** menu item is selected.

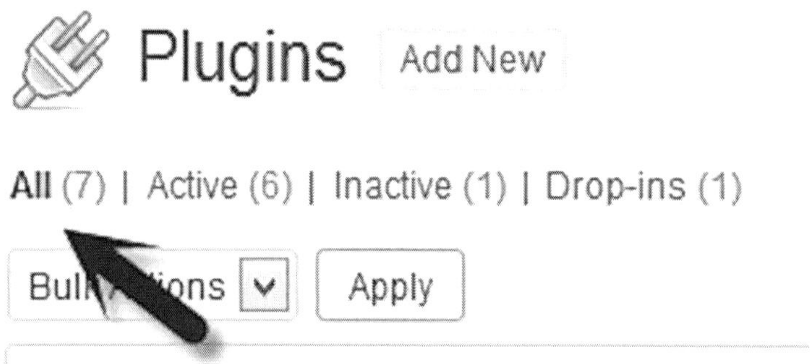

This is the filter that is currently set to show ALL plugins (active, inactive, etc).

We can view just the active, or just the inactive, by clicking those menu items.

NOTE: It is not a good idea to keep plugins installed that are inactive. If you do not need a plugin, uninstall it.

The "Drop-ins" menu may appear as you install more plugins. Drop-in plugins are special plugins that change the core functionality of Wordpress. This might be something like a caching plugin.

There may be times when another item appears in this menu labelled **Updates Available**. This will appear when there is an update available for one of your plugins and you can click this link to see which plugins have updates pending. However, I recommend you handle all updates as we saw earlier - by using the Dashboard -> Updates menu whenever you get notified there is something that needs updating.

We don't want to use either of the pre-installed plugins, so we can delete them now.

NOTE: Akismet is actually a good anti-spam plugin but it went commercial a while back, meaning it's no longer free if you have a commercial website.

Deleting plugins

To delete a plugin, it needs to be inactive. Therefore we need to deactivate the one we activated a few minutes ago before proceeding.

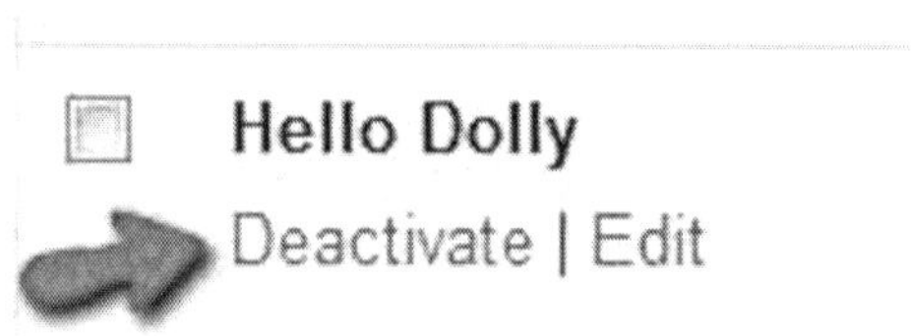

Just click the **Deactivate** link under the plugin.

To delete a plugin, just click the Delete link under the plugin name (the delete link only appears on inactive plugins):

You will be asked to confirm that you want to delete the plugin:

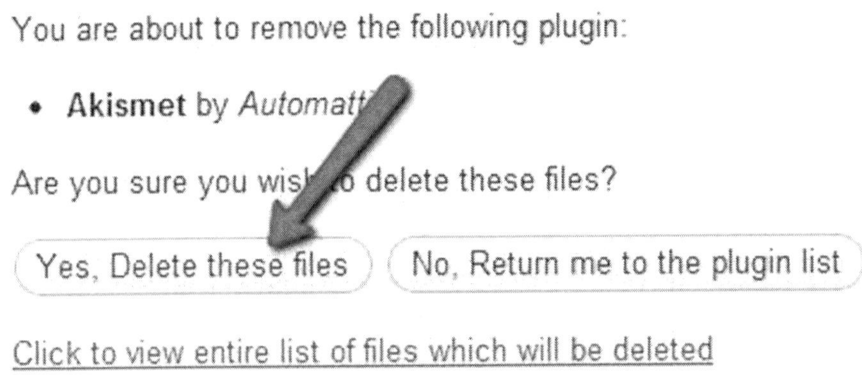

Clicking that button will delete the plugin and all its files from your server.

If you have more than one plugin to delete, there is a quicker way to remove multiple plugins in one go:

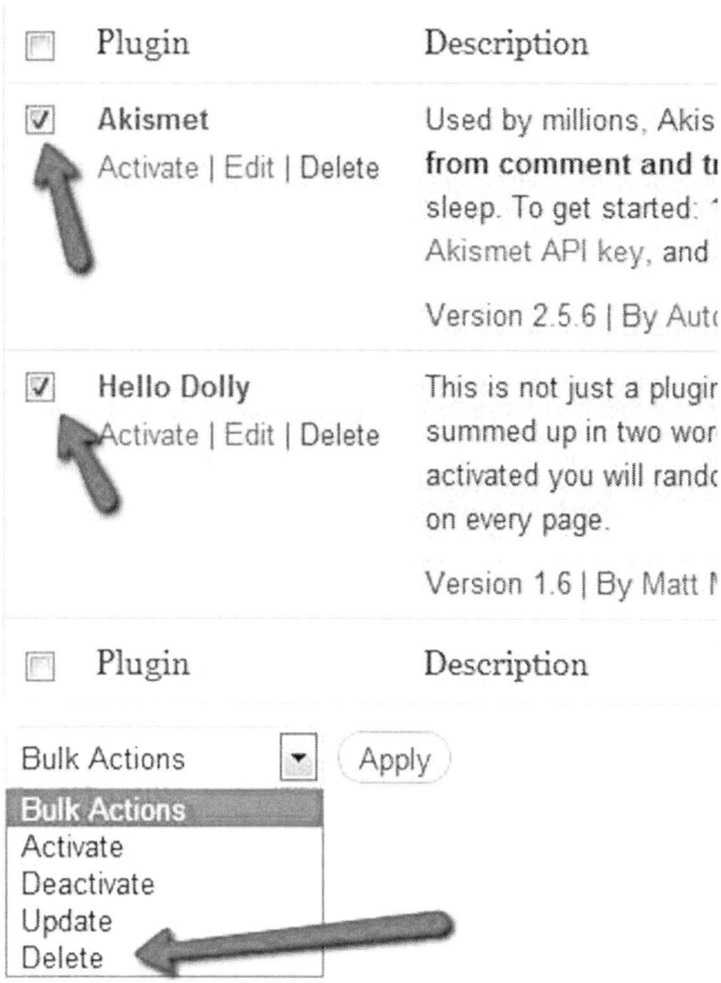

Just check the box next to each plugin you want to delete, then, in the **Bulk Actions** drop down box at the bottom, select **Delete**. Now click the Apply button to carry out the deletion. You will get a similar screen to the confirmation screen we saw a moment ago asking to confirm you want to delete all of the selected plugins.

NOTE: The bulk action feature also allows you to carry out other features on multiple plugins at once. These are Activate, Deactivate and Update.

Installing important plugins

OK, we now have no plugins installed. So let's go ahead and install 4 very important plugins, then configure them.

WP-DBManager

This plugin is VERY important because it will look after your WordPress database (that is where all of the information needed to create your website is stored). This plugin will not only keep the database healthy by optimizing it periodically, it will also make backups of the database at pre-arranged intervals, and send you a copy of the database via email. If you ever have to "reinstall" your site, these database backups are vital.

To install any plugin, go to the **Add New** Plugin screen by clicking the button at the top of the screen, or the link in the menu:

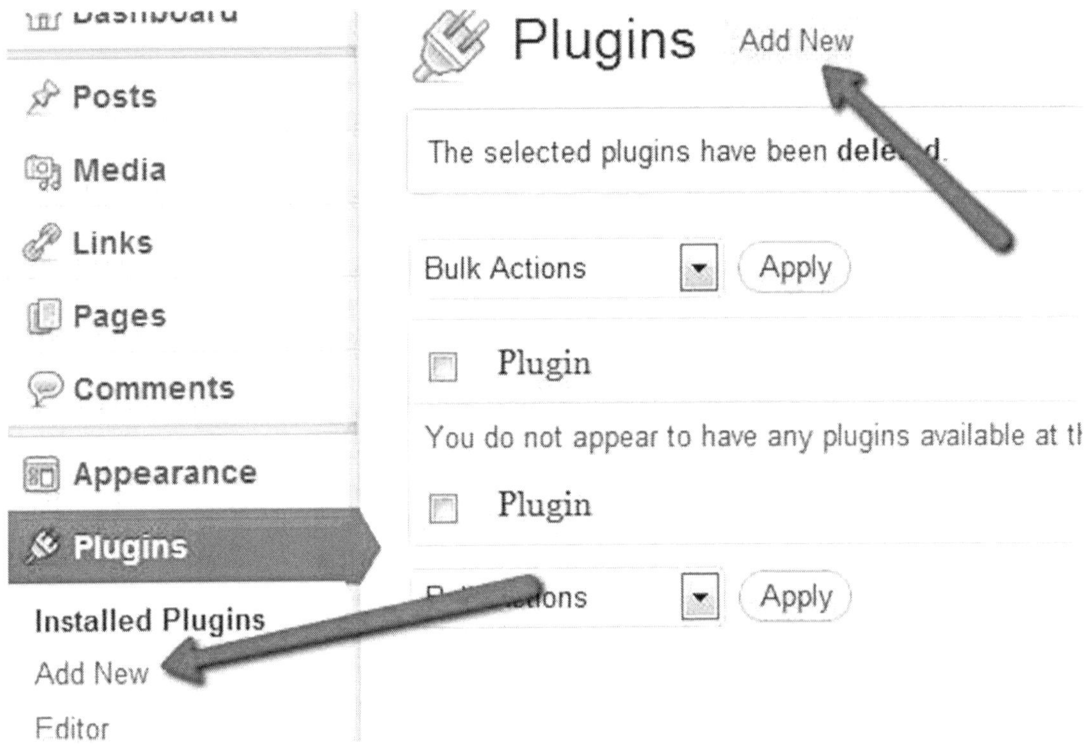

On the Add New screen, there is a search box. Type in **wp dbmanager** and click the search plugins button.

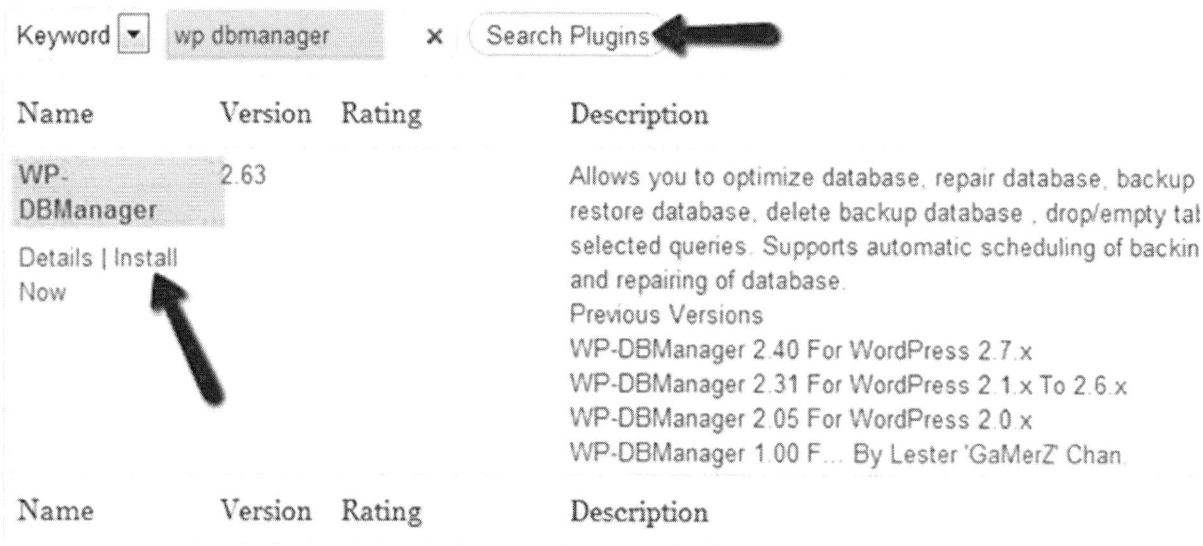

The WP-DBManager plugin will appear. Click the Install Now link underneath the plugin.

You'll be asked to confirm that you want to go ahead and install it.

After installation, you'll be asked what you want to do next:

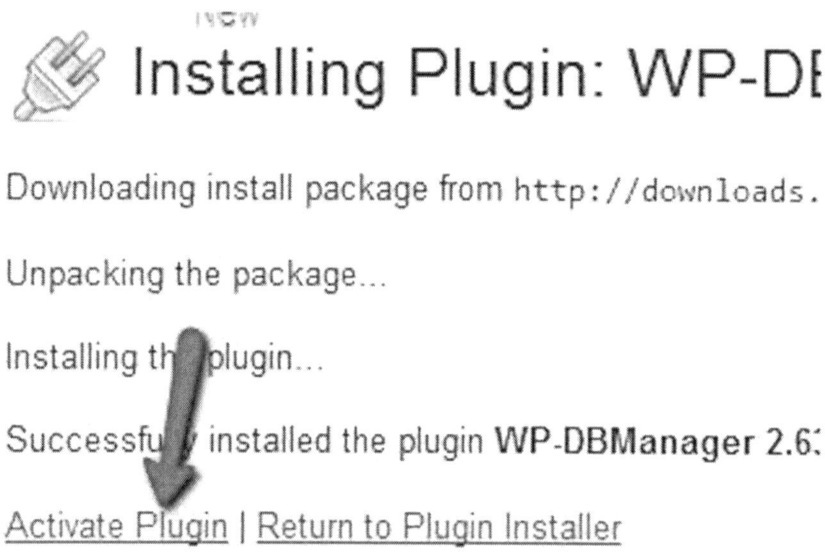

Click the link to activate the plugin.

Whenever you activate a new plugin, you'll usually get a new menu item in the Dashboard Navigation menu. This new menu item can sometimes appear inside the existing **Settings** menu, or it can appear as a new top-level menu item. With this plugin, we get the latter:

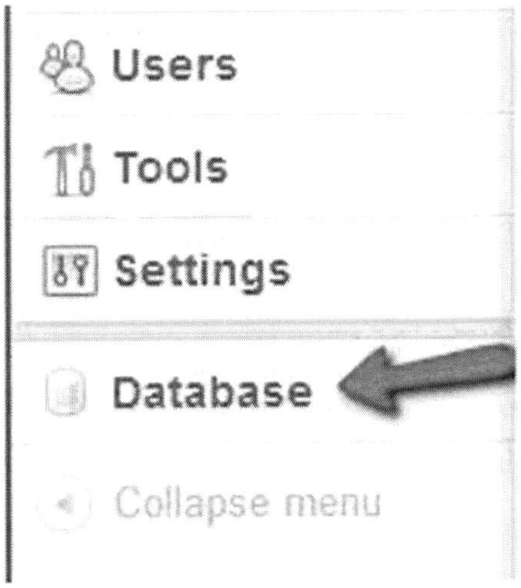

There is now a menu called "Database" in your Dashboard Navigation area.

Before we look at that in detail, there is one other thing you may have noticed. At the top of your screen there may be a warning that looks like this:

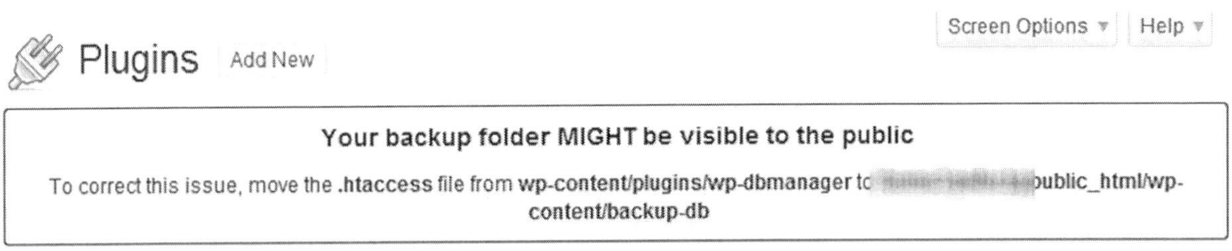

This is just a warning. While you can ignore it, it is always better to fix these problems. This plugin wants to protect the folder where backups will be saved. This is to prevent unauthorized people from downloading your database copies. To do this, we need to move & rename a file that was installed with the plugin. If you know how to use FTP, then you can use that. However, since I suspect many of you may not know how to use FTP, I'll show you how to do this in your cPanel.

Login to the cPanel of your hosting account.

Scroll down to the section on files, and click on the File Manager link.

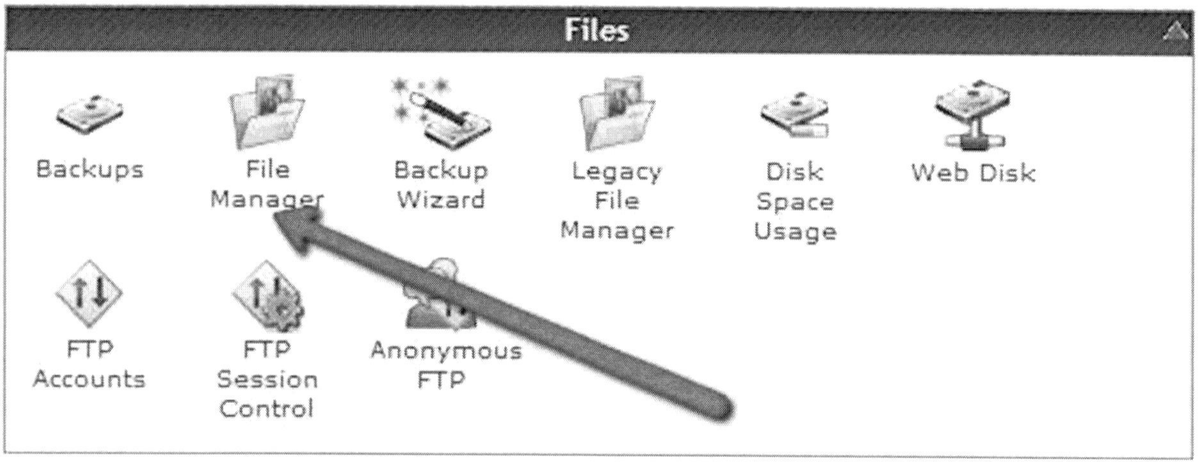

You will be asked where you want to login to:

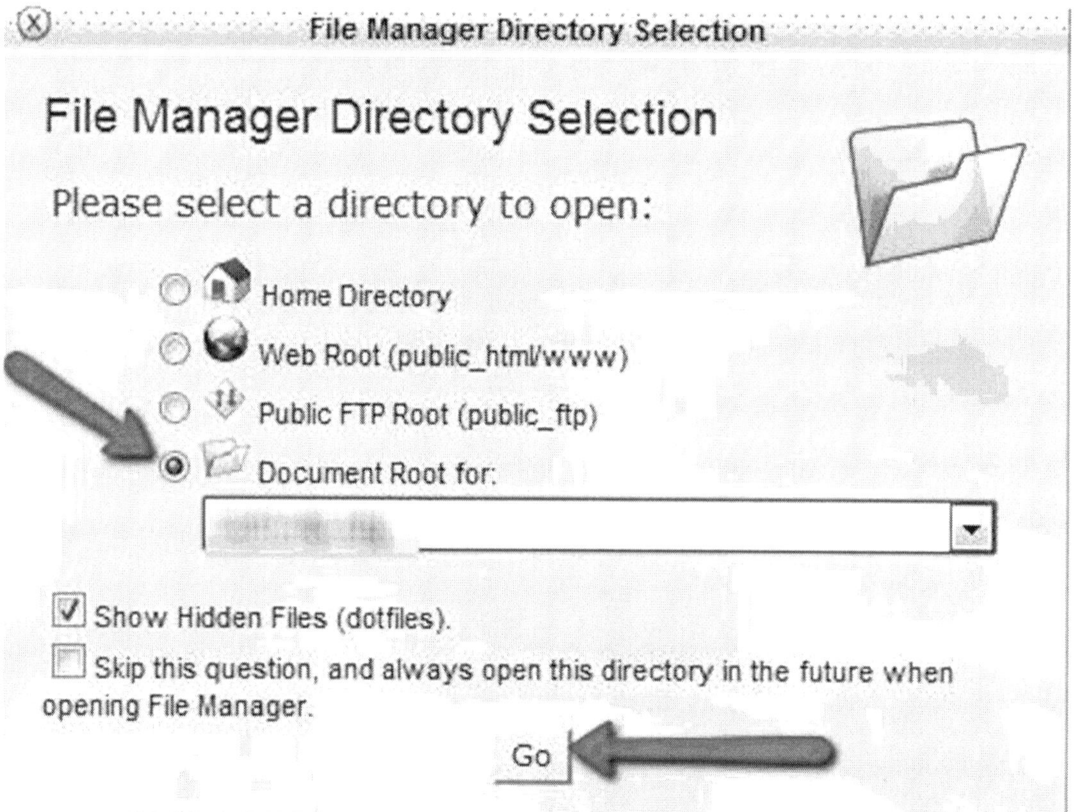

Select the bottom option of **Document Root for:** and select your domain name in the drop down box. Click the Go button to access your web space for the site. It will open in a new tab in your browser.

The file manager is very similar to the type of File Manager you have used with Microsoft Windows or on your Mac computer.

On the right hand side of the File Manager you will see the files & folders inside your currently selected folder (which is the document root we selected a moment ago). The left side you can see other folders on your server, but we can ignore those for now.

Glance down the column to the right of the folder list until you find **wp-content**. Double click the folder icon to the left of the folder name to open it.

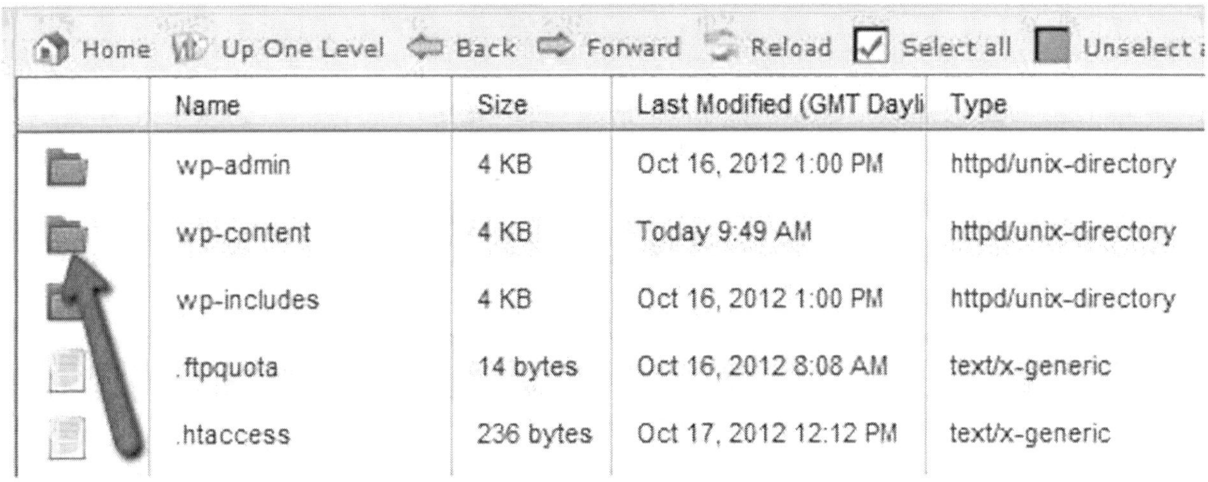

	Name	Size	Last Modified (GMT Dayli	Type
	wp-admin	4 KB	Oct 16, 2012 1:00 PM	httpd/unix-directory
	wp-content	4 KB	Today 9:49 AM	httpd/unix-directory
	wp-includes	4 KB	Oct 16, 2012 1:00 PM	httpd/unix-directory
	.ftpquota	14 bytes	Oct 16, 2012 8:08 AM	text/x-generic
	.htaccess	236 bytes	Oct 17, 2012 12:12 PM	text/x-generic

OK, you are now in the wp-content folder. Now look for the **Plugins** folder and double click the folder icon next to that:

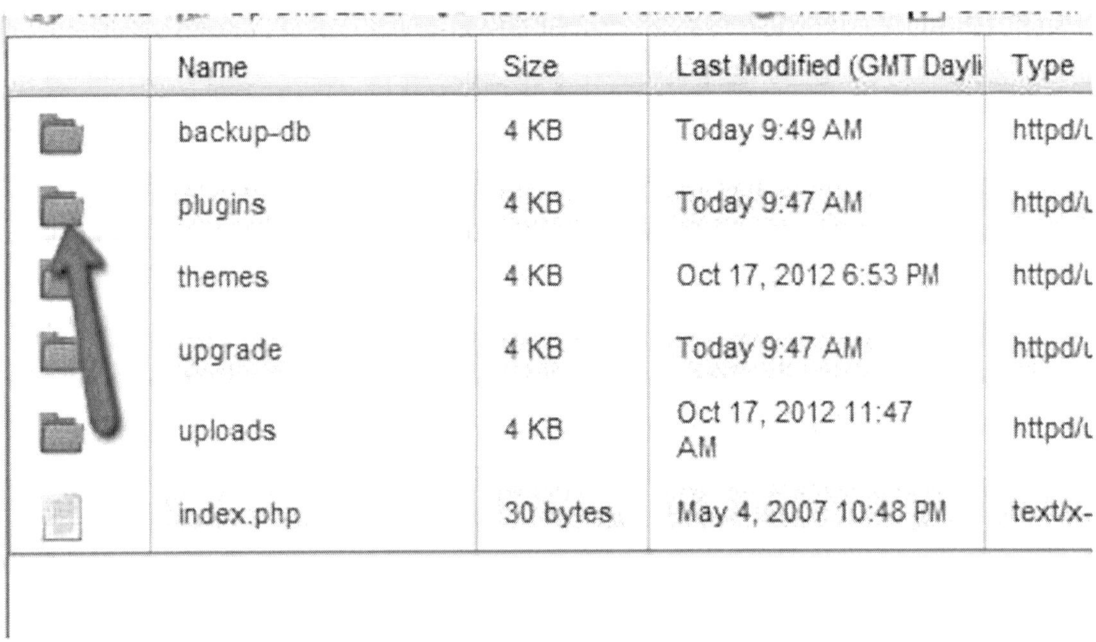

	Name	Size	Last Modified (GMT Dayli	Type
	backup-db	4 KB	Today 9:49 AM	httpd/ι
	plugins	4 KB	Today 9:47 AM	httpd/ι
	themes	4 KB	Oct 17, 2012 6:53 PM	httpd/ι
	upgrade	4 KB	Today 9:47 AM	httpd/ι
	uploads	4 KB	Oct 17, 2012 11:47 AM	httpd/ι
	index.php	30 bytes	May 4, 2007 10:48 PM	text/x-

We are now inside the plugins folder. Any plugins that you install will usually have their own folder within this folder. We want the wp-dbmanager folder, so find that and double click its folder icon to open it.

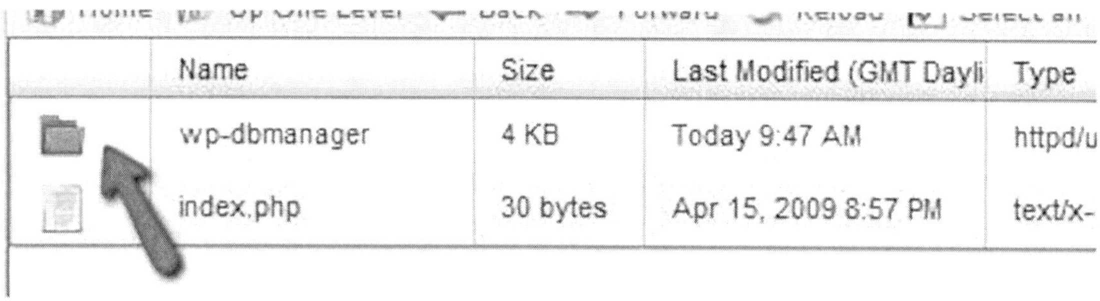

OK, great. You should now see a list of files. Find the one called **htaccess.txt** and right click on it to open a popup menu.

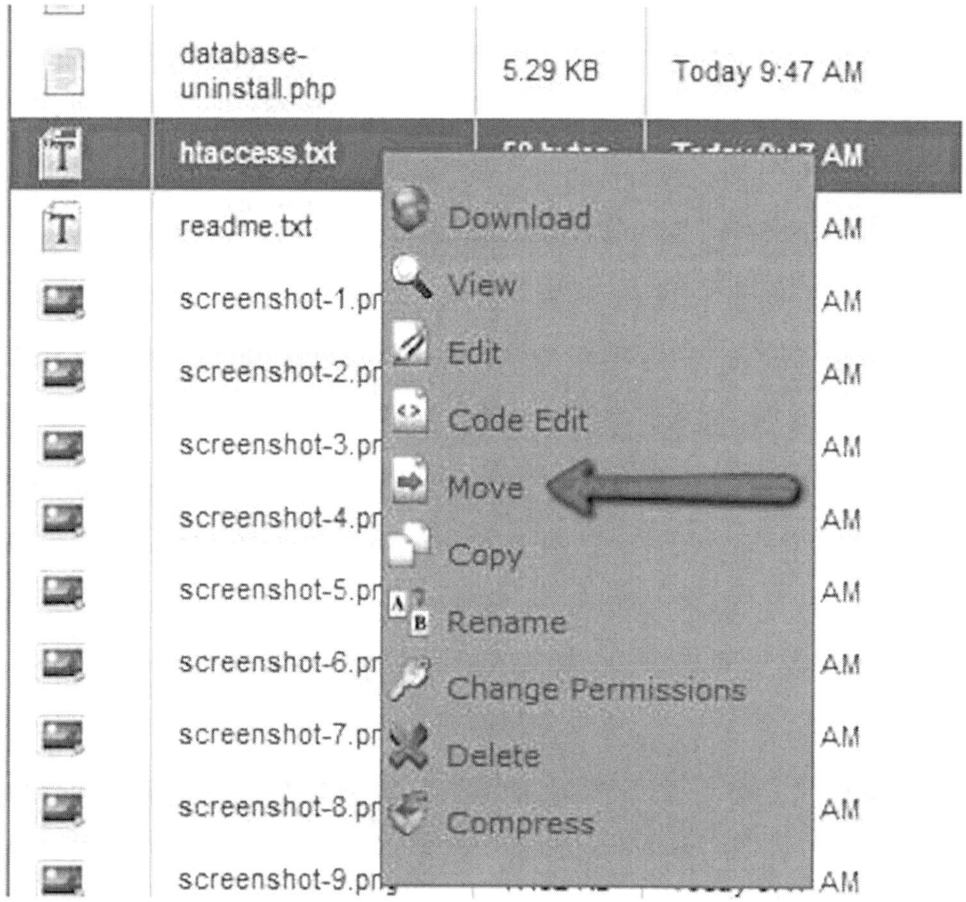

Select **Move** from this menu.

OK, now we need to go back and check the error message that we received in the Dashboard. Here is mine. I want to copy down the last part of the destination URL:

In my case, it's **wp-content/backup-db**. The chances are that yours will be the same.

Now in the File Manager, edit the line in the lower box so that after the **/wp-content/** part of the URL, it just says **backup-db** (as shown in the error message above).

Here is mine:

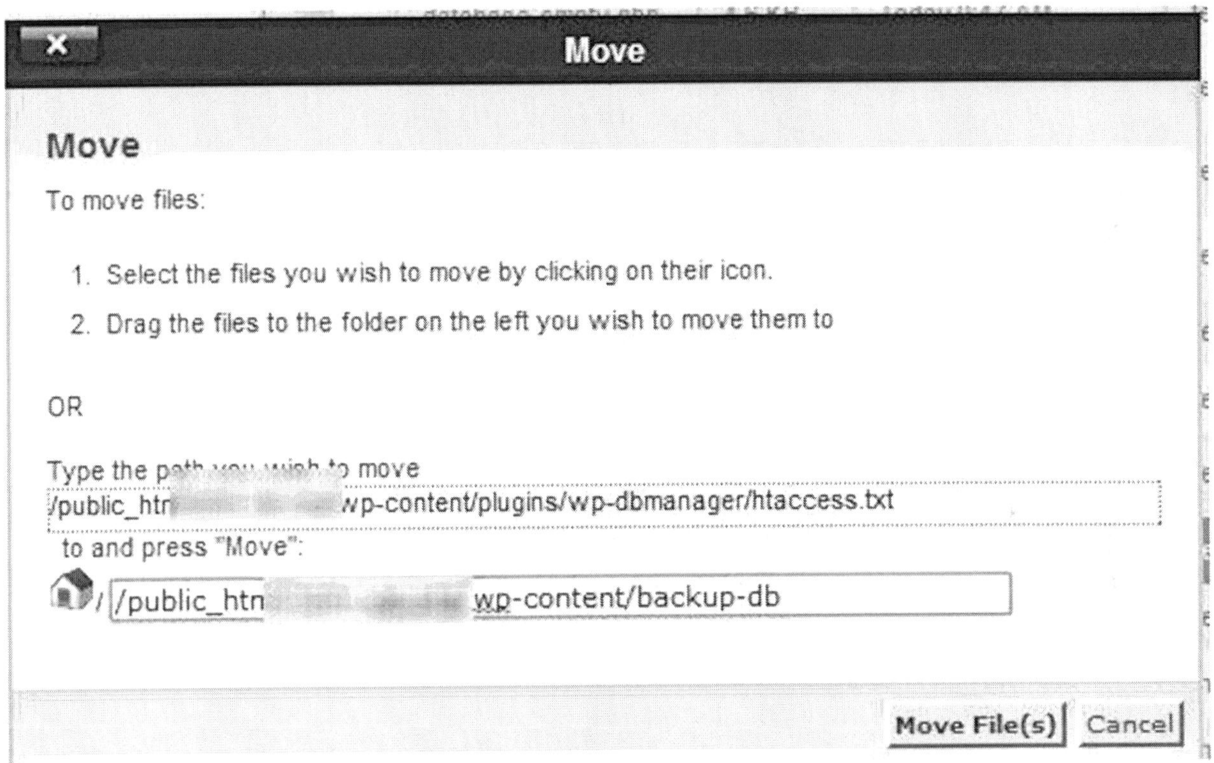

Click the Move File(s) button to move the htaccess.txt file.

OK, now we need to locate that file and rename it.

At the top of the File Manager, there is a button to move **Up One Level**.

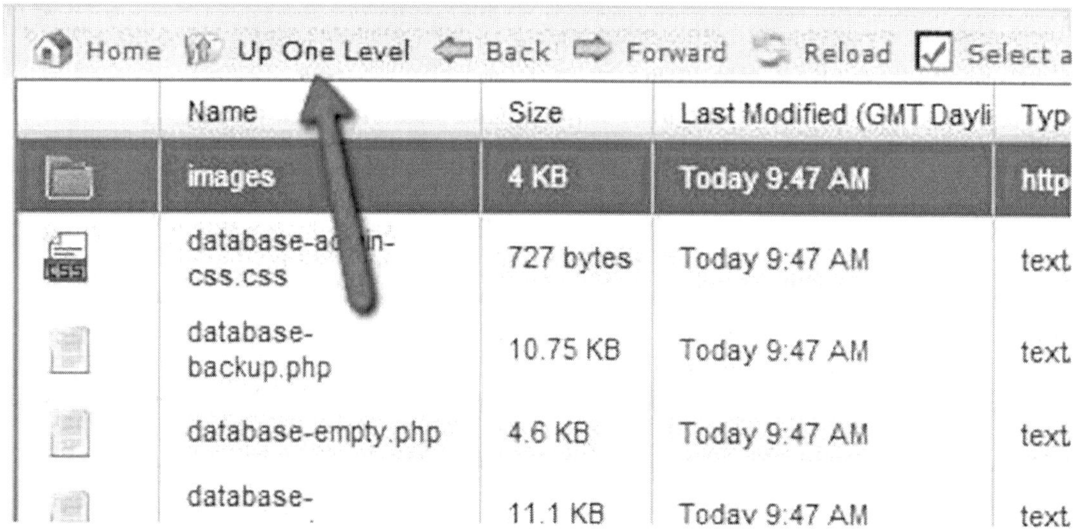

Click it.

Click it a second time and you should now see the backup-db folder:

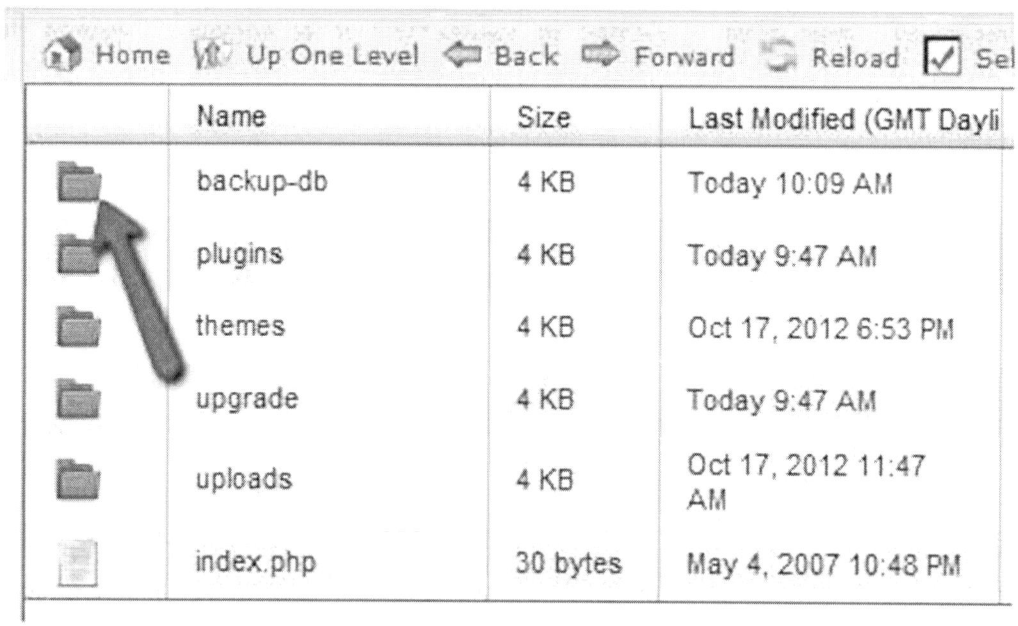

Double click the folder icon to the left of the folder name to open it.

You should now see the htaccess.txt file that we moved here:

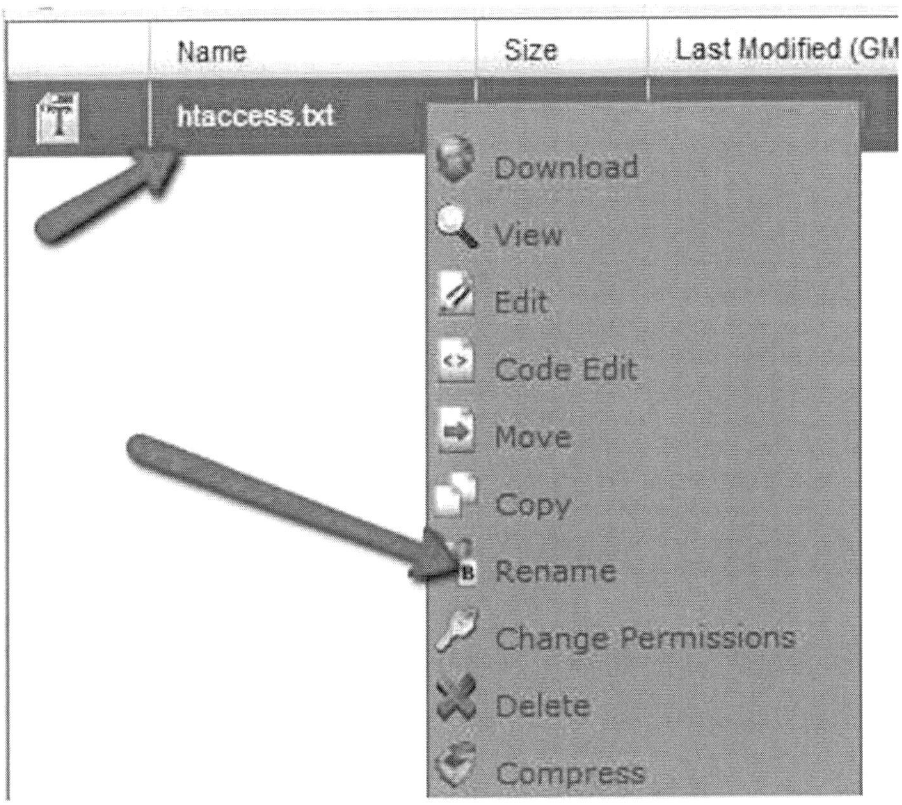

Right click the htaccess.txt file and select **Rename** from the popup menu.

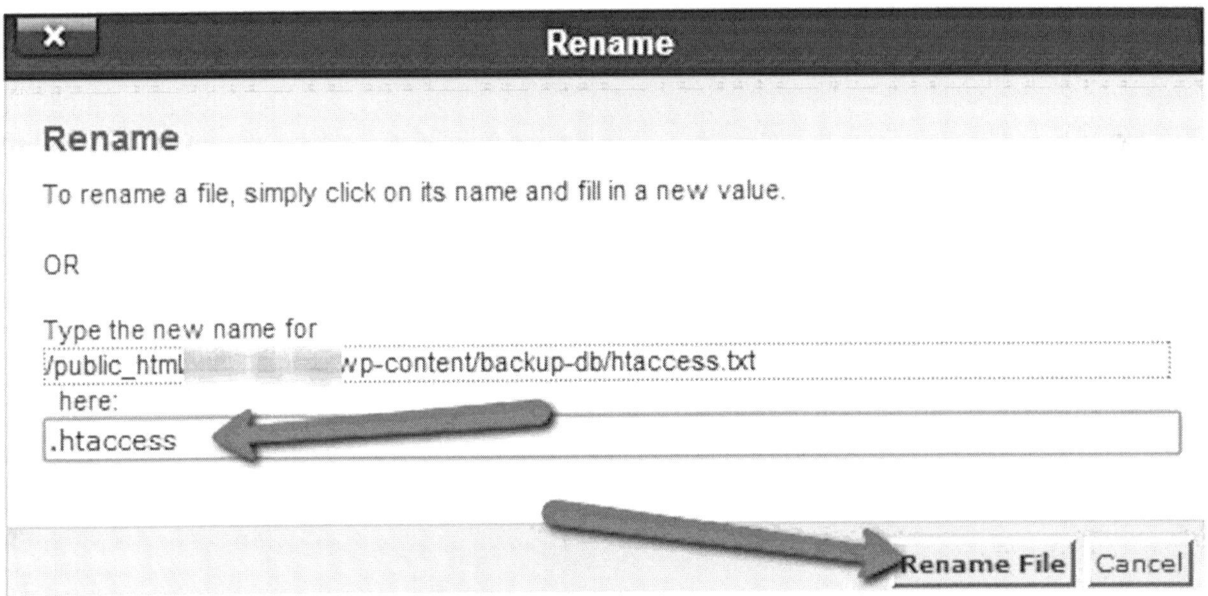

In the screen that appears, edit the lower box that contains the file name. Remove the **.txt** from the end of the filename and ADD a period (full stop) to the beginning of the filename. The filename should end up as **.htaccess**

Click the rename file button to complete the process.

You can now close the File Manager and logout of your cPanel.

Go back to your WordPress Dashboard where the error message is displayed and click the Refresh button on your web browser's toolbar. The error message should disappear.

Great. Let's configure the WP-DBManager plugin so we can start getting backups of our database emailed to us.

From the **Database** Menu, select **DB Options**.

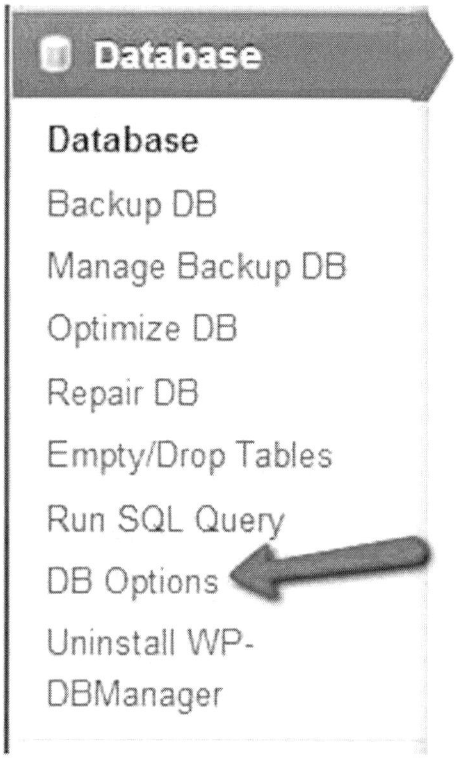

Just scroll to the bottom of that page and click the **Save Changes** button (I know you didn't make any changes, but click the button anyway). By doing this, you'll activate the plugin.

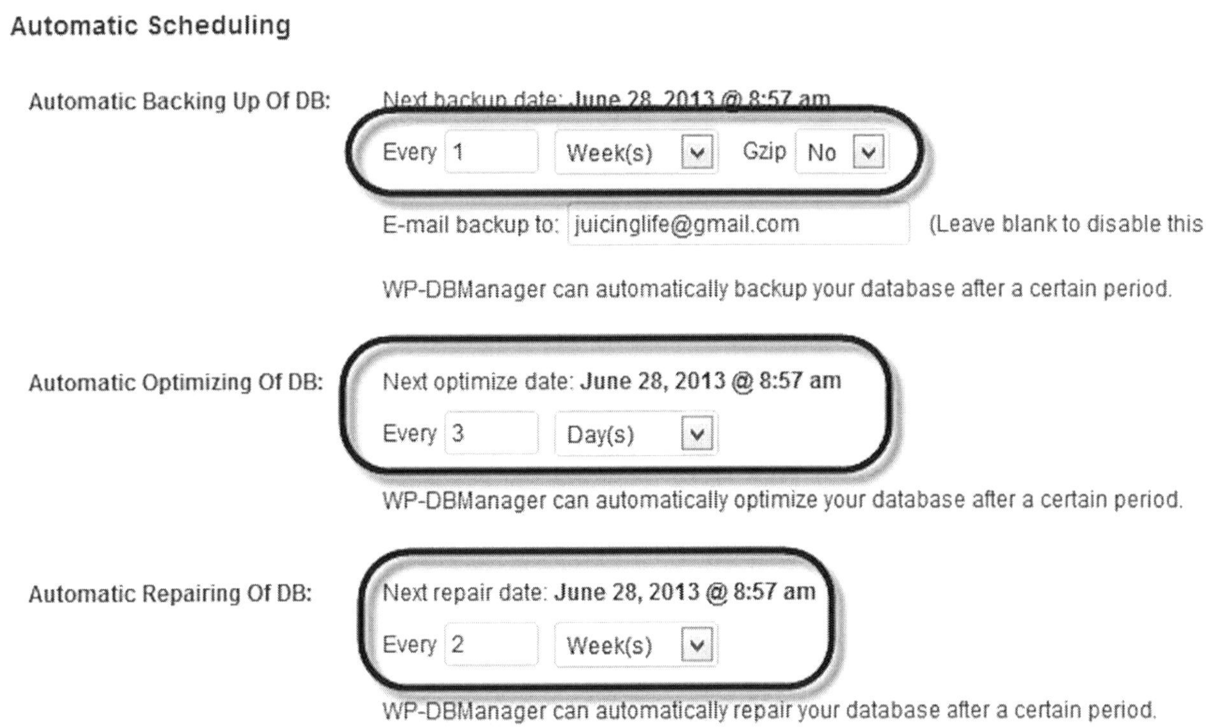

Now, under the automatic scheduling section you should see today's date and (serve) time. That means the first backup was created and emailed to you. It was sent to the same address found in the **Email Backup To** box on this page. That email will be the same one we filled in earlier, but if you want to change it to a different email, you can.

You'll see that automatic optimizing of the database will occur every 3 days, and automatic repair of the database every 2 weeks.

These are the default settings. If you add content to your site daily, you might like to get the backup sent more frequently than the once a week default (top box in the screenshot above), so you could change that to every 3 or 4 days, or whatever suites your needs.

The only other thing you may want to change is the GZip setting at the top. The default is no, meaning the backup is not compressed. Compressing makes the backup considerably smaller, so I do recommend you change this to Yes, and save changes.

Other than that, you are all set up with this plugin.

Go check your email to see if the first backup has arrived.

Contact Form 7

The Contact Form is another important part of a website because it allows people to contact you privately. The plugin we are going to install is called **Contact Form 7**, so go to the **Add New** plugin page and search for that exact phrase.

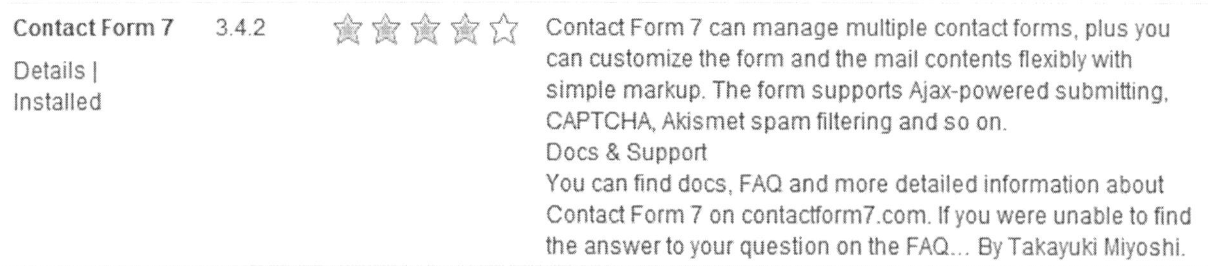

When you find it (it should be the first item in the list), click the Install Now link under the plugin name.

When prompted, activate the plugin. This one will create a menu in the Dashboard Navigation called **Contact**.

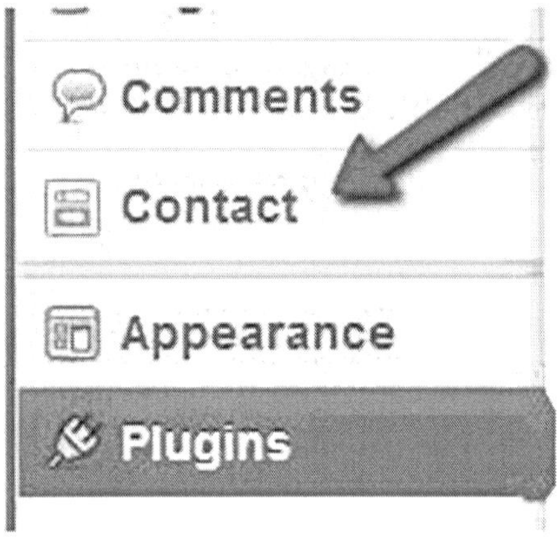

When you click on the menu item, you'll be taken to the contact form screen that shows all active contact forms (you can use this plugin to create different forms for different purposes).

There is one form in the list - the default one that the plugin set up. You can go in and edit this form by clicking the name of the form (Contact form 1), on the left. The title is a hyperlink to the form's editor screen.

We'll use the form as it is because it is fully functional and contains the important information.

What we need to do is copy the **shortcode** listed on the right.

[contact-form-7 id="50" title="Contact form 1"]

A shortcode is a convenient code for inserting something into a webpage. Some plugins use them, some don't. They make adding features to pages very simple.

Copy the code, and then go over to the **Add New** PAGE (NOT post) screen:

You'll have a new, blank page.

Add the word **Contact** in the title box, and paste the shortcode into the body of the page as shown below:

Click the Publish button on the right to publish this page to your site.

If you now visit your site, you will see that WordPress has automatically added a new menu item at the top, called **Contact** (the title of the page we just created).

Clicking it takes you to your new contact page on the site:

Great, now visitors can contact us.

WP-Policies

This plugin adds a few other essential pages to the website, like disclaimer, privacy and so on. It will actually create a wide range of "legal" pages. Some we need, others we don't.

Go to the Add New plugin and search for **wp policies**.

Install and activate the plugin.

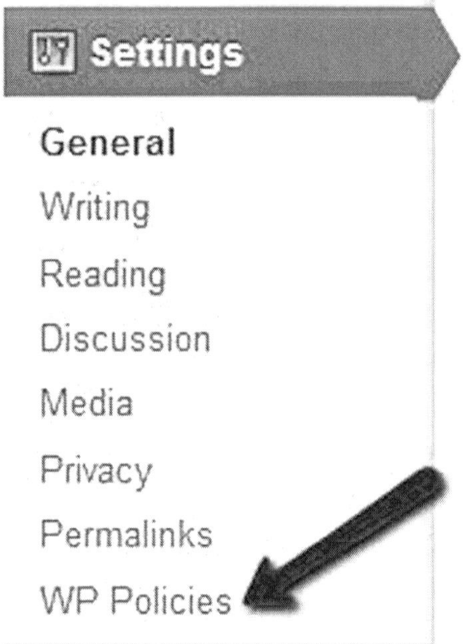

Click on the **Settings** menu followed by the **WP Policies** plugin.

NOTE: There may be a time in the future when you want to create your own legal documents, like privacy, disclaimer, terms of service etc. However, we'll use the default ones that come with this plugin for setting up the demo website.

On the settings page, scroll to the bottom.

In the Contact Details section, enter your details. These will be used when the plugin creates the various policy pages for your website.

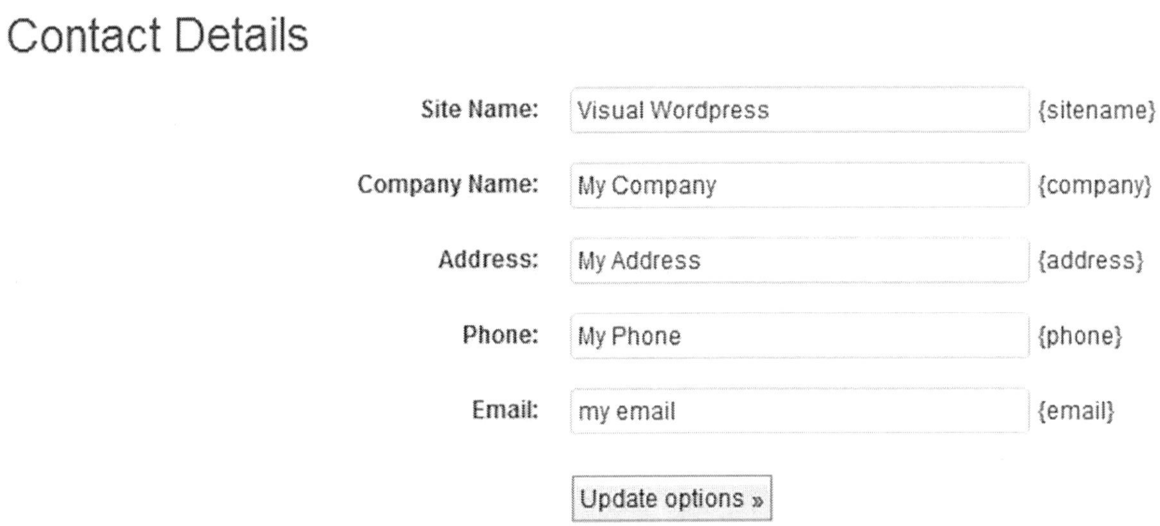

With that complete, scroll to the very end of the page.

Click the button labeled **Import Files.**

When the plugin reloads the page, you'll see a number of policy pages that have been automatically created for you:

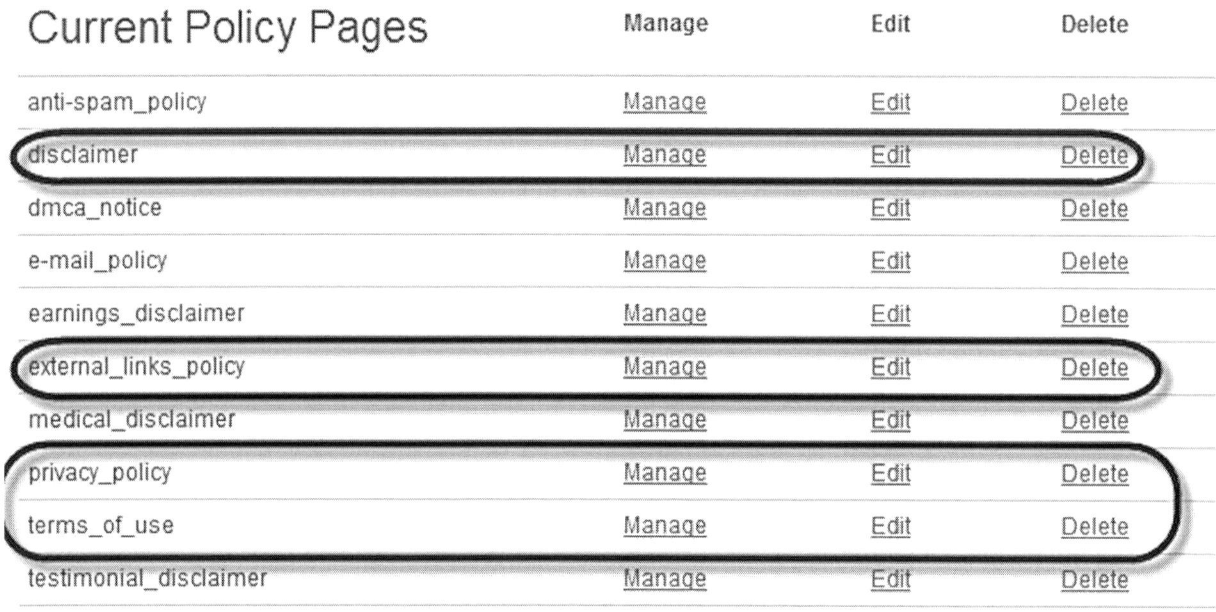

Current Policy Pages	Manage	Edit	Delete
anti-spam_policy	Manage	Edit	Delete
disclaimer	Manage	Edit	Delete
dmca_notice	Manage	Edit	Delete
e-mail_policy	Manage	Edit	Delete
earnings_disclaimer	Manage	Edit	Delete
external_links_policy	Manage	Edit	Delete
medical_disclaimer	Manage	Edit	Delete
privacy_policy	Manage	Edit	Delete
terms_of_use	Manage	Edit	Delete
testimonial_disclaimer	Manage	Edit	Delete

Depending on your site, you may need some or all of these policy pages. However, I am only keeping four on my site. They are: Disclaimer, External Links Policy, Privacy Policy and Terms of Use. I'll delete the rest by clicking the Delete link to the right of them.

I cannot suggest which policies YOU need on your site. That is something only a lawyer can tell you. If you want to keep them all, do so. You can add the ones that are important to your site later when we look at creating a custom menu.

Once you have deleted any policies you don't want, just click on the **Pages** menu in the Dashboard Navigation column and you'll see a list of your newly created pages:

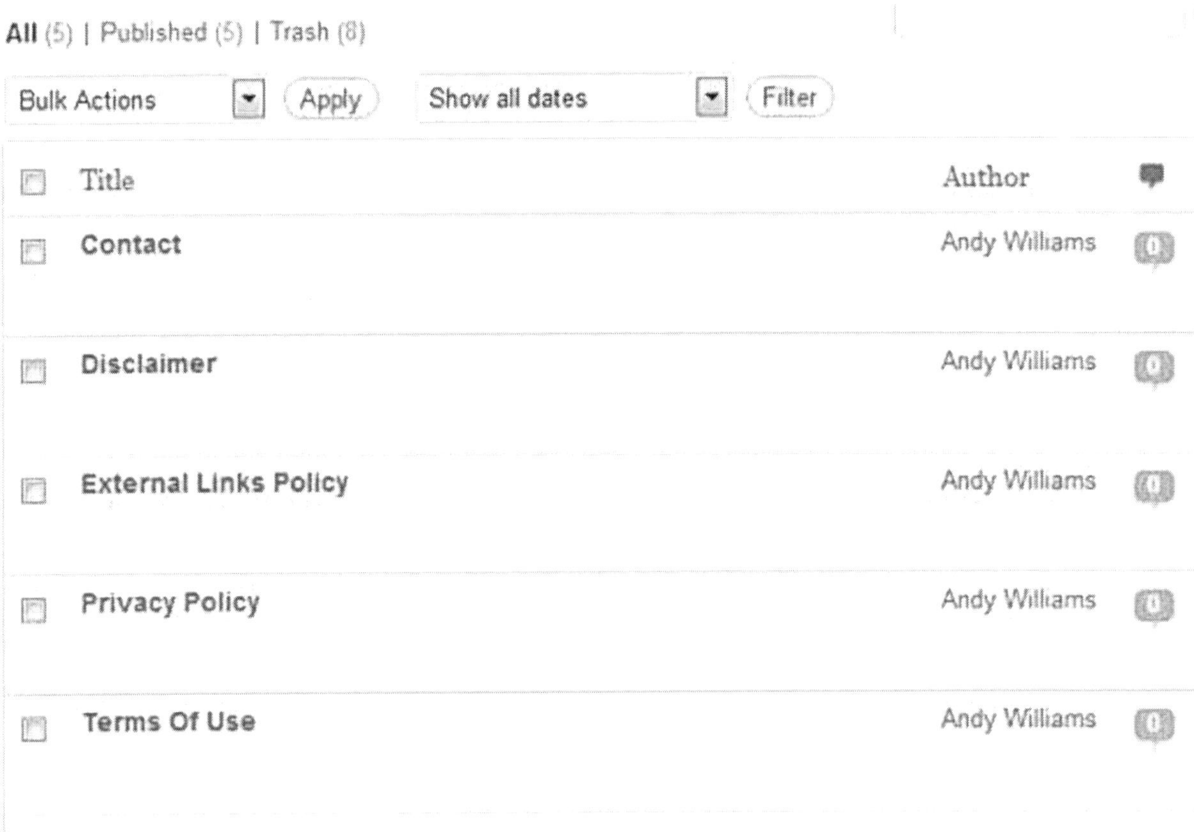

Clicking any of the items in this list will open the page editor screen.

When you get to the editor screen you won't see anything in the large content box, and you'd be forgiven for thinking there is no content on the policy page. However, click the Text tab of the WYSIWYG (What You See Is What You Get), editor and you'll see a reference to a file on your server. In this case it is called "disclaimer.dat". This file holds the content of the disclaimer page (you can edit this file in a text editor if you need to).

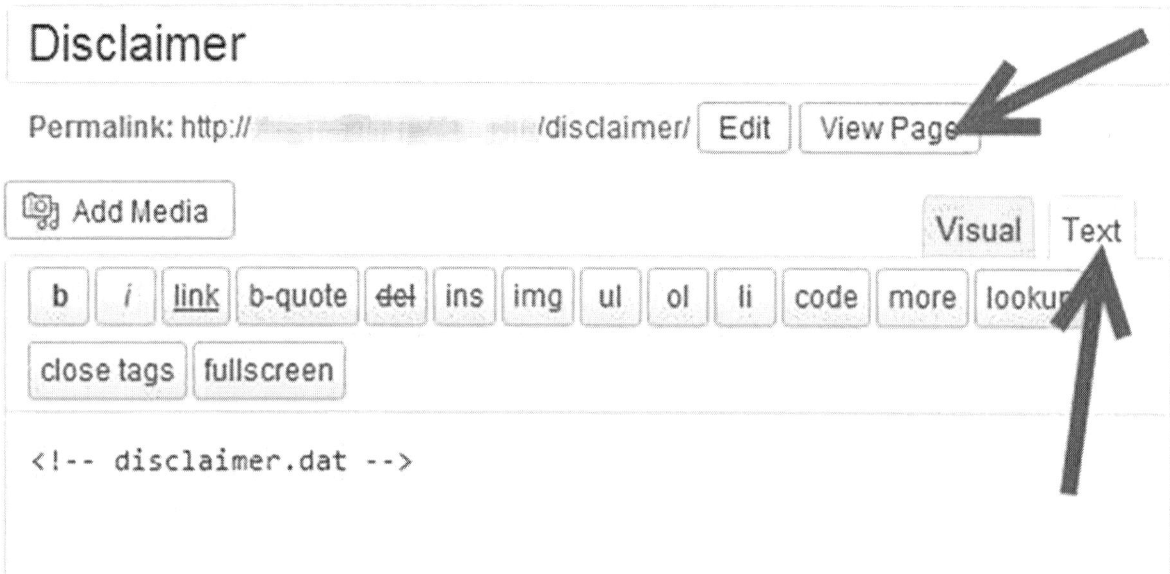

Do not try to edit the pages built with the WP Policy plugin or you could end up deleting the content from these pages. If you want to see what the policy looks like on your site, there is a View Page button in the editor screen (see above). Click it:

NOTE: If you don't want the hassle of leaving the Dashboard just to view your legal pages, simply right click over the View Page button and select the "Open Link in New Tab" option from the popup menu.

Unlike pages that we manually create, these ones are not automatically added to the navigation menu on your site. We will look at adding the important ones later on when we go over custom menus. For now though, let's look at the final essential plugin for your site.

WordPress SEO

Go to the **Add New** plugin page and search for **WordPress SEO**.

This is the one you want by "Yoast":

Install and activate the plugin.

This plugin installs a new menu in the Dashboard Navigation called SEO.

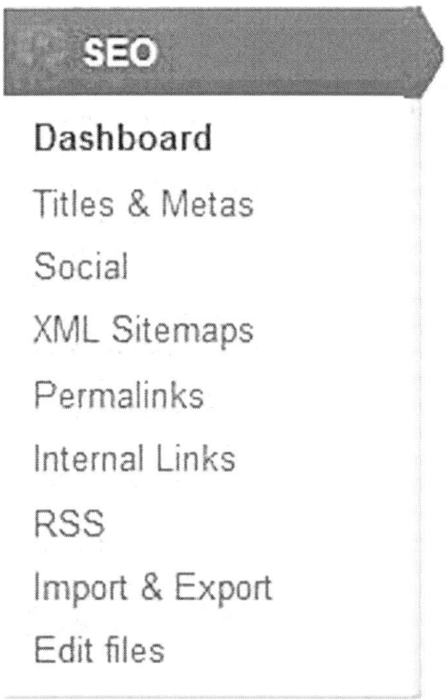

There are a number of options in this menu, but we'll only look at the essential ones.

The first item in the menu is **Dashboard**. If you click on that you can see a few settings - we'll leave all of these with their default values.

The next item in the menu is **Titles & Metas**. Click on it.

There are a number of tabs across the top of "Titles & Metas" and we will look at them, but first, on the General tab, check the **Noindex subpages of archives** checkbox and click the Save Changes button at the bottom.

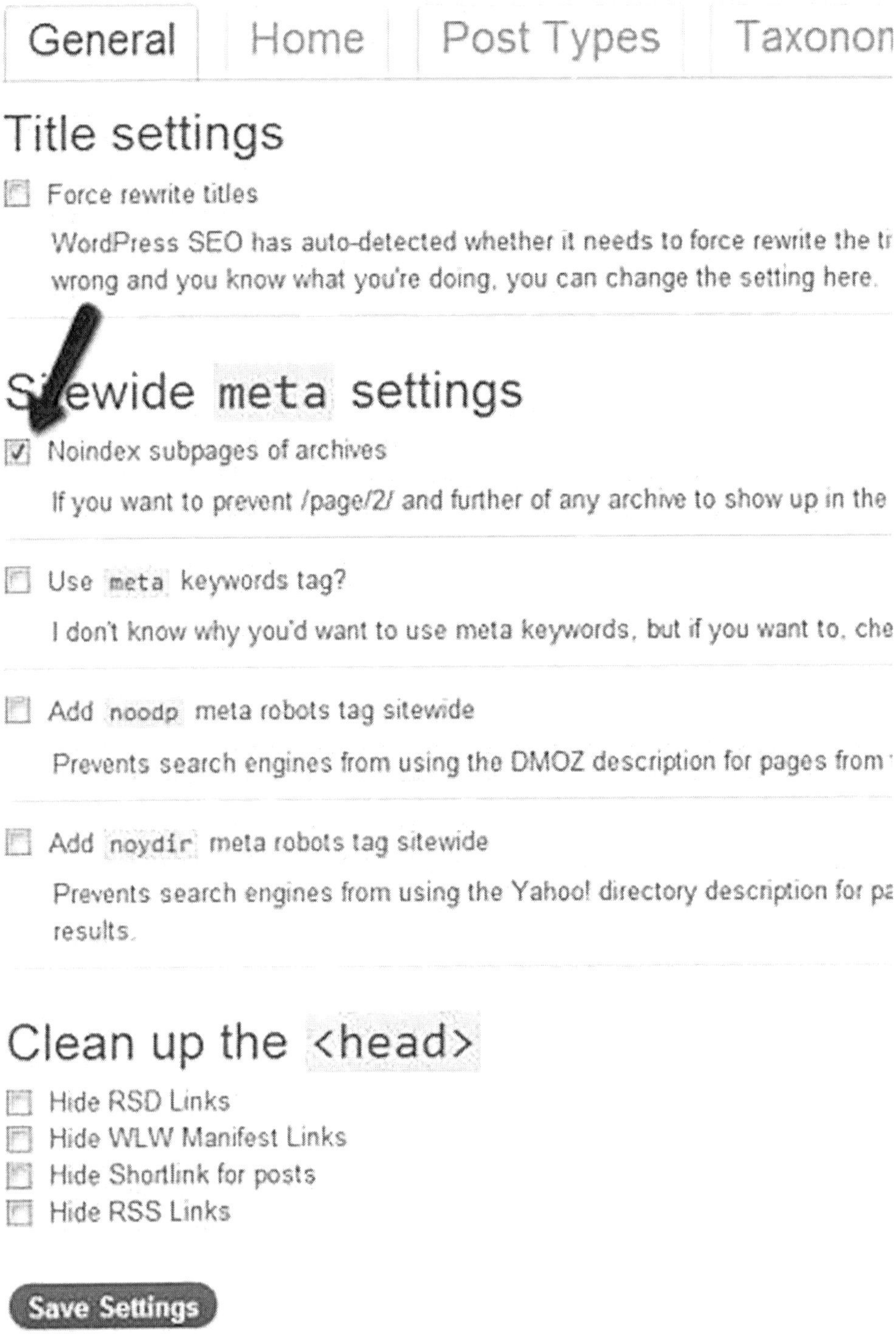

This setting will help prevent unnecessary duplication of content on your site.

OK, if you now click on the Home tab you will see the SEO settings for your homepage.

You will notice that the **Title Template** for your homepage looks like this:

%%sitename%% %%page%% %%sep%% %%sitedesc%%

This title has what the plugin calls variables. Variables are used to insert content dynamically into the title when the page loads. To see what each variable stands for, click on the Help tab. You'll see a list of all variables that are available to you:

Variables

These tags can be included in templates and will be replaced by WordPress SEO by Yoast when a page is displayed.

%%date%%	Replaced with the date of the post/page
%%title%%	Replaced with the title of the post/page
%%sitename%%	The site's name
%%sitedesc%%	The site's tagline / description
%%excerpt%%	Replaced with the post/page excerpt (or auto-generated if it does nc exist)
%%excerpt_only%%	Replaced with the post/page excerpt (without auto-generation)
%%tag%%	Replaced with the current tag/tags
%%category%%	Replaced with the post categories (comma separated)
%%category_description%%	Replaced with the category description

In the Homepage title, the %%sitename%% variable will be replaced with the site's name (which we have already set up in the General Settings of the site).

However, on the homepage, using variables does not make much sense since we are going to want the same title and description shown at all times for the opening page. This is not the case with posts as we'll see in a moment, but for the homepage, I suggest you actually write the title and description you want to use for it WITHOUT using variables. If you want to change the title or description in the future, you can come back and change it here.

Here is an example on my site:

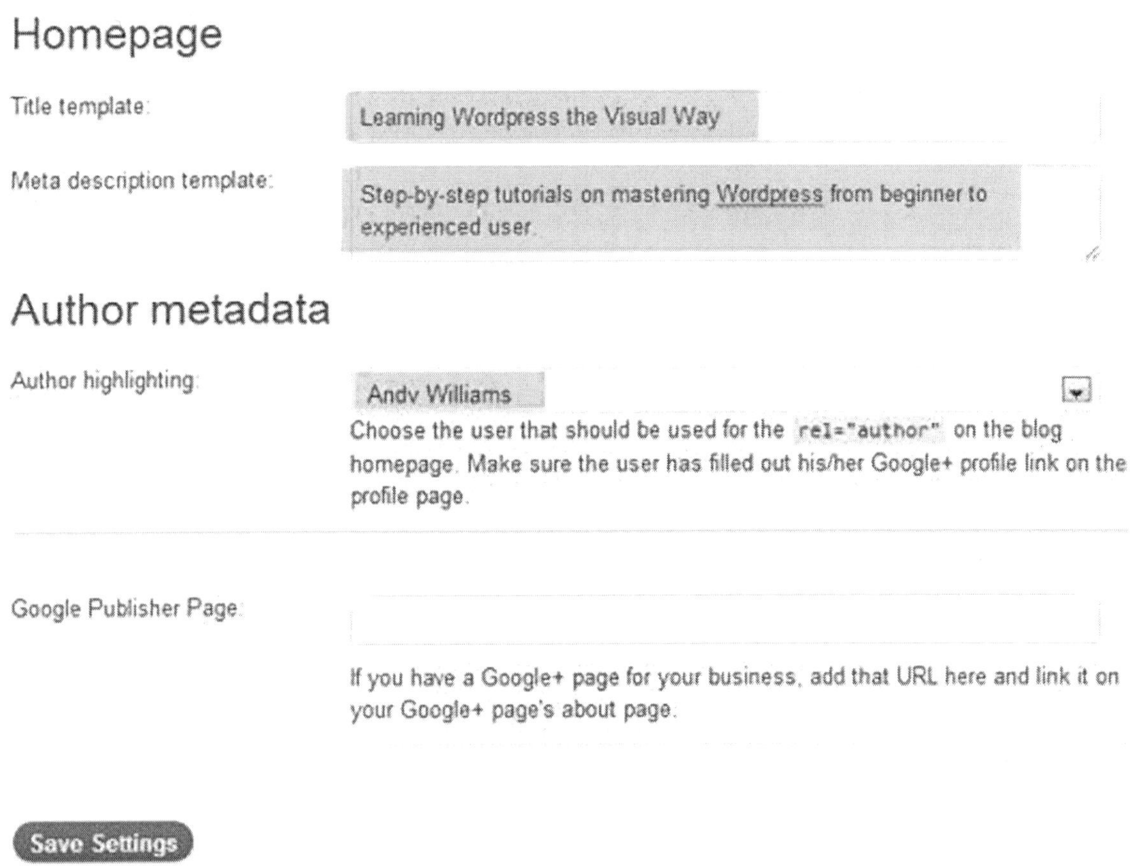

After entering the title and description for your homepage, select your author name from the **Author Highlighting** box and click the Save Settings button.

NOTE: The author highlighting box can be used to connect your website to your Google Plus account. While we won't be doing that in this book, selecting your author name from the box now gets you ready to connect the two together in the future if you decide you want to do that.

Click on the **Post Types** tab along the top.

This is where you can define how post titles and meta descriptions appear, as well as setting defaults on how the search engines will handle these pages.

What I recommend you do for ALL titles on your site is to use a combination of your site name and the post/page title. You can have your site name first or last (I recommend last), so that a post title on your site might look like this:

How to add a plugin to your site :: VisualWordPress.com

NOTE: The domain name I used in this example is not a real domain name - at least not mine. It is just used as an example.

Each post on our site will have a different title, so in the title box for posts, we MUST use a variable that represents the title - %%title%%.

We also want the site name included in the title, but that won't change for each post because the site name is always the site name. We can therefore type that in manually, but to get you used to using variables, let's use one for the site name as well.

So there are two variables needed for the post titles:

%%sitename%%

%%title%%

The title template would look something like this:

%%title%% :: %%sitename%%

Then whenever a post on your site is loaded in a web browser by a visitor, %%title%% will be swapped for the title of the post or page, and %%sitename%% will be swapped for your site's name.

OK, now we have that template, copy it into all of the title templates on the Post Type screen.

The next choice we have is what we want displayed for the Meta description. On posts, I recommend you use the excerpt of the post. The variable for excerpts is:

%%excerpt%%

Paste that into the Meta description box of the Posts section.

NOTE: We'll cover excerpts later when we look into writing posts, but basically when we add a new post to our site, we add in a short description of that post in an excerpt box. That will then be used as the post description when the page loads.

For the Pages and Media sections, leave the Meta description boxes empty. They are not important pages on the site (see the discussion earlier of pages v posts), so they don't need a Meta description tag.

Underneath the posts, pages and media sections you'll see some check boxes.

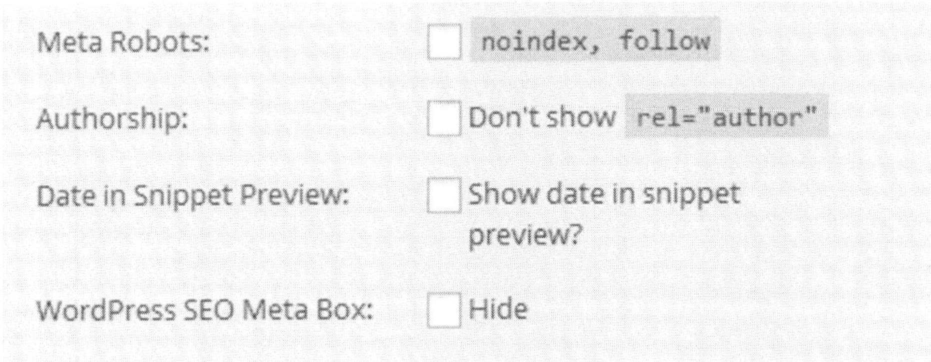

The top item is related to the Meta Robots. These tell search engines how to deal with that type of content on your site.

If you check the box next to **noindex, follow**, then Google will not index that type of content, but it will follow links on those pages. For our posts, this is obviously not what we want, so leave it unchecked.

The authorship option allows you to turn off the feature that adds your rel="author" details to that type of content. Essentially, the rel="Author" is a tag that this plugin will add to your web page to tell Google that you are the author. This also requires you to set up and and configure a Google Plus page. Setting up Google Plus is beyond the scope of this book.

The other two options can be ignored.

NOTE: The settings you see for posts, pages and media are global settings. All of these can be over-ridden at the individual post or page level, so we'll leave all of these unchecked.

OK, to summarize the changes we have made to Post types, we have set ALL title templates to:

%%title%% :: %%sitename%%

The post description was set to:

%%excerpt%%

All other settings are left blank.

Scroll to the bottom and click the Save Changes button.

Now click on the **Taxonomies** tab. These settings refer to category and tag pages.

We haven't looked at categories or tags yet, so this may be a little confusing. For now, just enter the values I tell you and we'll see how these affect our site later when we have some content up there.

Categories:

%%Category%% inserts the category name into the title. The description is the category description that we'll look at later when discussing categories.

I recommend that you select the **noindex, follow checkbox** for categories so that Google will read the pages and follow the links to the posts on your site, but NOT index the category page as this can contain a lot of duplicate content on the site.

NOTE: For experienced users, I actually recommend category pages be indexed (by un-checking this box), but you do need to make changes to your WordPress template and the way you use the category pages to prevent unnecessary content duplication. For this book, we'll stick with the easier option of checking the box.

Tags:

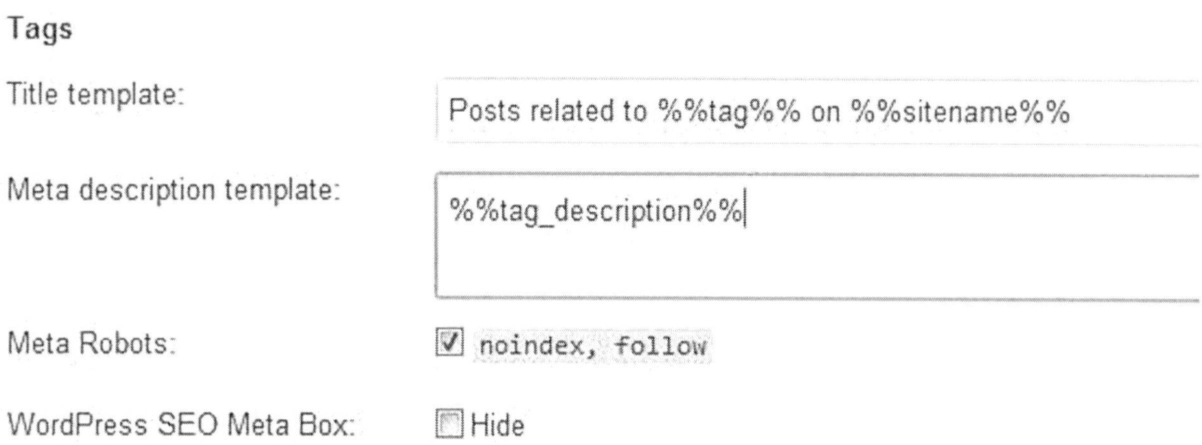

%%tag%% is replaced by the tag, and %%tag_description%% is replaced by the description we gave to that tag (we'll see this later when discussing tags).

Just like the category pages, I recommend you check the **noindex, follow** checkbox. This will prevent the search engines from indexing the tag pages, but allow them to spider the page, follow the links and find all of the posts on your site.

NOTE: Again, as with categories, I actually recommend advanced users allow the tag pages to be indexed, but you do need to customize your template/theme so that the tag pages don't end up with lots of duplicate content. This type of work is beyond the scope of this book.

Format:

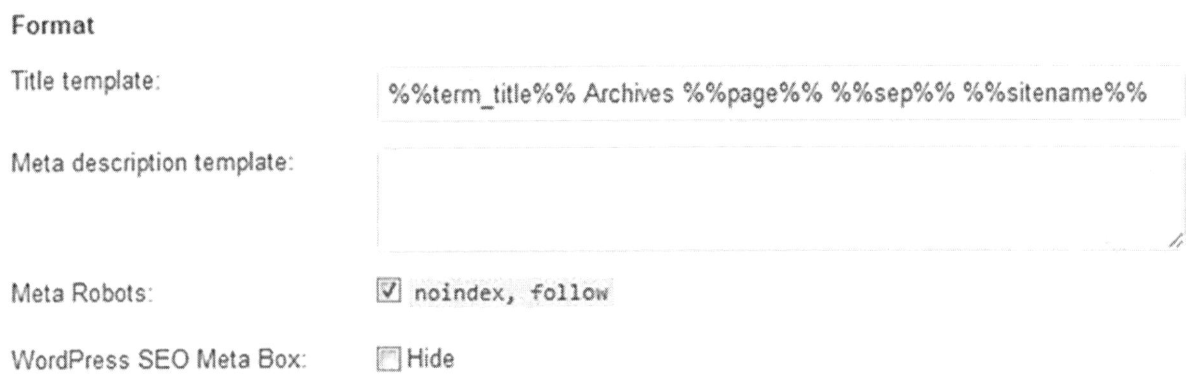

This one is just left at the default settings.

OK, the final tab is the **Other** tab. Click on it now.

This tab contains settings for some "archive" pages.

Here are the settings for **Author Pages:**

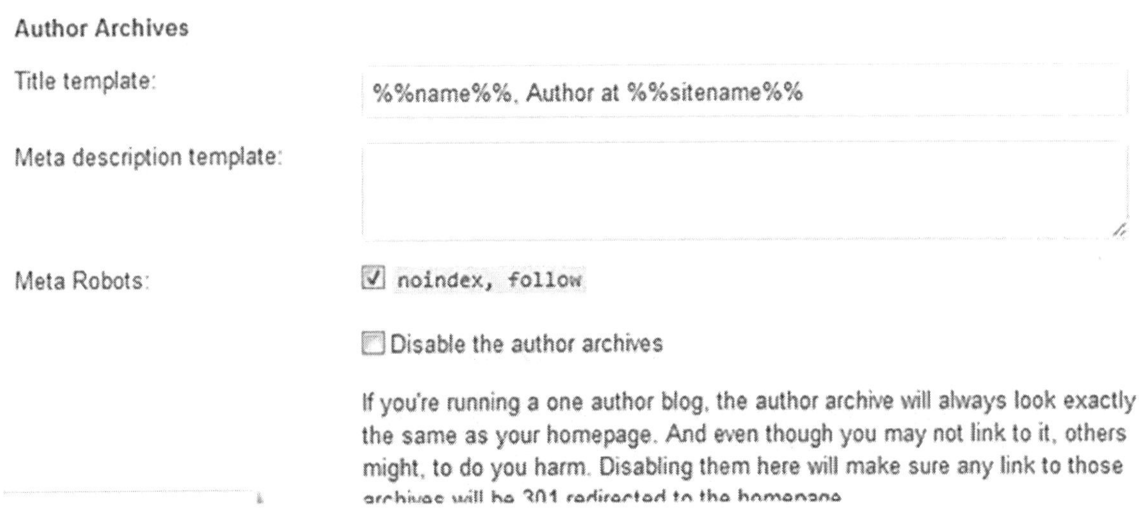

Make sure the Meta robots option is checked to **noindex, follow**. This again is to prevent unnecessary duplication of content on the site.

For **Date Archives:**

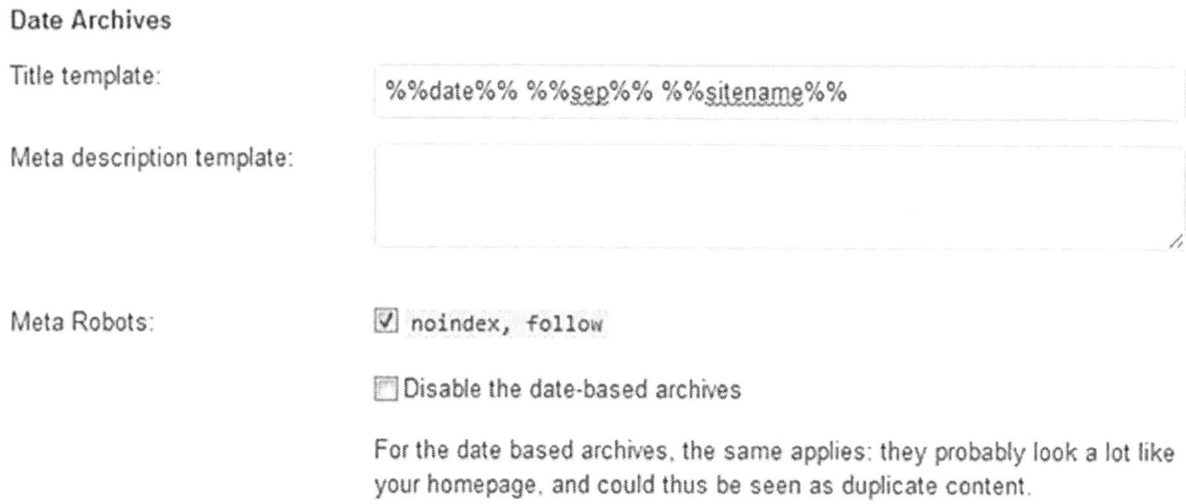

Again, **noindex, follow.**

And for the **special pages**:

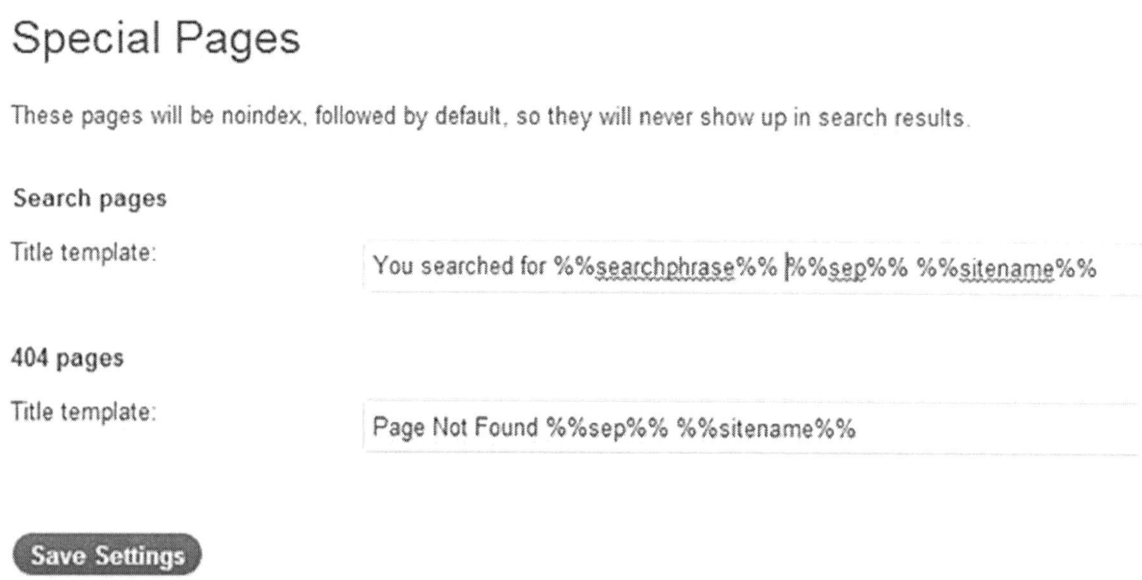

These format the titles for the search results (when using the built in search feature of WordPress), page and the 404 page is used when a page is not found.

Save settings when complete.

OK, we are finished with the WordPress SEO plugin settings for the moment, although we will see them again later in another part of the Dashboard.

There is a huge amount of functionality built into this WordPress SEO plugin. We won't be covering all the settings in this book. The only other option I want to cover here is the XML Sitemaps. Click on that option in the menu.

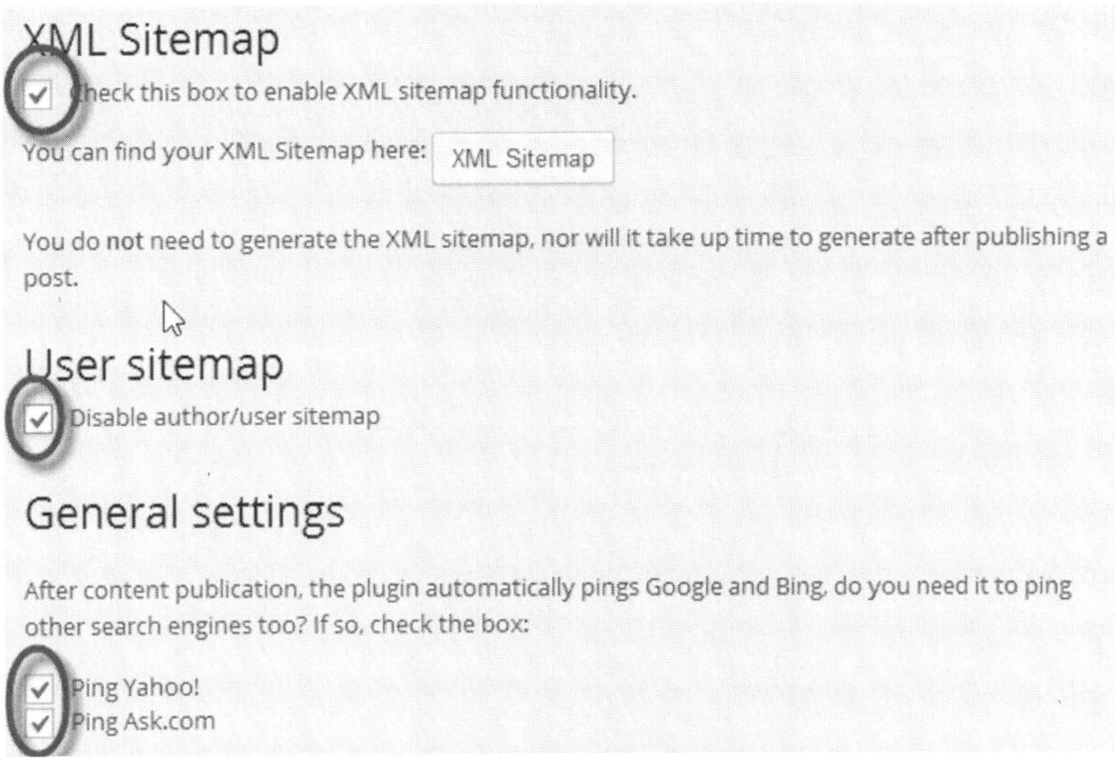

The top checkbox is to enable the Sitemap feature of WordPress SEO. If you decide to use a different plugin for sitemaps, make sure this one is unchecked. However, the sitemap features of this plugin integrate totally with the rest of the SEO settings on the site, so I recommend you use this one and check the box.

I'd also recommend you check the Ping Yahoo and Ping Ask.com boxes. This will let those sites know when new content is added to your site. We also have a long ping list that we set up earlier in the book when dealing with writing settings, so a lot of places will be informed when new content is added.

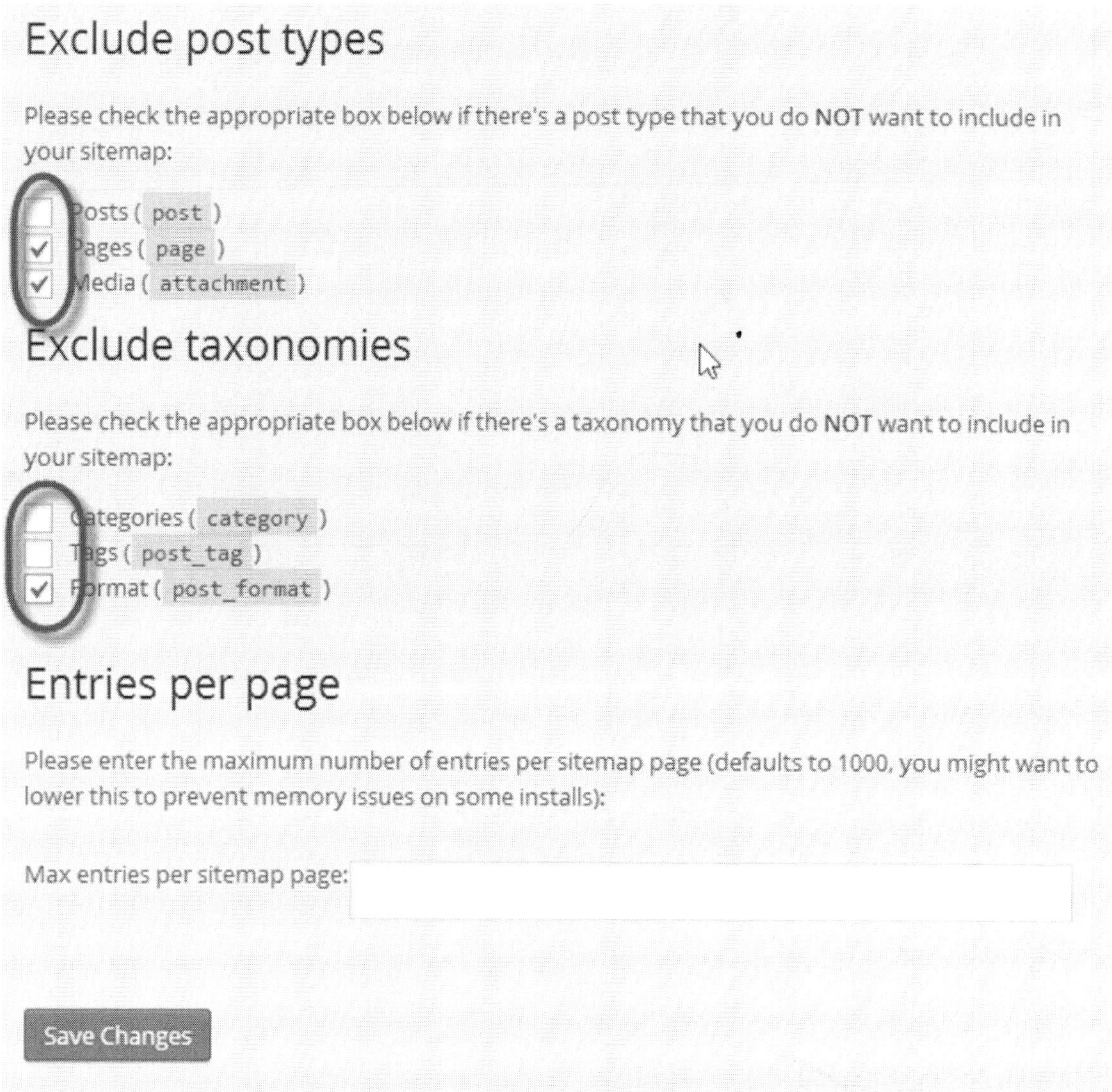

In the exclude post types, I'd recommend selecting media and pages. Any media we use will be embedded into a post and doesn't need a direct link in the sitemap. Also, since pages are only being used for our "legal" content, we don't need them on the sitemap. The only links we really want showing on the sitemap are our important posts.

Finally, you have the option to exclude Category pages, Tag pages or Format from the sitemap. I recommend you leave the first two unchecked so that they are included in the sitemap. You can check the Format (post_format) option. We have set up the SEO plugin to not index the category and tag pages, but we still want the search engines to find them and follow all links on those pages.

When you're done, click the **Save Settings** button at the bottom, and your sitemap will be set up.

You can now view your sitemap by clicking the button at the top of the XML Sitemap settings page. The sitemap will open in a new window (it won't be built until you save your changes).

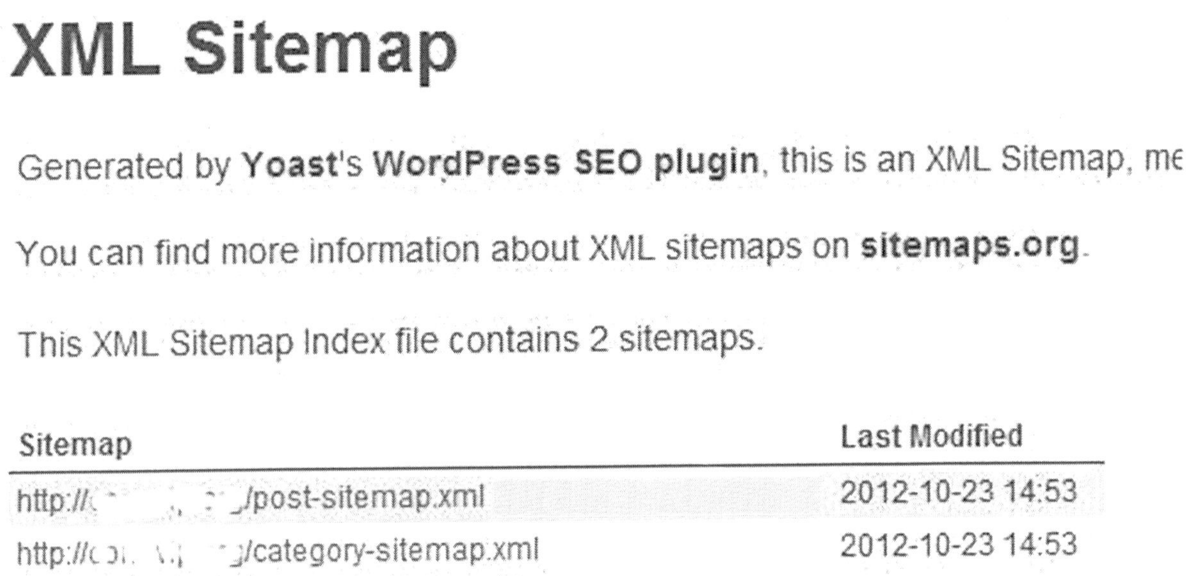

Assuming you have a post on your site, you will see at least two sitemaps, maybe more. There will be a sitemap dedicated to the posts on your site, one for the category pages, another for tag pages, and so on.

Another sitemap plugin I have used in the past did not separate out the sitemap entries like this, but lumped them all into one. I actually prefer that they be separated which is why I moved to using the Sitemap features built into the Yoast WordPress SEO plugin.

The only other setting you might like to change in this plugin is found on the permalinks page.

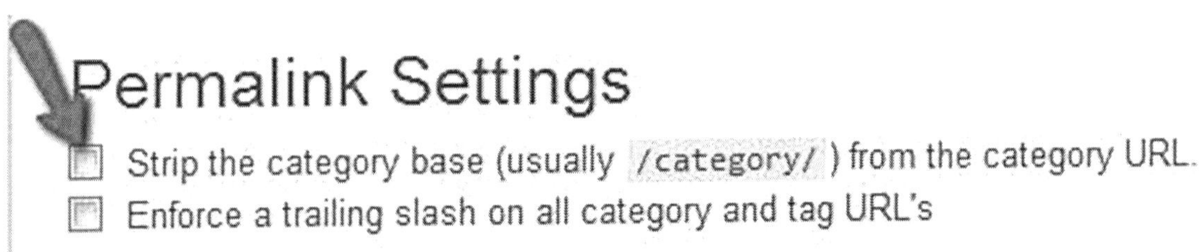

The top check box allows you to have the "/category/" part of a category page URL removed.

Remember we discussed the word **category** being inserted into category page URLs (and the word **tag** into tag page URLs) and how we could change that by entering a category base in the Permalinks settings? Well this option allows you to remove the word **category** altogether from the URLs of the category pages.

So, instead of creating a URL like this for my "plugins" category page:

http://visualworpdress.com/category/plugins

By checking that **Strip the category base....**option the URL would be this instead:

http://visualWordPress.com/plugins

What do I recommend? Well actually, I recommend you leave the word category in there. It doesn't do any harm and it does help identify that page to the search engines and visitor as a category page. The choice is yours. It's easy enough to change, but change it now if you are going to, before you start working on your site. Changing this later will change the URLs on your site, confusing search engines that have already indexed your old URLs.

We'll be looking at other WordPress SEO settings on a post by post (and page by page) nature, but for now we can forget about it and turn to another important part of your website - the comment system.

Tasks to complete

1. Delete any pre-installed plugins.
2. Install WP-DBManager and set it up.
3. Install Contact Form 7 and set up a contact page.
4. Install WP-Policies and create the "legal" pages.
5. Install WordPress SEO and configure it.
6. Set up the WordPress SEO plugin to handle your sitemaps.

Comments

I mentioned earlier that a lot of people turn comments OFF because they cannot be bothered with the work involved in moderating comments. The way I see it, the comments are part of the life and soul of a website and help to keep visitors engaged with you and your content. You NEED to offer them the chance to connect with you. Therefore, you really should keep comments turned on.

We have already configured the "discussion" settings to blacklist comments with known spam content (using the blacklist you found by searching on Google), but we can add another layer of protection - a comment spam plugin.

Let's install that plugin now.

Mouse over the Plugins menu and select Add New:

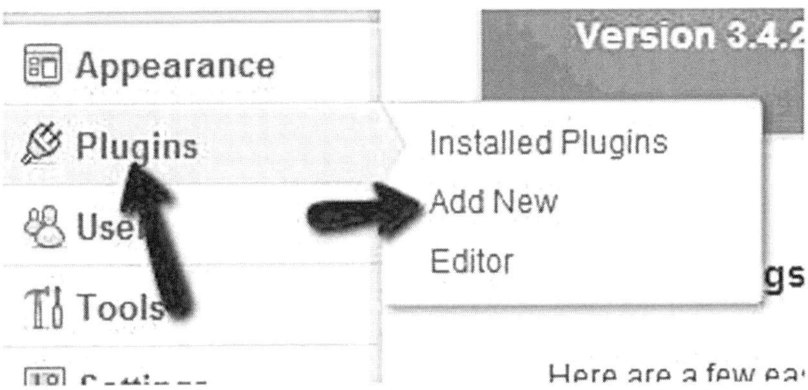

In the search box, type **growmap**:

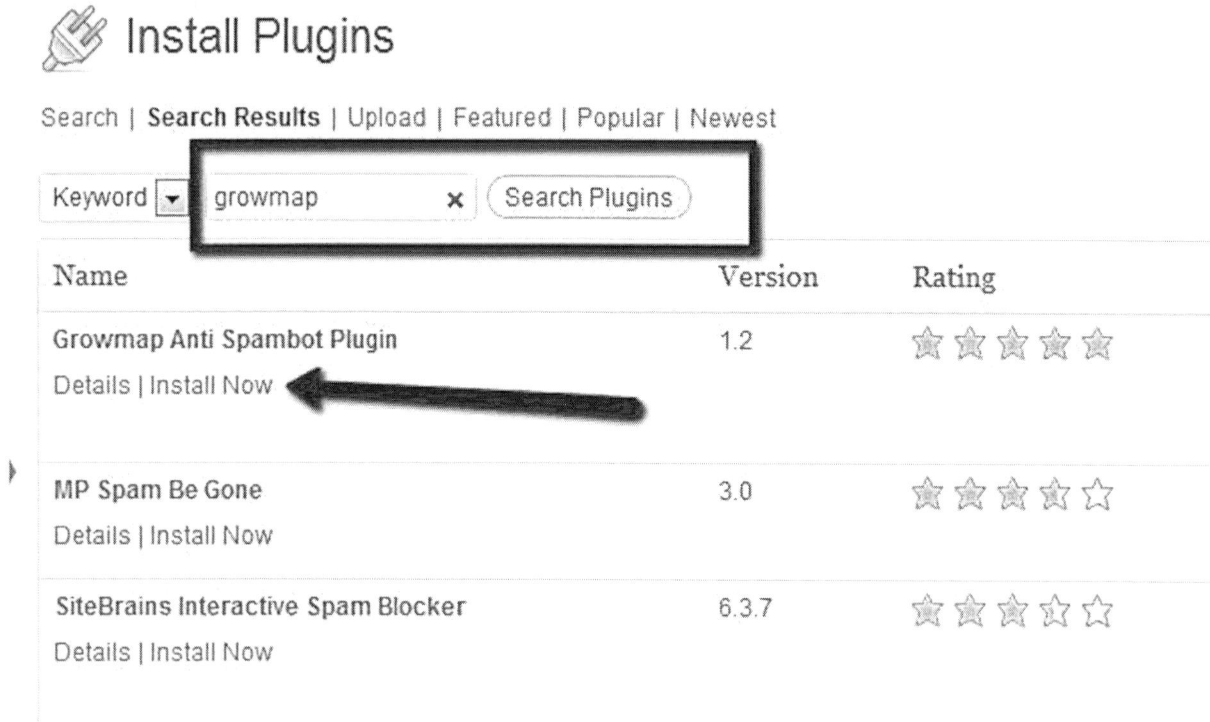

.. and click the Search button.

The plugin we are installing is called Growmap Anti Spambot Plugin.

Click the **Install Now** link under that plugin in the search results.

Once it is installed, you'll be prompted with a choice.

Click Activate the Plugin.

OK, that's it. The plugin has been installed.

If you mouse over the **Settings** menu you will find a new entry called G.A.S.P. These are the settings for this plugin, so click the link.

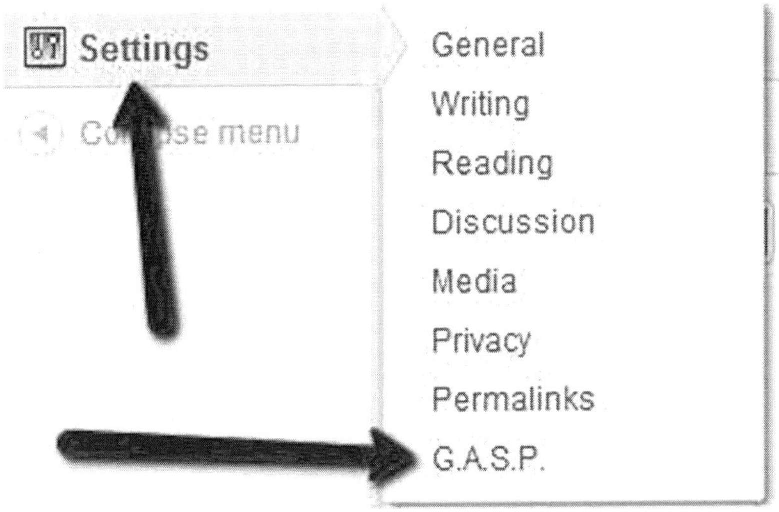

On the settings page there are quite a few options. At the very top:

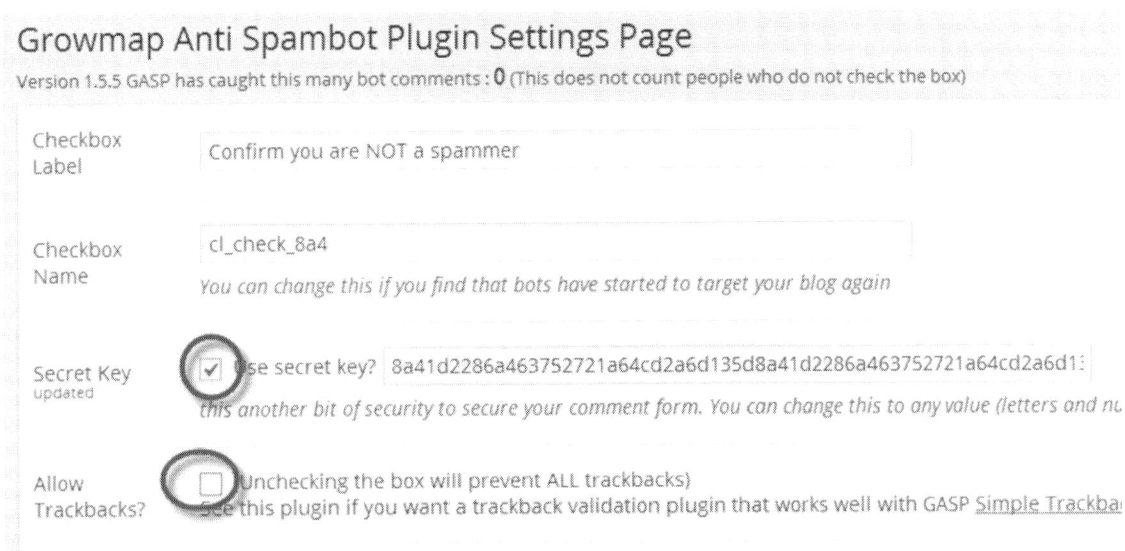

Check the **Secret Key** option, and uncheck the **Allow Trackbacks.** Trackbacks are often faked and are the cause of many spam comments. I like to cut them off here.

Now scroll down to the **Heuristics** part of the page.

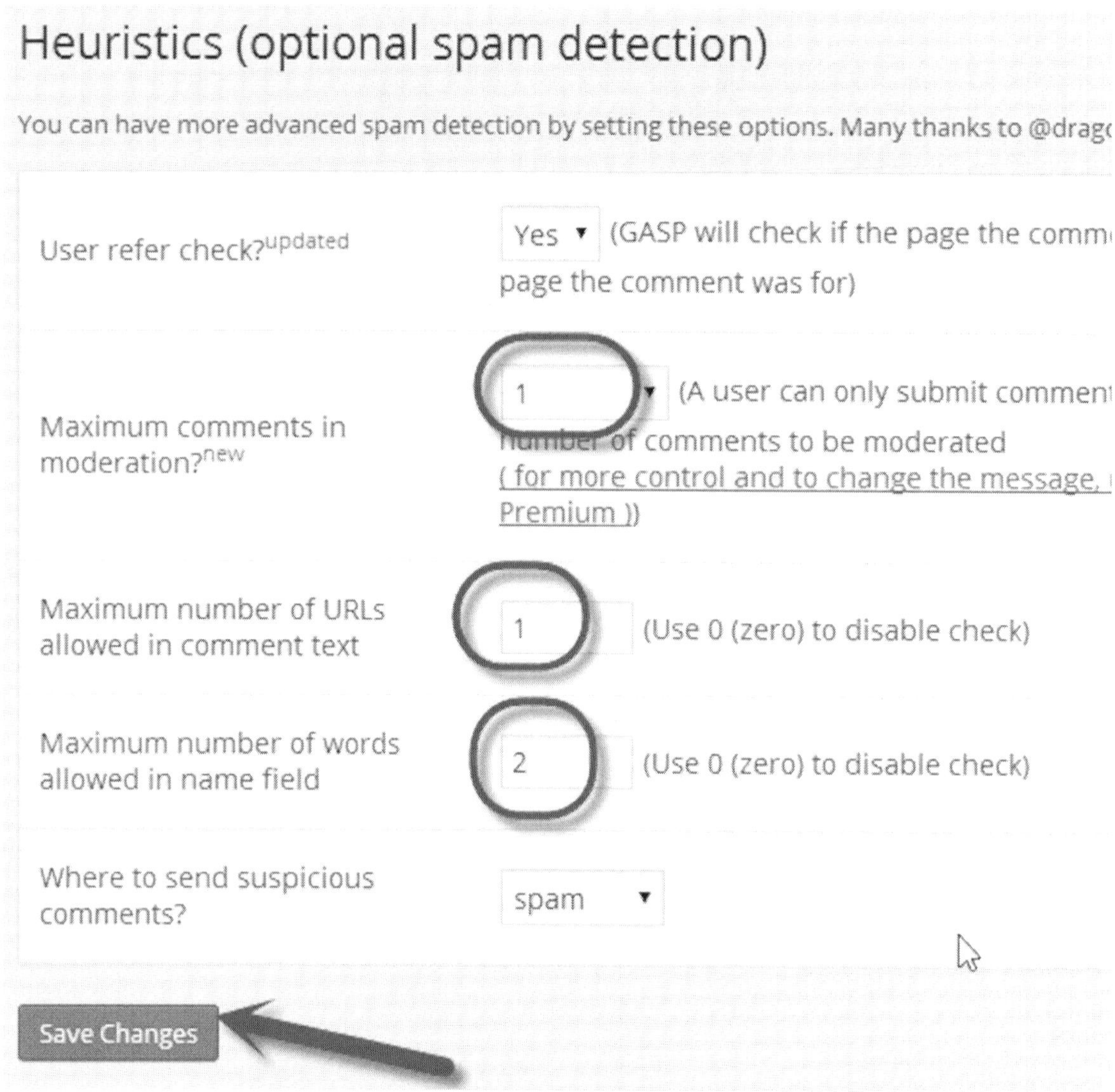

Change the **Maximum comments in moderation** to 1.

Change Maximum URLs in comment text to 1.

Optionally, change the maximum number of words in name field to 2. Some legitimate comment authors will add more than two words, but you can always check your spam folder for these that slip through. The problem with allowing multiple words in the name field is that spammers often use "money" phrases in their name field, to get a keyword rich anchor text link back to their site.

When done, click the Save Changes button.

Let's see what this plugin does (you will need to be logged out of your Dashboard to see the plugin at work).

If you look at the comment form on a post on your site, you'll see a little checkbox:

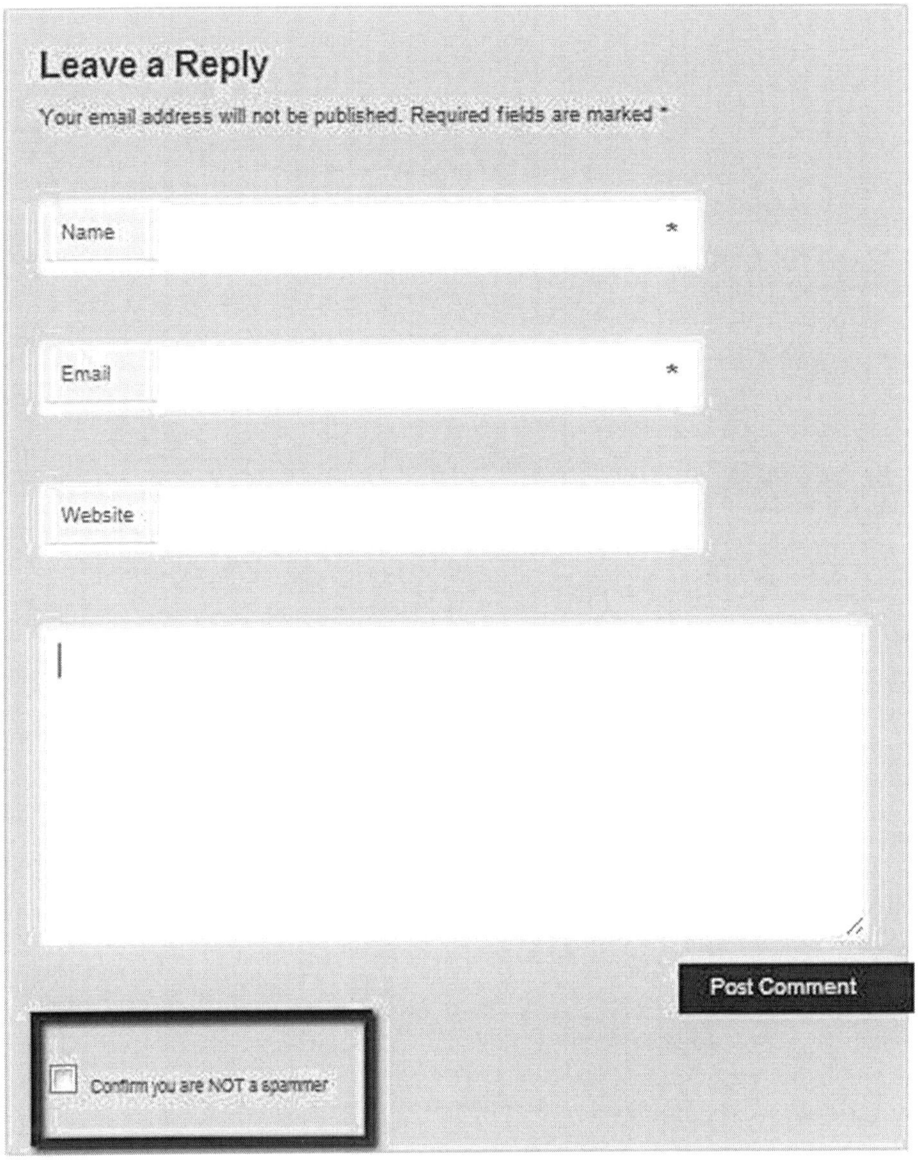

Most comment spam comes from "robot" software that won't know it has to check a box to post a comment. Anyone or anything that tries to leave a comment without checking this box will find their comment redirected to the spam folder automatically.

What if a legitimate person leaves a comment but forgets to check the box?

Well don't worry, they will get a visual warning that they forgot to check the box and have another chance to check it.

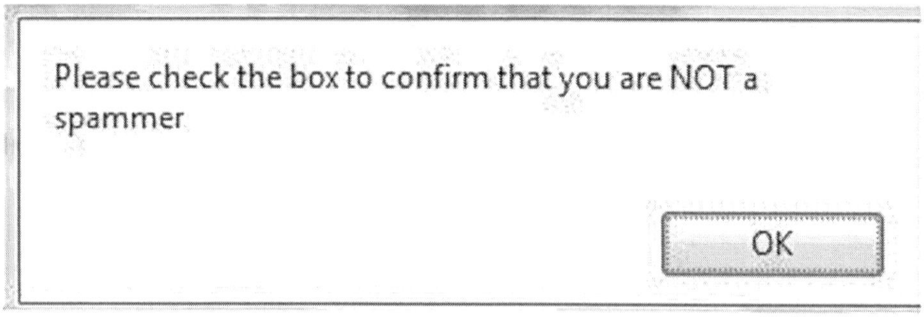

This is one of the best ways to stop large amounts of spam comments.

Moderating comments

When people comment, their comments won't go live until you approve them. This is how we set the site up earlier. If you had comments set on auto-approve, you'd most likely find so many spam comments on your site that you'd be pulling your hair out. Manual approval is the only way to go, and it does not have to take a long time.

Let's see how easy it is to moderate comments.

If you click on the Comments link in the sidebar of your Dashboard, you are taken to the comments section.

Across the top is a menu with Pending, Approved, Spam, Trash:

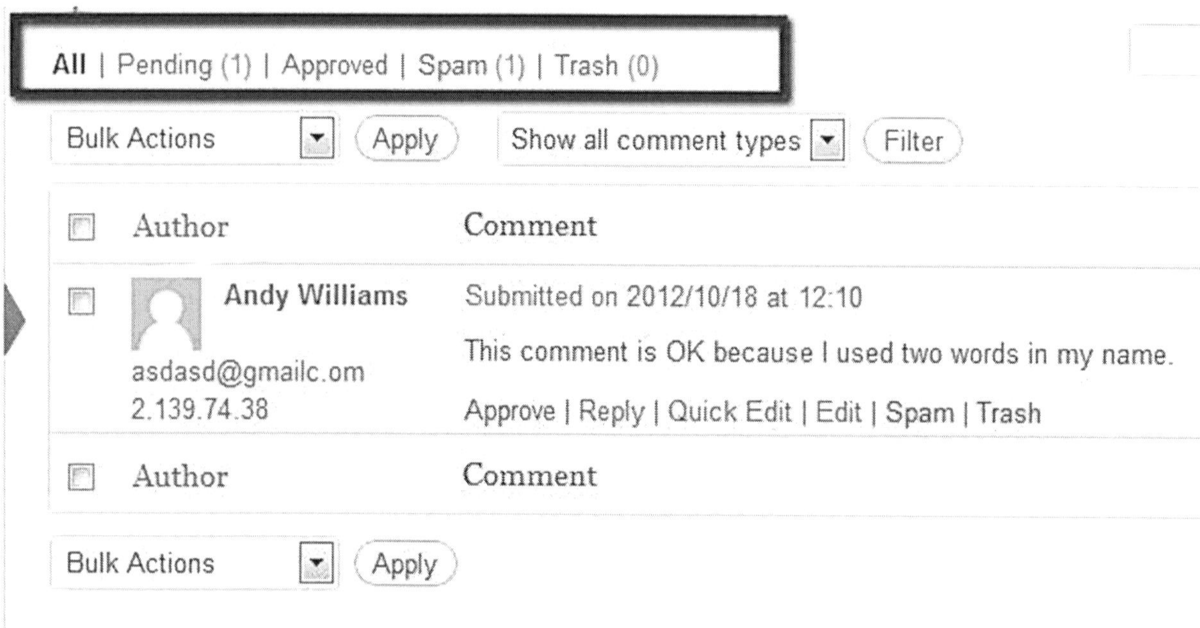

Lower down you can see a comment I added to my site. This comment was OK and passed all the tests - it did not have a URL in the comment, maximum two words in name, no words found in the blacklist, email address not in blacklist, etc.

If you hover your mouse over a comment in the list, a menu appears underneath that comment, which you can click to Approve, Reply, Quick Edit, Edit, send to Spam or send to Trash.

If the comment is OK, click the Approve link. If the comment is spam, click the Trash link (you don't need to use the spam link at all because we want to send all spam straight to the trash). You can also edit comments if you want to remove something or correct a spelling error – for example - from an otherwise good comment.

I recommend you don't reply to comments until you approve them. My typical workflow is this:

1. Moderate comments.
2. Go to the Approved comments by clicking the Approved link at the top.
3. Reply to comments that need a reply.
4. Go to Trash and empty it.

In the screenshot above, you will see that there is a (1) next to the spam link. That tells me there is one comment in the spam folder. It must have triggered one of the criteria we have set up for spam. Click on the spam link to see what the comment is:

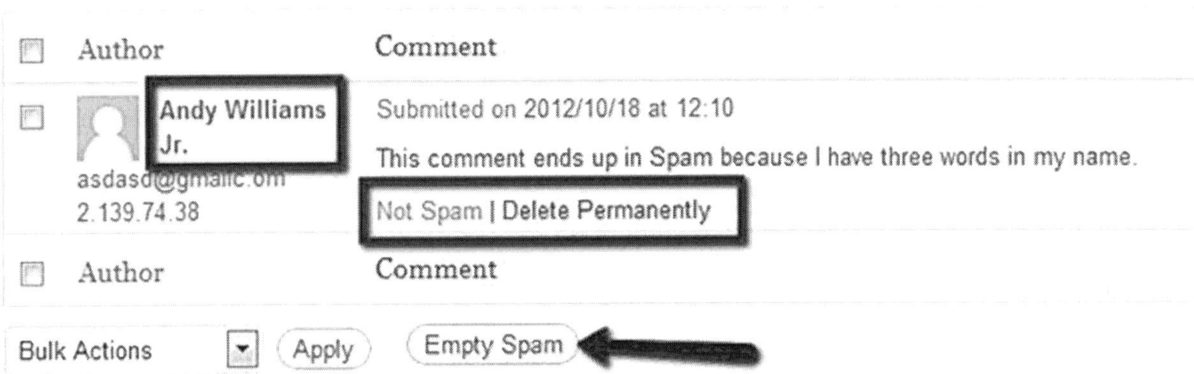

Looking at the comment, you can see that my name has three words so was sent to the spam folder. If you decide that a particular comment is not spam, mouse over it and the menu appears underneath. Click the **Not Spam** link and the comment will be sent to the **Pending** pile so that you can approve it.

Note that if all comments in the spam folder are actually spam, then you can click the Empty Spam button at the bottom to delete them all at once.

When you do delete spam, it is permanently removed.

The Trash folder holds all comments that were sent to the trash. Like the Spam folder, you can retrieve comments that are in the trash (if you need to), using the mouse over menu for any comment.

Finally, we have the Approved list. These are all comments on your site that have been approved. Click the link in the menu at the top to view them.

All comments in the Approved list have a mouse over menu as well, allowing you to **Reply** to the comment if you want to. You can of course change your mind about an "approved comment", and send it to Trash if you want to, or even unapprove it if you want to think about it.

What kinds of Comments should you send to Trash?

You will get a number of comments that say things you like to hear, like "nice blog", or "Great job". I suggest you trash all comments like this because they are spam comments. Their only purpose is to try and get a backlink from your site to theirs.

I recommend you only approve comments that:

1. Add something to the main article, either with more information, opinions or constructive information. That means never approving a comment that could have been written without that person ever reading your post. Comments MUST add something to your content. If they don't I suggest you send them to the Trash.
2. Never approve a comment where the person has used a keyword phrase for their name. You'll see people using things like "best Viagra online", or "buy XYZ online" as their name. No matter how good the comment is, trash it. What many spammers do is copy a paragraph from a good webpage on another website and use that as their comment. The comment looks great, but it was copied from another website.
3. I would suggest you never approve trackbacks or pingbacks. Most will not be real anyway.

With comments, be vigilant and don't allow poor comments onto your site as they will reflect badly on both you and your website.

Here are three spammy comments left on one of my websites. All three would go straight to the trash without hesitation:

Author	Comment
Del del_minter@yahoo.com 89.143.144.226	Submitted on 2012/09/27 at 3:12 am I could not refrain from commenting. Well written! Garden Furniture
Jason jasonphilips@gmail.com 178.73.216.89	Submitted on 2012/08/06 at 3:51 pm Very nice post. I just stumbled upon your blog and wished to say that I've truly enjoyed browsing your blog posts. In any case I will be subscribing to your feed and I hope you write again very soon!
Horizon Health and fitness EX : 58 An ellpitcal machine annettpassmore@googlemail.com 93.86.204.104	Submitted on 2012/08/06 at 2:38 pm In fact no matter if someone doesn't be aware of after that its up to other users that they will assist, so here it takes place.

None of these comments add anything to the article I wrote, meaning they made absolutely no reference to the post in question.

Did you also notice the name of the person in that last comment? That is an example of someone trying to get a keyword rich link back to their site.

Tasks to complete

1. Install Growmap and configure it.
2. Whenever there are comments on your site, moderate them. Delete any comments that are not "adding to the conversation".

Media Library

You can get to the Media Library either by clicking on the Media link in the menu, the media library sub-menu, or even when entering a piece of content:

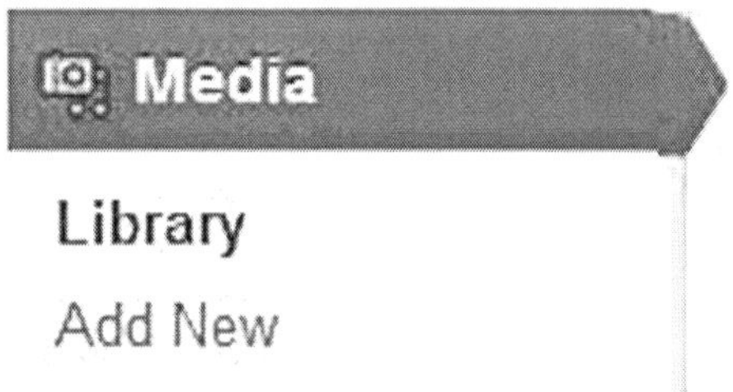

The media library is where you can upload images, videos and other files to use on your blog. It is a convenient place to hold all your media. Uploading stuff is really very easy.

You will usually add media directly from the **Add Post** screen when typing a piece of content. However, if for example you have a lot of images that you want to upload at any one time, it is often quicker to do it directly in the Media library.

How to Upload New Media

Uploading media is as simple as dragging and dropping it onto the large, box on the screen:

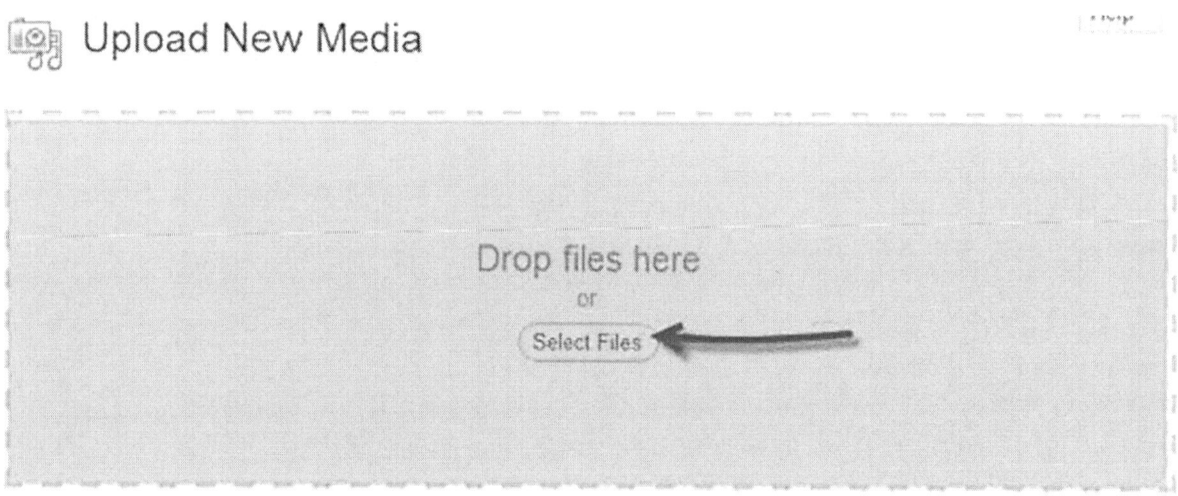

(You can also click the "Select Files" button and select them directly from your hard disk.)

To drag and drop something, simply open up Windows Explorer and find the item you want to upload. Click and hold on the item and drag it over to the rectangle in the media library and drop it (unclick the mouse button).

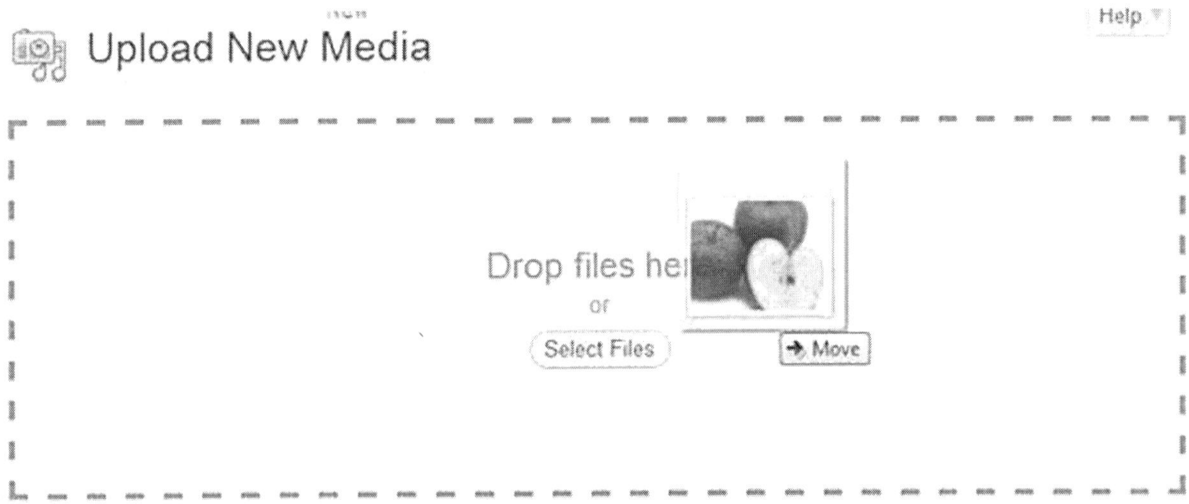

You can see I have dragged an image of apples over the box. When I drop it there, the image is uploaded to my library. When the upload is complete, you'll be shown a thumbnail of the image with a link to edit it:

Clicking on the Edit link opens the image in a new window where you see the image at full size. Under the image you can add some details:

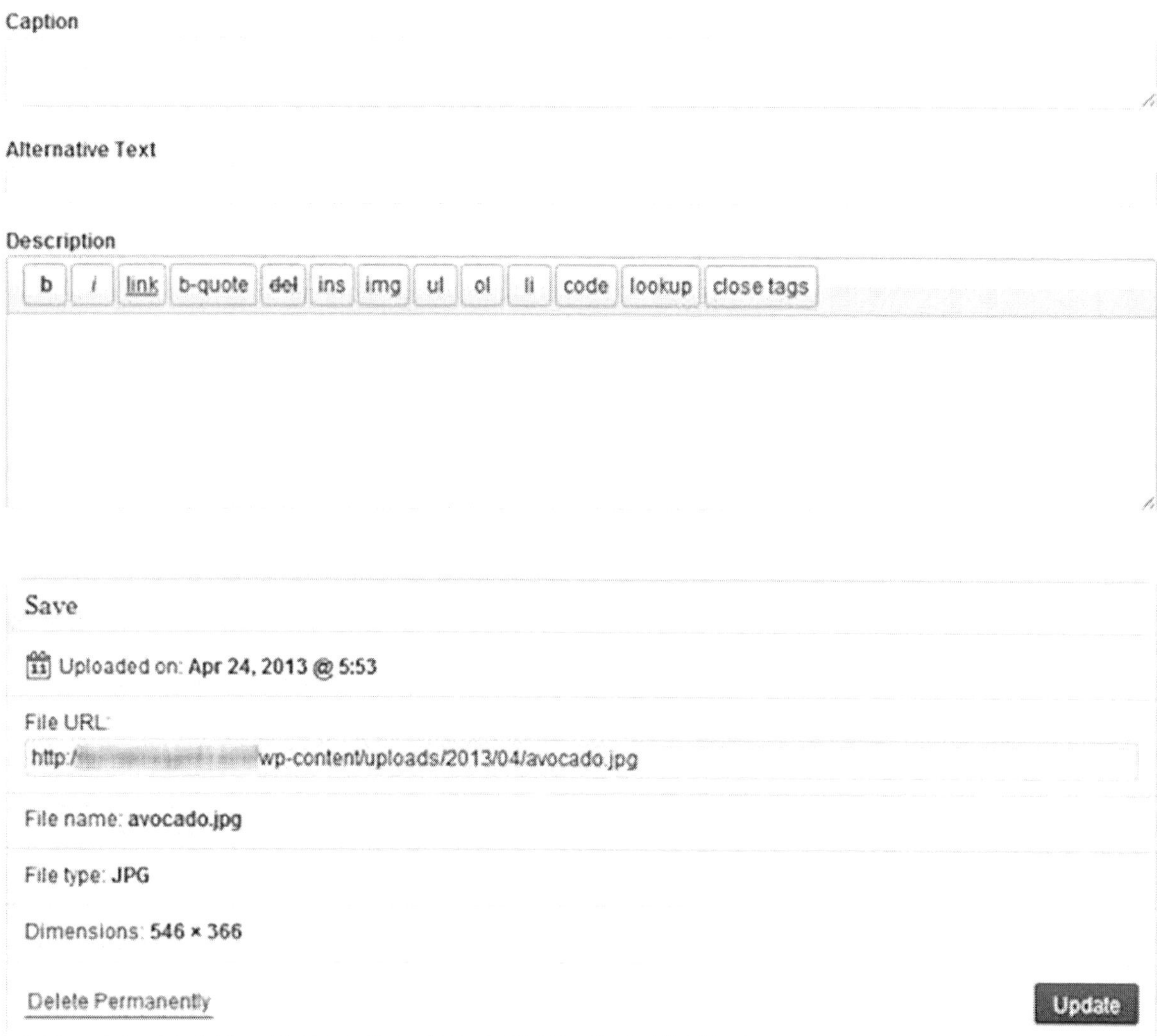

You can change/add a caption, the title, ALT text (which is the text shown to people who have images turned off in their browsers, e.g. visually impaired or blind people who will have text to voice software in order to read the page contents), and the description.

You can also grab the **File URL** of your newly uploaded image. If you copy that and paste it into a web browser's address bar, the image will load in your browser.

We will look at how to add an image (or video), to a post later in this book. But for now, just try uploading a few images to get the hang of things. Once uploaded, grab the file URL and paste it into your browser. Do they load?

NOTE: There are some file formats that WordPress will not let you upload for security reasons. PHP files are one example. If you want to upload a file so that you can offer it as a download on your site, but it is not accepted for upload, then zip it up and upload the zipped file instead.

All of the media in your library can be viewed on the Media library screen:

Each item has the now familiar mouse-over menu, which allows you to Edit, Delete Permanently, or View that media item.

There is a column showing you the date the item was added to your library.

There is also a column called "Uploaded To". This column lets you know if that image was used on a post or page.

Note that columns in the media library are sortable by clicking the title of the column. Furthermore, if there are columns you don't use and don't want to see, you can hide them by using the screen options. Remember those?

Just unclick whichever items you don't want to see. You can even specify how many media items you see per page in your library.

If you have a lot of media in your library, there is a handy search feature:

In the screenshot above, I searched for apples and the results returned the only media item called "apples". The search feature will look for your search text in both the title of the media and its description. If the word appears in either, it is shown in the search results.

Across the top of the media library, there are a few filtering options (depending on the types of media you have uploaded:

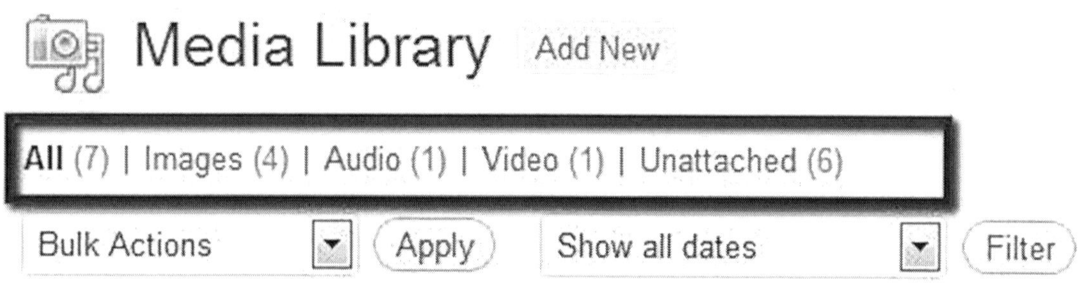

In the screenshot above, you can see there are 4 Images, 1 Audio file and 1 Video file.

If I want to see just the images, I can click this images (4) link and just those items will be displayed in the media list. Similarly I can choose to just show audio or video.

Finally in the media library you have Bulk Actions (something that can be applied to multiple items in one go), and a further way to filter your media. I mention these together because they are found together on the screen:

Next to each media item is a checkbox. If you want to delete several media items, you can check each one, and then select Delete Permanently from the Bulk Actions drop down box. Click Apply to delete the checked items.

To the right of that is a filter box that allows you to just view media that was uploaded in any particular month. Clicking on the drop down box only shows the months where media was uploaded, so just select the month of interest and click Filter. This is a great way of sorting through lots of media if you know you uploaded it last month, but cannot remember what it was called.

That's if for the Media Library for now. We will come back to this when we look at how to add content to your site using the **W**hat **Y**ou **S**ee **I**s **W**hat **Y**ou **G**et (WYSIWYG), document editor later.

Tasks to complete

1. Go and explore the media library. Practice uploading a photo, video or sound file and grabbing the URL.
2. Try using the search feature to find a specific piece of media in your library.

Pages v posts

When you want to add content to your site, you have two options. You can either create a new **Page** or a new **Post**. In terms of adding/editing, these two are very similar, but they are handled very differently by WordPress.

This may sound confusing to people who are new to WordPress (or maybe even new to website building). After all, isn't a post on your site a page? Doesn't a page on your site contain a post?

For some reason, WordPress creators decided to name these two types of content "posts" and "pages" and it does cause confusion. However, you DO need to understand the basic differences between them when it comes to building your site. The information I'll give you later will make it easy for you to decide which to use, so don't get hung up on these differences.

Since WordPress was originally designed as a blogging platform (i.e. to help build websites that were constantly updated with posts about whatever it was going on in that bloggers life), posts were designed for these regular updates.

WordPress posts are *date-dependent and chronological* and this separates them from Pages which are date-independent and not really related to any other piece of content on the site.

Posts were originally designed to be ordered by date, with a post you created yesterday logically appearing lower down the page than a post you make today. Newer posts are inserted at the top of the page, and older posts are pushed off the bottom.

It might help to think of an example.

Suppose you were keeping a blog about your weight loss program. On day one you weighed in at 210lb, so you write about that and what you have done for the day to help with your diet. Each day you write a new entry as a kind of personal journey on your weight loss progress.

When someone comes to your site, they see the daily posts in chronological order. This means visitors to your 'blog' can follow your story logically and see how your diet is working out for you.

This type of chronology is not possible to do with pages (well it is, but it takes a lot of effort plus plugins to achieve, so why bother?). Pages do not have any defined order within a site, though they can have a hierarchy with parent and child pages. We will look at this a little later on; so don't worry about it now.

OK, so the date-dependency is one important difference between WordPress posts and pages. What else?

Well, posts can be categorized, whereas pages cannot (at least not without plugins).

Suppose you were creating a site about exercise equipment. You might have a series of reviews on different treadmills, another set of reviews on exercise bikes, and so on.

Using posts allows us to categorize our content into relevant groups. If I had 10 reviews of various weight loss programs, I could create a category on my site called weight loss programs and add all 10 reviews to this category by writing them as posts.

Putting related content into the same category makes sense from a human visitor point of view, but also from the point of view of a search engine. If someone were on your site reading a review of the Hollywood Diet, it would be easy to take advantage of the features of posts in WordPress to also highlight some of the other diet reviews you have on your site. This can be done with posts (and we'll add a plugin called YARPP later to automate this), but it is a much more manual process if you tried doing the same thing with pages.

As well as categories, posts can also be tagged. Tags are an additional way to group and categorize your content. We'll discuss tags later, but for now, just realise that they can be used to further categorise your content to help your visitors and the search engines make sense of your project. It is possible to create tags for pages as well, but once again, only with plugins. However, we try not to use plugins unless they are absolutely essential as they do slow down the loading time of a website.

Another great feature of posts is that they can have **Excerpts**. These are short descriptions of the article that can be used by themes and plugins to create a Meta description tag, or a description of the article when linking to it. For example, below is a related posts section (created using the YARPP plugin that we'll install later), on one of my sites. It shows excerpts being used for the post descriptions:

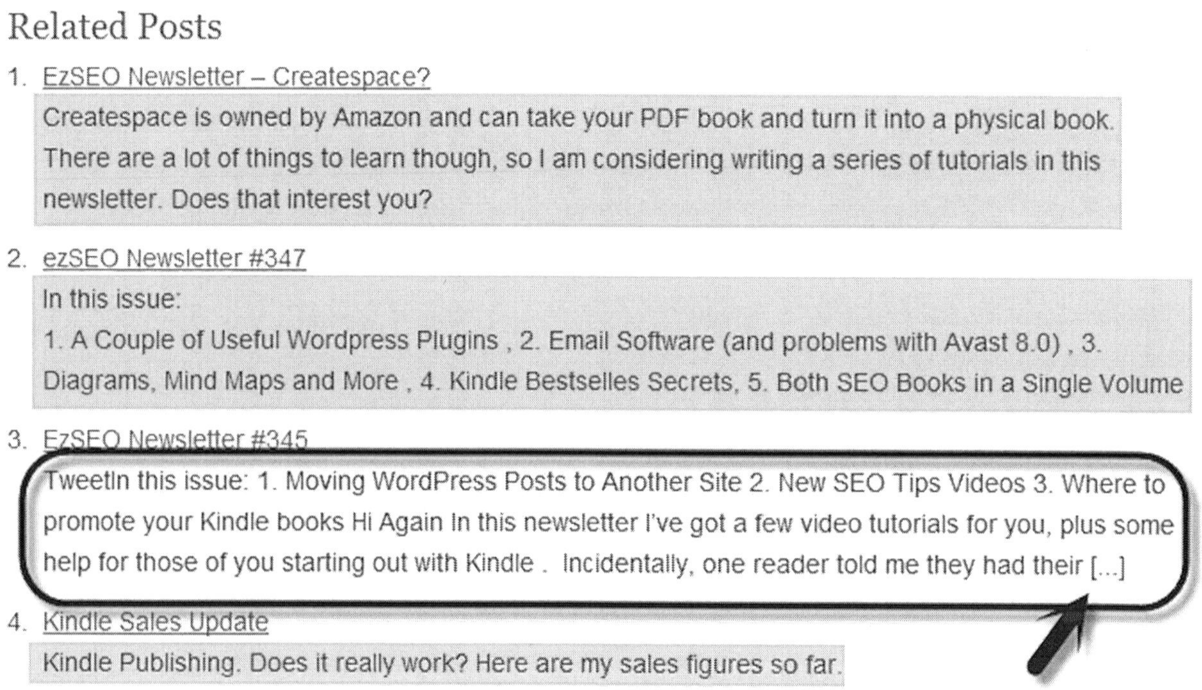

Without excerpts, the first X words of the article itself are used for the description (see item 3 in the screenshot above). This looks untidy since it finishes mid-sentence and uses a double or triple period (...) to signify that there is more to read. Also, bear in mind that the first sentence or two of the article does not always make the best description for the article.

Another important feature of posts is that they appear in your site's RSS feed. Remember, we talked about how important that was earlier in the book. Since RSS feeds are there to highlight the most recent posts, any important new content on the site should be a post so that it can be seen in your feeds.

One of the original differences between pages and posts was that pages could use different templates whereas posts could not. This meant that different pages on your site might have totally different layouts. This was not possible with posts. However, with the introduction of WordPress 3.1, a feature called **Post Formats** was introduced. We will look at this feature briefly when we add a post to the site, but for now, understand that post formats allow you to change the layout of your posts by selecting from a list of formats.

When to use posts and when to use pages

Not all webmasters agree on this, but I am going to give you a simple rule that will tell you when to use a post and when to use a page. This is the way I have built WordPress sites for myself and my clients for several years, and the system offers great SEO benefits as well as organizing content in a logical manner to help both visitors and search engines.

Before I tell you the rule, let me first distinguish between two types of content that you may have on your site.

The first type of content is that which is important to your niche and you want visitors to see. We will call this type of content, **Niche Content**. This will include all articles, reviews, etc. that you write for your site and your targeted audience.

The second type of content is that which you don't really care whether visitors see or not. The only reason we put it on the site is because we need to include it for various purposes. This type of content is frequently unrelated to any other. Typical examples would be a Privacy page, Terms of Service, Disclaimer, Contact page, and an About Us page (although a good 'About Us' page is one exception that we should make visible to our visitors). Apart from the About Us page, these others types of pages are what I call **Legal Pages**, since the only reason they are on the site is because we are required to have them there by law, or to comply with search engine rules.

OK, you get the difference?

Here is the basic rule.

Use Posts for Niche (topical), Content, and Pages for Legal Content.

Simple enough, but I am sure some of you may still not quite get it. You will when we start adding pages and posts to the website. Before we can do that though, we need to look at post categories and tags.

Tasks to complete

1. Go over this section until the differences between pages and posts are clear in your mind.

Categories & tags

Before we can start adding posts to our site, we need to think about the way the site will be structured and how the posts will be organized within the site itself.

We have already touched on categories and tags earlier in the book, and have set up the SEO settings for these taxonomies (organization of content). Let's now have a closer look at categories and tags so that you can fully understand them and add a few to your own site.

Both categories and tags are ways to categorize your posts.

All posts MUST be assigned to a category, but posts DO NOT have to have tags assigned to them. In that respect, categories are more important than tags.

Think of categories as the main way to categorize your posts, and tags as a further way to provide even more details about your posts.

Let's look at an example.

Let's consider a website about vacuum cleaners. What would the main categories be on a website about vacuum cleaners?

To think about this in a different way, how would you want to group the articles on your vacuum cleaner site so that related articles were in the same category?

Here are some ideas:

Dyson

Handheld

Dyson Ball

Eureka

Bagless

Cordless

Hoover

Upright

Canister

Miele

HEPA filter

All of these could be categories, but then you might get to the situation where one post might fit into several categories. While WordPress encourages this, I recommend you put each post into ONE category only. Thinking about one category per post actually helps you find the best categories for your site.

Of those ideas listed above, which ones would make the most sense if a vacuum could only be in one category?

How about “bagless”?

Nope. A vacuum could be bagless, upright and a Dyson.

The obvious categories from those listed above would be the categories that would only allow a post to be in one category - the brand names. My categories would therefore be:

Dyson

Eureka

Hoover

Miele

A Dyson DC25 vacuum cleaner review could only go in one category – the Dyson category.

So what about the other terms:

Handheld

Dyson Ball

Bagless

Cordless

Upright

Canister

HEPA filter

Well, these are perfect as tags because they add a little more information/detail about the post. For example, my review of the Dyson DC25 vacuum would be in the category Dyson, but could be tagged with ball, HEPA, bagless & upright.

The beauty (and danger), of using tags is that for every tag you use, WordPress will create a page just for that tag. In the example above, WordPress would create FOUR tag pages. One for “ball”, one for “HEPA”, one for “Bagless” and one for “Upright”.

The “HEPA” tag page will list all vacuums on the site that have been tagged with HEPA – it helps visitors find more HEPA vacuums if that is what they are interested in.

The "Bagless" tag page would list all vacuums on the site that were bagless (and therefore tagged with that term). A visitor on my site looking for a bagless vacuum could use the tag page to quickly see all available bagless vacuums that had been reviewed to date.

These tags also give search engines indications about our content, helping them understand what it's about so that it can rank better for related searches.

Tags are powerful. However, with that power comes some responsibility.

If you abuse tags, your site will become spammy. I have seen sites where posts have been tagged with 10, 20, 50, and even several hundred tags. Don't believe me? See this screenshot showing the tags for a post on one website I came across:

You don't need to be able to read the words in that screenshot to get the point. I've had to reduce the size of the screenshot to get all the tags into view. There are over 160 tags for that one article, and by the way, I happen to know that Google penalised this particular site.

Think about the problems of tag abuse by thinking how WordPress works and how it handles tags.

Every tag in that list will have its own tag page.

The biggest problem for that site is that many of the tags used on that post are not used on any other posts. That means there are 100+ tag pages with just a single post listed as using that tag.

To think about this in another way, if that was the only post on the site, there would be over 160 pages on it.

The way the webmaster used tags in this example is what Google would call "spam". Please, use tags responsibly!

Let's look at one more example.

Think of a recipe website about puddings, desserts, cakes and so on.

You might have main categories like:

Ice cream

Cakes

Muffins

Mousse

Cookies

These are the obvious categories since a dessert will only be able to fit into one of the categories. To further classify the recipes on the site, we'd use tags which would add a little more detail about each post.

What type of tags would you use?

Stuck for ideas?

Tags become more apparent when you look at a particular recipe. If the recipe was for chocolate brownies, then the category would be cakes and maybe you'd have tags like chocolate, walnuts, frosting. See how those tags compliment the category in helping to classify the recipe?

Those tags would be used on other posts too, e.g. banana cake (at least the way my mama makes it), would also be tagged with frosting and walnuts.

Chocolate would probably be a common tag in dessert recipes. Think of chocolate chip ice cream, chocolate mousse, chocolate gateaux, etc.

Do you see how the tags help define the article, giving a little more description about the contents of the piece? This is the mindset you are looking to develop as you utilize tags for your own website.

A few guidelines for using tags

1. Keep a list of tags you use on your site and make sure you spell them correctly when you reuse them. Remember, if you misspell a tag, another tag page will be created for the misspelt version.

2. Don't create tags that will only apply to one post. Remember, tags are there to help classify your content into groups. Most tags will be used several times on a site, and its use will increase as you add more content.

3. Only pick a small number of relevant tags per post. I'd recommend somewhere between 3 - 6 tags per post, but if some need more, then that's fine. If some need less that's OK too. This is just a general rule of thumb.

4. NEVER use a tag that is also a category.

Setting up categories & tags in your dashboard

Categories and tags are properties of posts, so you'll find the menus to work with them under the Posts menu of the Dashboard navigation.

Categories and tags can either be set up before you start writing content, or added as you are composing it. The most common method is to set up categories before you begin, but add tags while you are writing your post.

I recommend that you create a description for all tags and categories, and to do that, you will need to go into the pages using the links in this menu.

OK, let's go and set up a category first. Click on the categories menu:

On the right you will see a list of any existing categories. There is only one - uncategorized, that WordPress has set up for you. Since this is the default category on the site (See Writing Settings), we want to change this to be a default category and one that means something to our site. If you mouse over the category title, you'll get the menu appear underneath it:

The Quick Edit will allow you to change the category name AND the category slug. The slug is just the text that is used in the URL to represent the category of the post. Remember we set up Permalinks earlier to look like this:

/%category%/%postname%/

The %category% variable is replaced by the category slug and the %postname% variable will be replaced by the post name slug.

To create the category slug, WordPress uses the same text as the category name (converted to lowercase), with any spaces bridged by a dash.

Therefore a category name of **juicer reviews** would have a default slug of **juicer-reviews**, but you can specify your own slug if you prefer not to use the WordPress default.

Since we want to add a description to every category we create (to be used as the category Meta description), we need to click on the **Edit** link to give us access to all settings for that category.

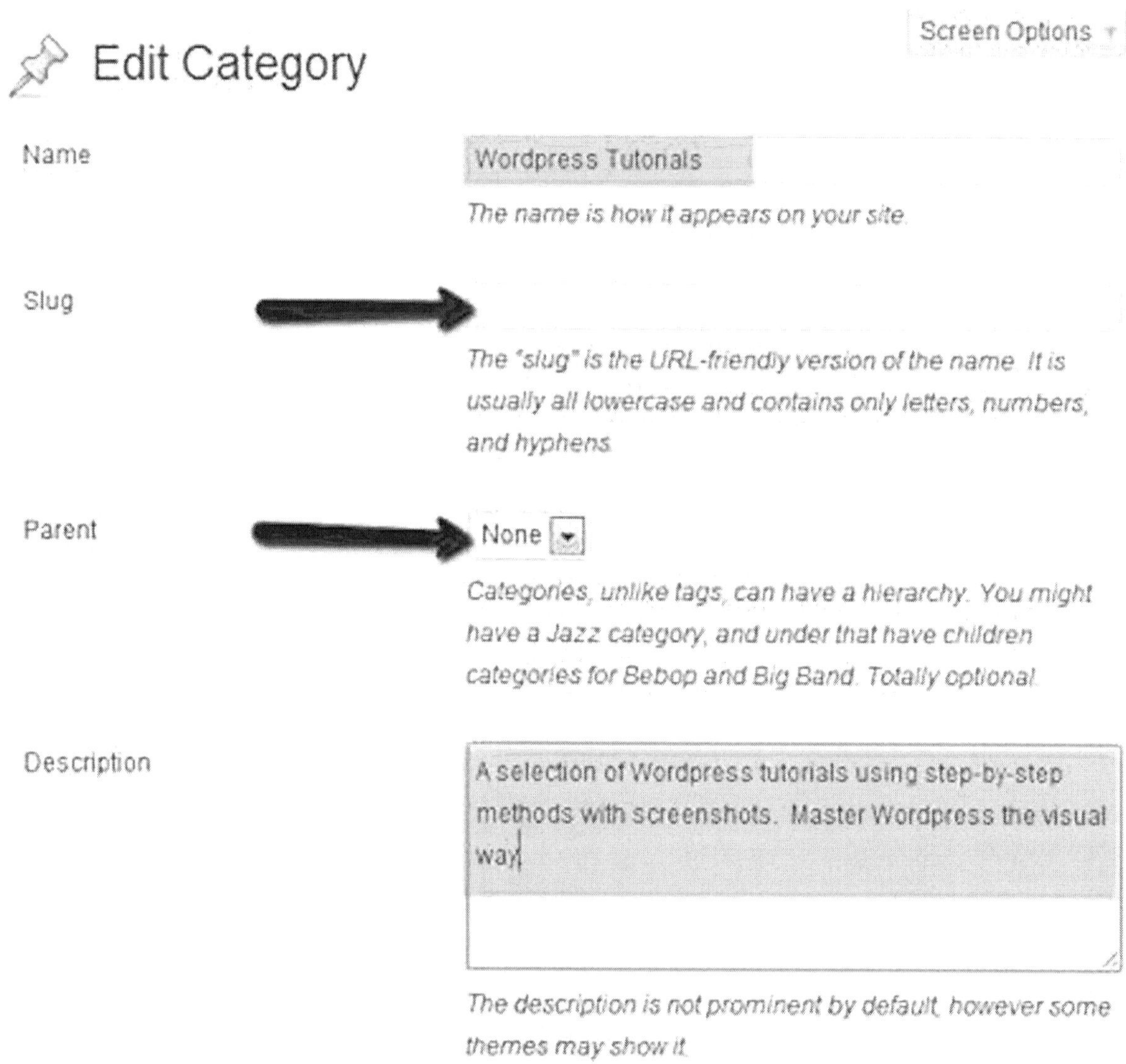

I have entered a new category name for my default category (the default is the one that is selected when you create a new post). You can of course change this by selecting a different category as appropriate.

I have left the slug empty. When I save these settings, WordPress will use **wordpress-tutorials** as the slug. Therefore the URLs of the posts in this category will look like this:

http://visualwordpress.com/wordpress-tutorials/installing-plugins

I have added a description that will be used as the Meta description of the category page, but I have not selected a parent category.

NOTE: If you have installed the Wordpress SEO plugin by Yoast, you will have more options on your category edit screen. We will look at these in a moment.

Parent categories & hierarchy

Categories can be hierarchical. In other words, you can have categories within categories.

An example might be a website on car maintenance. I might have a category called Toyota, but then want sub-categories called Engine, Brakes, and Exhaust etc.

Therefore the parent category would be Toyota. When I create the engine, brake & exhaust categories, I'd select Toyota as the parent.

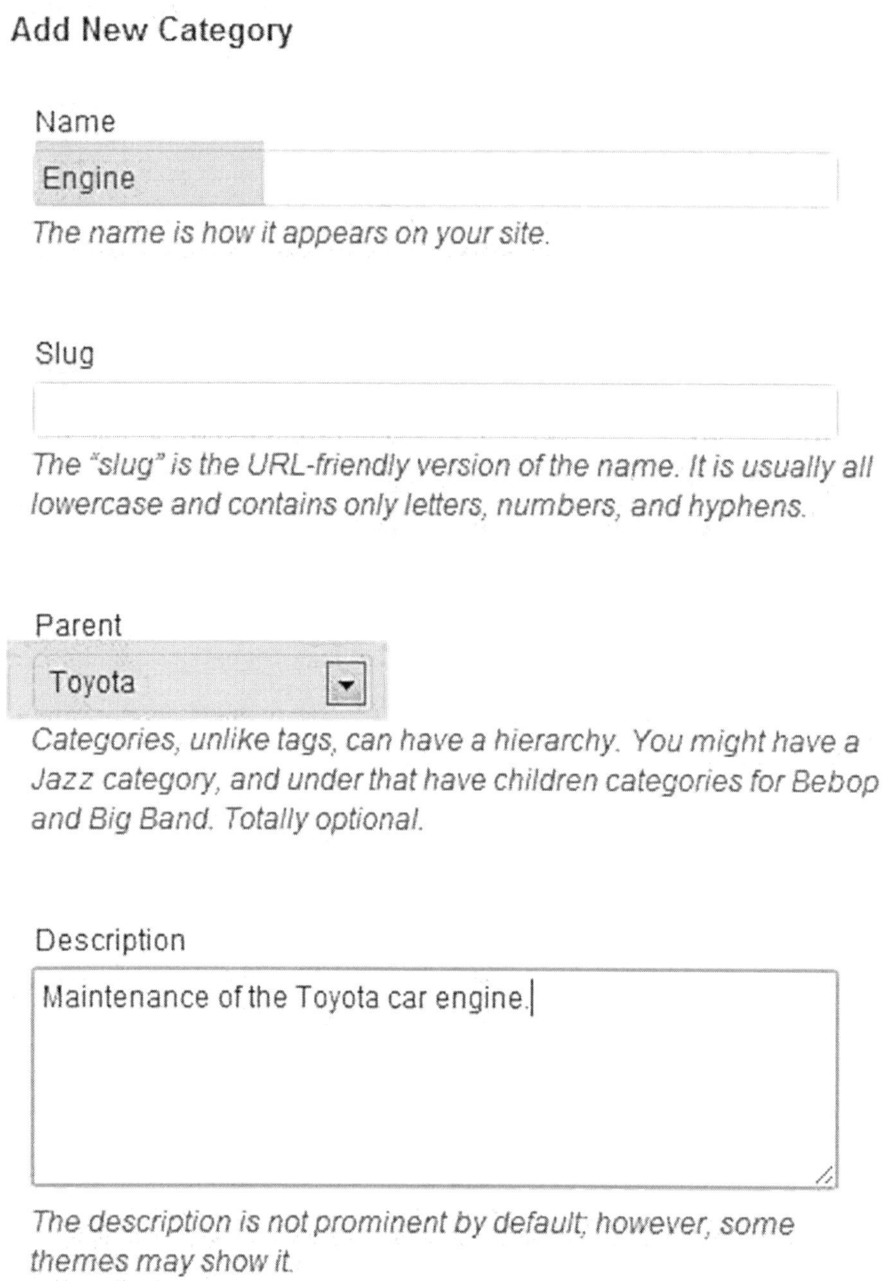

In the list of categories you can spot parent/child relationships within categories because they are shown in the table as a line next to the child. The child is indented:

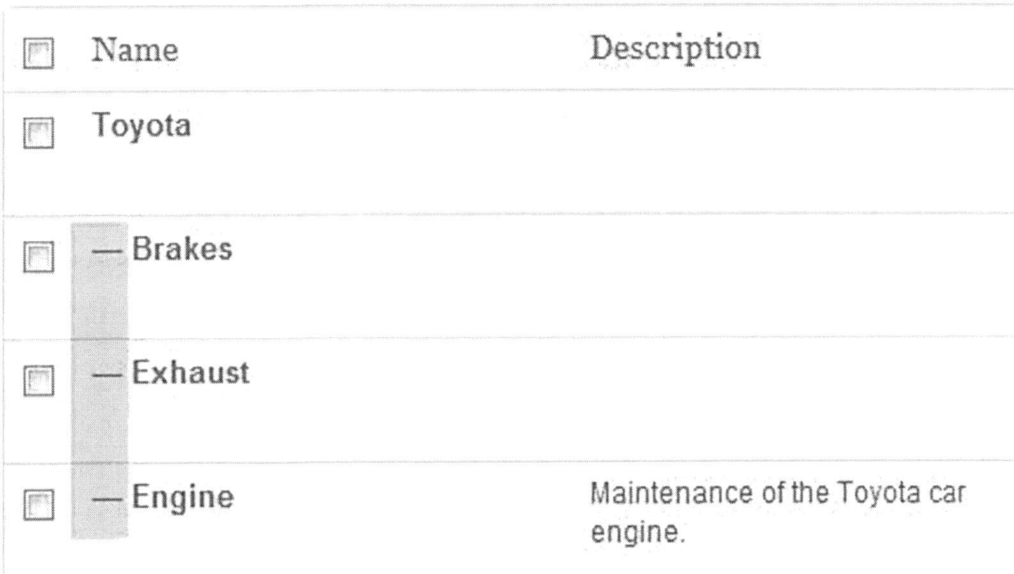

On my website, I could then have a menu item called Toyota, which opens up when you mouse over to include the child categories.

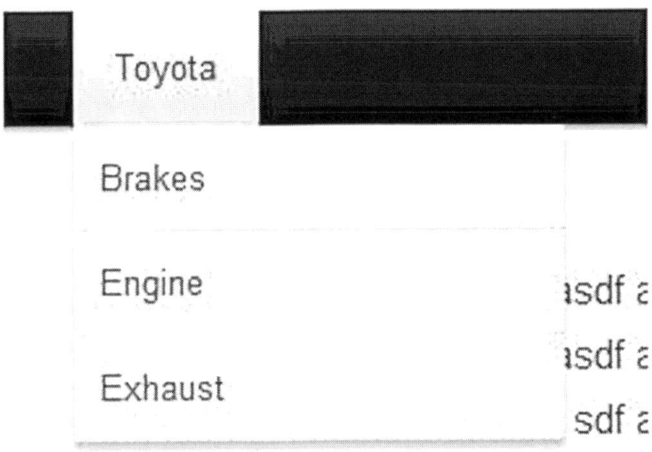

Parent - Child categories are very useful for tidying up the categorization on your site.

Imagine if you had 10 brands of cars, and 10 different areas on maintenance for each type of car. That would require 100 categories which would be too many to display on a website. By using parent-child categories, you can just have the 10 brands as the parent categories on your site, with the maintenance sections only visible on mouse-over as children to the parents.

Adding a new category

Adding a new category is easy. Fill in the title, slug (if you want to), and a description. Then select a parent if applicable. Click the **Add New Category** button and your new category is ready for use.

If you go to the category list and click the Edit link of a category, you'll actually notice more settings than just Title, Slug, Parent and Category. These additional settings are only seen when you go into full edit mode, and they are added there by the WordPress SEO plugin by Yoast that we set up earlier.

Here are those WordPress SEO Plugin settings:

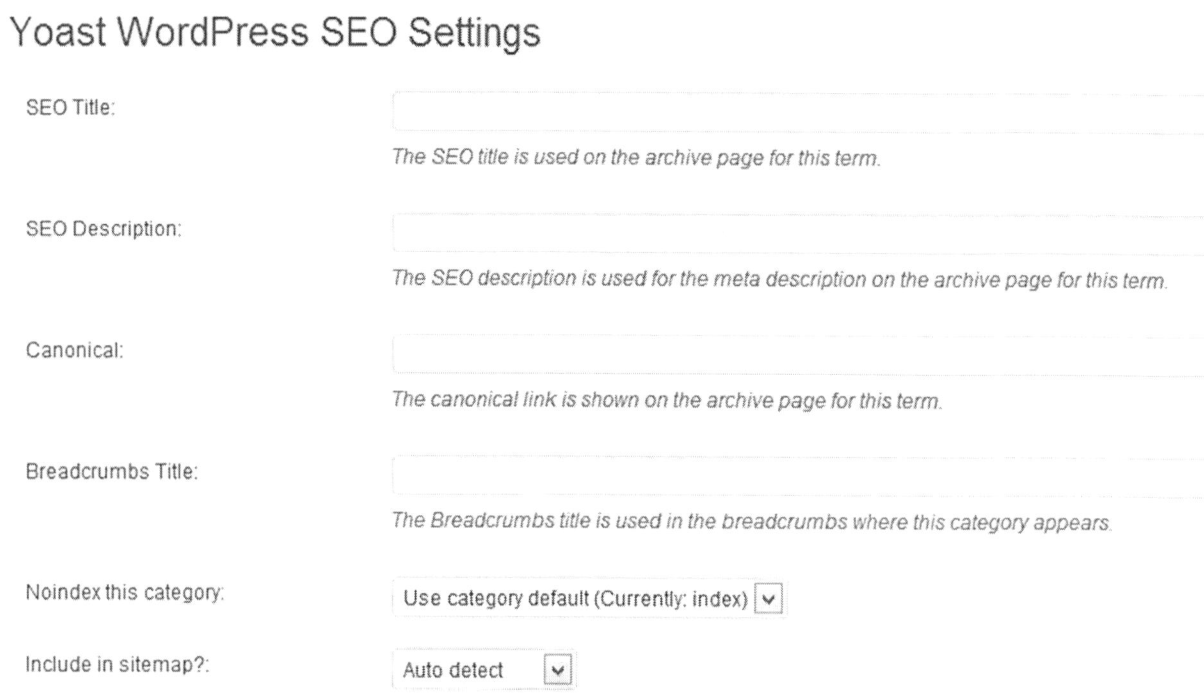

You can actually ignore these settings because WordPress does a good enough job of handling categories. There is only one setting here that is worth thinking about now, which is the **Noindex this category** drop down box.

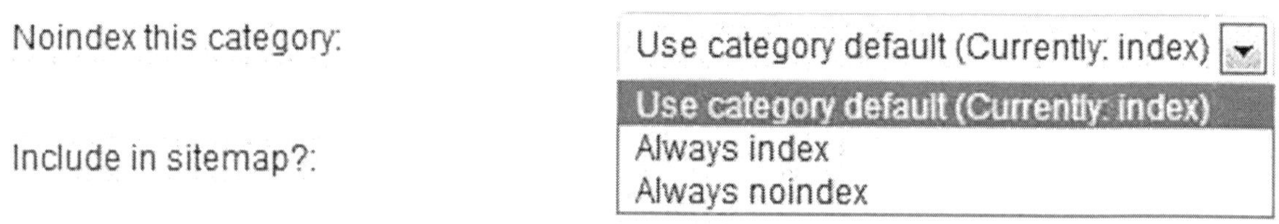

This allows you to set up some categories to be **noindex** with the search engines. Although this isn't something you normally want to do, it does highlight the fine level of control that this plugin adds to WordPress. We'll see more of this fine level of control when we add new content later.

Adding Tags is very similar to adding categories except tags cannot have a parent child relationship with each other.

For every tag you enter, add a description to explain what that tag is being used for. That description will then be used for the Meta description of the tag page; this is how we set it up within the SEO plugin, remember?

Similar to the categories, the **Add Tag** screen has just a few options - Title, Slug and Description. You only need to fill in the Title and Description because WordPress will handle the slug for us. However, if you go in and edit an existing tag, you will see extra Yoast WordPress SEO plugin settings for the tag. Again, these can be ignored for now, because WordPress handles tags very well.

While I expect you will add tags directly on the **Add Post** screen as you write your content, I do highly recommend you come back to this section every time you use a new tag, just to fill in a description for those tags you create. When you make a new tag on the **Add Post** screen, you don't have the option of adding the description there and then, but it is important to add one nonetheless.

Tasks to complete

1. Set up a few categories for your site.
2. Think about possible tags and keep a list on a notepad.
3. Make sure to add descriptions to every tag and category that you add.

Writing posts

Whether you are writing posts or pages, the main content editor is the same.

To create a new post on your site, click the Posts -> Add New link in the Dashboard navigation menu.

The Add Post (and Add Page) screen has a lot of information on it. Let's look at the **W**hat **Y**ou **S**ee **I**s **W**hat **Y**ou **G**et (WYSIWYG) Editor first.

WordPress WYSIWYG editor

The toolbar of the editor (the place where you add your content), looks like this:

You'll see on the top right there are two tabs - Visual & Text (the Text tab was called the HTML tab in previous versions of WordPress).

The Visual tab is where you can write your content using WYSIWYG features. On this tab you'll see text and media formatted as it will appear on the website once published. This is the tab you will want to use for most of the work you do when adding new, or editing existing content, on your site.

The other tab - Text - shows the raw code that is responsible for the layout and content of the page. Unless you specifically need to insert some code or script into your content, stick with the Visual tab.

On the toolbar, the button at the far right (see screenshot above), opens up more features (tool buttons), of the toolbar. Some of the features are well worth using, so click on that button. Your toolbar will now look like this:

The two rows of buttons allow you to format your content visually. If you have used any type of Word Processor before, then this should be fairly intuitive.

I won't go through the functions of all these buttons. If you want to see what each one does, move your mouse over it and you'll get a toolbar tip appear giving details.

Adding content to your site is as easy as typing it into the large box under the toolbar.

As you write your content you can select text and then click a toolbar button to format the selected word(s). Make it bold, or change its colour, make it a header, or any of the other features offered in the toolbar.

You can easily create headlines from the drop down box (far left, bottom row) on the toolbar. Write the headline, select it with your mouse, and choose the header you want from the drop down box:

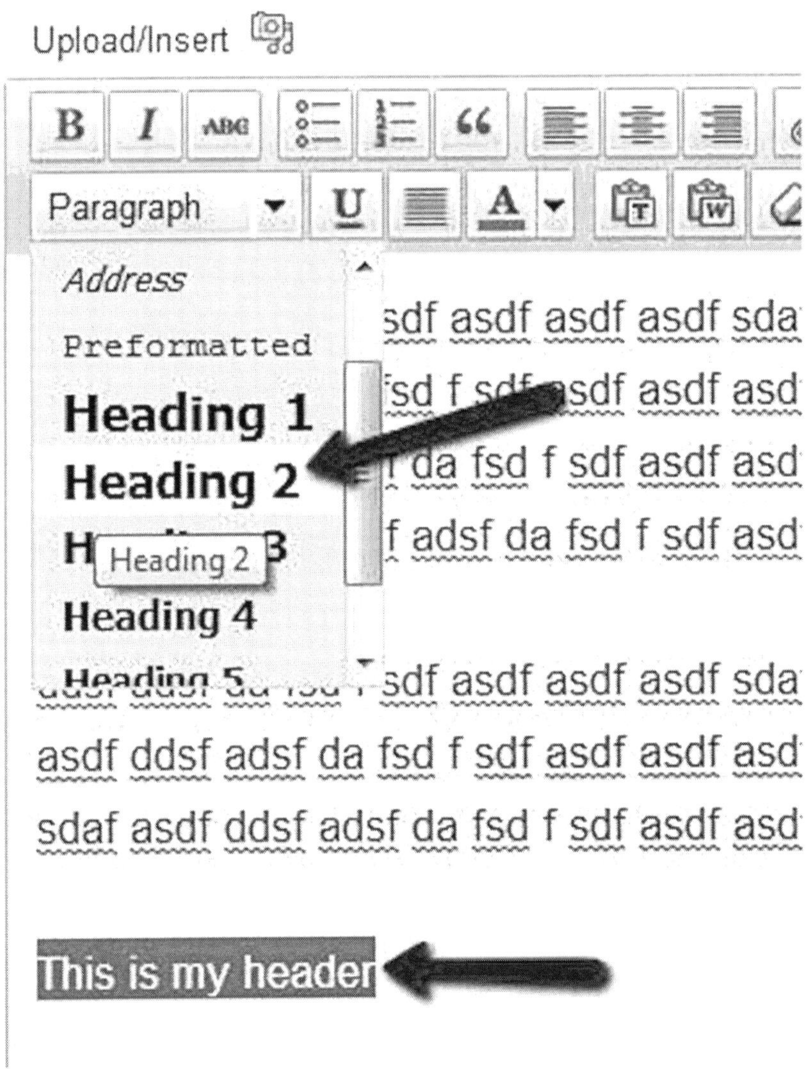

NOTE:

WordPress templates typically show the title of your post as an H1 header at the top of the page. This is the biggest header available and is equivalent to the **Heading1** in the drop down selector. You should not use more than one H1 header in your article, so DO NOT use any **Heading 1** headers as you write your content. Use **Heading 2** for sections of your article, and **Heading 3** for sub-headers inside **Heading 2** sections of your content.

OK, it's now time to go ahead and write an article (post), for your website.

As you write your article, you may want to insert an image or some other form of media. We looked at the Media library earlier in the book, but let's now go through the process of adding an image to an article we are currently working on.

Adding images

Position your cursor in the article where you want to add the image. Don't worry too much about getting it in the right place because you can always re-position it later if you need to.

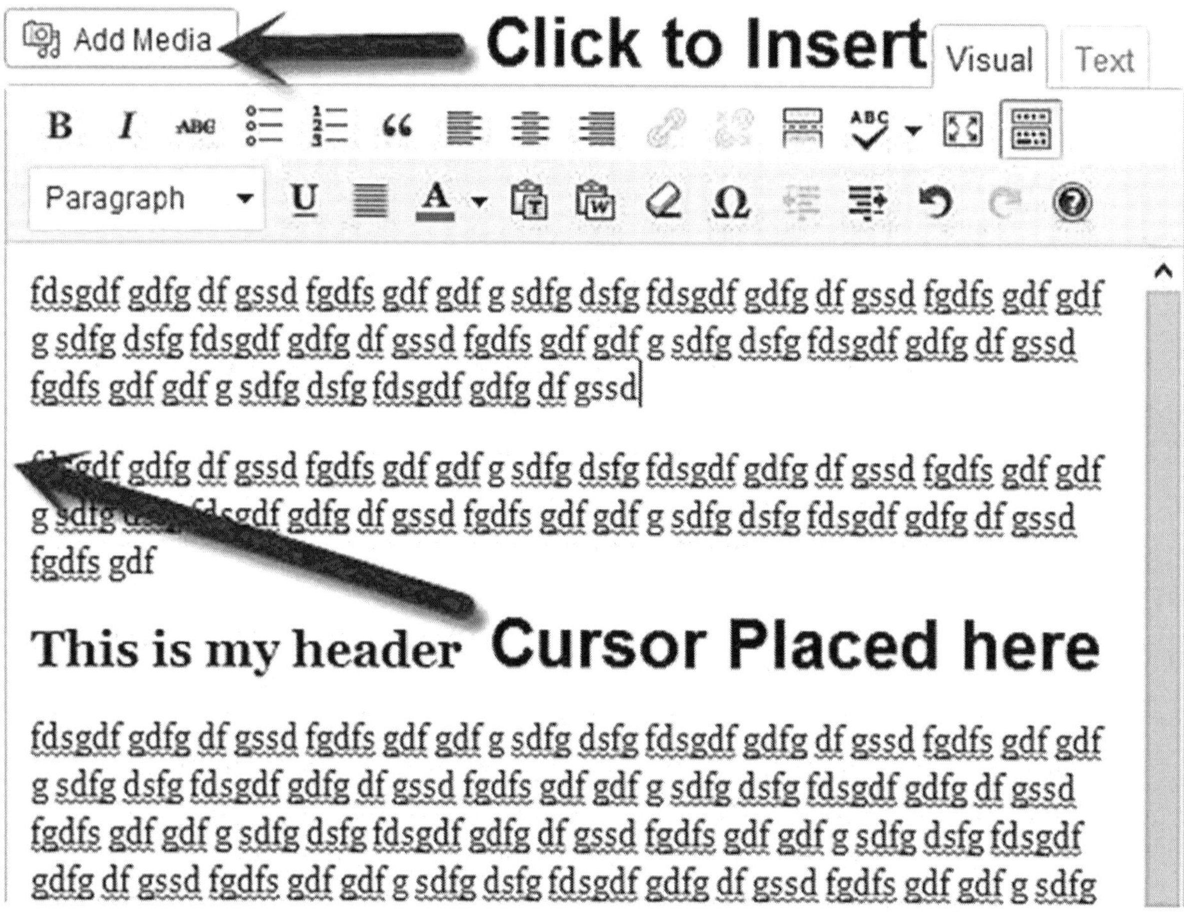

When you click the button at the top to **Add Media**, you'll get the popup screen that we've seen previously:

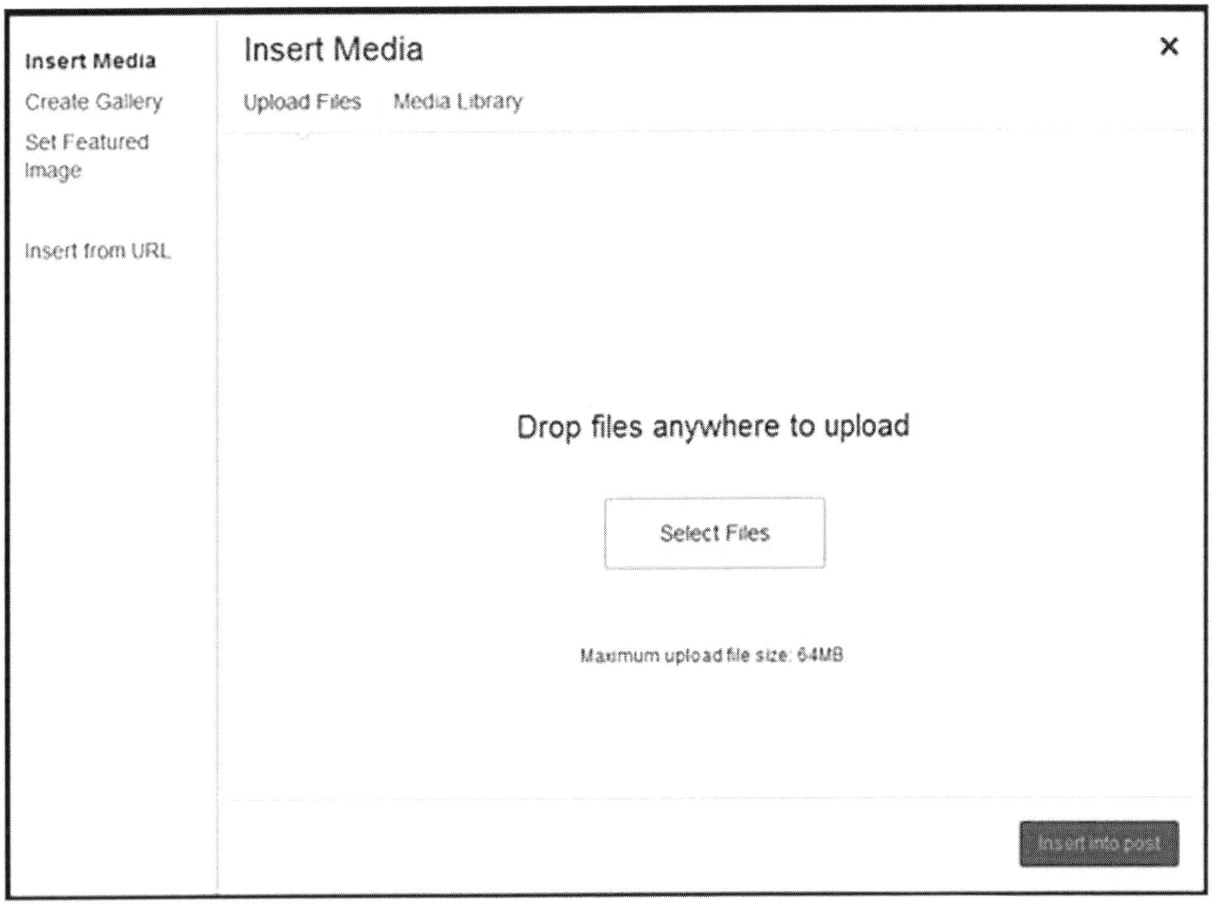

From this screen you can upload an image (or other media), from your computer by dragging-and-dropping it into the main rectangle containing the **Select Files** button. You can also add from a URL, or preselect a file from your Media library.

Let's add an image from our Media Library that we uploaded earlier. Click the Media Library tab on this screen.

When you click on the image you want to insert, a check mark appears in the top right corner. The image details are shown on the right side, and can be edited (Title, Caption, ALT text, Description, Alignment & Size).

I want my image aligned left, so need to select **Left** from the Alignment drop-down box.

Note that if you select an alignment for your image, the text will wrap around that image. If you leave it at the default **None**, then there is no wrapping of text around the image.

I also want my image size to be full size, so I'd select **Full Size** from the size drop-down box.

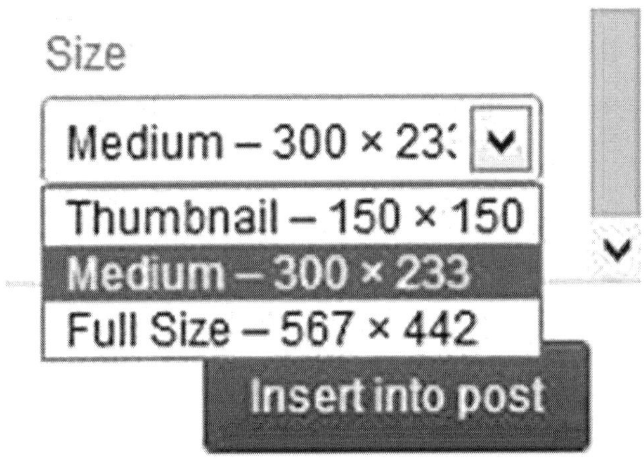

Once I have made my selection, I click the **Insert into post** button at the bottom.

Here is that image inserted into my post at the position of my cursor:

If you have the position wrong, you can simply click and drag the image to a different location.

If you find that the image isn't inserted as you intended (e.g. you forgot to align it so don't have word-wrap), click on the image and two buttons will appear. The one on the right will delete the image so that you can start again, and the one on the left will re-open the properties screen so you can edit the image properties as required.

Click the button on the left to open the properties screen:

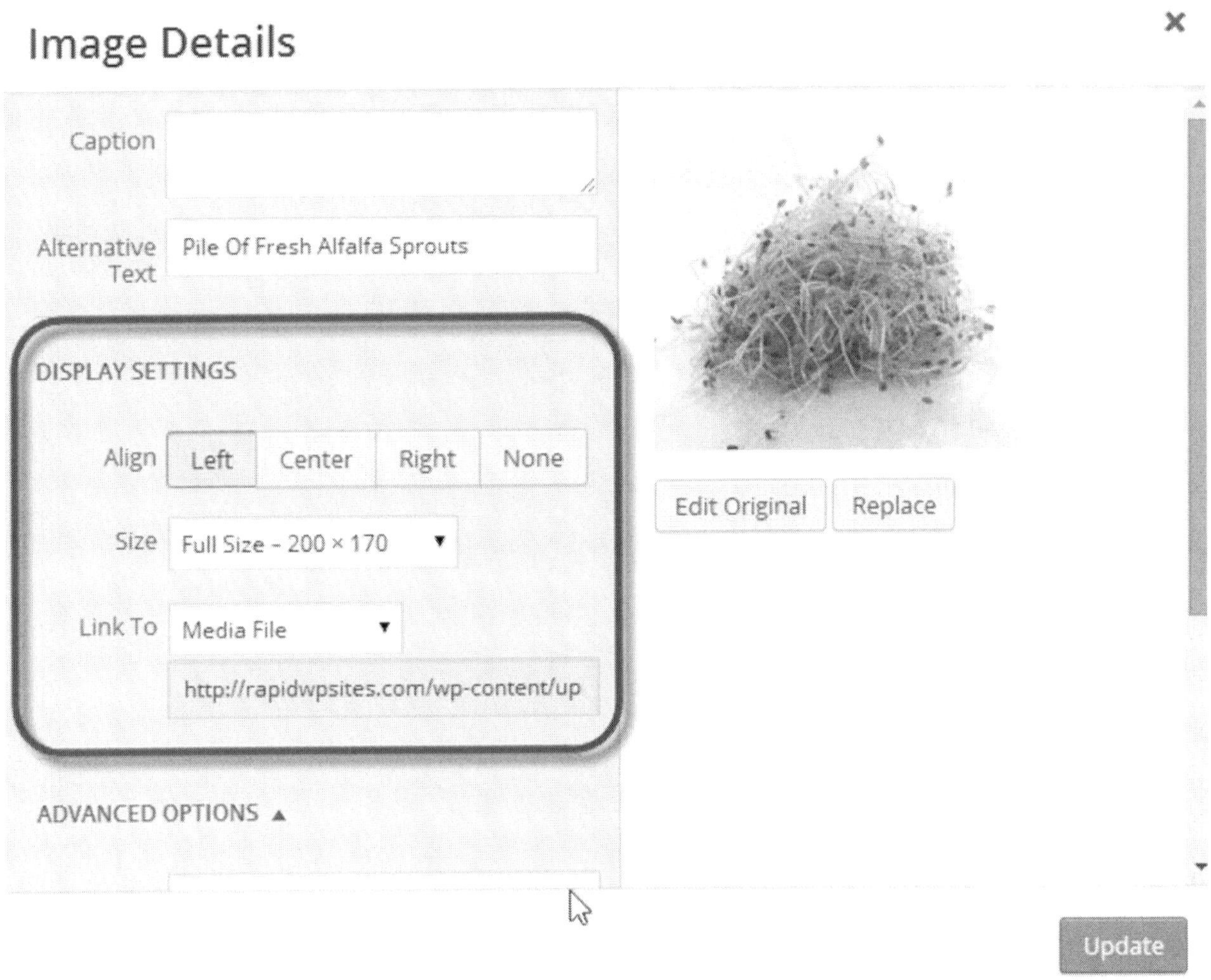

Notice that on the left, there is a **Size** drop down box. This offers you a thumbnail or full size image, or a **Custom Size** which allows you to enter the exact dimensions you want.

Below these settings you'll see some **Advanced Settings**:

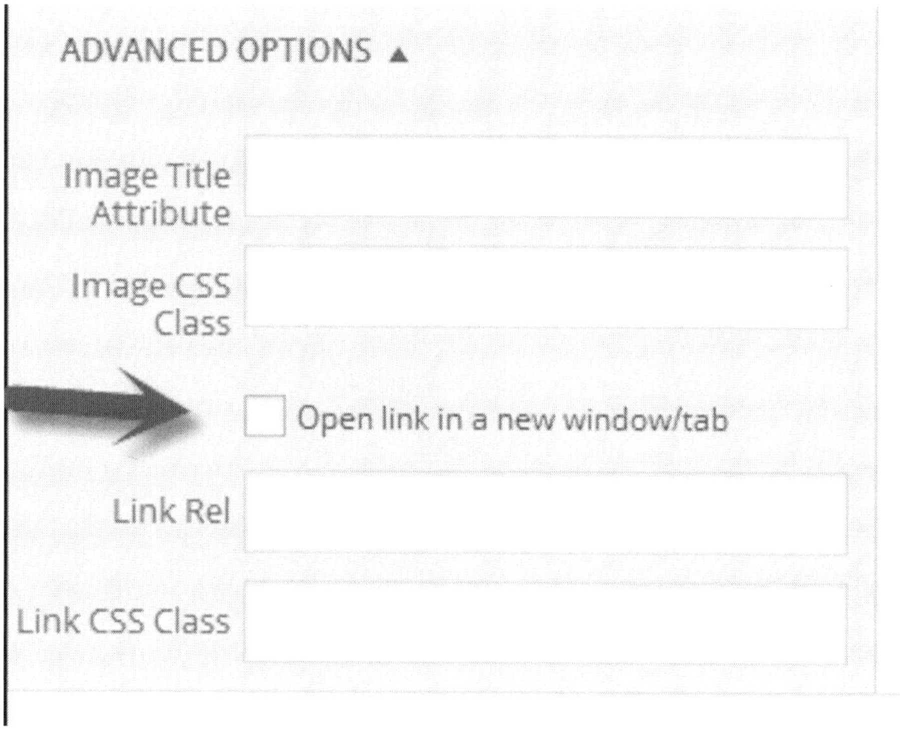

One advanced feature that you may find useful is the check box to "Open link in a new window/tab". This is useful when your image links to another web page and you want that link to open in a new browser window.

You can insert videos from your Media library in exactly the same way.

OK, now go on to finish your first post.

There are a few things we need to do before we make our article live. Let's go through the complete sequence from start, to publish:

1. Add a title.
2. Write & format your post using the visual text editor (WYSIWYG).
3. Select a post format if available.
4. Select a category.
5. Add some tags.
6. Add an excerpt.
7. Select a date/time if you want to schedule the post for the future.
8. Publish/Schedule the post.

OK, so we have completed down to step 2.

Post format

Not all WordPress themes use Post Formats. The Twenty Eleven theme that we are using does, so let's look at what these post formats are. On the right of your screen you see the Format options.

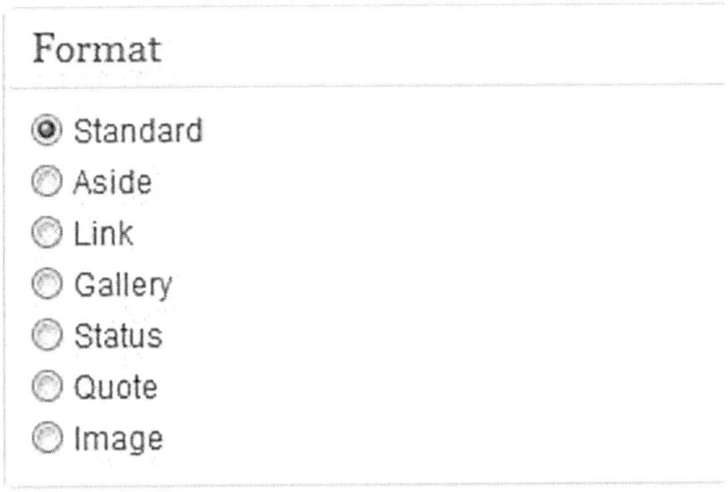

Since most, if not all of your posts, should use the default (Standard format), we won't go into details in this book about other formats. Most people just won't use them and not all templates support them. If you are interested in post formats, experiment with them and then view your post to see how it looks. You can also read more about Post Formats on the WordPress websites:

http://codex.wordpress.org/Post_Formats

The next step in our publishing sequence is to choose a category. Choose just one category for each post. You can add a new category "on the fly" from within the Add post screen, but if you do, remember to go in and write a description for the new category so it can be used as the meta description of that category page (remember the WordPress SEO plugin we set up earlier is expecting a description for categories and tags).

Select 3-5 tags for the post. Add your chosen tags to a list that you maintain so you can reuse (with correct spellings), those tags on other posts. You can enter tags, even if they don't already exist, simply by typing them into the tag box. When you are finished, click the **Add** button to the right of the tags box.

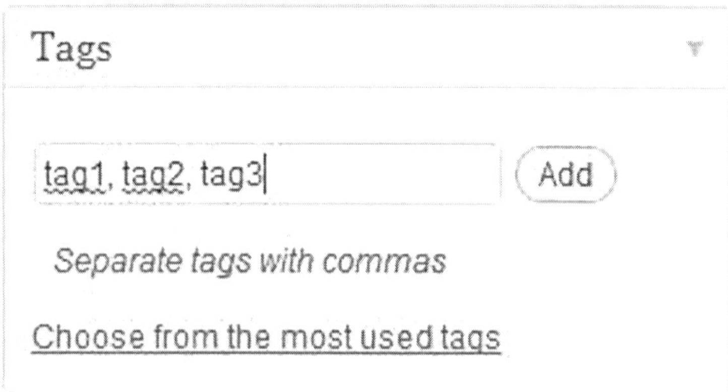

As you add and use more tags, you can click on the link **Choose from the most used tags** and a box will appear with some of the tags you've used before. You can just click the tags that apply, and they'll be added to the tag list of your post.

If you add "new" tags when entering a post, I recommend you go into the Tags settings to write a short description for each one. Yes it takes time. However, this will be used as the Meta description of the tag page because we set this up using the WordPress SEO plugin earlier.

Next up is adding an excerpt to your post. This should be a short description that you want to show your visitors. Its purpose is to encourage them to click through and read the article. This excerpt will be used as the Meta description tag of the post, as well as the description of the post in the "related posts" section, which is displayed at the end of each article you publish (see the YARPP plugin later).

To enter the excerpt, scroll down below the WYSIWYG editor until you find the box labeled excerpts: If you do not see it, click the screen options button on the top right, and make sure the excerpts box is checked. While you are in the screen options, I recommend you check ALL of the boxes. As you work out what you need and what you don't, you can uncheck those that are not of interest.

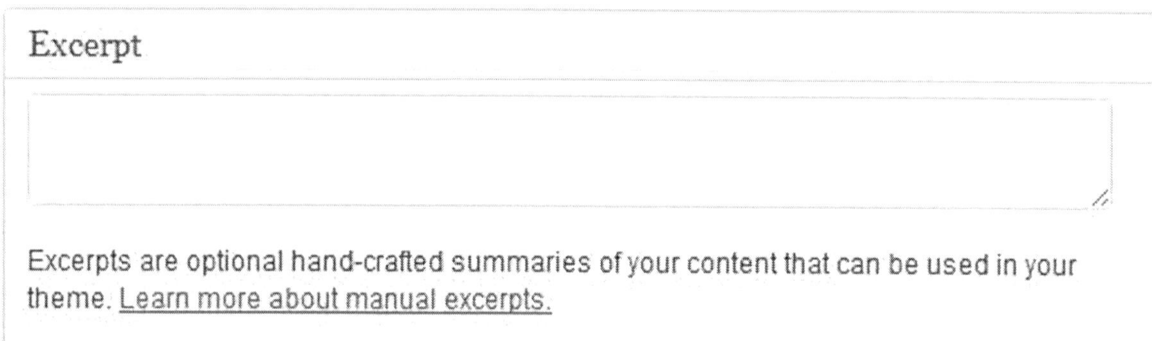

Enter a three to five sentence paragraph to encourage the click.

OK, the next step in the process is deciding when you want the post to go live on your site. If you want it up there immediately, then click the Publish button. If, like me, you are writing several posts in a batch, it is a good idea to spread the posting of the content out a little bit. Luckily, WordPress allows us to schedule the posts into the future.

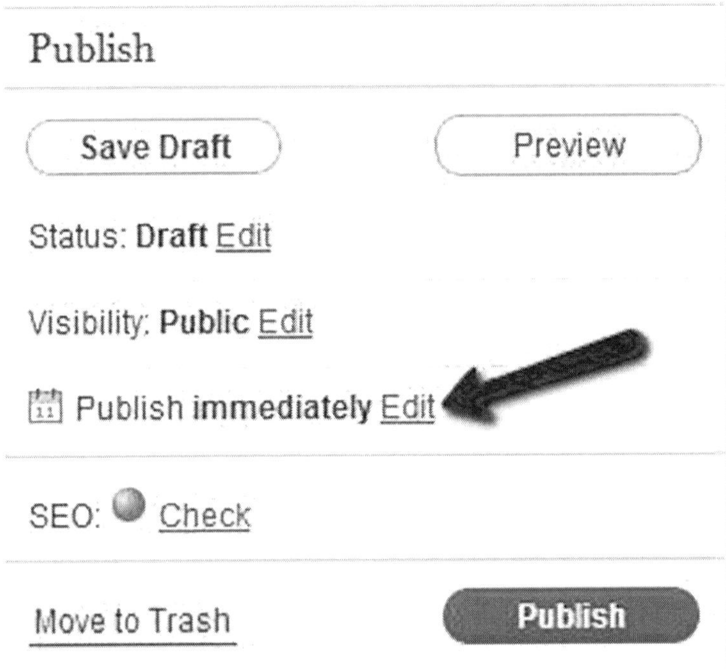

In the Publish box over on the right side, the default is to publish **immediately**. However, there is an Edit link that you can click which opens up a calendar for scheduling:

Enter the date and time you want to publish the post and then click the OK button.

The publish button now changes to Schedule.

Click the Schedule button to schedule the post.

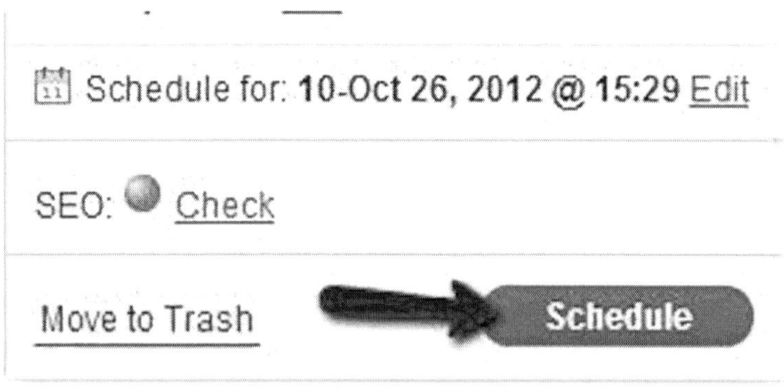

That's it. You've just published or scheduled your first WordPress post.

Before we move on, there is one last thing to cover here. It's the way that the WordPress SEO plugin we installed earlier is integrated into the Add Post (and Add Page), screen.

If you scroll down a little, you should come across the **WordPress SEO by Yoast** section.

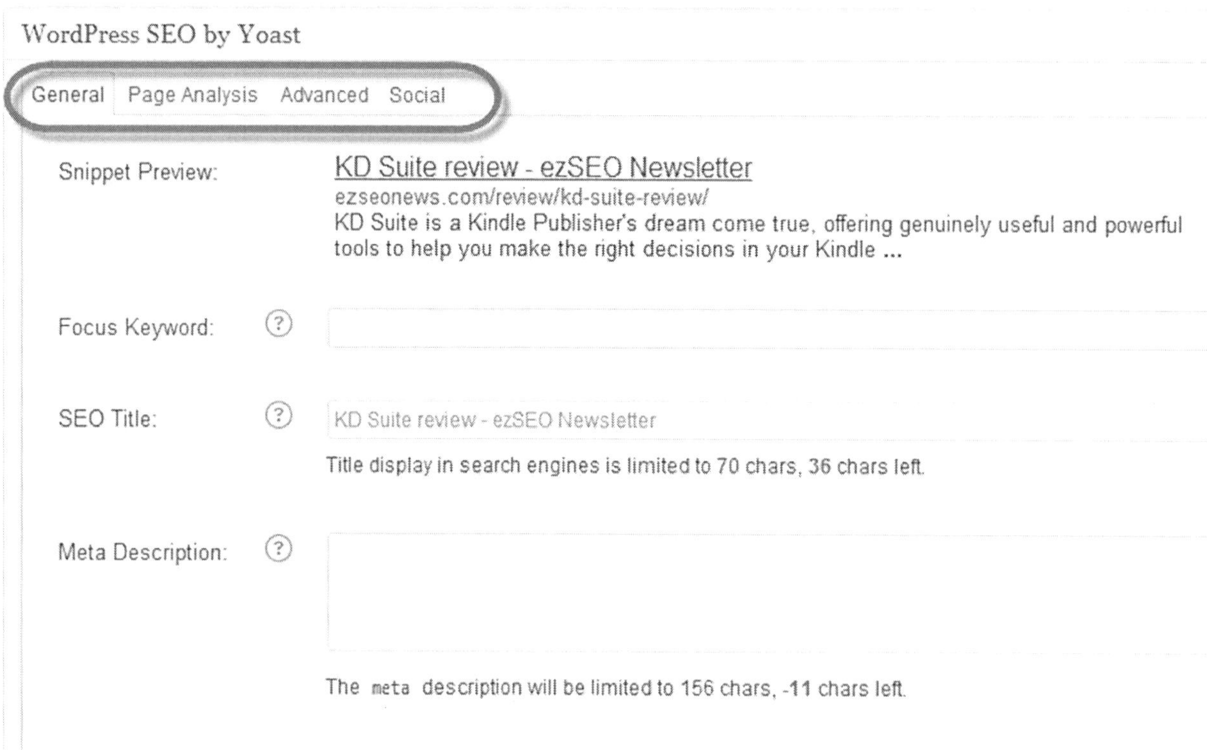

NOTE: If you don't see this section, make sure it is checked in the screen options (top right).

There are 4 tabs across the top of these settings. You can ignore the **General** tab as we have already entered a title and Meta description (the excerpt). The **Focus**

Keyword can also be ignored. It was useful in the past when optimizing a web page, but today, that kind of thing can easily get you into trouble with Google.

Similarly, ignore the **Page Analysis** tab as that relates to optimization of the web page for your focus keyword. You'll only end up in trouble using this.

The important settings that we might be interested in are on the Advanced tab, and even then, only the ones at the top of that section:

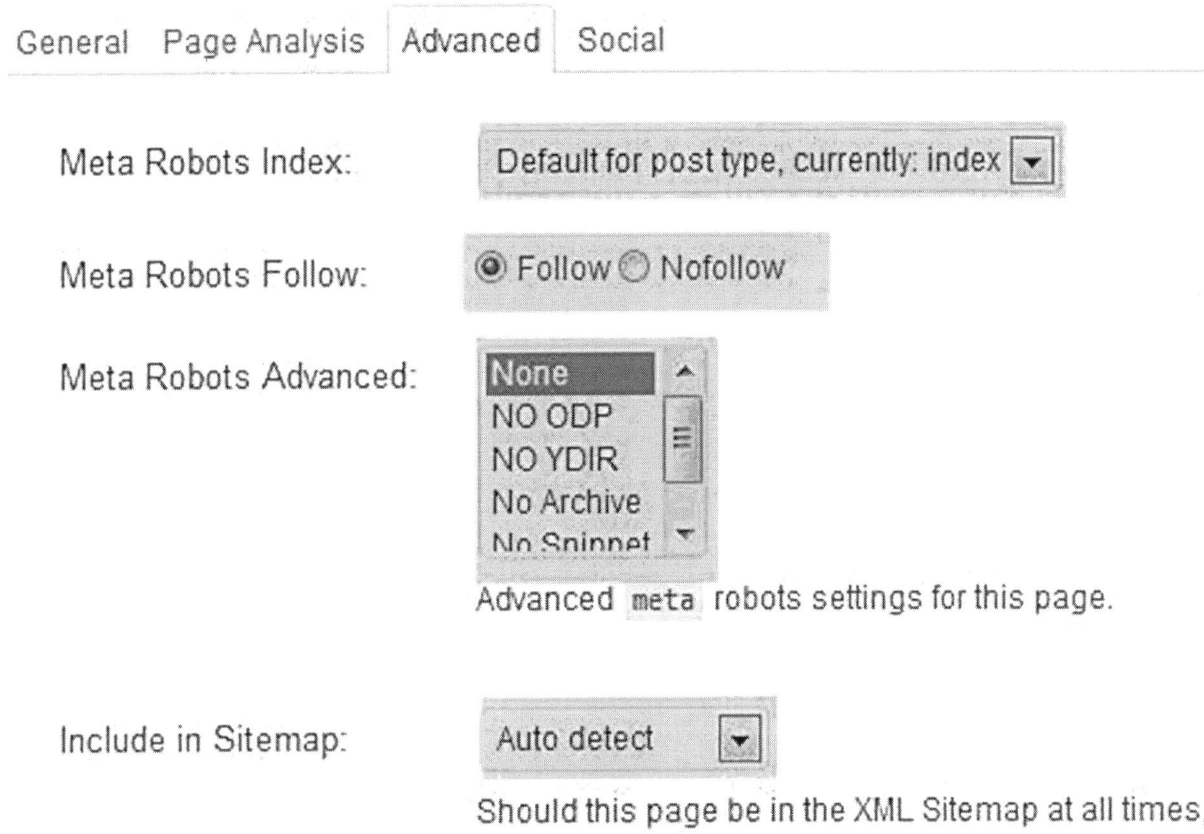

I have highlighted the only settings you really need to know for now.

These settings give us fine control over how the search engines will deal with this post. Not all posts, just THIS post. With this fine level of control, we can treat every post and page on our site differently if we want to.

The top setting is Meta Robot Index. The default settings were set up when we installed the plugin. Essentially we want ALL posts to be indexed. If we want to make a particular post noindex, we can do it here with that top drop down box.

The next setting is whether we want links on the post followed. Default is yes but we can set them to nofollow. I don't recommend changing this unless you know what you are doing.

The Meta Robots Advanced allows us to set a few other Meta tags on our pages.

No ODP and No YDIR can be ignored.

No Archive tag tells Google not to store a cached copy of your page

No Snippet tells Google not to show a description under your Google listing (nor will it show a cached link in the search results).

The only one you may want to use here is the No Archive option, but only in very special circumstances. There are times when we don't want Google to keep an archive (cached version), of a page. We can set the Meta tag to say No Archive for any post or page with these settings, thereby preventing the search engines from keeping a backup of the page.

Why might you want to do this? Well, maybe you have a limited offer on your site and you don't want people seeing it after the offer has finished. If the page was archived, it is technically possible for someone to go in and see the last cached page at Google, which will still show your previous offer.

The social tab of these settings can also be ignored. It might be something you want to look into when your site takes off though.

Editing posts

At some point, after you have written a post, you may want to go in and edit or update it. This is an easy process. Just click on the **All Posts** link in the **Posts** menu. It will open a screen with a list of posts on your site.

Now it's just a question of how to find the actual post you want to update or edit. There are two ways of doing this. One is from within your Dashboard using the available search and filtering tools. The other method is one I'll show you later by visiting your website while you are logged into the Dashboard.

For now, let's look at how we can find posts from within the Dashboard:

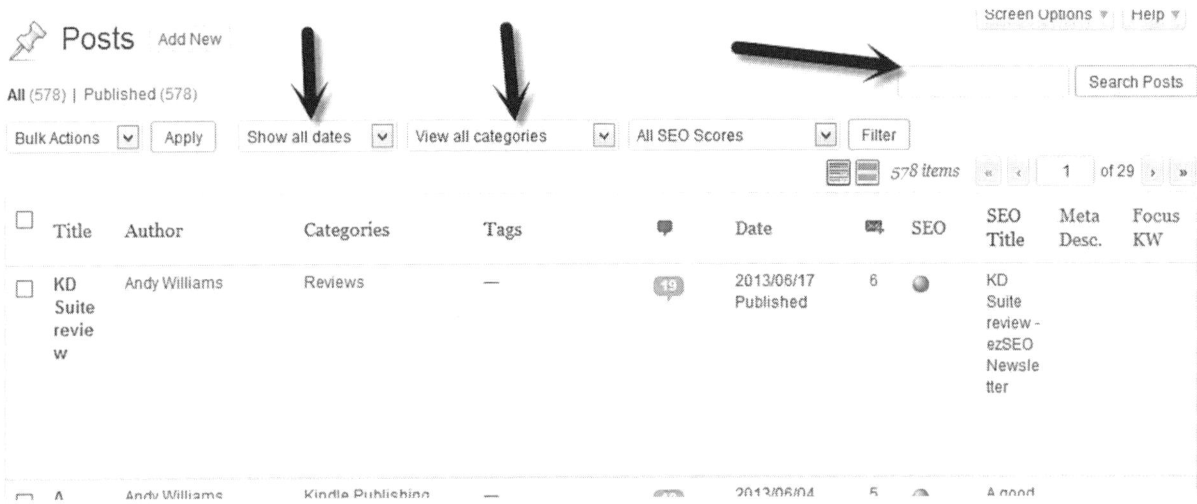

Firstly, if you know what month you wrote the post, you could show all posts from that month. I don't use that feature as it's easier using other methods.

Alternatively, you can search for a post by showing just those posts within a certain category. You can do this by selecting the category you want to search from the "View all Categories" drop down box at the top.

Perhaps the easiest way of all is to use the Search Posts feature. Type in a keyword phrase you know is in the title, and then click the **Search Posts** button.

Once the list of matching posts is displayed, mouse over the one you want to edit to bring its menu into view, and select edit. Or, a simpler way is to just click the title of the post.

This takes you back to the same editor screen you used when first creating the post. Make your changes in there and just click the **Update** button to save your modifications.

NOTE: Whenever you make changes to a post, WordPress keeps a record (archive), of those changes. At the bottom of your Add/Edit post screen is a section called **Revisions**. If you don't see it, make sure it is checked in the screen options from the top.

You can view any previous version of the post by clicking the date link. This does not lose the current contents; it just opens a viewer screen where you can see what that version looked like:

At the very top you can see the revision you are looking at. It will be the revision you clicked on in the previous screen. The content of that revision is highlighted in yellow in my screenshot. This is the content of the post for that date.

You can also see further down there's a list of all revisions with the currently published revision selected. You can view the contents of any revision simply by clicking on it in the list. The preview will appear at the top of the screen.

What is useful is the **Compare Revisions** button. This will compare a currently published version with the revision you are previewing.

Older: 16 October, 2012 @ 10:40   Newer: 24 October, 2012 @ 11:32 [Current Revision]

```
- Welcome to WordPress. This is your first post. Edit or delete it, then start blogging!

+ Welcome to WordPress. This is your first post. Edit or delete it, then start blogging! ;-)

+ http://youtu.be/YersIyzsOpc

+ <a href="http://com-vip.org/?attachment_id=34"><img class="alignnone size-full wp-image-34" title="apples" src="http://com-vip.org/wp-content/uploads/2012/10/apples.jpg" alt="" width="284" height="221" /></a>

+  
```

At the top of each revision is the title. The one on the right is also labeled as the "Current Revision". This is the one that is published live on your site. The older version is on the left.

If you decide you want to revert back to an earlier version, you can click the **Restore** link next to the version you want to return to. WordPress won't ask for confirmation before restoring the old version, but it doesn't matter. If you make a mistake, just return back to the list and restore the one you actually wanted.

Tasks to complete

1. Enter a post. It doesn't have to be real post and you can always delete it afterwards. I just want you to get used to writing content in the WYSIWYG editor. So add text and an image, and then play around with the image alignment and settings.
2. Publish your post and go to your site to see how it looks in your web browser.
3. Go back and edit the post.
4. Now scroll to the bottom of the page and look at the revisions section. Check out the differences between two different versions of your post, and try reinstating an older version. Then change it back to show the later post again.

Making it easy for visitors to socially share your content

Having great content on your site is one thing, but getting people to see it is something else.

One of the ways people find a website is through the search engines. They search for something and Google shows them the most relevant links. If we rank well enough for a particular search term, the web searcher may land on our page.

Another way people can find our content is via social media channels. Places like Facebook, Google plus, and Twitter are good examples. To make this more likely, we need to install a social sharing plugin on the site. A social sharing plugin will add buttons to the website that allow people to share the content they are reading by the simple click of a mouse. Social sharing buttons make sharing easy, and therefore more likely.

There are a number of great social sharing plugins, so you can actually choose whichever one you want. The one I recommend you start off with is called **Add Twitter, Facebook Like, Google plus one Social share**.

Search the plugins for that and you'll find it:

Add Twitter, Facebook Like, Google plus one Social share Details | Installed	2.4.0		Author Site| Plugin Home Page This plugin is the most efficient way to integrate the important social share buttons like twitter, facebook like, google +1 (plus one), LinkedIn, stumbleupon and Pinterest in three different position and styles. Automatically display the social share buttons Above the post, below the post, both above and below or floating left side of post. Flat/Round borde... By Kunal Chichkar.

Install and activate the plugin. You'll then find the settings for the plugin inside the main **Settings** menu.

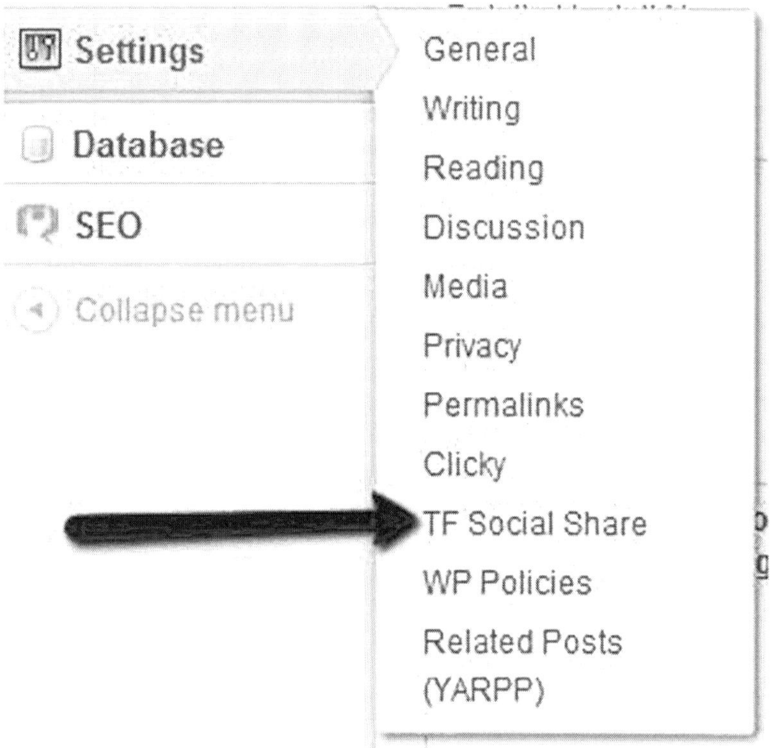

Go to the settings menu so we can access and setup the plugin.

Let's go through these settings bit by bit. At the top you can define which buttons you want to appear on your site:

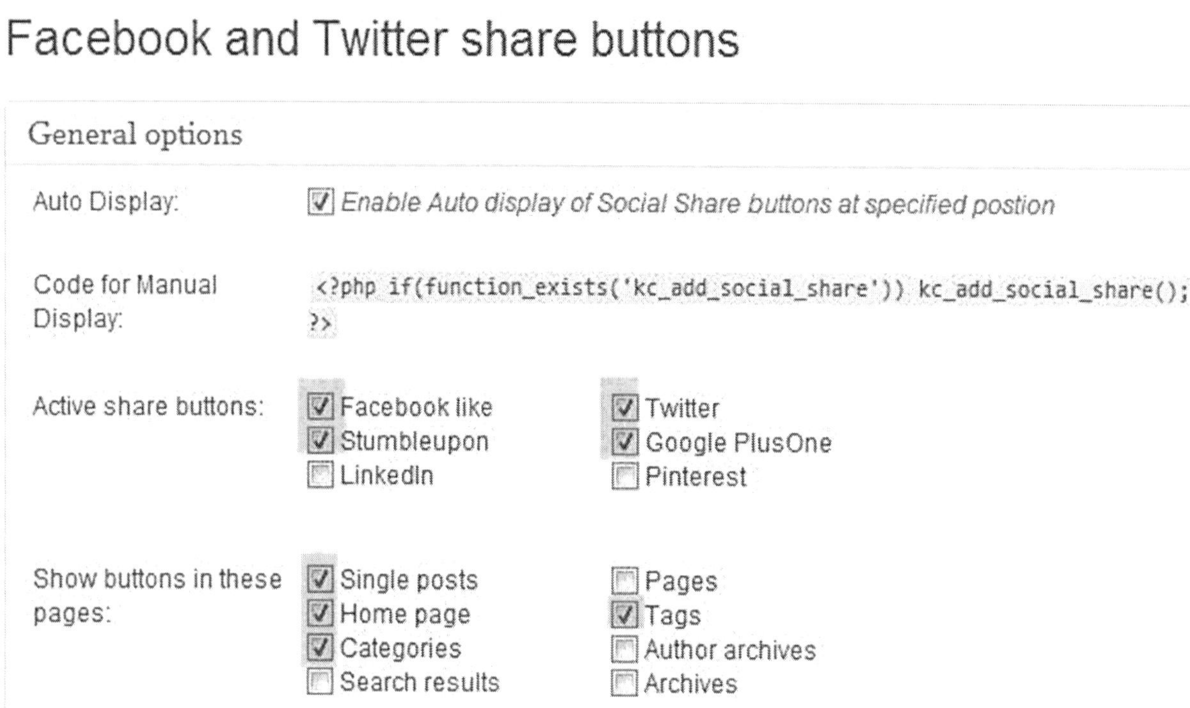

You can select whichever ones you want. I don't typically select Pinterest unless my site has a lot of images that I want shared. I also don't include LinkedIn unless the site is more business orientated.

Once you select which buttons to show, you can then select where to share them. I'd recommend you put them on any post or page you want shared. That means **single posts**, **home page**, **categories & tags**.

Before we move onto the next set of options, make sure that the **Auto Display** check box is checked at the top.

OK, next we decide where on our content the buttons should appear. I usually choose above and below, but you can play around with these settings and decide on something you like.

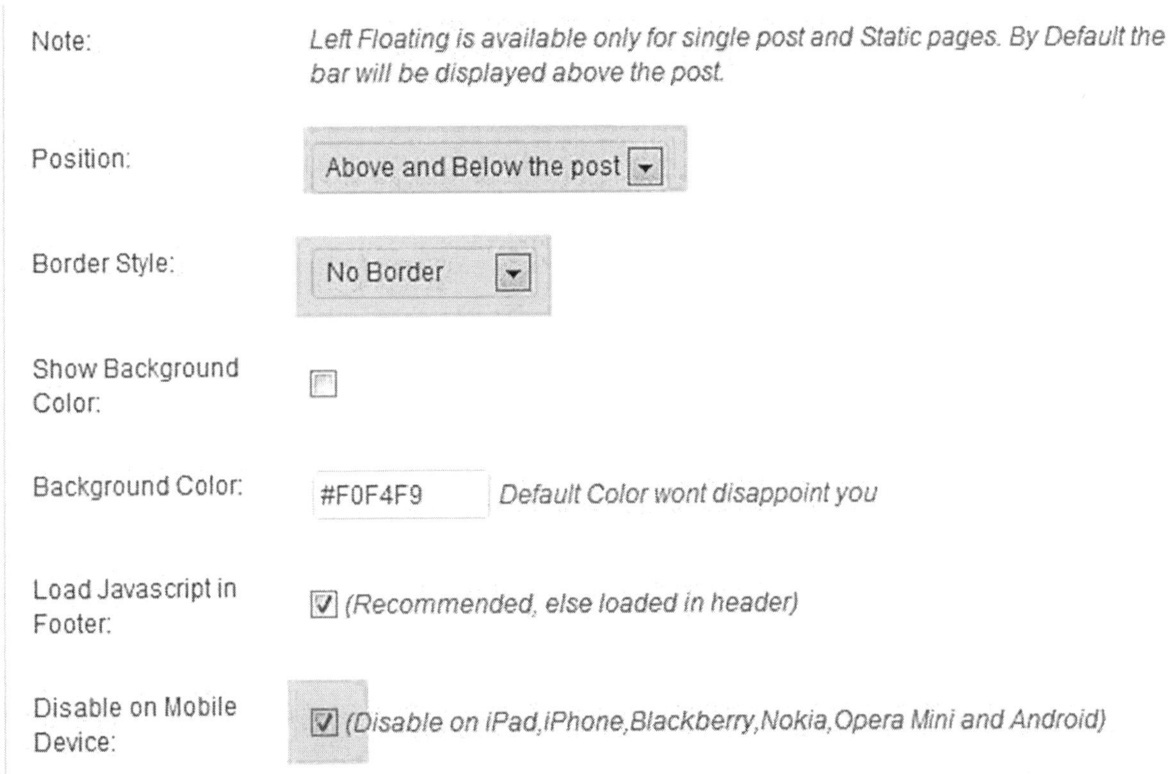

I recommend you uncheck the border (which draws a box around the buttons) and remove the check next to **Show Background Color**. Your buttons will then look more integrated into your site's pages.

The disable on mobile devices is checked by default. That is probably because they found some problems displaying these on mobile devices. Therefore, I'd leave that unchecked for now, but try it later on when you have a change to view your site on an iPad, Android tablet and Smartphones.

Next, if you have a Twitter ID, add it without the @ symbol.

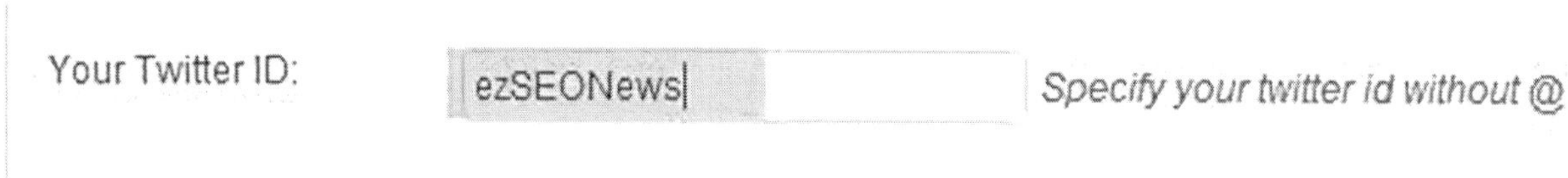

The next set of options is only valid if you chose to display the buttons on the left side (when you chose the position of the buttons).

If you are displaying the buttons on the left side, you can play with these floating options to make sure they look OK on your site.

The final settings are for width and count display.

You can leave these at their default values and only come back to change things if you find a problem with how the buttons look on your pages.

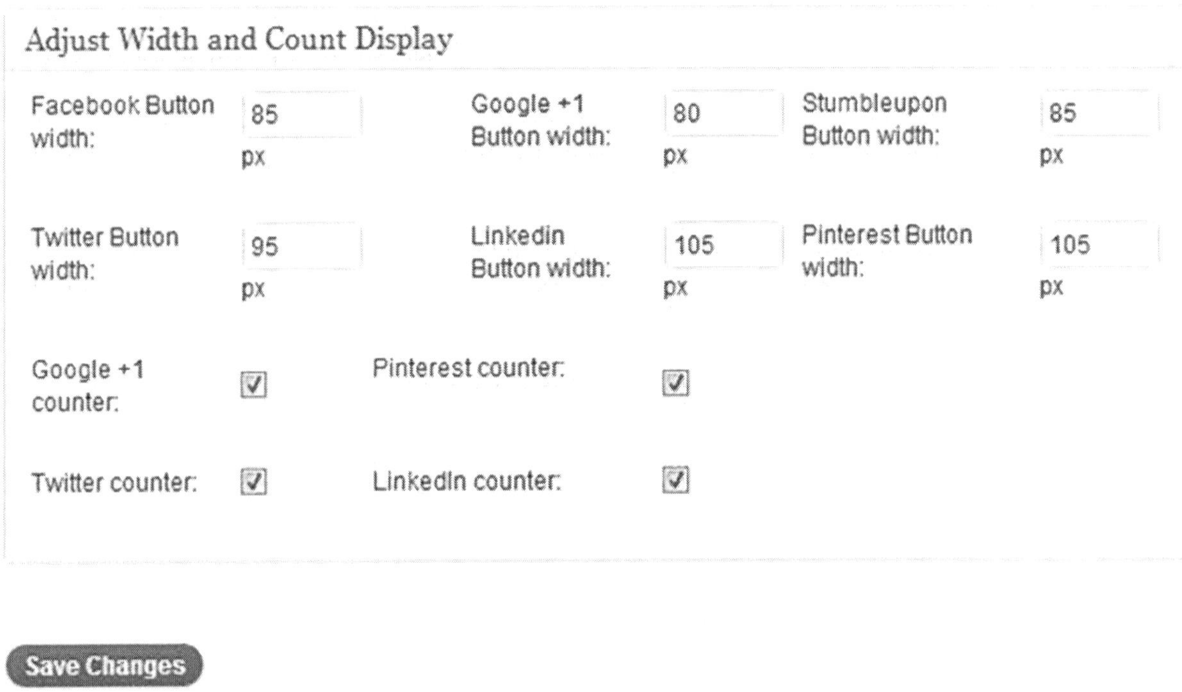

OK, click the **Save Changes** button and then go visit your website.

Other social share plugins

Over the years I have tried lots of social sharing plugins. Some work great, while others only seem to work on some websites and not others. If you find the plugin above does not work properly on *your* site, here are some others to try that I have personally used and like. In no particular order:

1. Social Essentials by Shane Melaugh - http://goo.gl/wBkqo
2. Slick Social Share by Remix4 - http://goo.gl/dBNJS This one creates a

floating bar that contains your social sharing buttons.
3. Facebook,Twitter,Google plus one Share Buttons by Jeriff Cheng http://goo.gl/JAkyN

Tasks to complete

1. Install the social sharing plugin and set it up to suit your needs.

Differences with pages

As we discussed earlier, pages are different to posts. On the Add/Edit Page screen, it all looks very similar, but there are a few notable omissions - namely no categories or tags! There is also no box to add an excerpt. These are no great loss to us, as we don't use pages for important articles/content on the site.

We do, however, have a couple of options for pages that are not found in posts - Page Attributes:

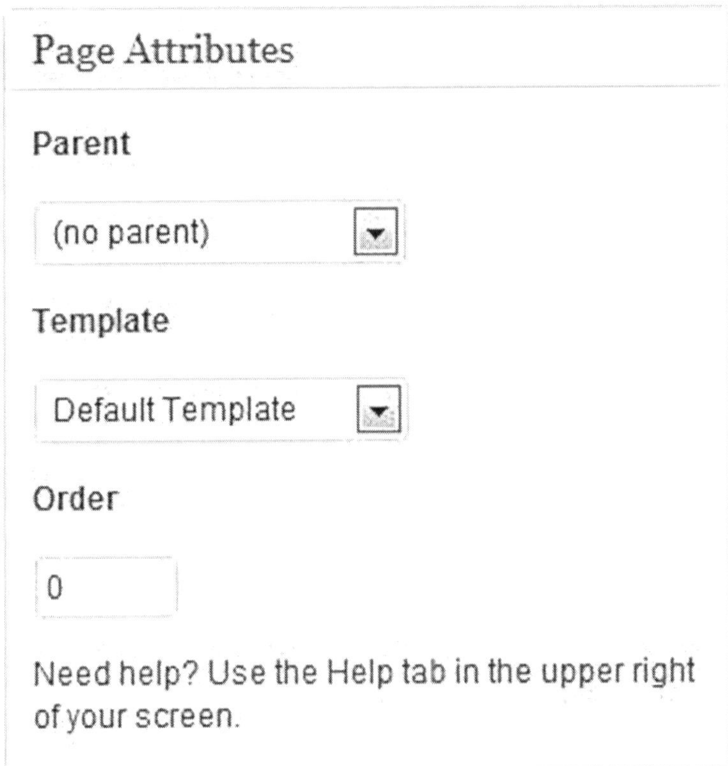

Since we are only using pages for our "legal" content (and "About" page), these new settings don't really apply to our site. However, you might be interested, so I'll explain what they are.

The page attributes allow you to do the following: Set up parent-child relationships between your pages, choose a template for your page, and set the order of your pages. Let's look at what this means to you.

A Parent Child relationship between pages is similar to the relationship we saw earlier with categories. Any page can have a parent page, and the level of parent-child relationships can be many levels deep.

For example, you might have a page called Disclaimers.

You might then set up other pages on your site called Medical Disclaimer, Outbound link Disclaimer, Affiliate Disclaimer and so on. For each of these pages you make the **Disclaimers** page the parent. We therefore have this type of relationship:

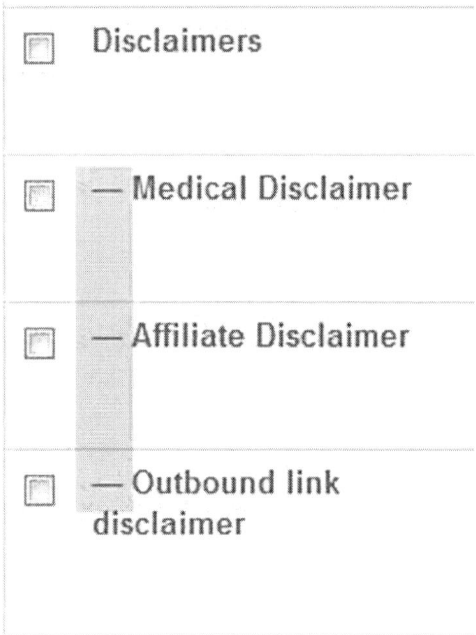

With WordPress templates, like the Twenty Eleven template we are using here, it recognizes and handles this type of parent-child page relationship, so when adding these pages to the navigation bar, you get this dropdown menu:

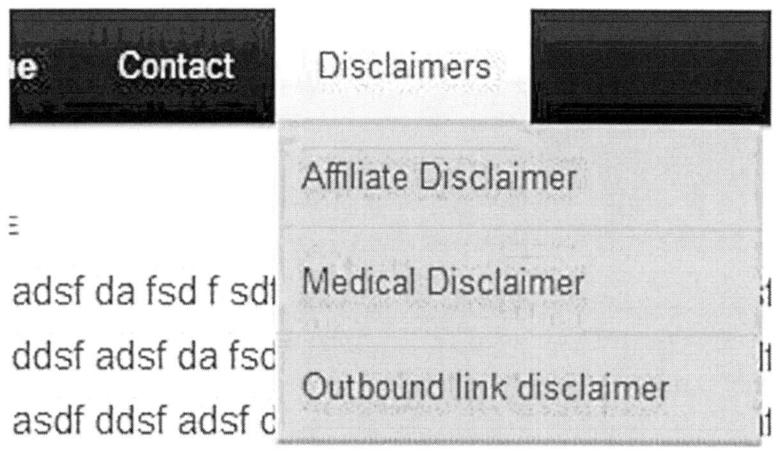

The child disclaimers are listed underneath the parent page. This saves space on the navigation menu.

The biggest problem with parent child pages is that not all themes support them. Because of this I don't bother using parent child pages. Instead, if I want to create the type of hierarchy seen in the menu above, I will create a custom menu, which we'll look at a little later on in the book.

The next Page Attribute is the Template.

The templates you have available for your pages depend on the theme you are using. Some themes don't have any additional page templates, while others may have several. As you can see, the Twenty Eleven template comes with a total of three templates to choose from.

The **Default Template:** Shows main content but no sidebar.

The **Sidebar template:** Shows the main content with a sidebar.

The **Showcase template:** I'll leave that for you to find out.

For any theme you use, you'll need to read the documentation (or experiment yourself), with the page templates to see what they each do.

The final Page Attribute is the order. This is where you can supply a numerical value to order your pages (number 1 being the first page). This is only useful when you leave the responsibility of creating navigation bars to WordPress. If you haven't set the order, then WordPress uses its own default values for deciding which page should be listed first.

We won't be setting the page order for our "legal pages" because we will create custom menus later. These custom menus will show our pages EXACTLY as we want them, without the hassles of setting up parent-child pages or changing the order.

Tasks to complete

1. Go and look at the Page Edit screen. Note the page attributes box. Have a look at the settings by pulling down the drop down box to show the page templates.
2. Set up a parent page and two or three child pages. There doesn't have to be any content on them. Once done, check out the menu on your site to see how WordPress handles parent-child pages.

Internal linking of posts

One of the best ways of keeping visitors on your site is to interlink the content on your pages. There are a few ways of doing this.

The basic way is to manually add links from one page to another. This is easily done in the WYSIWYG editor.

Just highlight a word or phrase that you want to link to another post on the site:

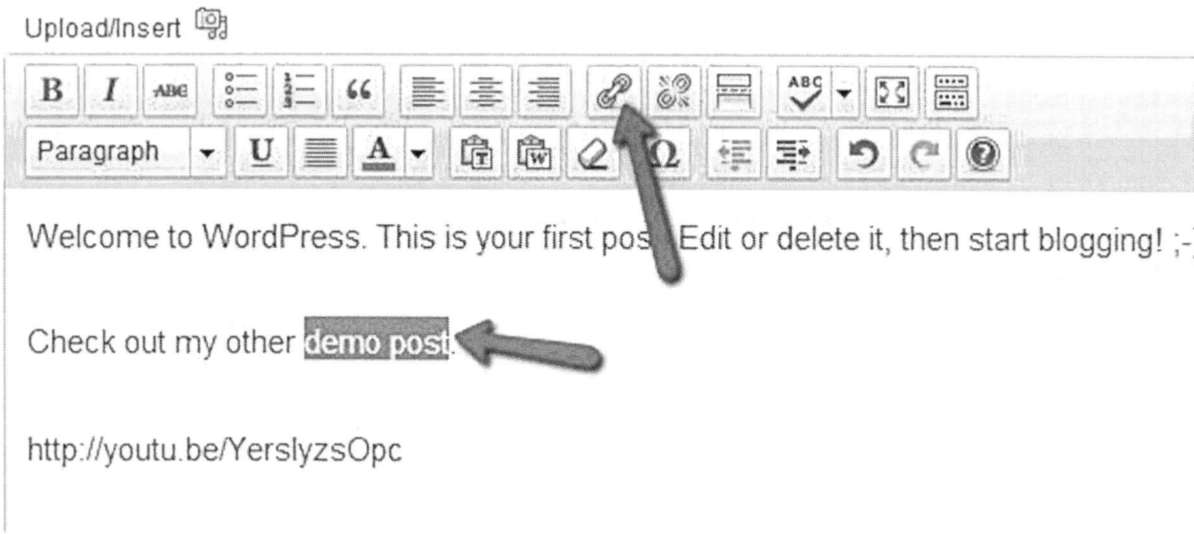

.. and then click the link button in the toolbar. A popup box will appear asking for details of where and how you want to link to that other page:

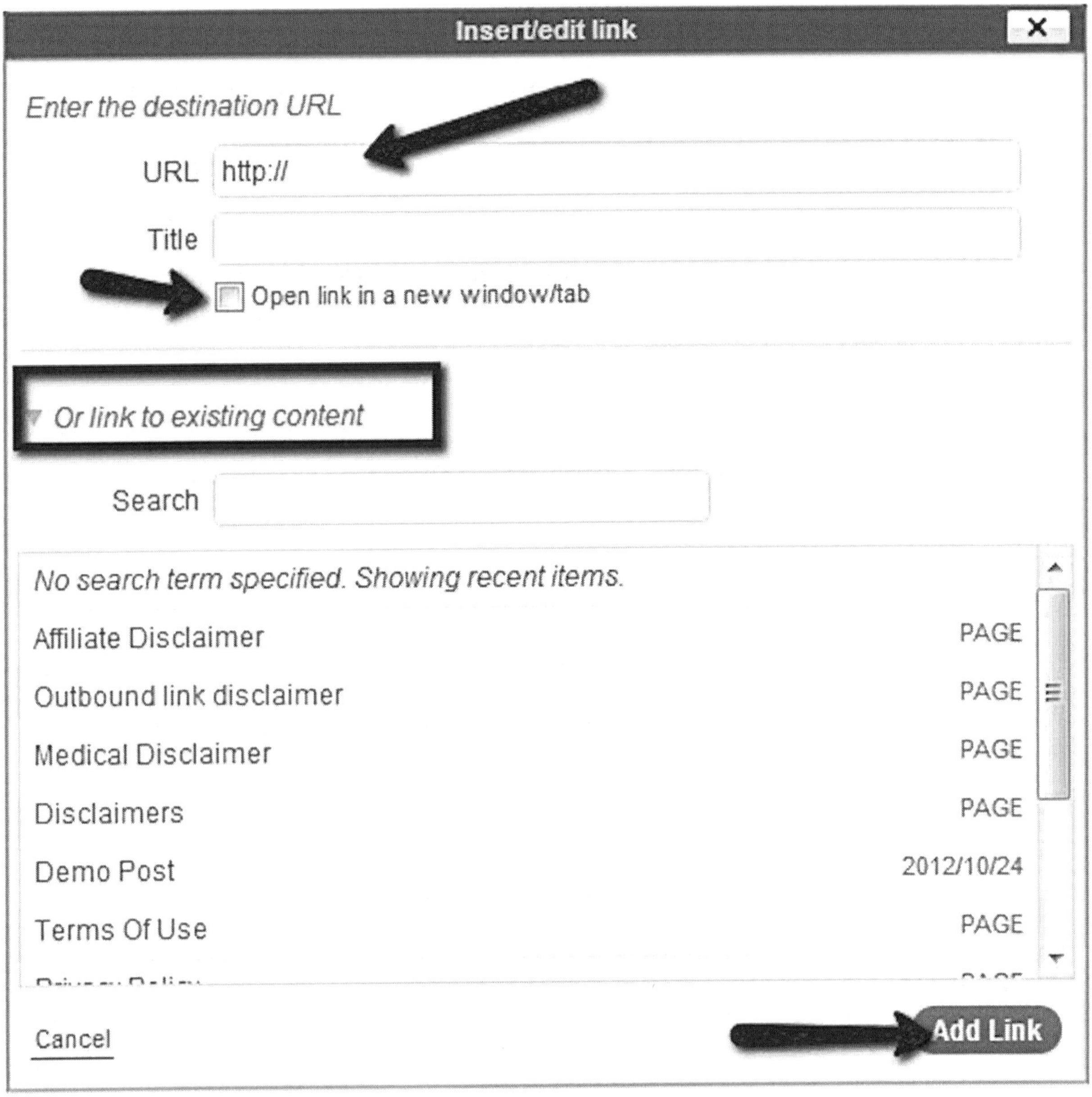

The very top box is asking for the URL of the webpage you want to link to. I recommend you ALWAYS begin this with http:// or your links to other sites won't work.

If you know the URL of the webpage, that's fine. Just paste it in. I usually open the webpage in a separate tab of my browser and copy the URL from the address bar to paste into the URL box.

If you are linking to a webpage on your own site, there is a link labeled **Or link to existing content**, which if you click, opens a box at the bottom that lists all of the content on your site. There is a search box there to help you find stuff more easily. Once you see the page you want to link to in this list, just click it. The URL and title will be filled in for you by WordPress.

WARNING: I recommend that with all internal linking on your site you leave the title attribute BLANK. The reason is simply that Google are on the warpath. They are penalizing websites that appear to be over-optimized and the link's title attribute has been one place that spammers have abused in the past. Adding in any kind of keyword rich title could eventually cause your site problems. So be safe, and leave the link's title tag empty.

Your final choice for the link is whether to open it in a new window or not. I have a general rule of thumb with this option. If I am linking to another page on my own site, I open it in the same window (so leave that checkbox empty). If I am linking to a page on another website (and may therefore lose the visitor from my own site), then I'll have the link open in a new window/tab, by checking that box.

With all the settings filled in, click the Add link button to add the link to your article.

OK, that's the 100% manual way of inter-linking your content.

One way I recommend you inter-link your content is with a plugin called **Yet Another Related Posts** plugin. This plugin allows you to set up a "Related Articles" section at the end of your posts. This will automatically link to articles that the plugin deems related (according to parameters you set up).

Go to the **Add New** Plugin screen and search for **yet another related post**.

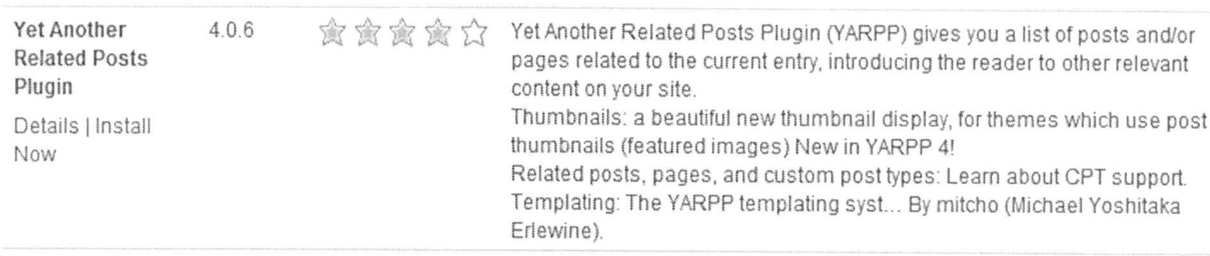

Install and activate the plugin.

You will now find the YARPP settings inside the main settings menu:

Click on the link to the settings so we can set this up.

The first thing to do when you get to the YARPP settings page is open up the Screen Options at the top:

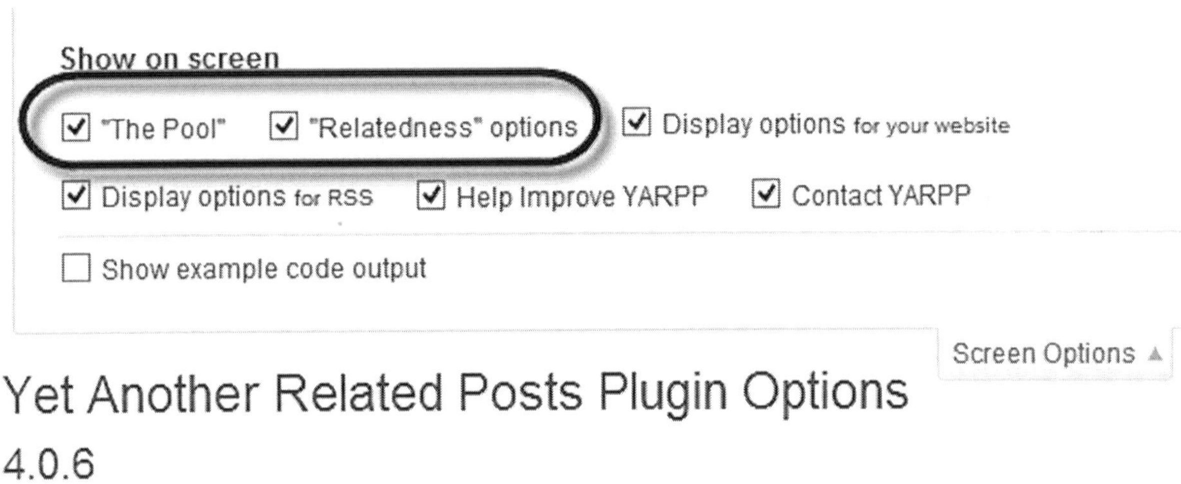

Check **"The Pool"** and **"Relatedness" options**.

The pool is something you might want to switch off at some point. I don't use it, but I always suggest turning everything on until you get an idea of what a thing does. At that point you can decide whether to turn them off or not.

OK, let's set up the plugin.

So the top options on the page are the "Pool":

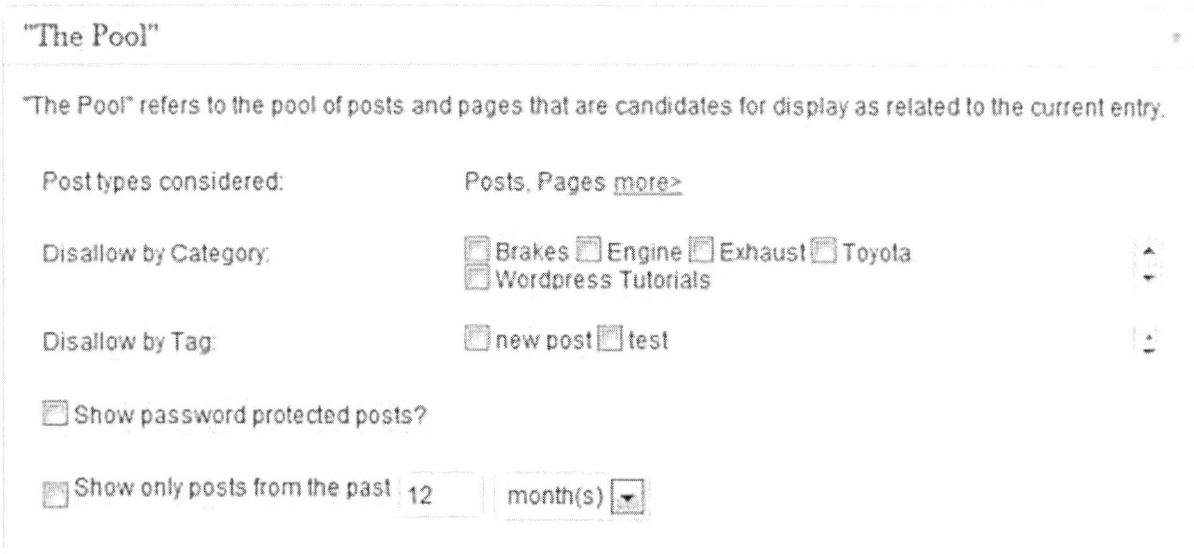

You can leave these options set at their defaults. The Pool does give you some power over what posts are shown in the related posts section of your articles. You can decide not to allow posts to be included based on category or tag. You can also show password protected posts or only posts from the last X number of months, weeks or days.

Since I leave everything at the default level, I turn this off in the screen options.

Next up are the relatedness options.

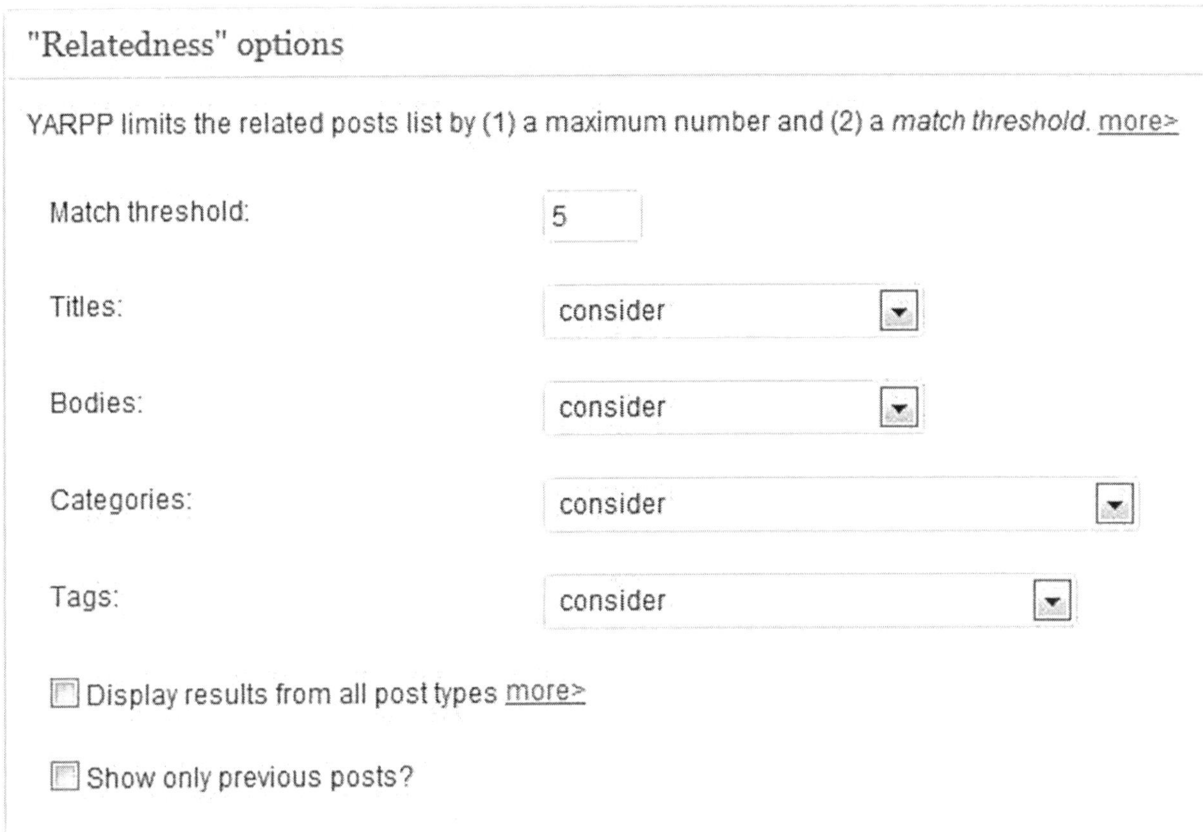

Again, for now you can leave these options set at their default values. The only thing you might like to play with is decreasing the **Match Threshold** if you are getting a "No related posts found" message at the end of your posts. I'd consider reducing this to a 4, then a 3, then a 2, then a 1.5 and so on, until the related posts are (1) shown, and (2) related to the post/article they appear on. This is something you can only really do when you have a number of posts on your site.

For now, leave everything as it is and when you have more content, check out the related post section after each post and play with the threshold until you're happy.

Next up are the Display options. These basically tell the plugin how you want your posts displayed in the related posts section.

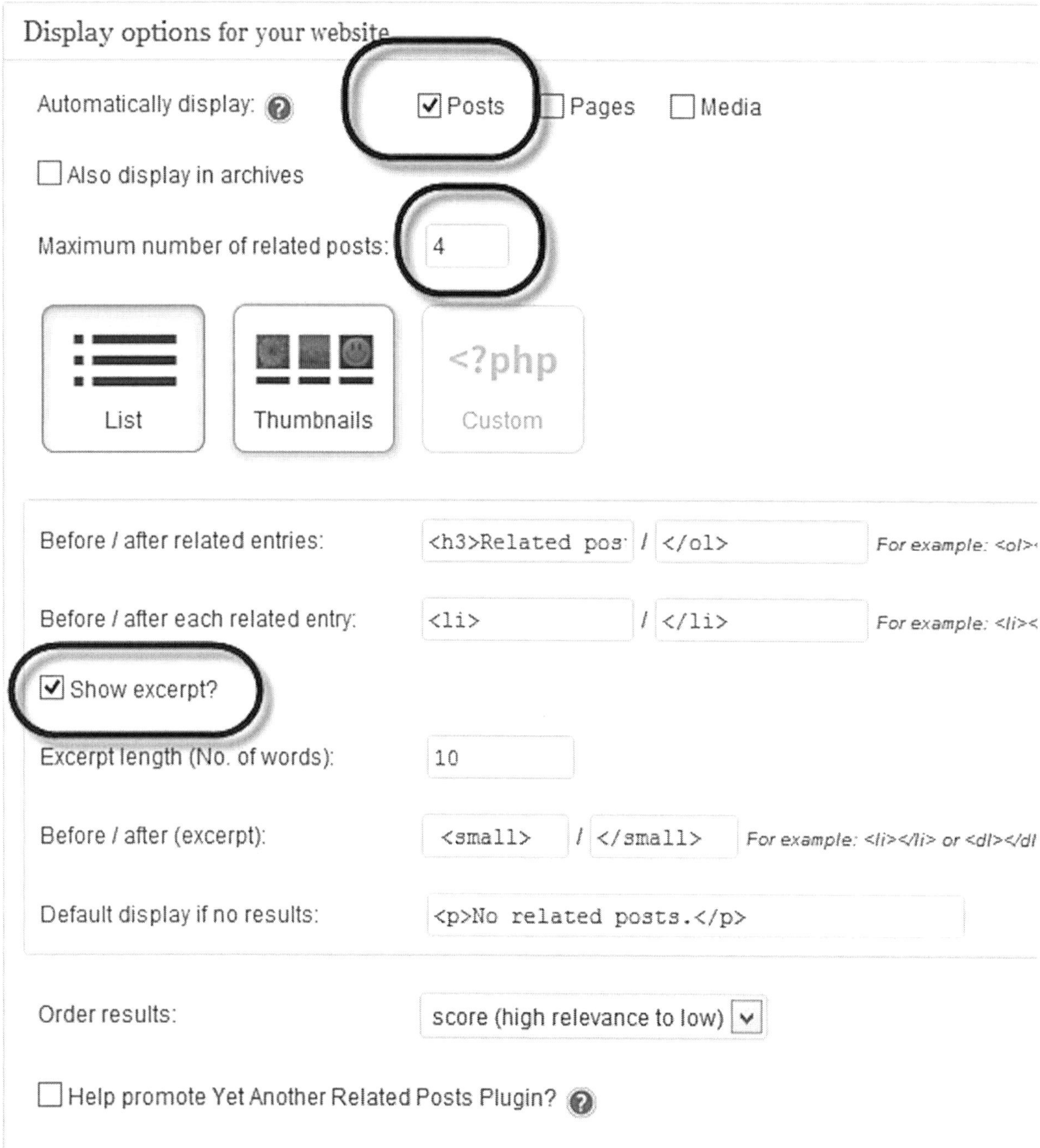

At the top, make sure **Automatically display** in posts is checked. You might like to uncheck this if you decide later to include related posts in the sidebar instead of at the end of each post. Wait until we cover widgets before you decide.

Next you can choose the maximum number of related posts to show. The default is 4, but you might like to reduce this to 3.

Check the box labeled **Show Excerpts?** (this will show the post description with a link).

That's it for this section of settings.

The last option in these settings is to display related posts in feeds.

Leave this UNCHECKED.

Now save the changes.

NOTE: You can create your own templates for formatting related posts using this plugin. Since this requires some PHP knowledge, we won't be covering it in this book. However, if you are interested in exploring more options for the display of your related posts section, look at the help documents of this plugin. You will find links to the YARPP website & forum in the top right of the settings screen.

Here is an example of a related posts section on one of my sites using this plugin.

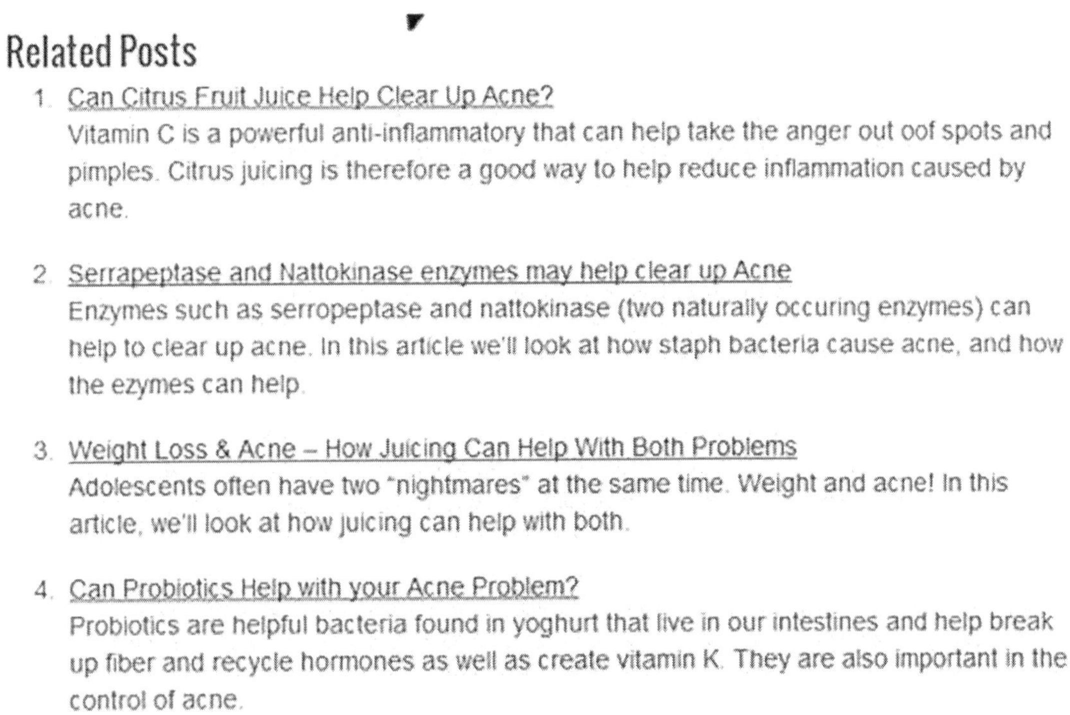

Related Posts

1. Can Citrus Fruit Juice Help Clear Up Acne?
   Vitamin C is a powerful anti-inflammatory that can help take the anger out oof spots and pimples. Citrus juicing is therefore a good way to help reduce inflammation caused by acne.
2. Serrapeptase and Nattokinase enzymes may help clear up Acne
   Enzymes such as serropeptase and nattokinase (two naturally occuring enzymes) can help to clear up acne. In this article we'll look at how staph bacteria cause acne, and how the ezymes can help.
3. Weight Loss & Acne – How Juicing Can Help With Both Problems
   Adolescents often have two "nightmares" at the same time. Weight and acne! In this article, we'll look at how juicing can help with both.
4. Can Probiotics Help with your Acne Problem?
   Probiotics are helpful bacteria found in yoghurt that live in our intestines and help break up fiber and recycle hormones as well as create vitamin K. They are also important in the control of acne.

This related posts section was on a post about acne. Can you see the benefits?

People who are reading the main acne article are shown other articles related to the condition. It gives us another chance to keep the visitor on our site.

We have looked at two ways we can inter-link our content. Firstly we can manually create links within the content. Secondly we can use a plugin like YARPP to show related posts to our visitors.

The last option I like to use is a plugin that I can set up to control internal linking on a much more automated basis, and without losing control over the linking.

I have written an article on internal site linking using this plugin. If you are interested, you should read that article here:

http://goo.gl/mYDvx

Tasks to complete

1. Install YARPP and configure it.
2. Go and edit an existing post, or create one for this exercise and add links manually to a couple of other pages on your site (or on another website altogether).
3. Open the page in a web browser and check that the links you added work properly.

Homepage of your site - blog or static?

WordPress is a tool that was created initially for blogs. That is, websites that publish date-related content as posts. The way in which WordPress handles these posts by default is to post them on the homepage, with the latest post at the top of that page. In the settings, we saw that we could define how many posts to include on a page with the default set at 10. That means the last 10 posts published on the site will show up on the homepage in chronological order, with the latest post at the top and older posts below. As you post more content to the site, the older posts scroll off the bottom of the homepage and are replaced by the newer ones at the top.

If that is the type of site you want, then that's fine. You can ignore this section and leave things at their default settings.

Personally, I like to create a homepage where I have more control over the content being displayed. I like to create the homepage so that it always displays my "homepage article". The homepage article is there to help visitors find their way around my site. This type of organisation is typical of non-WordPress sites. The good news is that it's easy to do in WordPress. You just need to write the "homepage article" as a PAGE, not a POST.

Once you have created that article, go to the Reading Settings inside the main settings menu of the Dashboard Navigation.

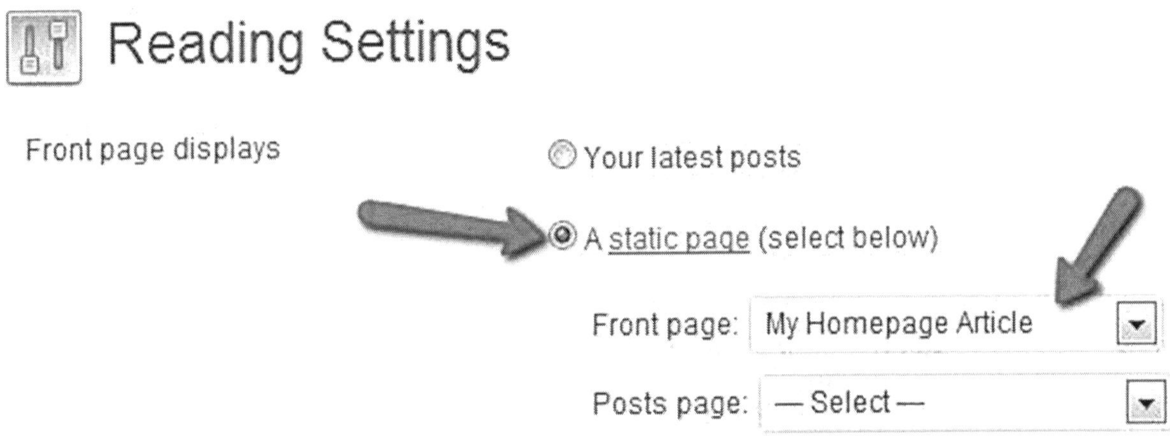

At the top of the screen there are two radio buttons with **Your latest posts** selected as default. You need to select the **A static page** option.

Now two drop down boxes will appear. The top one labelled **Front Page** is the one we are interested in. Simply click on the drop down box and select the page you created with your homepage article.

At the bottom of your page, click on the Save Changes button.

OK you are all set. Go to your homepage and you'll see the main article being displayed. No matter how many posts you add to your site, that homepage will not change (unless you change it).

OK, I hear your question.

"If the homepage just shows the same article, how are people going to find all my other content on the website?"

Well, that's where the sidebar, widgets and custom menus come in. We'll look at those next.

NOTE: If you have completed this exercise to turn a page into your homepage and you are not seeing the sidebar on the homepage, go in and edit the page and change the page temple to one that uses a sidebar. On the Twenty Eleven theme, that option is **Sidebar Template.**

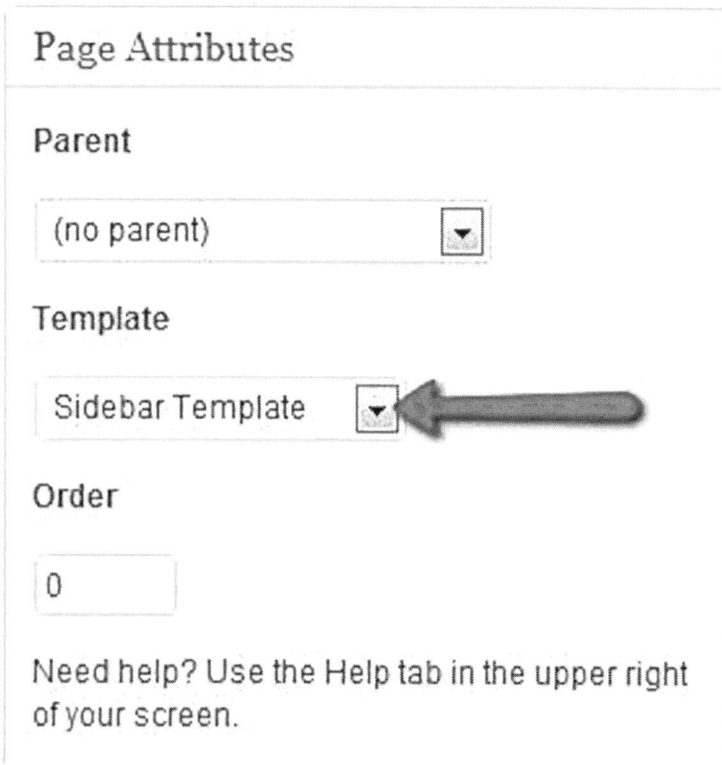

That will force the homepage PAGE to use a template with a sidebar, which we'll need in the next section.

Incidentally, if your site is showing a comment form on the homepage and you want to turn this off, just go in and edit the page again. There is a section there called Discussion (if you don't see it, check the screen options at the top).

Simply uncheck the option to **Allow comments** (and trackbacks and pingbacks if you wish), and then re-publish the page by clicking the update button.

Tasks to complete

1. If you want your homepage to show the same article, create a PAGE with that article, and then go and edit the Settings -> Reading so that the page you created is static on the front page.

Widgets

Widgets are basically plugins that allow you to easily add visual and interactive components to your site without needing any technical knowledge.

If you want to add a list of recent posts, you can do it easily by using a widget. Perhaps you want to add a poll to your site? Well, that can be done with widgets too.

When a designer creates a WordPress theme, their initial drawing will probably have "widgitized" blocks drawn onto it, so that they can visualize which areas will accept widgets. Maybe it will look something like this example (with the red/shaded areas able to accept the widgets):

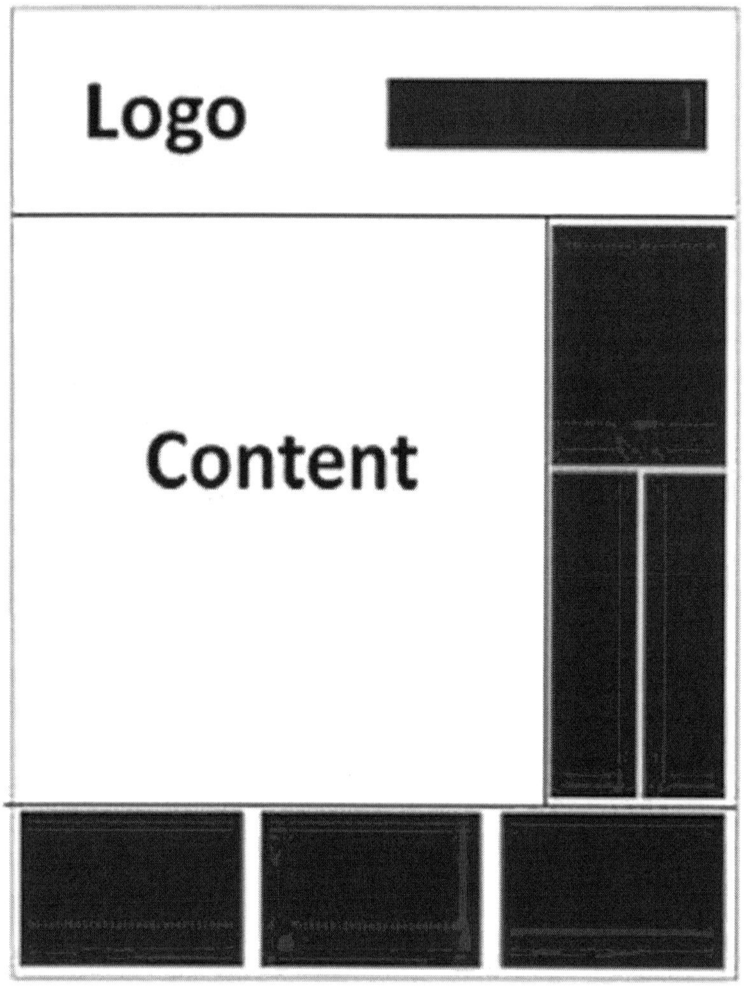

The usual areas that accept widgets are sidebars and footers. However, some themes have extensive widget capabilities, with even the entire homepage being widgetized.

We'll have a look at the standard widgets that come with WordPress in a moment, but first, let's see which areas of the Twenty Eleven theme can take widgets.

Login to your Dashboard and go to the Appearance -> Widgets menu.

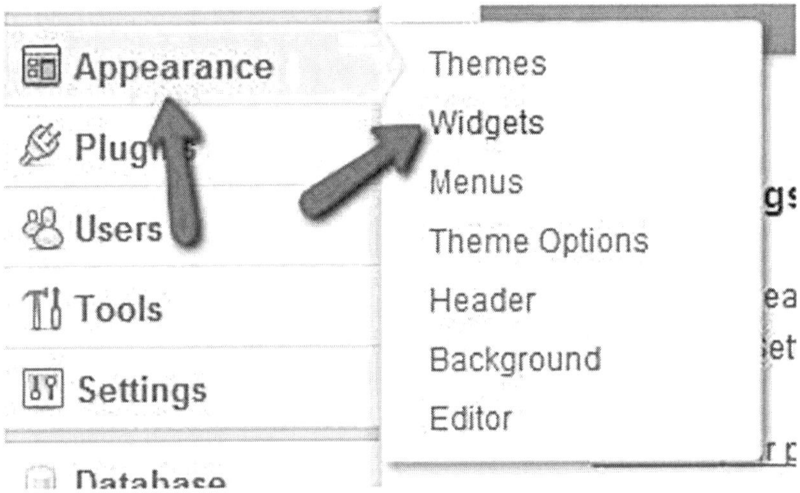

This will take you to an area where you can set up the widgets on your website. On the right you'll see some collapsible rectangles that represent the areas on the site that can accept widgets. As I have mentioned before, this will be different for each template, but for the Twenty Eleven theme, this is what we've got to work with:

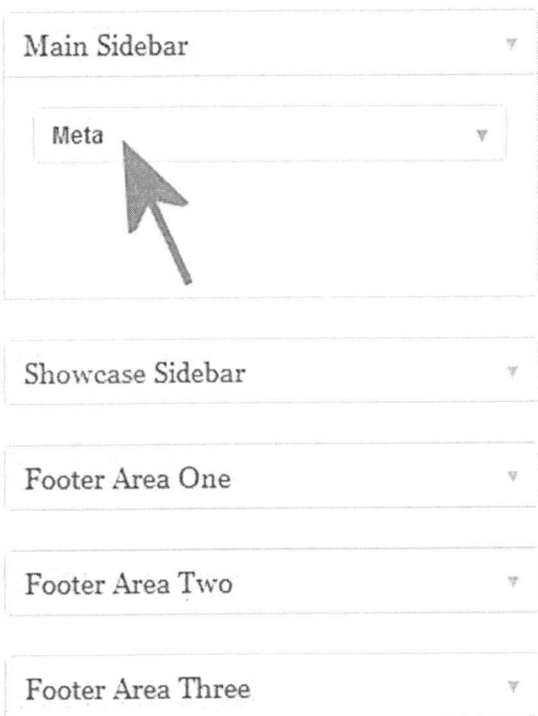

There are 5 areas of the website that can accept widgets.

The Main Sidebar: That's the sidebar that appears on your homepage, all of your posts and whichever pages use the sidebar template. You'll notice that there is already a widget in that area of my site. It's called Meta, and that adds some links to the main sidebar that you can see below:

If you remember, when we were clearing out the pre-installed widgets, I left that one in there so I could have a quick-link to login to my website. If I wanted to remove those links from my site, I'd simply delete that widget.

There is also an area called Showcase Sidebar, which can accept widgets. This is the sidebar that is shown on pages (not posts), that use the Showcase page template. If you want to experiment with the showcase page, do so (the sidebar may not appear where you expect it to).

The other three widgetized areas on the Twenty Eleven theme are the three footer areas, which represent the left, middle and right positions.

Let's add a simply text widget to each of these areas so we can see the effects on our site. A text widget is a widget that will display text (or HTML), in a widgetized area of your website.

Let's do it together so you can get a feel for how to use these widgets.

Click on the little arrowhead pointing down in the top right hand corner of the **Footer Area One** widgets area. This will open it up.

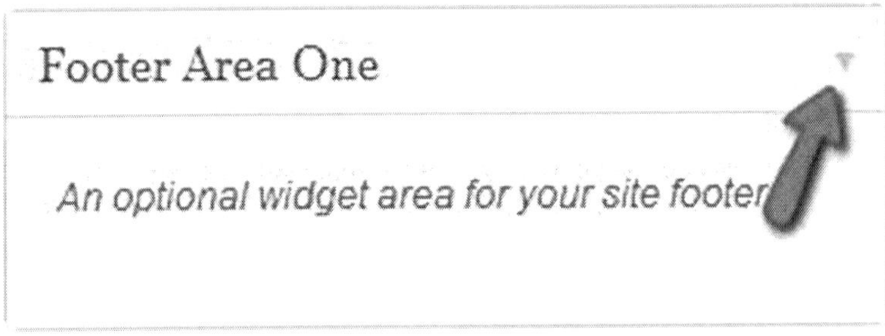

Now click and drag a text widget from the **Available widgets**, and drop it (by releasing the mouse button), in the Footer Area One.

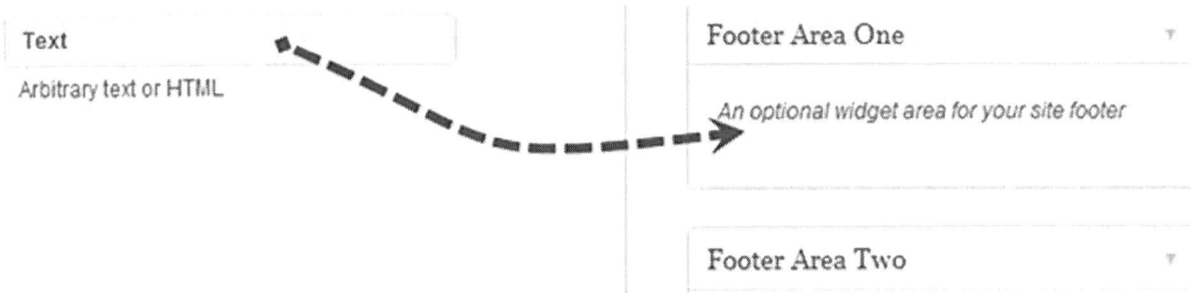

The text widget will open up for editing its settings.

At the top of the text widget you can enter a title. Enter Text Widget 1.

In the big box underneath (which would normally hold the text or html code you wanted to insert into your page), enter the same thing - Text Widget 1.

When done, click the Save button, on the bottom right side, to save your widget settings.

Repeat for Footer Area Two and Three, but change the text widget title and text to Text Widget 2 and Text Widget 3 respectively.

Now go and view your website. Scroll down to the footer area:

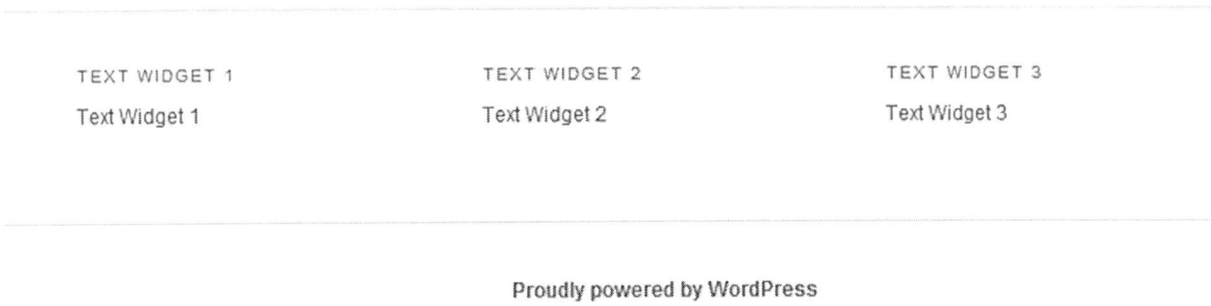

You can see that the three widgets you added appear in the bottom left, middle, and right positions of the footer. These areas correspond to the three widgetized areas. Cool eh? Using the text widget you can add any text or HTML to these areas of your website.

When playing around to see what widgets do and how they appear on your site, I recommend filling in all of the settings for the widget. In this example we entered a title and the main text. We can see how the WordPress template handles the formatting of the title and the text. The title is all uppercase and the main text is normal.

Let's have a look at the standard widgets that are already installed.

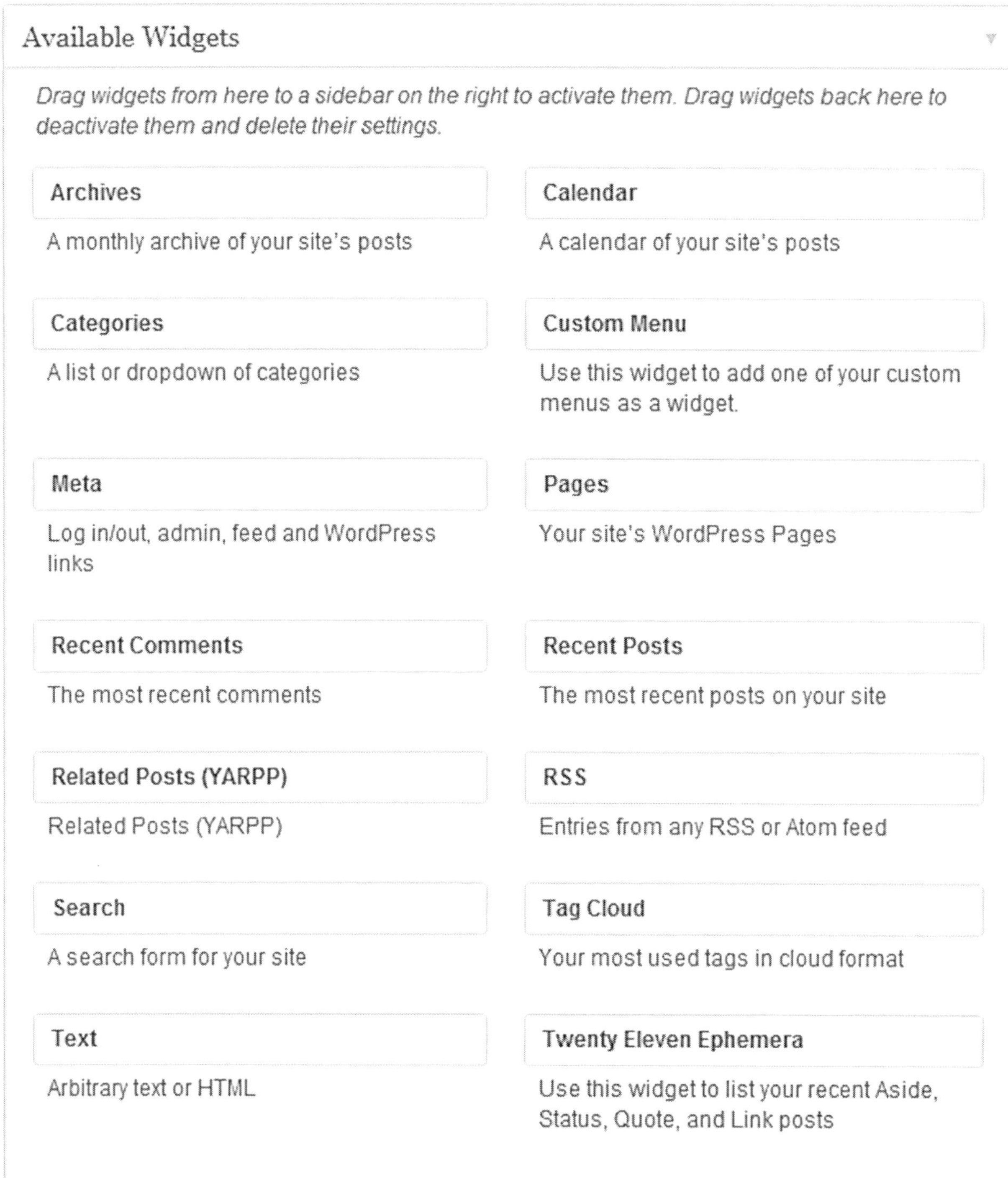

I am not going to go through these, as they are fairly self-explanatory. Besides, you can always add them yourself and see what they do, and remove them just as easily if need be.

Hopefully you can now see the potential of widgets.

You are not just limited to the widgets that come pre-installed with WordPress. Many plugins or services provide their own WordPress widget so that you can add new features to your website as you build it up. For example, you'll notice that there is a YARPP widget that was installed with the Yet Another Related Posts plugin. That widget will add a list of related posts to your sidebar in case you don't want them displayed after the post (which we enabled in the settings previously by choosing to automatically show related posts after the article).

Basic HTML

One thing that will come in handy is some simple HTML code that you might like to use in widgets. You can add HTML to a text widget. For example, if you want to add some text with a link to another page, you'd just look up the HTML below for creating a hyperlink and insert it into your text widget accordingly.

A hyperlink

<a href=”URL”>LINK TEXT</a>

Just replace URL with the web address of the page you want to link to, and the LINK TEXT with the word or phrase you want linked.

Example:

If you are interested, you can read my review of the <a href=”http://blenderreview.com/waring”>waring blender</a> for more details.

It I entered that into a sidebar text widget, it would look like this on my site:

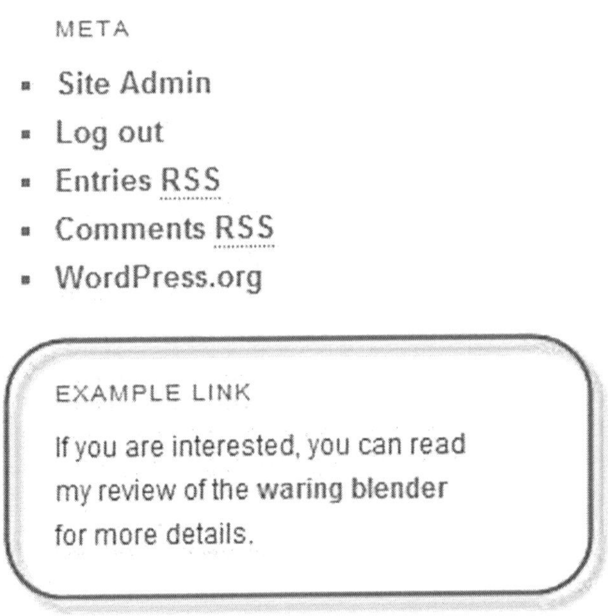

I added a title to the text widget (Example link). You can see the phrase "waring blender" is a link to the URL I specified in the HTML.

An image

To insert an image, here is the HTML:

<img src="URL" width="XX" height="YY" />

Replace URL with the URL of the image (upload it via the media library and grab the URL there), XX is the width in pixels and YY is the height in pixels. If your image is the correct size (which it should be to keep image load times to a minimum), then you can leave out the height and width parameters and the code just becomes:

<img src="URL" />

For example, using an image from my media library, I grabbed the URL for the image and inserted it into a text widget. This is what it looks like:

A numbered list

The HTML for a numbered list is a little more complicated.

```
<ol>
  <li>item one</li>
  <li>item two</li>
  <li>item three</li>
</ol>
```

You simply replace item one, item two, item three and so on with whatever you want displayed. You can add as many items as you need. Just repeat the <li>**item**</li> code once for each item you want to add.

For example, here is some code which shows a numbered list for my top three tablet recommendations.

```
<ol>
  <li>Asus 301</li>
  <li>Asus 201</li>
  <li>Apple iPad</li>
</ol>
```

.. and this is what it looks like in a sidebar text widget.

NOTE: The text you add for an item CAN be a hyperlink. Just construct it from the HTML I showed you above.

A bullet list

A bulleted list is almost the same code as the numbered list with one modification.

Instead of the code opening with <ol> and closing with </ol>, a bullet list opens with <ul> and closes with </ul>. The "ol" stands for ordered list (ordered by number), whereas the "ul" stands for unordered list.

```
<ul>
  <li>item one</li>
  <li>item two</li>
  <li>item three</li>
</ul>
```

Here is my widget now:

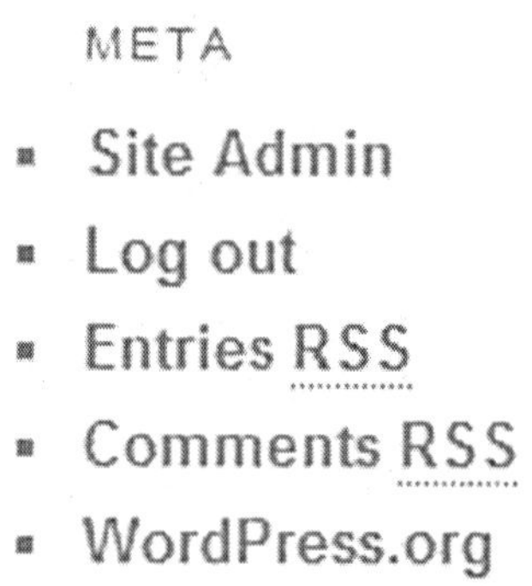

That should give you enough HTML to get you started with text widgets.

There is one other widget that I do want to discuss in a little more detail. It goes hand-in-hand with one of the features we haven't looked at yet, which are custom menus. The widget itself is used to display a custom menu in a widgetized area. We therefore need a custom menu first, so that's where we'll begin

Tasks to complete

1. Go and explore the widgets area. Add some widgets to your site and then view the site in your browser to see what they do and how they format the information.

2. Add in a text widget and experiment with the HTML code I gave you in this chapter. Try adding a text widget to the top of the sidebar with a photograph of yourself (or your persona image), and a brief bio.

Custom menus

To add or edit a custom menu in WordPress, go to the **Menus** item inside the **Appearance** menu:

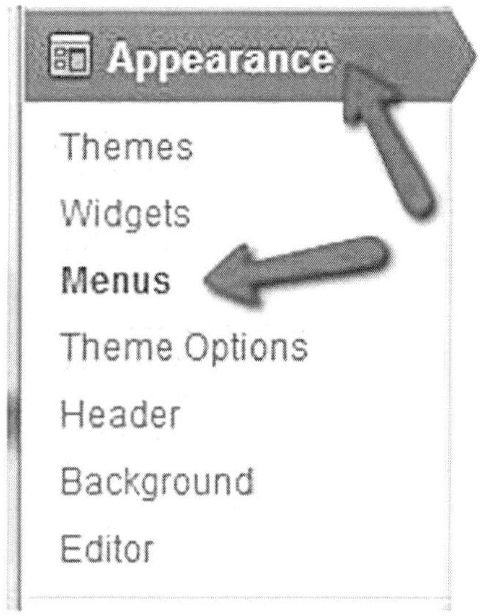

If you have been following along as you've read this book, you will have noticed that every time you created a new page, WordPress added it to the menu on your site.

NOTE: When the WP policies plugin created a lot of pages for us, these were not added to the menu. Pages only get added to the menu when we actually go in and create the page manually.

Here is the menu that WordPress has built for me:

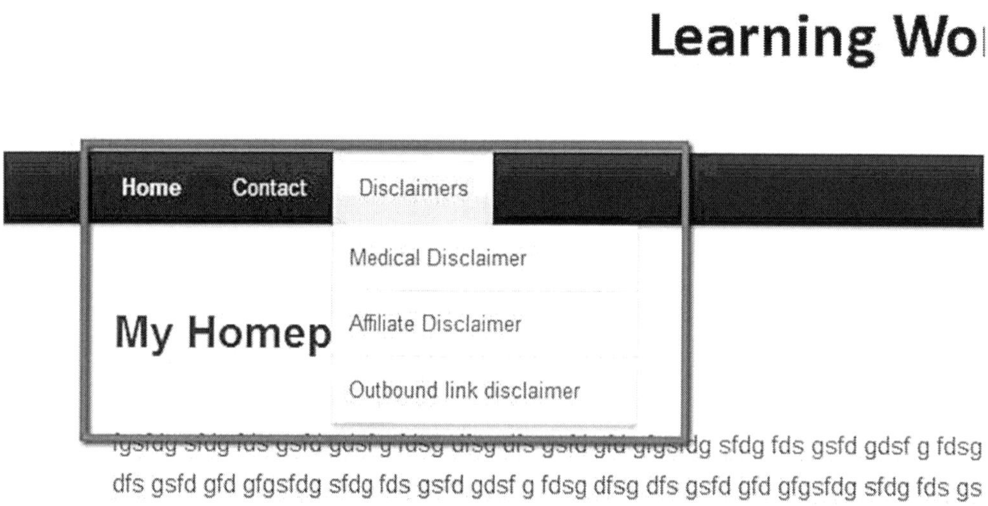

This is not how I want my navigation menu to appear. The good thing is I don't have to put up with it, because I can create my own custom menu.

Let's now design a custom menu to replace the one above.

In the custom menu screen, the first thing you need to do is click the **create a new** menu link.

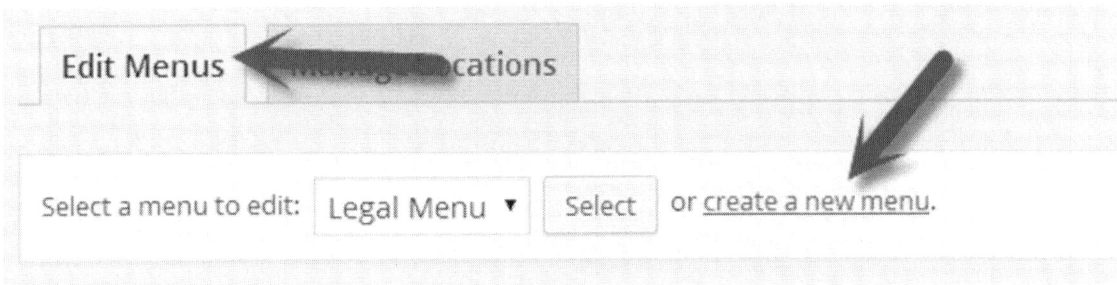

Type in a name for your menu (I've called mine "Top Menu"), and then click the **Create Menu** button.

When the page refreshes, immediately click the **Save Menu** button.

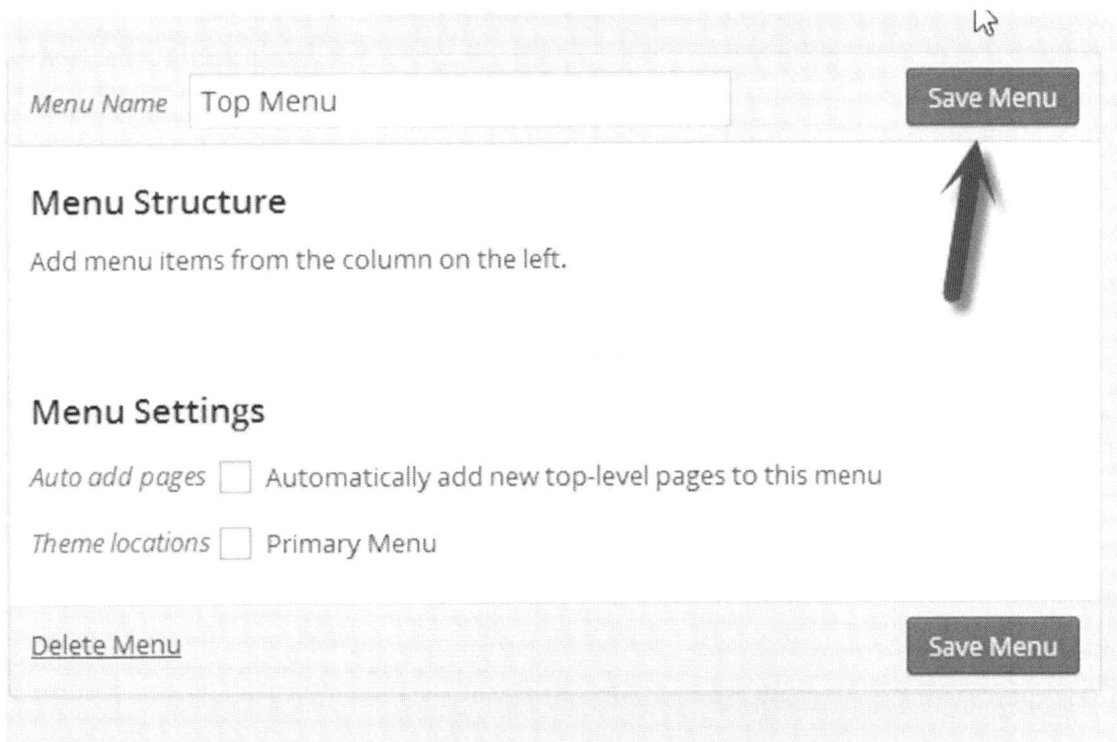

At the top of the screen you'll see a tab labeled **Manage Locations**.

Click it.

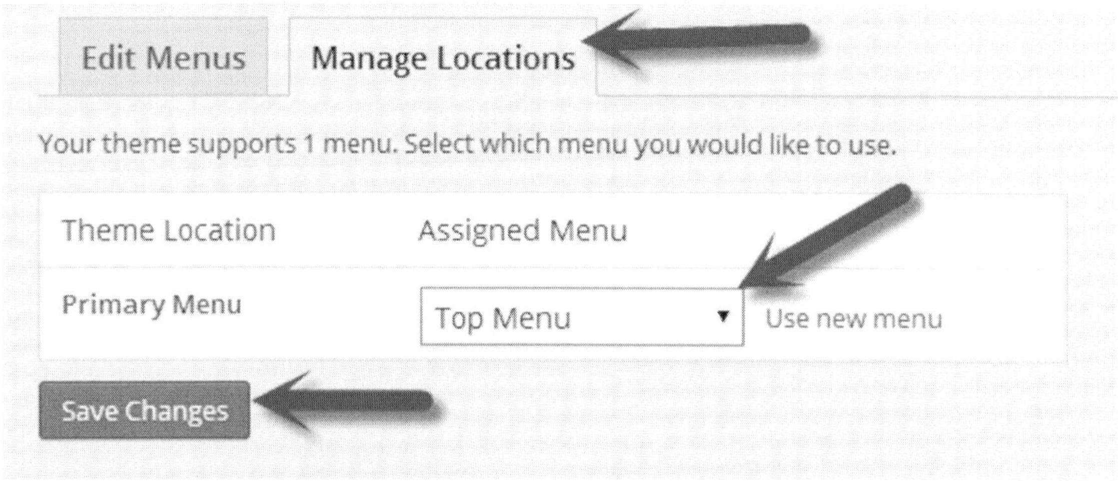

This screen tells us how many custom menus our theme supports. The Twenty Eleven theme supports only one - the **Primary menu.**

That is the menu we want to replace.

NOTE: This limit on the number of custom menus supported does not affect your ability to put custom menus in the sidebar, as that is controlled by a plugin, not the theme.

OK, from the drop down menu labelled **Primary Menu**, select the menu you just created and then click Save. That tells WordPress we want to use our own menu and not the one WordPress created for us automatically.

Since our custom menu is presently empty, if we now check our site, the old menu has gone. Go and visit your homepage to check. The menu should no longer be there. If it's still visible, make sure you have saved the menu AND saved the menu selection for the Primary location.

OK, time to build our new menu.

Building a menu is easy. For the most part, you can select from the lists that WordPress gives us on this screen. However, for the first link in my menu, I want a link called "Home" that links back to my homepage. To add this, we need to add a **custom link**. A custom link is just one we need to build ourselves as opposed to selecting it from the list that WordPress presents us with.

On the left you'll see a box labelled **Links**.

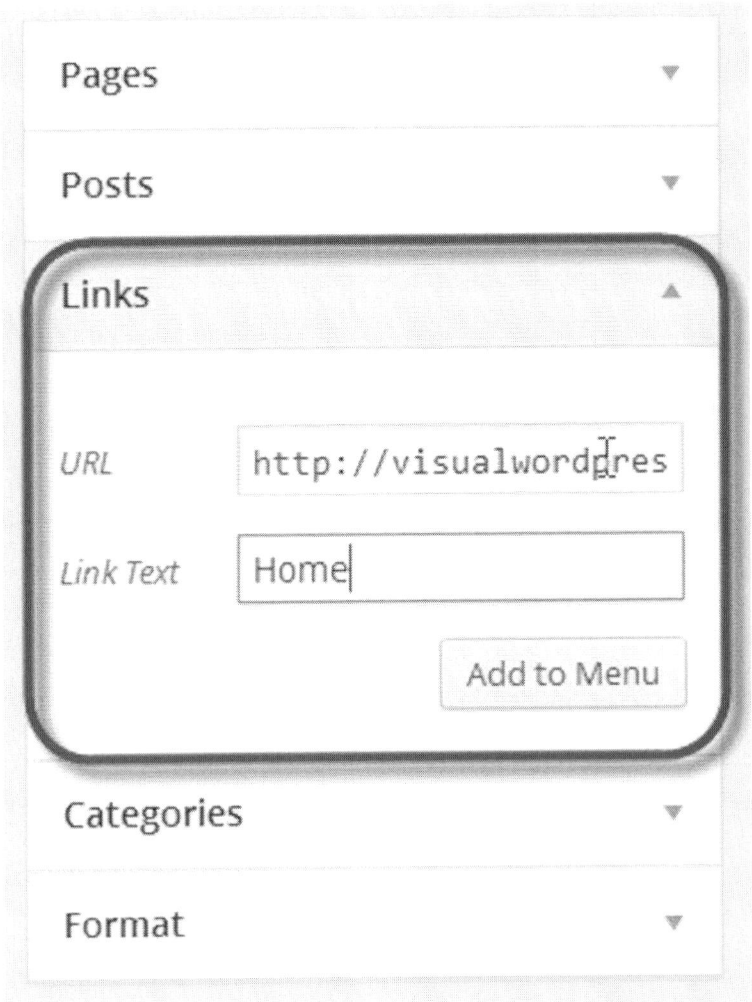

Just enter your homepage URL (making sure to include the http://), in the URL box. Next, add the text you want displayed for that menu item in the Label box. And finally, click the **Add to Menu** button.

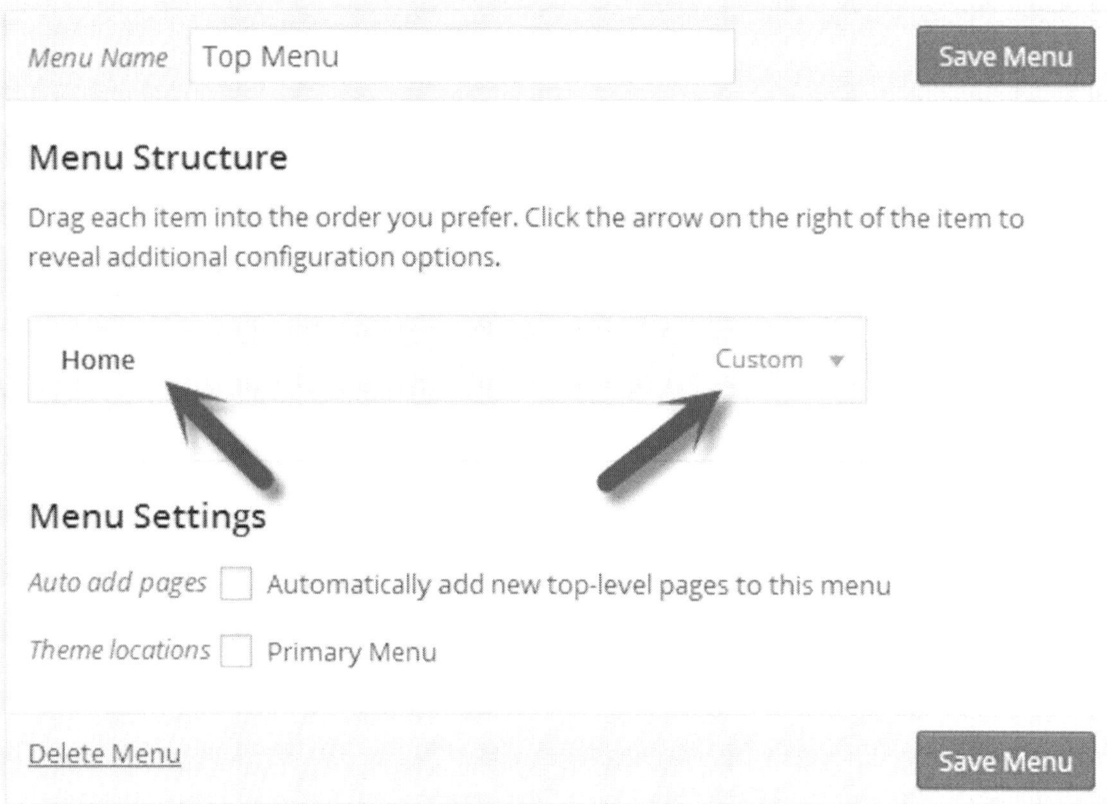

A box now appears in the menu we are building on the right.

Notice that the box has an arrowhead on the right side labelled **Custom**. The box is currently collapsed, but it can be expanded with that arrowhead where we can access to some of the settings:

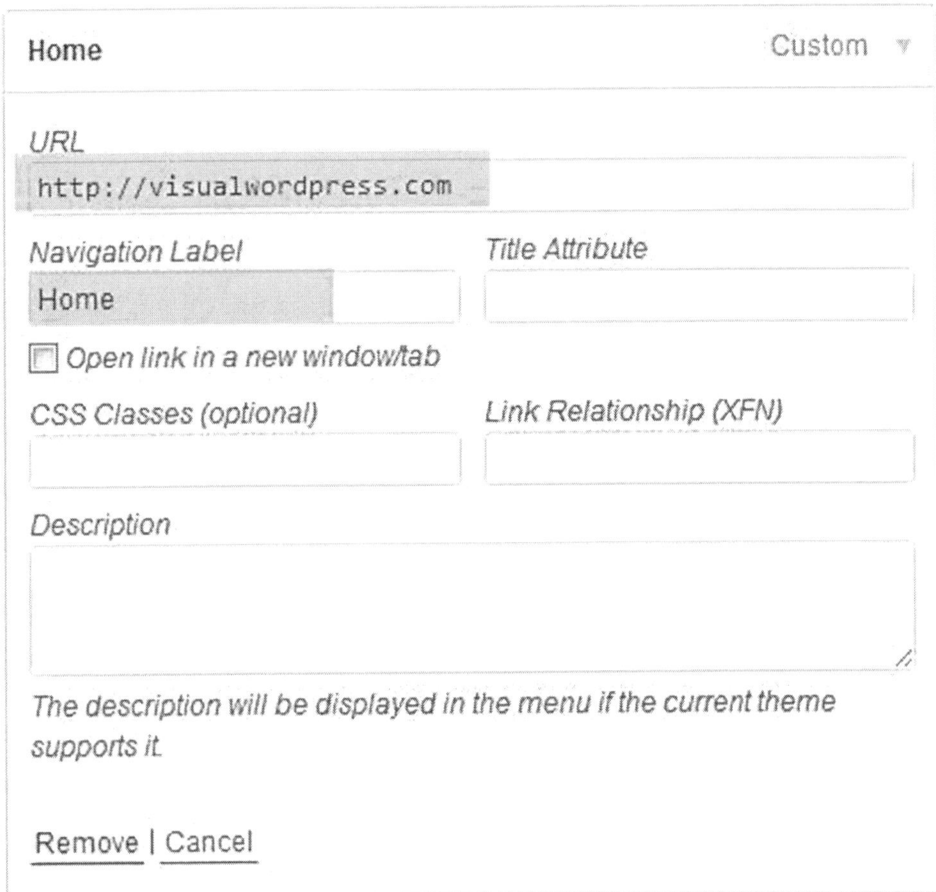

Yours will have fewer settings in it than mine because some are hidden by default. To see all of the settings that are visible in my screenshot, simply check the boxes in the **Screen Options** (top right). The only box in the screen options that I would leave unchecked is the **Format** box. You can uncheck others later, once you know what they do and whether or not you need them.

The main settings for each link are as follows:

• **URL** - the URL (web address), that you are linking to.

• **Navigation Label** - the text that is displayed for the link.

• **Title Attribute** - Do NOT use this; leave it blank. Remember we mentioned earlier about getting into trouble with Google for stuffing keywords into a link's "title" attribute?

• **Open link in a new Window/tab** - useful if you are linking to another website, but all links to pages on your own site should have this option unchecked.

• **CSS Classes** - don't worry about this. It's an advanced feature for people who want more control over the way the menu links look.

• **Link Relationship (XFN)** - this can actually be useful on occasions if you want to set the "nofollow" attribute on a link. I set links to all "legal" pages as "nofollow", and this is the box where I do that. We'll see it in a minute as I continue to construct my menu.

NOTE: Nofollow simply tells the search engines not to follow the link. It's a good idea to nofollow links to sites you don't really trust.

• **Description** - is sometimes displayed by the theme, but not all themes support this attribute. I would therefore ignore this feature and even uncheck it in the screen options.

OK, with the home link in my menu, my site now has a functioning custom menu:

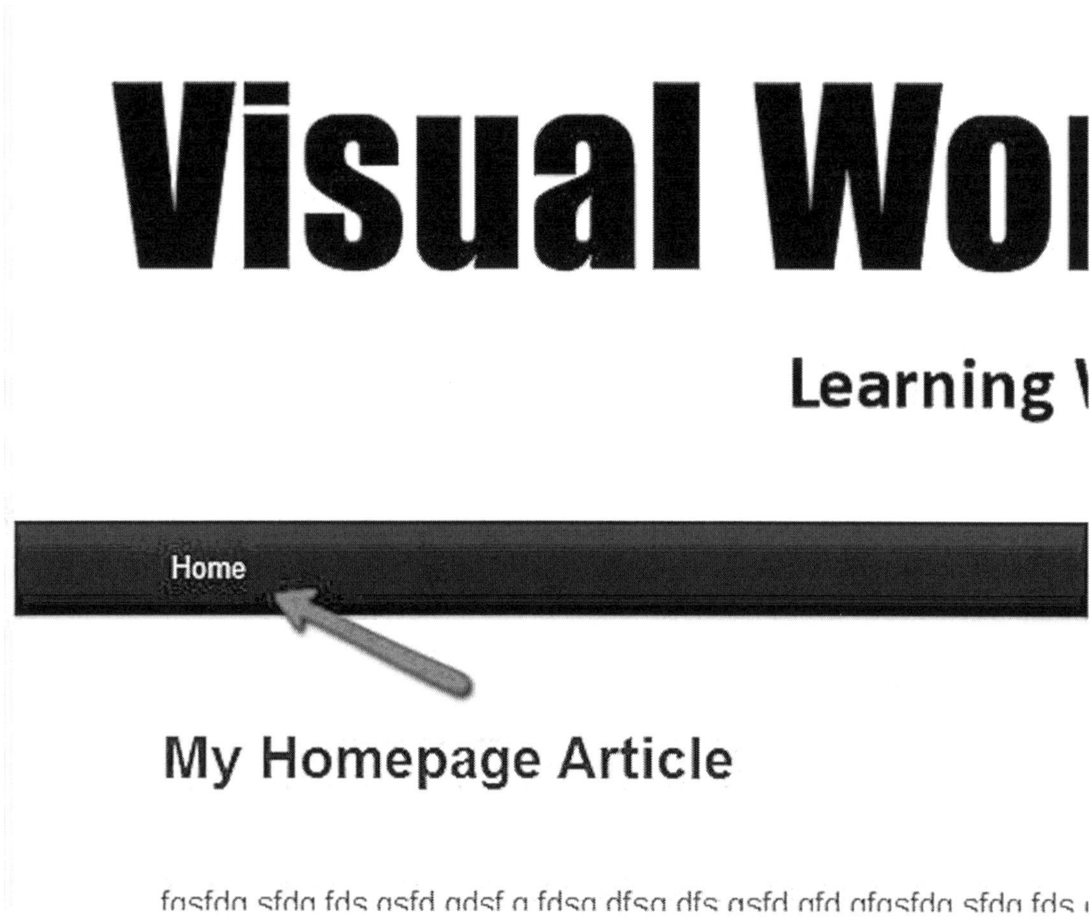

There is only one link in the menu, but it's a start. Let's add some more.

As we move down the options on the left (underneath the **Custom Links**), is the **Posts** section:

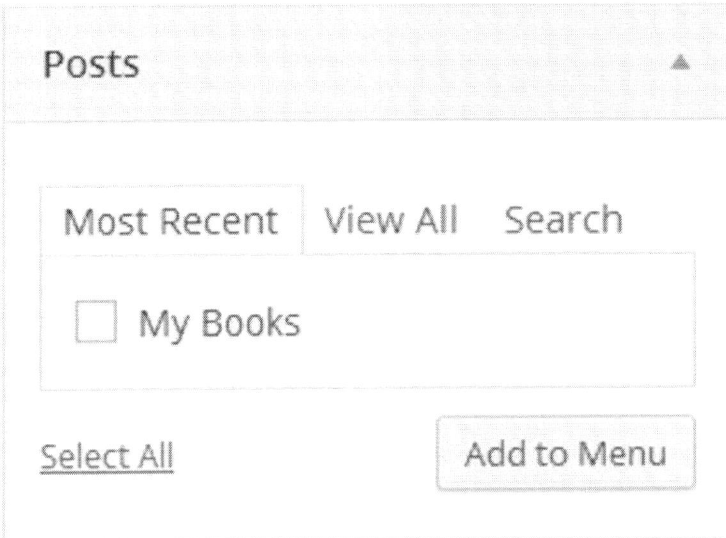

This section lists the most recent posts on your site, though there are tabs to view *all* posts and even search for posts. If you want to add a link to a particular post in your menu, select the check box next to that post and click the **Add to Menu** button. The post will then appear in the menu. I don't want any POSTS in my menu at the moment, but I do want some PAGES. That's the next section down:

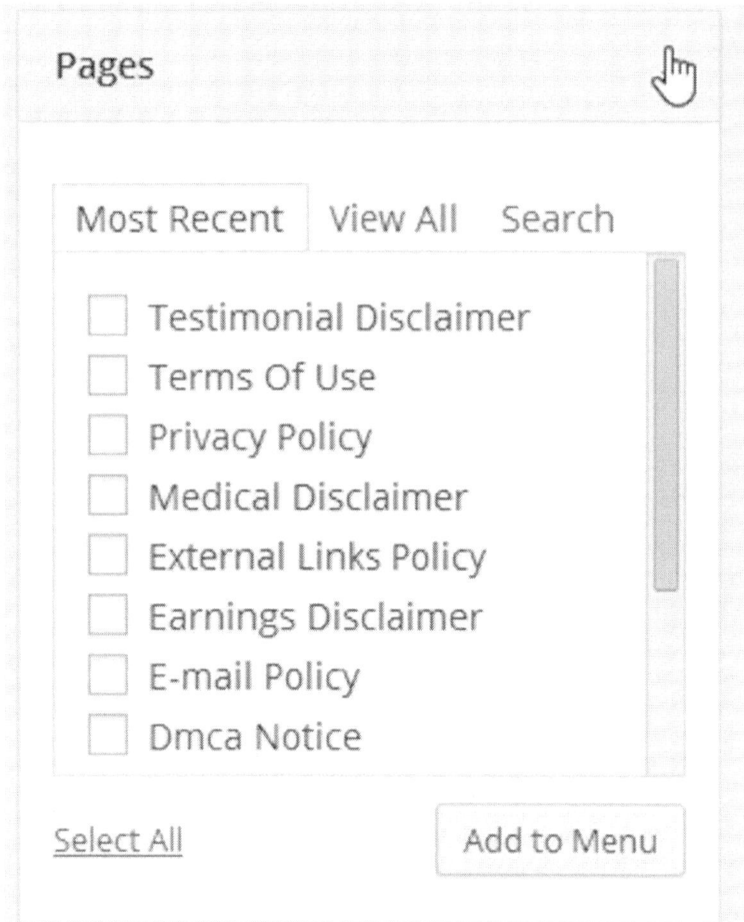

Just select the pages you want included in your navigation menu and then click the **Add to Menu** button.

The pages will now appear in the list on the right. There are three other types of links we can add to our custom menu; the most useful being Categories and Tags:

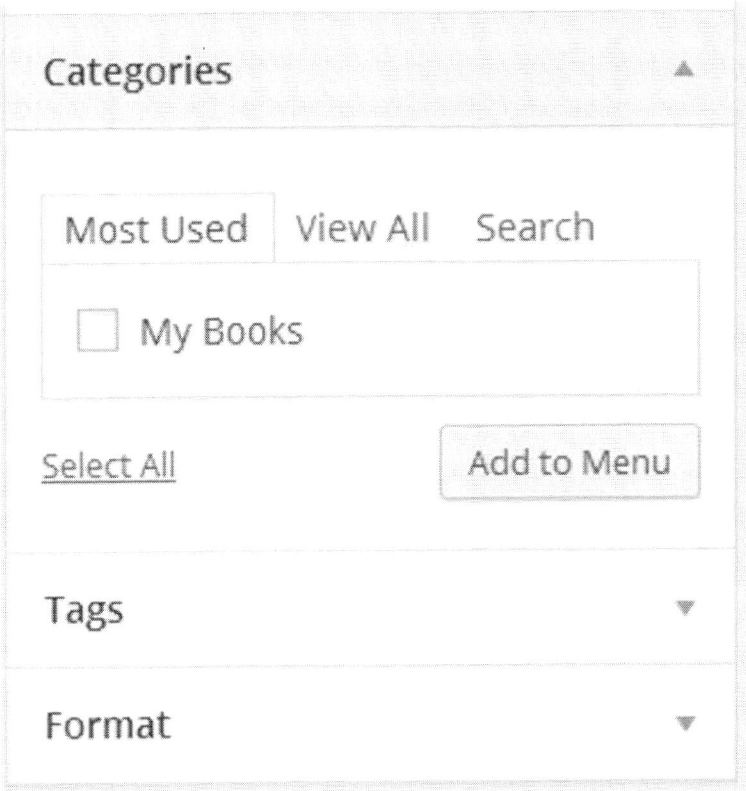

These options allow you to add links in your menus to category pages and tag pages.

If there are important category or tag pages on your site, it might be something you want to add to your own menu (or maybe a custom menu in the sidebar using a custom menu widget!)

OK, I have now added all of the links I want in my menu bar, but there's a problem; on the site, it's looking kind of messy!

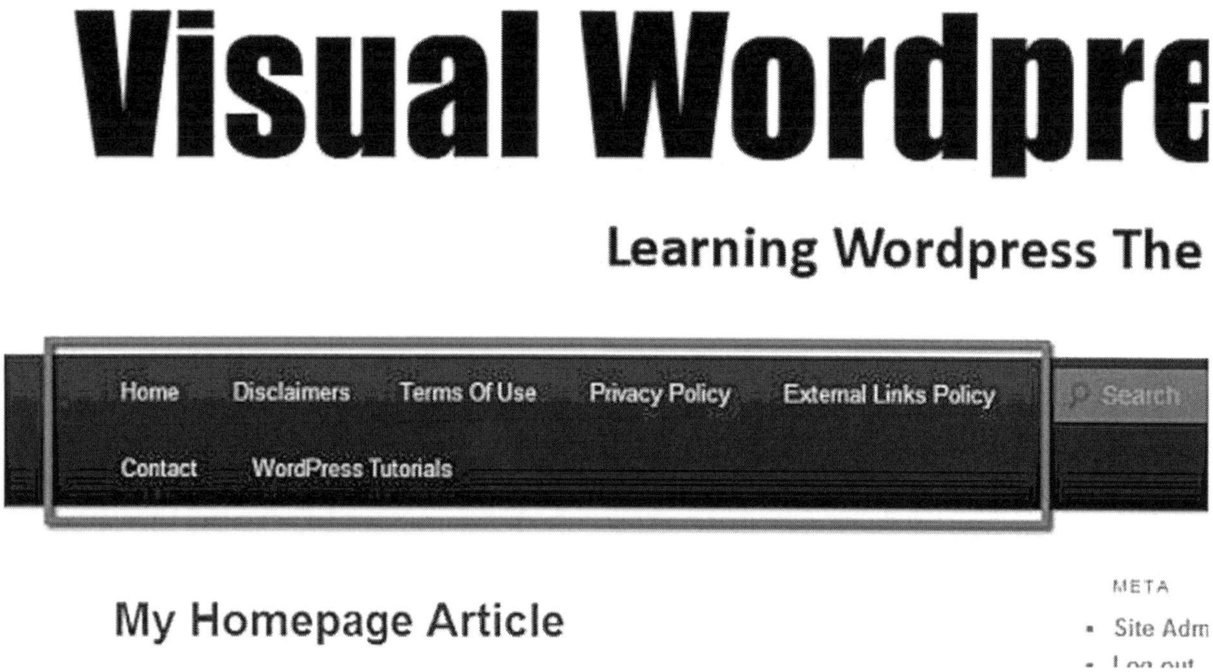

I would like to have my menu bar display in this order: Home first, WordPress Tutorials next, then Contact, and finally a hierarchical menu that lists all of the disclaimers and “legal” pages. OK, so let’s re-organise the menu items.

The Custom Menu Designer has the drag and drop feature. This means you can click and hold down your mouse button to pick up a menu item, drag it to the place you want it located, and then unclick your mouse button to drop it there. That is the simple procedure of how we can re-order the items in our menu in just a few seconds.

After dragging my menu items into the order I want them to appear, this is what I now have:

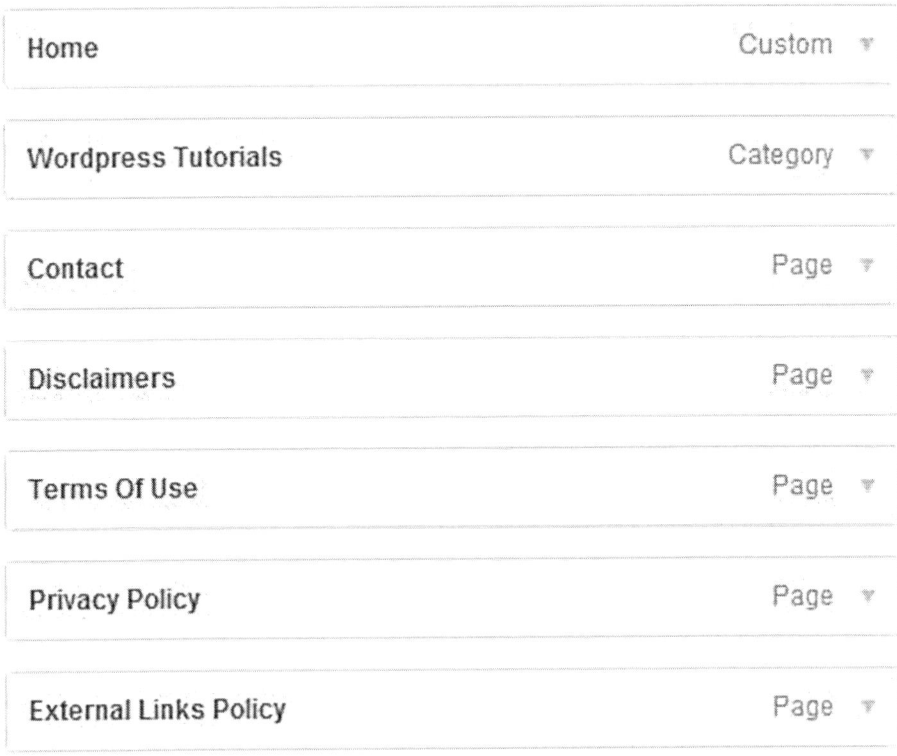

The only snag now is getting those legal pages into a hierarchy, with the last three items appearing as a drop down menu of the Disclaimers menu. But don't worry, that's easy too.

To create a “child menu”, drag the menu item to the right a little, just underneath the item you want as its parent (see below):

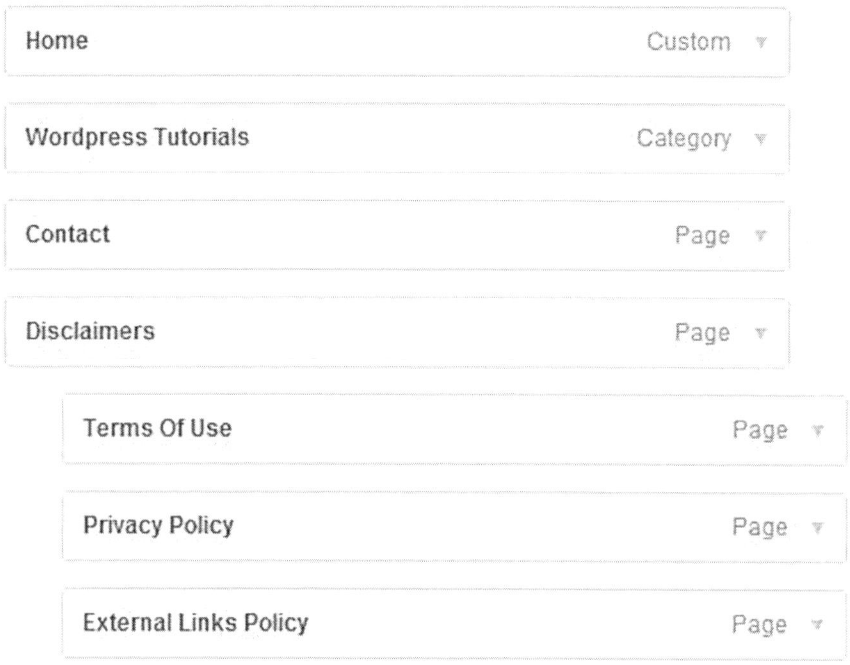

Do you see how the Terms of Use, Privacy Policy and External Links Policy are all lined up and indented under the Disclaimers menu item? That makes them child menus of the Disclaimers menu. So on my site now, the menu system looks like this (after saving everything of course).

Do you see how powerful the custom menu designer is?

We don't have to rely on WordPress to create the site navigation. We can easily create a navigation menu system without the fuss of using parent/child pages and setting page order. If you design your own navigation menu, you get more flexible menus. In other words, menus that display exactly as YOU want them to.

OK, so one final thing. Any custom menu you create can be added to a sidebar using the custom menu widget. I'm just going to create another menu quickly so I can show you how this works.

First, I need to add a new menu:

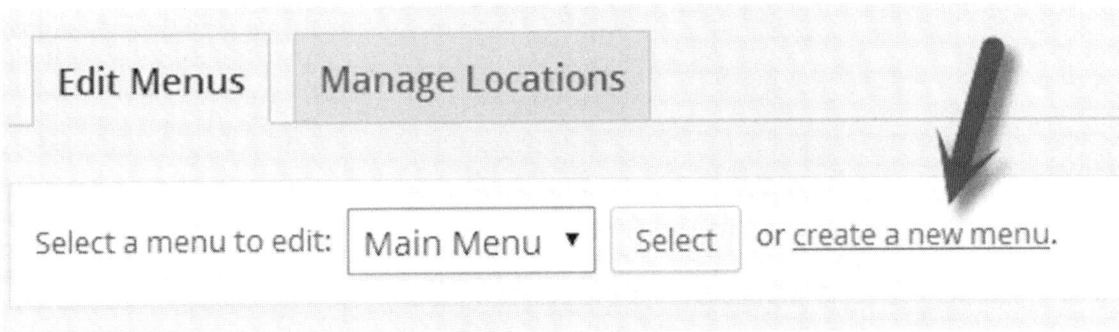

.. add a name, and click **Create Menu**.

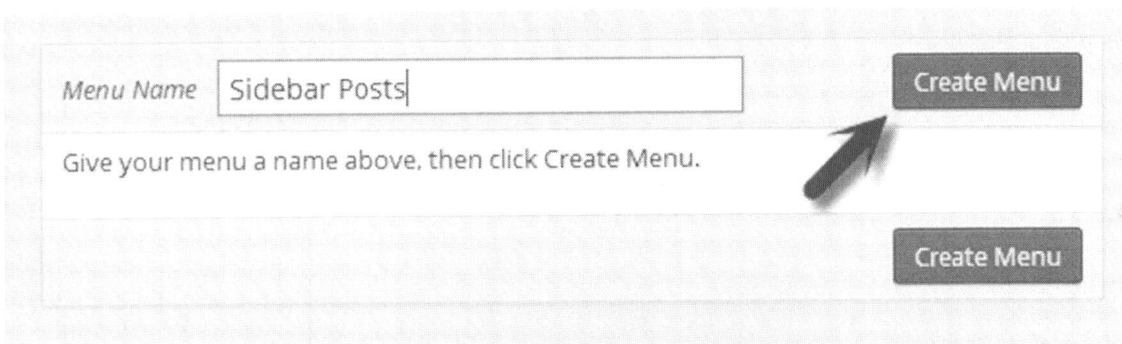

I'll just add a couple of posts to the menu using the Posts selector and then save my new menu.

OK, now it's time to head back to the Appearance -> Widgets screen.

When you get there, drag a custom menu widget into the Main Sidebar:

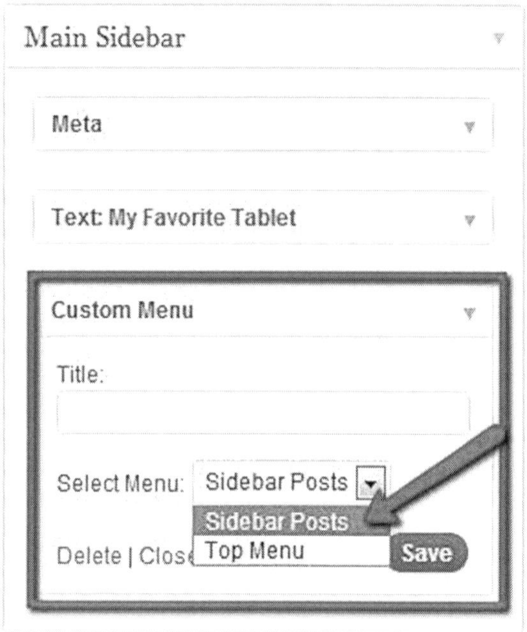

You can add a title for the widget and select the menu you want displayed. Save the widget, then check out the sidebar on your homepage. Here is mine:

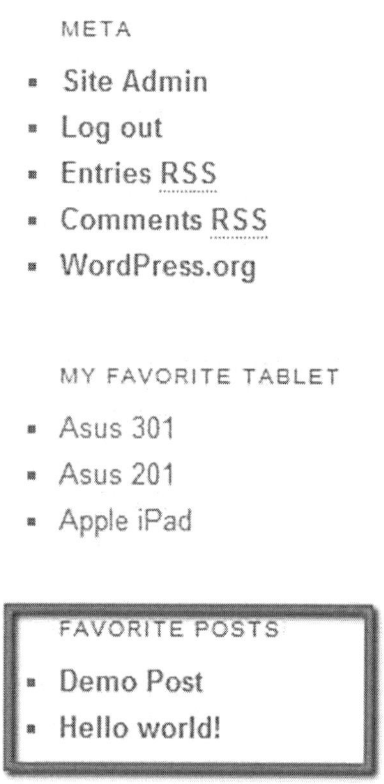

You can create custom menus for all kinds of things. These may be top review pages or important tag pages. The point is this; custom menus give you the flexibility you need as you design and develop your website.

Tasks to complete

1. Go and experiment with Custom Menus.
2. Create a menu with a "Home" link and links to the "legal" pages on your site. Don't worry if you're unsure about what you want to add to the menu(s), as you can always update things later. And of course, any changes will be effective immediately, the moment you hit the Save button.

Viewing your site while logged in

Something special happens when you are visiting your website while logged into your Dashboard.

Earlier, when we were looking at the User Profile, we made sure an option was checked - **Show Toolbar when viewing site.** Let's have a look what happens with that option enabled.

Login to your dashboard and then open your website in another tab of your web browser.

What you'll see is a very useful "ribbon" across the top of your website:

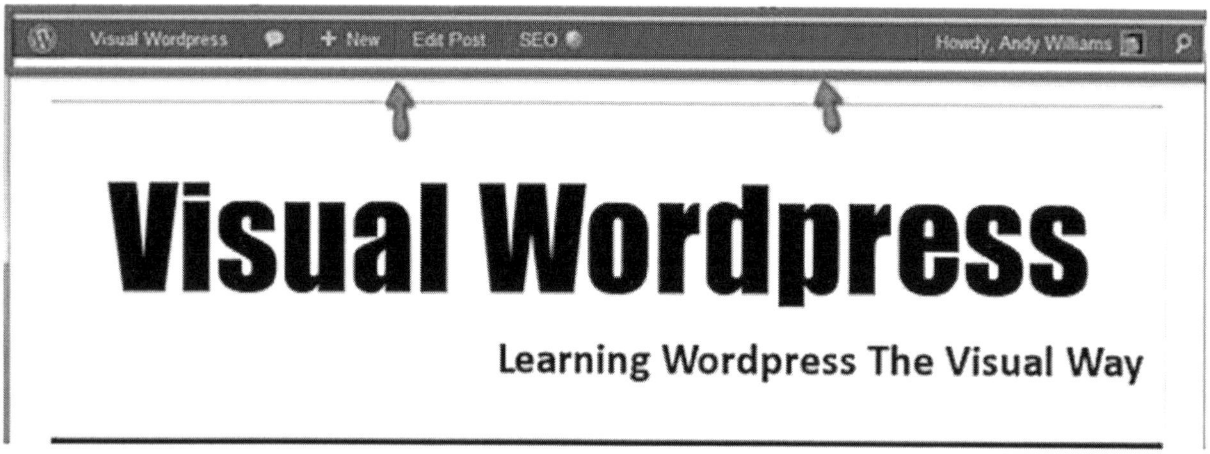

This ribbon gives you access to some important WordPress features. For example, if you want to edit a page or post on your website, you can visit your website, find the post, then click on the edit post link in the ribbon bar (you can see it in the screenshot above). That link will open up the post in the WordPress Dashboard ready for editing.

The ribbon is very useful as you browse your site. If you find errors, just click the **Edit Post** link, fix the issue(s), and then click the Update button.

The other main features of the ribbon are the two drop down menus:

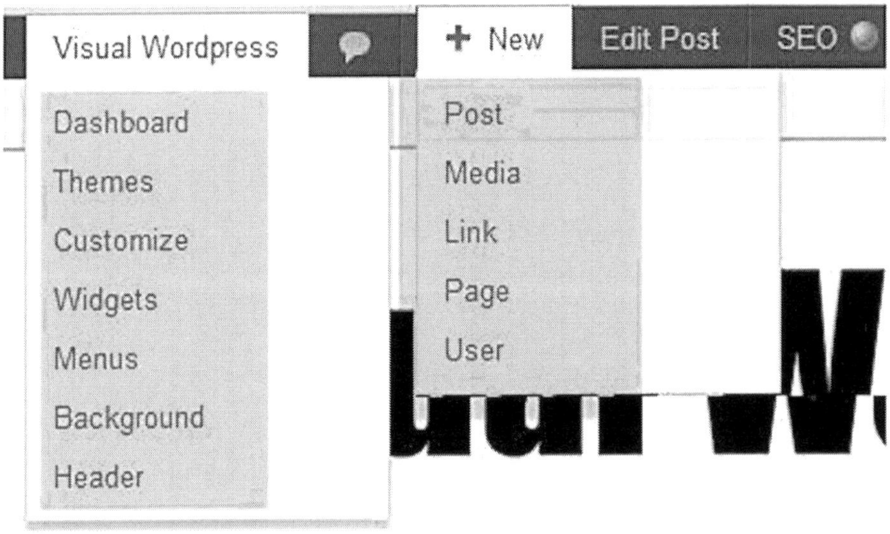

The first one gives you access to your Dashboard, Themes, Customize, Widgets, Menus, Background and Header settings.

The other menu allows you to add a new Posts or Page, access Media, add a Link, or open the new User setup page. Now some of these features won't be much use, but it is nice having them there in case you need them at any time.

The biggest benefit of this ribbon, to me, is the Edit Post link AND the speech bubble.

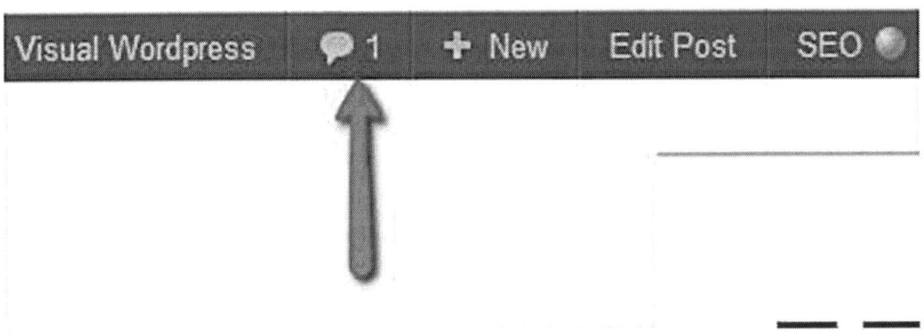

See that number one next to the speech bubble? That means there is a comment awaiting moderation. Clicking the speech bubble will open up the Dashboard at the moderate comments screen.

Tasks to complete

1. Login to your site.
2. Open the site in a new tab in your browser.
3. Explore the ribbon bar at the top and see what quick options are accessible from it.

WordPress security

WordPress has often been criticized as being too easy to hack. There have been a lot of cases where people have lost their WordPress site after a hacker gained access to it and wreaked havoc. Several years ago, one of my sites got hacked so badly that I just deleted the whole thing and let the domain expire. At that time, I didn't have a reliable backup system in place. It is therefore wise to take the security of your site very seriously.

Earlier in the book we set up a plugin which is sending us database backups every week or so via email. That's a great start, but the plugin does not backup everything we need to restore a site. It doesn't backup the theme, plugins, or any customizations we may have made.

To create a complete backup of my sites, I use a script that I bought called WP Twin. This script creates a perfect backup of a website (which includes things like theme settings and plugins). If a site of mine ever did get hacked again, I could restore the entire project with a few simple clicks of the mouse (or even move the site to an entirely different domain).

WP Twin is a premium script that isn't cheap. Knowing that most people have a tight budget when starting out, I had a look around for a free alternative. I found one that has good reviews, but have not used it myself. It's called Duplicator and you install it the same way you do for any plugin. Just search for Duplicator in the add plugins screen of your dashboard.

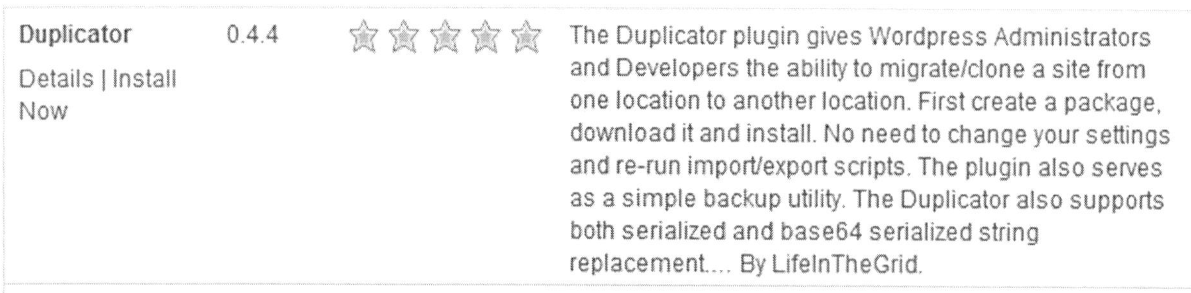

Disclaimer: I have not used this plugin so cannot show you how it works or personally vouch for it in any way.

What this plugin will allow you to do is take an exact snapshot of your site and all its data, which would then allow a complete reconstruction of the site if anything bad happened. I would keep the database backups coming via email as well, but Duplicator will provide you with another layer of cover should you ever need it.

Another layer of protection is to **always upgrade WordPress** as soon as there is a new update available.

The WordPress team fix security leaks as soon as they are found. Therefore, if your Dashboard says there is a WordPress upgrade; install it as soon as possible to make sure your copy of the software is up-to-date with any bug fixes and or new security patches.

Finally, I also use a script on all of my sites that helps protect against hackers. It is a commercial script, but it is cheap. I have used the script (on over 100 websites), ever since I lost that site to hackers. I haven't had any problems with hackers since. The script is called WP-Secure and you can read about it here:

http://goo.gl/fKud9

Tasks to complete

1. Always keep WordPress up to date.
2. Install a backup plugin, like Duplicator, and make a full backup of your site.
3. Consider getting the WP-Secure plugin and installing it to prevent hackers from gaining access to your site.

Monitoring website traffic

Every Webmaster wants to know how many visitors their site is getting and how those people are finding their pages (through search engines, via social media channels, etc.).

Fortunately there are a number of good, free solutions to give you this information.

The tool I use on my own sites is called Google Analytics, but it is complex and perhaps overkill for someone just starting out. I'd therefore recommend you use a free service like Get Clicky - http://clicky.com/

Head on over there now and sign up for an account.

The signup process is just a simple form that asks for your email, real name, username, and password. Then of course it asks which domain you want to track. Just enter the full URL of your website.

After signing up, you'll be logged into your account preferences. You don't need to do anything in there (unless you want to). For now, just click through to your Dashboard:

When you get there it will look a little empty:

It will remain empty too, at least until you add some tracking code to your website so that Get Clicky can monitor visitors on your site.

To add this code to your site, I recommend another plugin by the same guy that created the WordPress SEO plugin. This one is called "Clicky by Yoast".

Go to your Dashboard Plugins area and click on **Add New**. Then search for **Clicky by Yoast**.

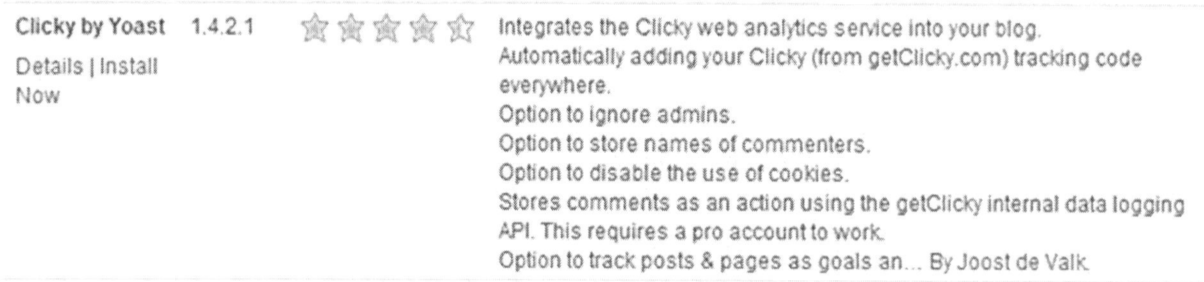

Install and activate the plugin.

You'll find the settings for the plugin inside the main Setting menu of the Dashboard Navigation:

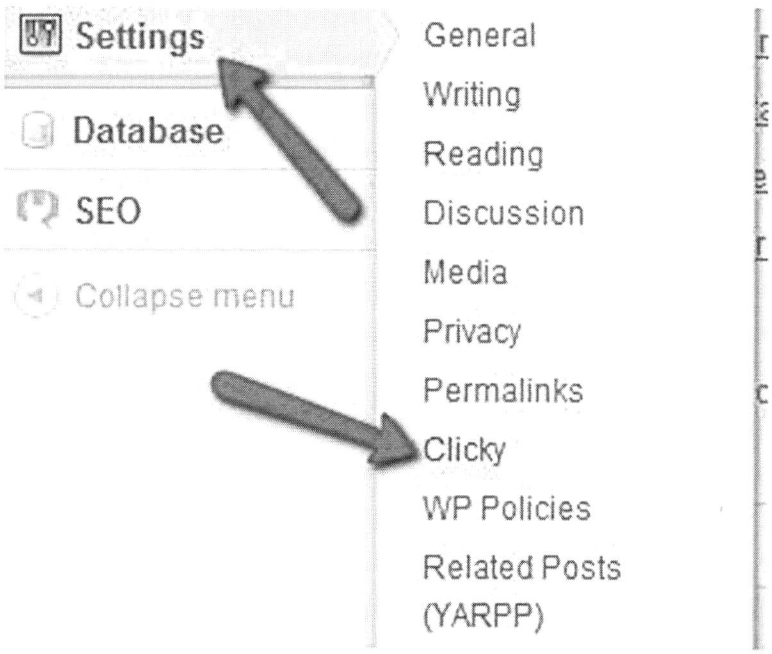

We need set up the plugin so that our website can communicate with Get Clicky. Click on **Clicky** in settings menu to open up the options for this plugin.

Open the Get Clicky website in another tab of your browser and login.

You should have the Clicky settings in your WordPress Dashboard open in one tab, and your Get Clicky account opened in a second tab.

Click on the **Preferences** link over at Get Clicky:

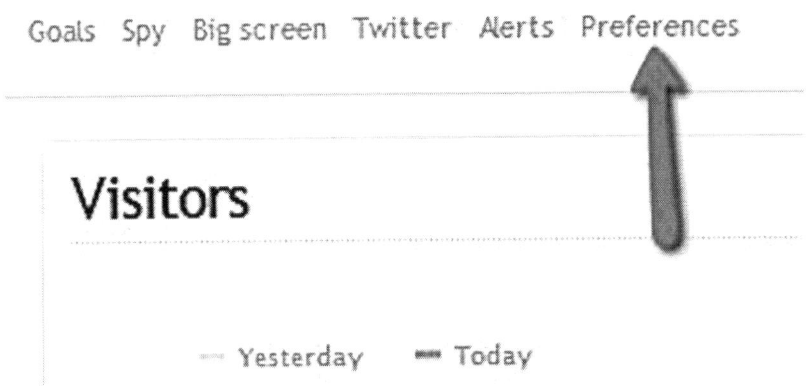

You'll see information about your site that you'll need to use in order to set up the plugin (I've blurred out my own data):

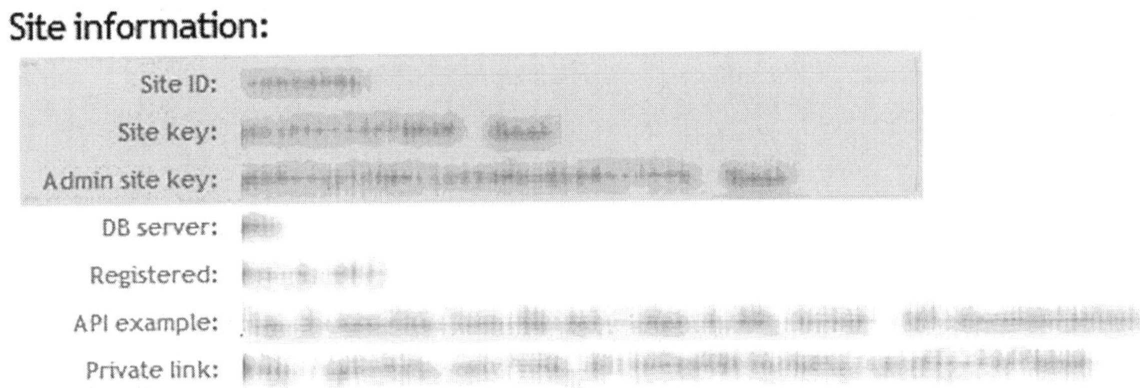

Copy the **Site ID**, **Site Key**, and **Admin site key**, from the Get Clicky website, and paste them into the Settings of the WordPress plugin.

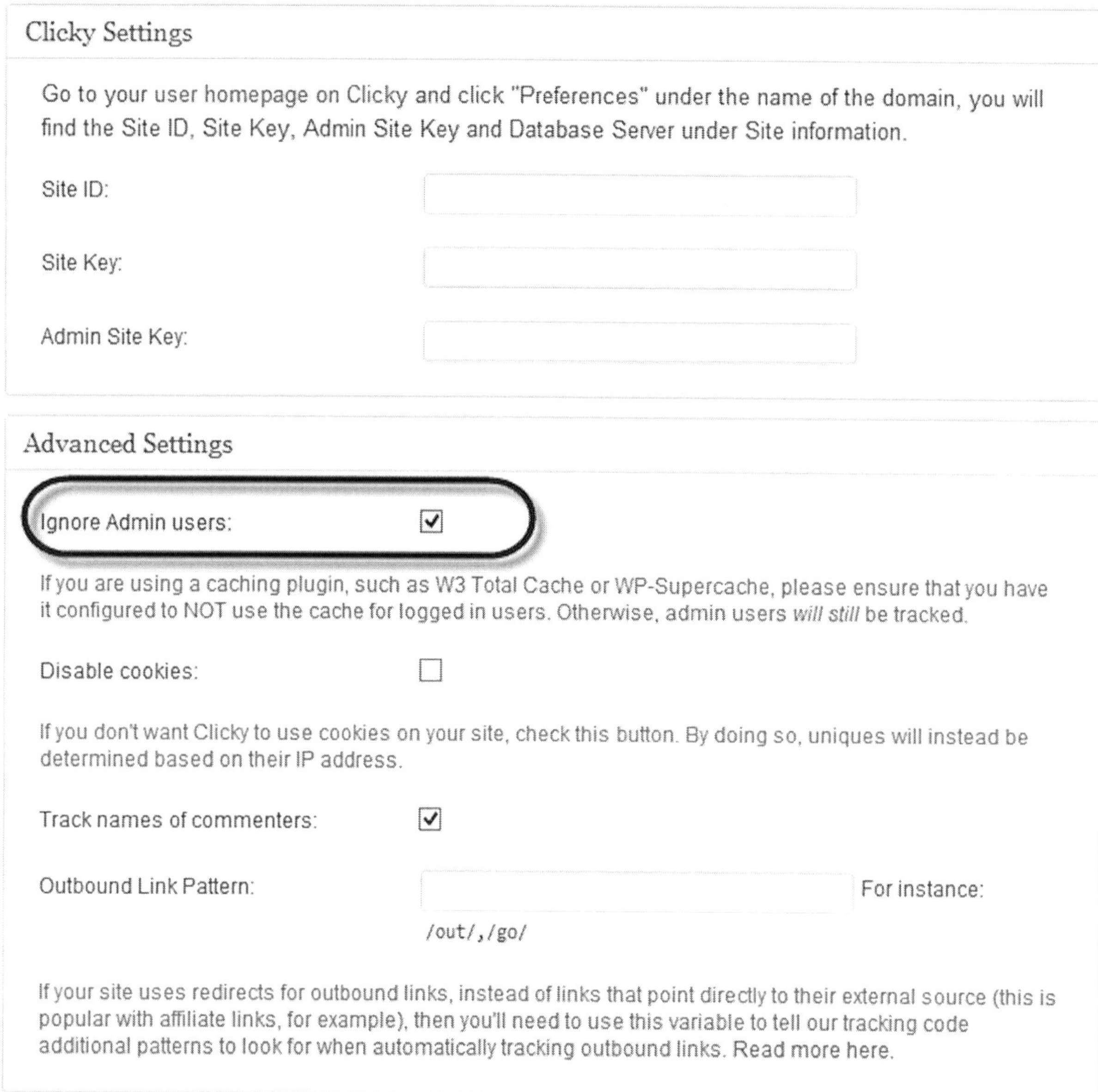

Make sure the Ignore Admin Users is checked so that your own visits are NOT tracked when you are logged into your Dashboard.

Next click on the **Update Clicky Settings** button at the bottom. That's it, you're all done here.

When someone visits your website, the plugin sends information about that visit to your Get Clicky account.

When you want to check how many visitors you are getting on your site, you can login at Get Clicky and use the tools they provide for visitor analysis. We won't go into more details here about how to use Get Clicky. If you want more help on that, you can read the Help section on their site. Alternatively, you can just go over there and explore the options.

As your site grows, I'd highly recommend you look into Google Analytics and make the switch. It's the best free tool out there and gives a wealth of information about your visitors.

Tasks to complete

1. Set up an account at Get Clicky.
2. Install the Clicky plugin and configure it as above.
3. Go over to the Clicky website and explore the tracking options. Use their Help if needed, so that you can find your way around the data and make sense of what it all means.
4. When you have time, look into Google Analytics.

Search Engine Optimization (SEO)

Search Engine Optimization has changed a lot in the last couple of years. It has always been one of the most important aspects of building a website because it helps you to rank better in Google, and consequently get more traffic and make more sales from your pages (the latter only being important if your site is commercial of course).

Today, things are very different. If you overdo your optimization, Google are likely to penalise you and dump your site out of their search engine.

If you ask Google about the best way to optimize your site, they'd probably tell you to avoid Search Engine Optimization altogether and just focus your efforts on the 'visitor experience', and not to worry about the search engines.

Despite sounding like a lost cause, you should still consider a number of "best practices" as you build your website. I will list the main things to consider here, but if you want a more in-depth discussion about SEO, I'd highly recommend my own book on the subject called **SEO 2014 & Beyond :: Search Engine Optimization will never be the same again**.

It's available in Kindle Format on Amazon:

Search Amazon for: **B0099RKXE8**

Main points for safe SEO

1. Always write content for the visitor, not the search engines.
2. Always create the highest quality content possible and make it unique. More than that, add something to your content that is not found on any other websites covering the same or similar topic, for example, your personal voice, experience or thoughts.
3. Engage your visitor, and allow them to open discussion with you via the built in comments feature.
4. Never try to write content based on keyword phrases. Always write content around a topic. E.g. don't write an article on "best iphone case", write an article on "Which iPhone Case offers the best protection for your phone?" See the difference?
5. As a measure of whether your content is good enough, ask yourself if you could imagine your article appearing in a glossy magazine? If you answer no, then it's not good enough to publish on your own website.
6. DO NOT hire people to build backlinks to your site. If you want to build some links, create them on quality websites that point back to yours. More on this in my SEO book mentioned previously.

7. Add a social sharing plugin to your site so that people can quickly share your content on social channels like Facebook, Twitter, YouTube and Google Plus etc.

The best advice I can give you for present day SEO is to read and digest Google's Webmaster Guidelines. They are there to help us create sites that will rank well in their Search Engine Results Pages, aka SERPs. You can read those guidelines here:

http://goo.gl/PyMip

Wordpress SEO

There are a number of ways you can improve the on-site SEO of your Wordpress site. While some of the basics are included in this book, I wrote a separate comprehensive book on the subject of Wordpress SEO. You can find it by searching Amazon for B00ECF70HU.

Tasks to complete

1. Read Google's Webmaster Guidelines over and over again until you know them off by heart. They really are very important and will benefit you in the long run; providing you adhere to their suggestions of course

Where to go from here?

We've covered a lot of ground in this book. You should now be confident finding your way around the WordPress Dashboard.

You have installed WordPress, installed the essential plugins, and configured everything so that your site is now ready for content.

So what's the next step?

Create impressive content!

Everything we have done in this book has been to achieve one main goal. Get your site set up & ready to accept your content. You can now concentrate on publishing content while WordPress takes care of the rest.

Here is your plan going forward.

1. Create a post.
2. Publish it.
3. Rinse and repeat steps 1 and 2.

If you want a "static" homepage rather than one showing your recent posts, create a PAGE with the content you want displayed there. Then set up the reading settings so that this page is shown permanently on your site's front page. You can then go back to the 3-step process outlined above

Create a post, publish & repeat.

I have created a website all about Wordpress where you can find more tutorials or ask me questions. The website is at:

http://rapidwpsites.com

Good luck!

Andy Williams

http://ezSEONews.com

Useful resources

There are a few places that I would recommend you visit for more information.

http://ezSEONews.com - This is my site where I offer free help and advice to webmasters. While you are there, sign up for my free weekly newsletter. You can also look through past issues and read articles on a variety of topics related to building WordPress sites.

SEO 2014 & Beyond :: Search engine optimization will never be the same again (http://goo.gl/rJ6b4)- This is my book on the new SEO. I say the "New SEO" because SEO changed forever in 2012. Many books, websites and courses that are on sale today are way out of date when it comes to SEO. Following their advice could get your site banned in Google. My book is bang up to date.

Google Webmaster Guidelines (http://goo.gl/cRq7a) - this is the webmasters bible of what is acceptable and what is not in the eyes of the world's biggest search engine.

Google Analytics (http://www.google.com/analytics/) - the best free analytics program out there. When you have some free time to learn how to use Google Analytics, I recommend you upgrade from Get Clicky.

Google Webmaster Tools (http://goo.gl/JkGqv) - This is a set of tools built to help webmasters. It is also a route by which Google can send you messages via email if there are any problems or other things you should know about regarding your website.

Please leave a review on Amazon

If you enjoyed this book, or even if you didn't, I'd love to hear your comments about it. You can leave your thoughts on the Amazon website.

If you don't feel you can leave a review, I'd really appreciate it if you could click the Like button, and click some of the tags on the page (or add your own). They are found near the bottom of the page and will help other people find the book when searching Amazon.

The Book on Amazon by searching for **B009ZVO3H6**

WordPress SEO

How to SEO Your WordPress Site

By Dr. Andy Williams

ezSEONews.com
CreatingFatContent.com

Version 1.0

Introduction

Search Engine Optimization (SEO), is the process webmasters go through to encourage the search engines to rank their pages higher in the search results. Typically it involves working on the site itself. This is called on-site SEO, but it also involves working at site promotion, and that is what's known as off-site SEO.

Sites can be built in a number of different ways (PHP, HTML, Flash, etc.), using a wide variety of site-building tools, with common examples being Dreamweaver, Drupal, and WordPress, to name just three. Most websites and blogs share certain features that we can control, and use, to help with the on-site SEO. These features include things like the page title, headlines, body text, ALT tags and so on. In this respect, most sites can be treated in a similar manner when we consider on-site SEO. However, different platforms have their own quirks, and WordPress is no exception. Out-of-the-box WordPress doesn't do itself any SEO favours, and can in fact cause you ranking problems. This book will concentrate specifically for the on-page SEO of WordPress sites, highlighting the problems, and working through the numerous fixes.

By the end of this book, your WordPress site should be well optimized, without being 'over-optimized' (which is itself a contributing factor in Google penalties).

1. The Biggest Sin - Duplicate Content

One of the main considerations when working on a WordPress site is duplicate content. For example, every post you create will also be posted on several other web pages within the site. Whether that post is shown in its entirety on all these pages, or as a shorter 'excerpt', is often controlled by the site's theme. Some themes will let you choose, whereas others will not.

So What Does This Mean to You, the SEO?

When a post is made on a WordPress, it may be published on all of the following web pages on that website, and at the same time:

1. Homepage
2. Post page. Every post is given its own web page.
3. Category page(s). Posts are assigned categories, and the category pages show all posts in that particular category.
4. Date archive page(s). These are pages that show all the posts made on a given date.
5. Tag page(s). Tag pages are another way of organizing your content. You can assign several words or phrases to each post, and for every word or phrase, a tag page is created. These tag pages show all posts that have been tagged with the specific word. Therefore if you used a tag 'blue widget' on five posts, the blue widget tag page will show all five posts.
6. Author page. This is an archive showing all of the posts made by a particular author.

That's six areas where the exact same post may show up!

If you assign just one category to a post, and one tag phrase, that means each post could appear on six web pages of the site **AT THE SAME TIME**. While I recommend you only assign a single post to just one category, tags are different. If you use tags, I'd recommend 3-5 per post. That would take the count up to nine or 10 pages showing identical content.

This type of duplication is bad (very bad!)

So the general rule that I recommend is to only include the 'full post' on ONE webpage of your site. On any other page where that post appears, you should be using excerpts, or in some cases just the title.

Having a high level of control is vital to removing this type of duplication, and the process begins by choosing a good template. The template should allow you to specify what you want posted on each of those six areas of potential duplication. I will therefore look at themes shortly, and explain what you need to look for when choosing a theme of your own.

First though, we should mention web hosting.

2. WordPress Web Hosting

OK, so you may be wondering why I am talking about web hosts. After all, isn't this supposed to be a book about WordPress SEO?

Yes, it is. However, the speed at which your site loads (and even the uptime of your site), are factors that are taken into account by search engines. Slow loading websites, or those which are unavailable for long periods of time (because the host server is down), suffer poorer rankings because of it. Sites which go down frequently, negatively impact the reputation you have with your visitors too.

There are many types of webhost, and lots of different plans that come with each one. You can get shared hosting, a managed or unmanaged Virtual Private Server (VPS), or a Dedicated Server. There are even some hosts that specialize in WordPress site hosting (although not all that advertise 'WordPress hosting' are setup specifically for it). I also know of one host that specializes in hosting WordPress sites that is built with the Genesis WordPress theme.

So which should you go for?

Well, that will depend on how much money you have available for your hosting. If you have a good budget, I would recommend going with a true 'WordPress optimized' web host. Here are two of the better known options:

1. WPEngine
2. WebSynthesis - This is hosting specifically designed for StudioPress themes (Genesis Framework), which we will look at in the next section of this book.

Links to both of these can be found on the book resource page here:

http://ezseonews.com/wpseo

If you visit those hosts, you'll notice that they are quite pricey, starting at $27/$29 per month for a single website. I have never used these personally, so cannot comment on their reliability. I do suggest you read the small print though, for whatever hosting package you decide to go with. The first host listed above has a price of $29 per month, but that only allows you 25,000 visitors a month in traffic. That is less than 850 visits a day, and for big, popular sites would be a problem.

2.1. Shared Hosting & Dedicated Servers

Most hosts offer a wide range of packages, from simple shared hosting, to dedicated servers (where you basically are given a computer and told to get on with it).

Dedicated servers, and unmanaged VPS hosting, both require a certain level of technical know-how, so I don't recommend you consider those unless you are technically capable.

For most people, shared hosting will be the best option because of the lower costs, especially for new sites. However, shared hosting is generally the most unreliable in terms of uptime and server response times (how long the server takes to respond to a request to show your web page).

As you look for a host, if you know of a website that is hosted with a particular company, I suggest you sign up for a free (or paid), account at Monitis.com and setup a 'monitor' to check the site every 5 minutes for response time. This will give you a good idea of how reliable that hosting company actually is.

See http://ezseonews.com/wpseo

Two of the most popular shared hosting companies are Hostgator and Bluehost. I have tried both, and until recently, Hostgator was the one I would have recommended. However, they have since 'upgraded' the server I was on, and uptime and response times plummeted as a result. Here is a screenshot from Monitis showing the details for one of my Hostgator hosted websites:

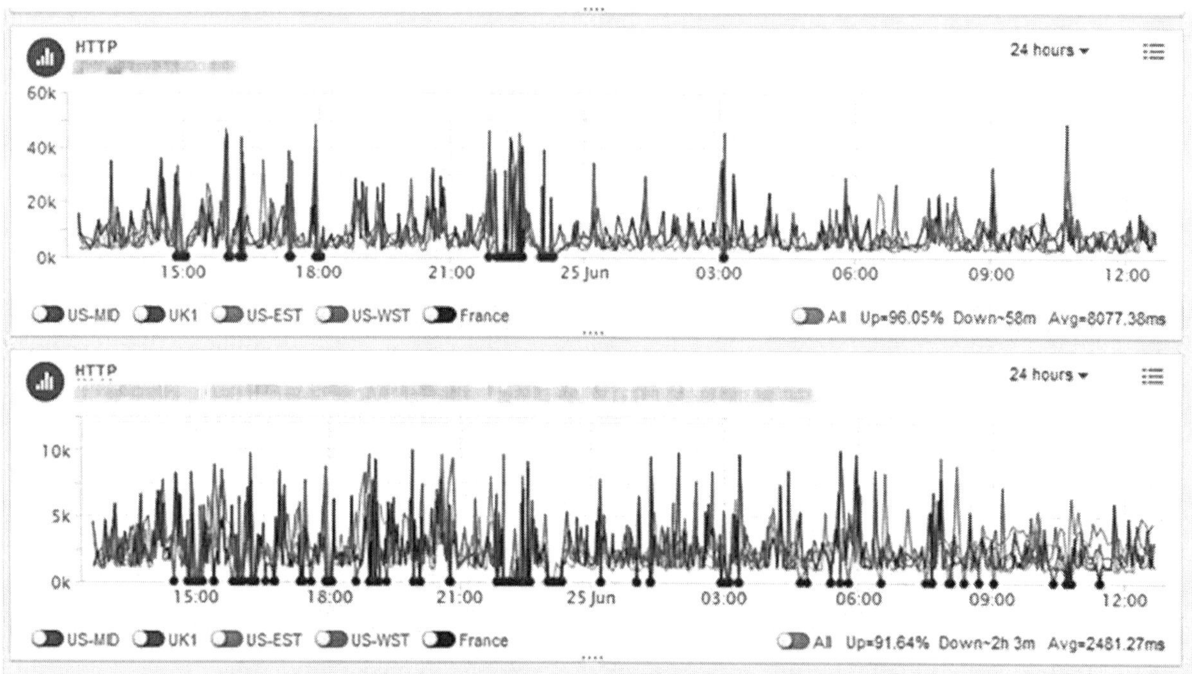

Look at all those peaks (these indicate when the server took longer to respond), and the small circular dots on the baseline (where the server did not respond).

The top graph is the homepage of the site. Over a 24 hour period, the homepage was down for 58 minutes, and the server response time was over eight seconds! That means it took eight seconds on average (although there are a lot of peaks over 40 seconds), to connect to my server, and that's even before the webpage started to download.

The lower graph is an internal page on the same site. This page gets less traffic so should have better response times - which it does - at around 2.5 seconds. However, that page was down for over two hours in the previous 24 hours.

I moved this site from Hostgator to Bluehost, but I found Bluehost to be just as unreliable. I guess Hostgator and Bluehost (being two of the most popular shared hosting companies); have suffered because of their own success.

I eventually found a host that I am happy with. They are called StableHost (http://ezseonews.com/stablehostreview).

StableHost offers free CDN with their hosting (which basically means your site is served from a network of servers around the globe). My site is hosted on their 'En-Basic' Enterprise hosting package, costing $19.95 per month at the time or writing. I have enabled CDN on the site (which only takes two minutes to setup), and here is the data from Monitis for the last 24 hours.

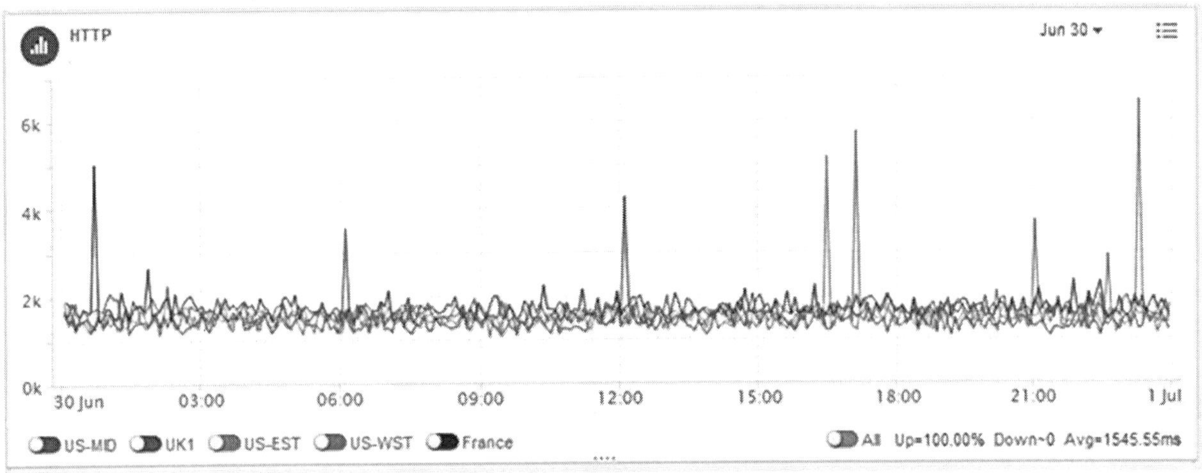

That's 100% uptime and a response time of around 1.5 seconds.

An inner page:

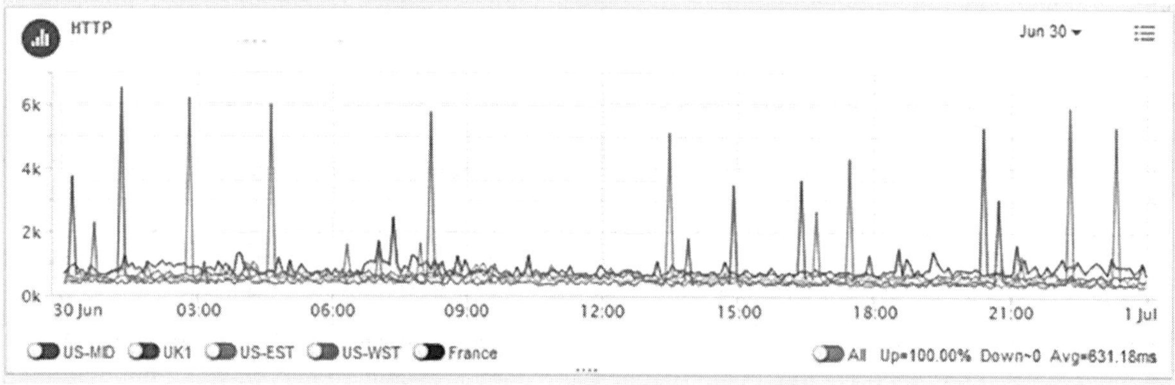

The inner page was down for one minute, and response time was 0.65 seconds.

You'll notice that there were far fewer peaks in response times on StableHost, and when there were peaks, it was a maximum of around 6 seconds, compared to the 40+ second peaks on Hostgator.

What all of this shows you, I hope, is that not all hosts are equal. If you want reliable hosting, go for the best that you can afford (and remember price does not necessarily correlate with quality). My order of choice would be:

1. WPEngine OR WebSynthesis.
2. Enterprise level hosting on StableHost, using CDN. http://ezseonews.com/stablehostreview
3. Shared hosting, but buyer-beware!

3. Themes & Theme Settings

There are lots of great themes out there, many of them are free. However, I don't generally recommend free themes, and here's why:

- They may not get updated.
- Some might include malicious code.
- A number of them contain footer links back to the creator's website (or any website they choose), which is really bad for SEO.
- They could be poorly written, and therefore slow to load.

There is one free theme that seems to have a huge following though, and is therefore updated regularly. It's called Atahualpa.

http://wordpress.org/themes/atahualpa

If you want to go down the free route, this is a good one to choose.

I have two recommended commercial themes for WordPress:

1. Genesis
2. Thesis
   Both of these can be found at http://ezseonews.com/wpseo

Both of these are 'frameworks'. Essentially a framework powers your WordPress site, and you change the appearance of your site by installing child themes, or skins that work with the framework.

Both Genesis and Thesis are excellent choices, though it has to be said that there is more of a learning curve with Thesis. For this reason, I recommend Genesis to my own students, and use it on *all* of my own sites. It's highly customizable, there are lots of child themes to choose from, and I can completely control the duplication issues that WordPress causes (see chapter one if you need to recap).

If you want to use a different theme, here is a five point checklist to help you decide:

1. Theme is fast loading.
2. Theme allows you to control how posts appear on all of the six 'potential duplication areas' of your site that we looked at earlier. You should have the options of full post, excerpt, or just the title.
3. Theme has at least one sidebar.
4. Theme allows one (or two) menus at the top of the website.
5. The theme does not include any mandatory links or attributions in the footer.

Points 2-5 can be answered by the theme's support desk. What about the first point though? How can you tell the load speed of a website, and check for potential problems with a template? You'll be pleased to know that this can be done quickly and simply.

For this we can use a free service at GTMetrix.com

GTMetrix allows you to analyse the page load times of any web page you want.

Find a site that uses the theme you are interested in using, and enter the URL of that site into GTMetrix. This tool then breaks down the page load speed into elements, and tells you exactly how long each element takes to load.

First the summary:

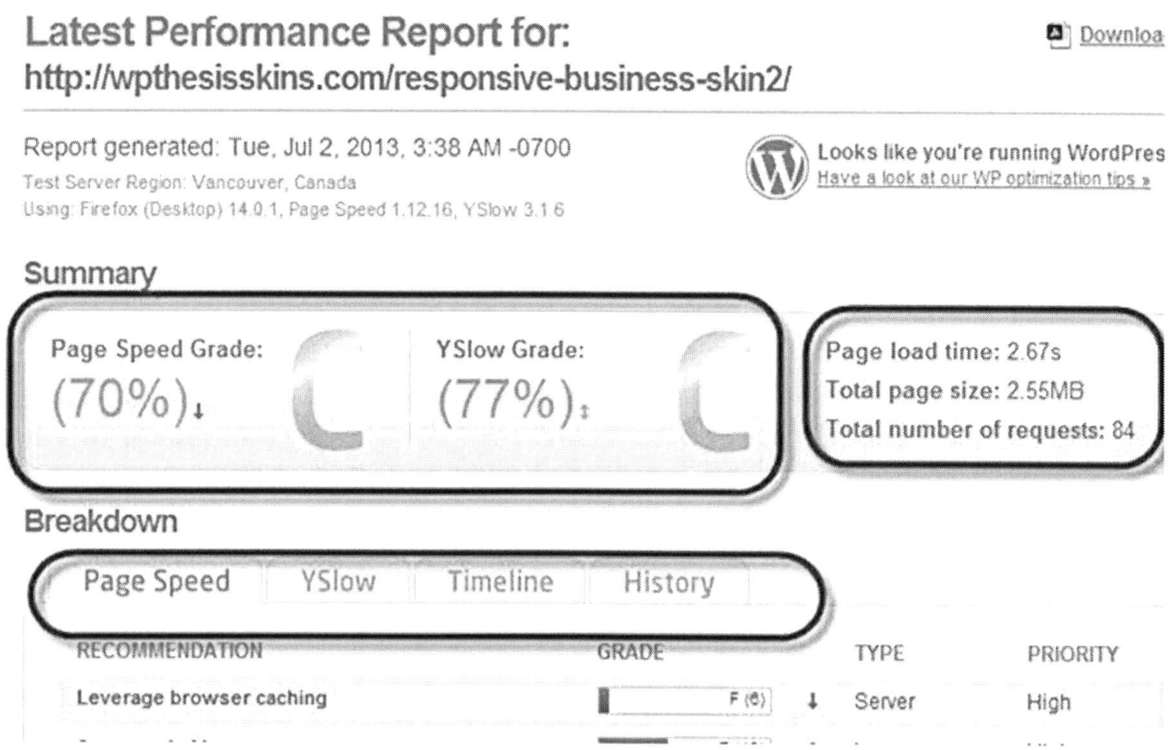

The summary gives you an A, B, or C rating of the page speed. You also get to see the page load time in seconds, the total page size, and the number of requests that were needed to download the page.

You should be looking for A or B ratings.

Under the main summary are 4 tabs: Page Speed, YSlow, Timeline, and History. The Page Speed and YSlow tabs offer advice on how to speed up the website. Click on any entry in these tables for an expanded view that shows you specifically what you need to do to fix an issue.

The timeline tab offers an interesting view of the page load speed. It tells you exactly how long each element on the page took to load. This is where you can get information on any 'theme-specific' problems.

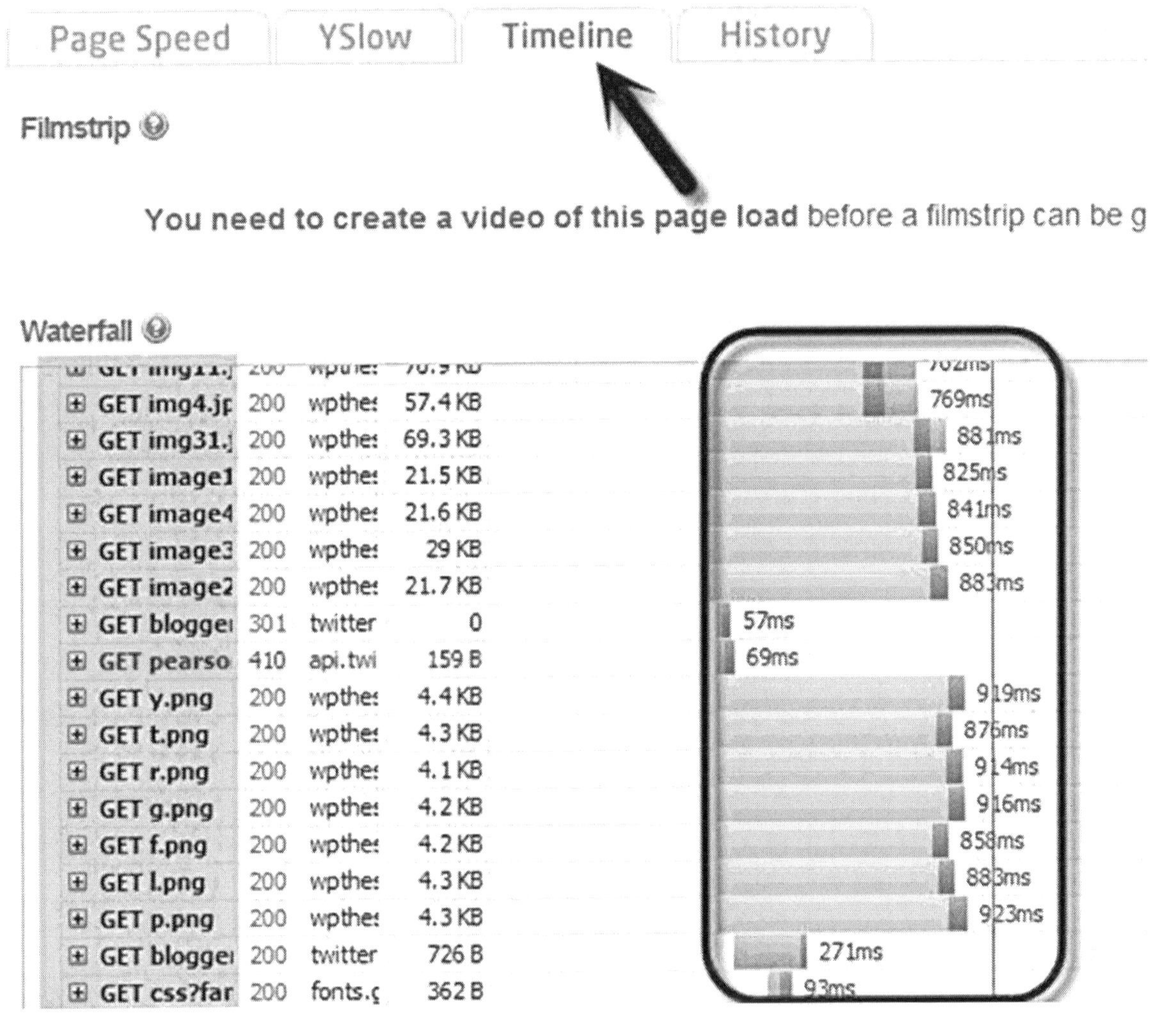

On the right hand side you can see the times taken to load each element. The timings are in milliseconds (1000ms equals one second).

On the left hand side you get a list of the page elements. If you move your mouse over an element, it will expand to show you the full URL of that component. For example, the element below took over half a second to load:

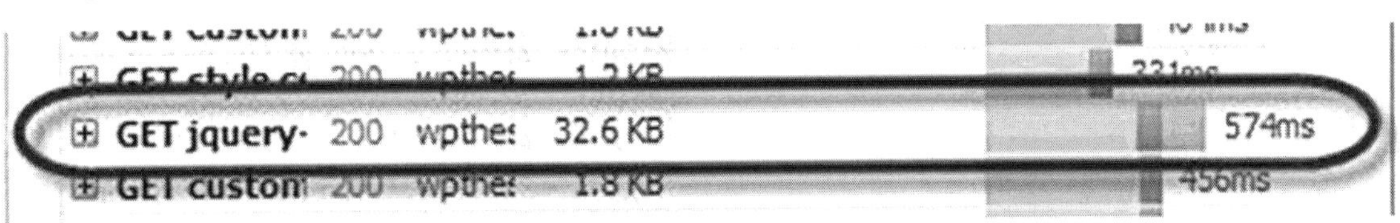

When I place my mouse over the element to check what it is, I see this:

In this case, it tells me that the element is related to the theme.

By looking for slow loading elements on the page, and checking whether they are related to the theme you want to use, you can make judgments on the how well that theme is optimized.

TIP: You will find that a lot of the slower loading elements on a page are images. Some images are related to the theme, whereas others are not – they are merely images added to a post. Don't worry about any slow loading image if it is not part of the theme.

Also, look for any element that has a large file size as these take longer to download. Here are a few in the theme I am testing:

The images of the demo theme are 1024 pixels by 485 pixels on their server. So the theme needs large images if you want to use its Slideshow feature. This means you will have physically large image files as well, although you could most probably reduce their size in KB using various techniques.

NOTE: If you use the Chrome Browser, you can install an extension called 'PageSpeed' (by Google). This will give you a measurement of how fast the site loads. Anything over 85 is considered a good score.

Here is the PageSpeed score for the same theme demo site shown in the GTMetrix example above:

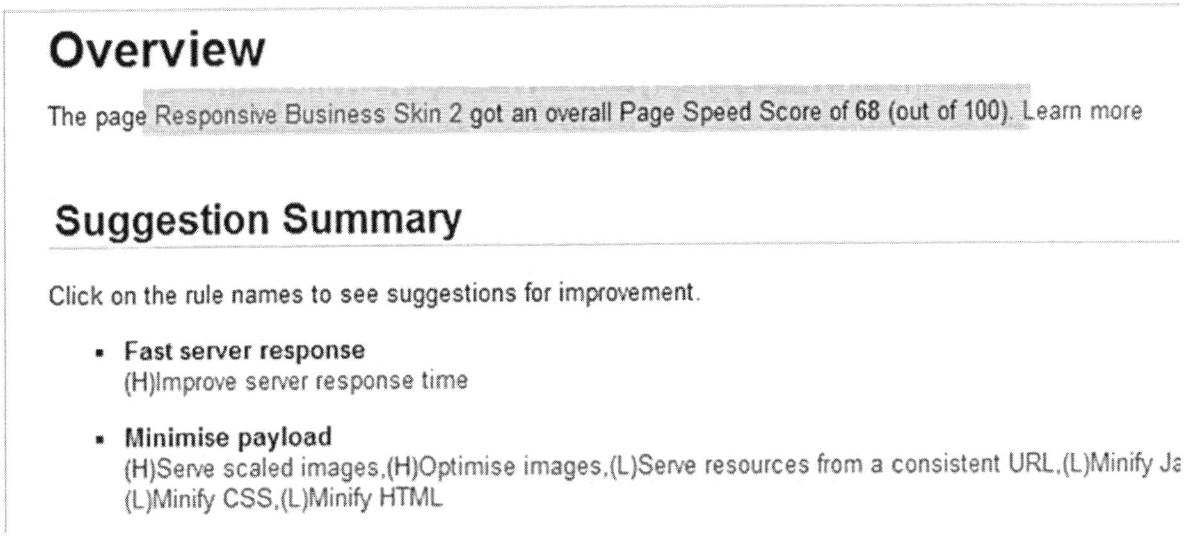

One final thing to be mindful of is that it's unlikely the demo sites set up by theme vendors use caching plugins, or a content delivery network (CDN). That means the speeds you see with tools like this will probably be faster once it is setup on your server and properly optimized. With this in mind, don't concentrate too much on the page load times reported, and instead, look for large files that the theme uses, as these may cause speed problems on *any* server.

Hopefully you have seen that choosing a theme is not just as simple as finding one that looks good and using it. You need to make sure it will load fast too, and not contribute to longer loading times, especially if you go with cheaper, shared hosting.

For the rest of this book, I am going to be using the Genesis theme framework for most examples. If you haven't chosen a theme yet, or want my recommendation, go with the Genesis framework, and choose one of the child themes that you like.

If you are already using a different theme, don't worry, you can still follow along with all of the SEO advice given in this book.

3.1. Installing a Genesis Child Theme

This is a three step process:

1. Install the Genesis Framework.
2. Install the child theme.
3. Activate the **child theme**.

That's all there is to it.

The Genesis framework is needed by the child theme, so needs to remain installed on your server.

Once you have your child theme installed and activated, I recommend you **uninstall** all other themes that may be in your WordPress Dashboard. The reason for this is that old themes can often be routes taken by hackers to gain access to your site. We really don't want to give them that chance! So delete all themes (and plugins), that you are not using.

4. Google Tools

Google offer some great tools to webmaster, for free. I use them, and I recommend you do too. The three I am specifically referring to are Google Webmaster Tools, Google Analytics and Google authorship.

4.1 Google Webmaster Tools

Why should you use Google Webmaster Tools (GWT)?

Here are some good reasons:

- Get notified by Google if there is a problem with your site. Google will send you messages if, for example, your backlink profile looks spammy, or if your site is using an old version of WordPress, etc. They will also notify you if they detect malware on your website.
- Discover any HTML problems with your site. You can then follow the suggestions that GWT gives you to resolve the issue(s).
- Submit and check your sitemap (which can speed up indexing of your website).
- Select a geographic target audience. For example, if your website targets UK customers, but your site uses a .com extension, you can use GWT to tell Google that you want your site to be given more consideration in the UK.
- Check how well your site is being indexed by Google.
- Identify crawl errors. Google will tell you the URLs that it had trouble crawling, and the page which linked to that URL, thus allowing you to quickly identify and fix broken links on your site.
- Request Google removes specific URLs from their search results.
- Get a complete list of all links that point to your website (at least the ones that Google knows about). This can be very useful, especially in identifying links from spammy sites, which you can then disavow with the Google Disavow tool.
- Identify keywords that people are using to find your site. Google shows you the number of impressions in the search engines, how many clicks you got, the click through rate (CTR), and average position in the SERPs (Search Engine Results Pages). The CTR can be very useful for finding pages that may need their title/description tweaked so as to try and improve the CTR.

GWT offers a useful set of tools for all webmasters. I highly recommend you sign up and add your website(s) to your account, so you can track them all.

Sign up here: http://bit.ly/oGe6PP

4.2 Google Analytics

Google Analytics is a free visitor tracking tool, which is far more powerful than many commercial tools that are available.

Reasons to use Google Analytics (GA) include:

- See details of your visitors, like the search term they used to find your site, how long they spent on your site, which browser they use, what country they come from, and so on.
- Get real time statistics, showing how many people are on your site right now, and which pages they are viewing, etc.
- Connect your Google Analytics account to your GWT account, and Google AdSense account, for even more tracking features.
- Split-test different versions of, for example, a sales page.
- Set up custom alerts, to notify you about the things that are important to your business.
- Monitor mobile traffic.
- Lots of other features...

Sign up here: http://www.google.com/analytics/

Once you have signed up for Google Analytics and registered your site with them, you'll be given some tracking code to insert into your website. Whichever theme you use, you should have an easy way to insert your analytics code. Here is a screenshot for the Genesis theme (**Genesis -> Theme Settings** menu):

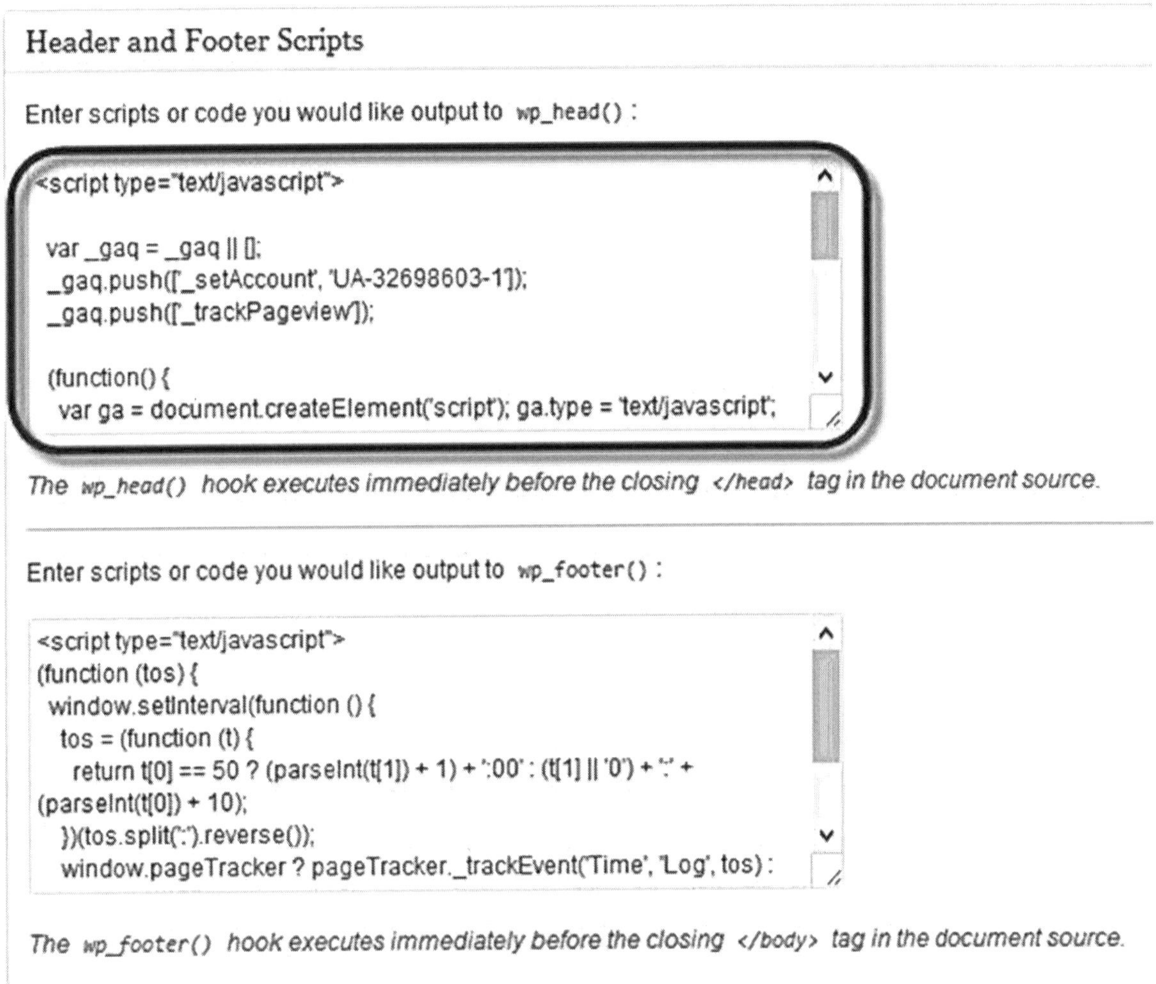

If possible, insert the analytics code into the wp_head() section of your website.

There are some known issues with Google Analytics and the way it reports 'time on site' and 'bounce rate'. For that reason, I have also inserted another script into the wp_footer() area of my theme (see screenshot above). You can read more about these issues, and grab the code yourself here:

http://bit.ly/KbUvs9

4.3 Google Authorship

Google authorship is not so much a tool, as something you setup between your website and your Google plus profile. By linking your website content to your Google Plus profile, you get these three benefits:

1. Tell Google that you are the author of the content. If someone then steals your work and reposts it on another site, Google knows that you were the true, original author.

2. You can have your Gravatar image (globally recognized avatar), show up next to your content in the search results, which in turn can add social proof to your listing, and increase click through rates (CTR).
3. Build Author Rank. This is thought to be an increasingly important ranking factor. The more Google trust an author, the higher they will rank that author's work.

We will revisit Google authorship later in the book, and I'll show you how to set it up so that the posts on your site (and on guest blogs), are assigned to you.

5. Screen Options

The WordPress Dashboard has some settings hidden away in the top right corner of its screen. You should see the link to **Screen Options**, and they control what you see on the screen when you are moving around the dashboard. The screen options are a series of checkboxes which you can check or uncheck depending on what you want displayed.

These screen options change depending on where you are in the dashboard. For example, if you are editing a post, the screen options will be specific to that task:

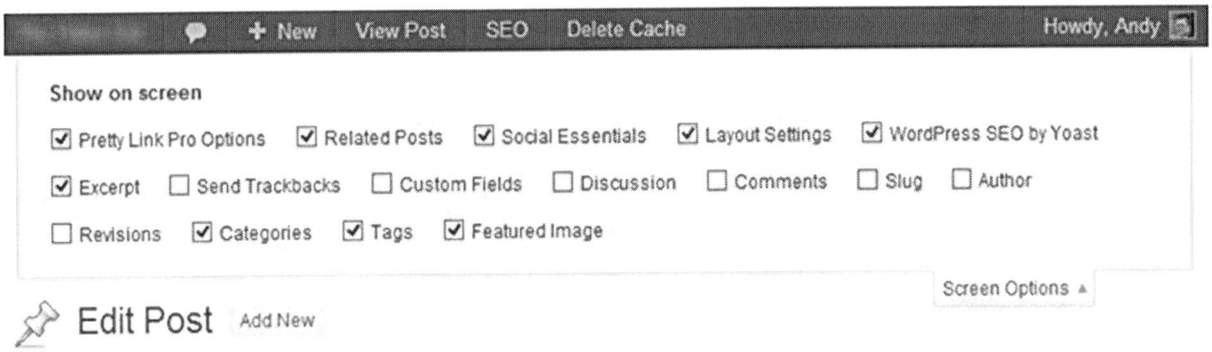

If there is something you do not use, you can uncheck it and it disappears from your dashboard, helping to reduce any unnecessary clutter.

As another example, here are the screen options when editing the settings of the YARPP WordPress plugin (which we will look at later):

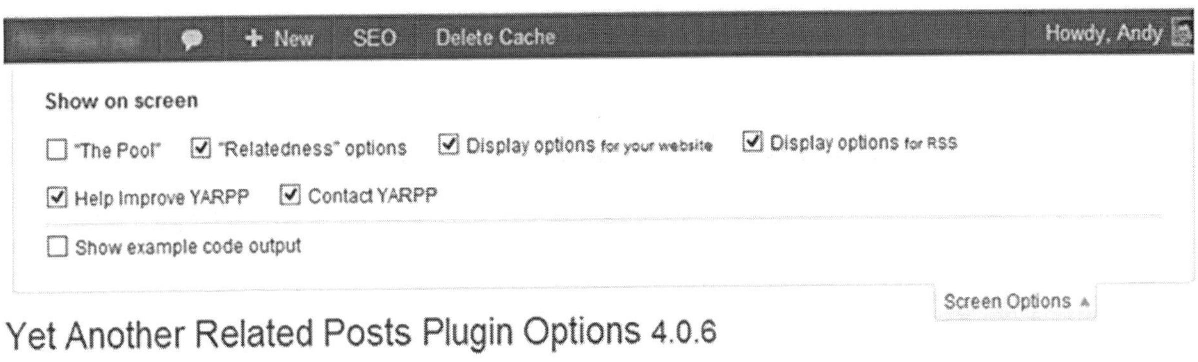

If you are ever looking for something mentioned in this book, or any other, but don't see it in your dashboard, then check the screen options. There's a good chance you have that particular box unchecked.

6. WordPress Settings Menu

During the initial setup of a WordPress site, it's a good idea to go through the Settings menu first to make sure everything is set up properly. You will find this settings menu in the left sidebar of your Dashboard. Mouse-over the word 'Settings' and a popup menu will appear displaying the options. Click on the word 'Settings' and that menu integrates into the sidebar, below the main Settings heading:

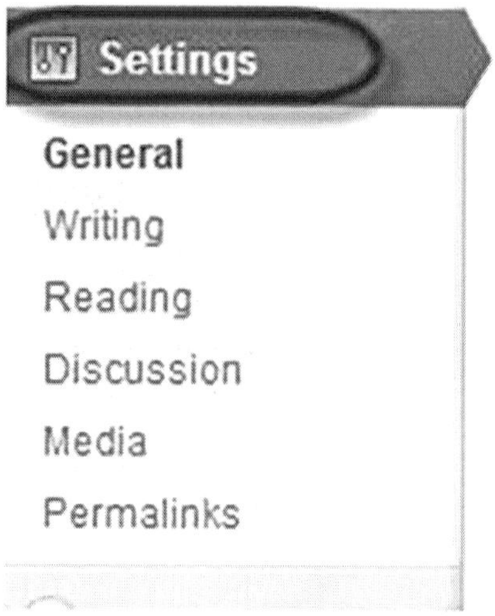

Once we install a few plugins later on, there will be more items in the Settings menu, but we'll deal with those as and when we get to them.

Note that I will only be covering the settings that are specifically related to good SEO.

6.1. General Settings

Site Title & Tagline

The top two items in the General settings are Site Title and Tagline. Later in the book we will look at creating a custom logo image and using that on the website, but until you create & upload that image, the Site Title and Tagline entered here will be displayed at the top of every page on your site.

DO NOT stuff keywords into the site name or tagline fields. Your site name will most probably be based on your domain name, and the tagline should be a short sentence specifying your site's goal, philosophy or slogan.

There is a good article on creating a tagline on the Copyblogger website:

http://www.copyblogger.com/create-a-tagline/

If you need help with yours, I suggest you read that.

E-mail Address

The only other setting we need to concern ourselves with on this page is the email address. This will be used by WordPress, plugins, and a free external service (Gravatar.com). We'll be looking at these later, so your email address needs to be correct.

6.2. Writing Settings

In terms of SEO, the only setting we need to change here is the **Update Services**. These are a list of web services that get notified whenever new content gets published on the site. Having a good 'ping list' will help your content get indexed quicker too.

Search Google for "WordPress ping list" and you'll find a list of sites to include. Simply copy and paste the list into the Update Services box, and then save your settings.

6.3. Reading Settings

Latest posts vs. static page

At the top of the Reading Settings is the **Front page displays:**

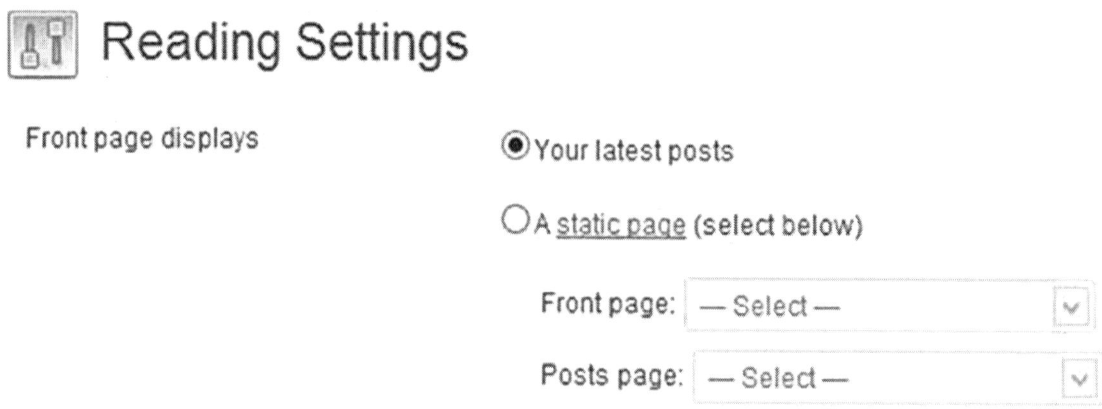

This will tell WordPress which if the two options to use for the homepage on your site. You can select:

1. **Your latest posts**
2. **A static page**

If you want to have a static page as your homepage, i.e., an article that does not change, you can create that article as a WordPress 'Page', and then select that page here to use as the homepage (front page).

In this book, we will be using a Genesis theme, and the home pages in Genesis are widgetized. If you're not sure what that means, don't worry. Just realise that it's good, and we'll look into it later in the Homepage section of this book. To take advantage of this fantastic Genesis homepage feature, you need to leave the settings here to show 'Your latest posts' on the front page (which is the default setting).

Next up on the Reading Settings is deciding how many posts to display on the homepage and archive pages (like category page, author page, etc), and decide what information is shown in RSS feeds (something WordPress generates for your site).

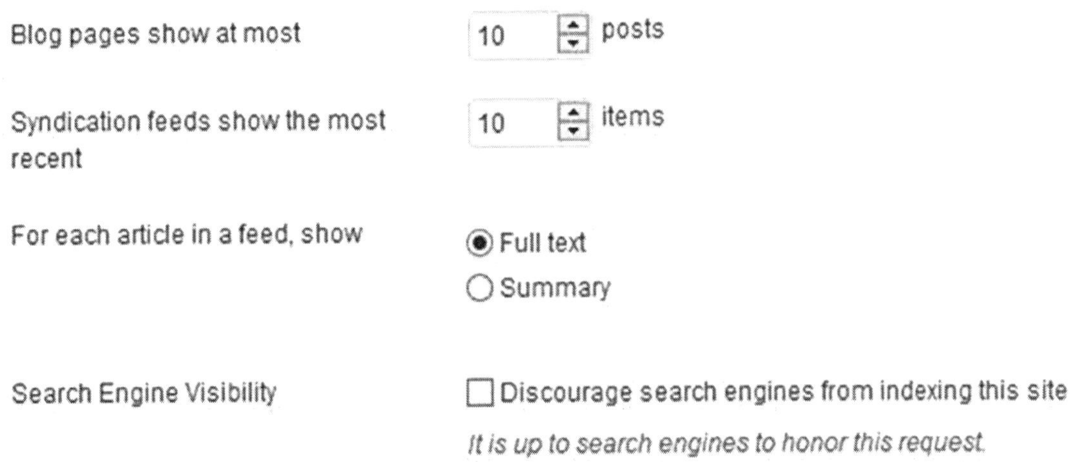

The default setting is 10, which means WordPress will show 10 posts on the homepage, 10 on the category pages, and 10 on the author page, etc. If there are more than 10 posts to show, then the remainder will be added, in batches of 10, to additional pages, and you'll get a next/previous type navigation to move between them.

I would recommend you leave the '**Blog pages show at most**' set to 10.

Beneath that is the '**Syndication feeds show the most recent**' option.

WordPress creates RSS feeds for your site (see my WordPress for Beginners book if you want to read more on this - http://www.amazon.com/dp/B009ZVO3H6). Your site will have a main feed, plus there will be feeds for category pages, tag pages, and so on. This setting tells WordPress how many items to include in the feed. With Google's Penguin algorithm looking at the over-optimization of inbound links, I'd limit the RSS feed to a maximum of 10. In the past, webmasters have included 100 items (or more), and that would mean any site that is displaying your RSS feed will contain 100 links back to it. Before Google Penguin, that was OK, but not now. So I would suggest leaving this number set at 10.

You now have to decide what the feed contains, i.e., all the content of your posts, or just a summary of them. Select '**Summary**' because otherwise you are making if far too easy for scraper software tools to copy (steal), your content. These software tools monitor RSS feeds and strip the content out. Your content is then likely to be posted on one or more spammy sites around the internet, and that's not good.

Later in this book we will look at Google Authorship, and one reason I recommend you use this is to tell Google that you are the author of the content. Essentially, when it's set up, any new posts you add to your site will automatically be tagged in Google with you as the author. Then if someone does steal your work, Google knows who the real author/owner is, and rewards you in its search results pages.

The final option on this page is '**Search Engine Visibility**'. When some people develop a website, they want it to be finished before the search engines come to spider the site. This option allows you to do just that. By checking the box, your website will basically tell the search engines to ignore it until you decide the time is right, and uncheck this option.

I recommend you leave this box unchecked from the start, that's unless you have good reason to not want the content indexed as you create it. As I add content to a website, I *want* Google to find and index it as soon as possible. If they see new content being added over a short period of time, they'll know the site is under construction and needs to be spidered more regularly so as to keep their index up to date. By leaving this option unchecked, you are encouraging the search engine spiders to crawl your site, and that's a good thing.

6.4 Discussion Settings

The Discussion Settings refer to the commenting system built into WordPress.

Google likes to see visitor interaction on a website, so this is an important part of your WordPress SEO, and so you'll want to keep the comments enabled.

At the top of these settings, you will see:

These boxes should all be left checked.

The first option means WordPress will try to send a notification to any blog you link to in your posts. This lets a site owner know you have linked to them, and can sometimes result in a link back.

The second option is the first one in reverse. If someone links to your site, then WordPress will notify you so that you can see who's linking to you. This has been abused by spammers and you will get a lot of false positives here, but you'll still get these even if you disable this option.

The final option simply tells WordPress to allow visitors to comment on your posts. This is what we want - visitor participation.

The '**Other comment settings**' section has a few more options:

Check the first box so that anyone leaving a comment must enter a name and an email address.

The second box should be unchecked unless you are creating some kind of membership site where people need to register in order to participate.

Leave the third box unchecked too, unless there is a reason why you want to close comments on older posts. I personally like to keep comments open indefinitely, and if there is a post where I want to close them, I can do that in the 'Edit Post' screen, just for that one post.

The fourth checkbox will enable nested comments. This is something that not only makes the comments look better, but more intuitive for your visitors. This is because replies to a specific comment will be nested under the original, and this in turn makes following the conversation much easier.

The next option allows you to spread comments across pages once you get over a certain number of remarks on the main post page. This is a good idea if your site gets a lot of comments, because the more you have, the longer the page will take to load. If you anticipate a lot of comments, enable this option. You can also specify here whether you want comments to be shown with the oldest or newest first. I personally think it makes more sense to have older comments at the top. That way, the comments are chronological, but this is a personal preference.

Next on this page is the '**E-mail me whenever**' settings. Do you want to be notified when someone comments on a post? If so, make sure that option is checked. I recommend you check this so that you get instant notifications of any new comments posted on your site. This means you get to reply quickly. Fast responses to comments are important, and it makes the visitor feel that you care. Practising good interaction means there's a much better chance the commenter will come back and visit your site again.

The second email option is to notify you when a comment is held for moderation. You can uncheck this, because in a moment we will tell WordPress to hold ALL comments for moderation, and we are already getting notified every time someone posts a comment anyway.

In the '**Before a comment appears**' section, check the first box, and uncheck the second.

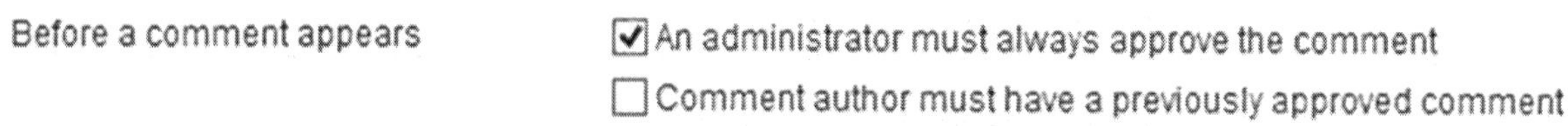

This will force ALL comments to appear in a moderation queue, and will only go live on your site once you approve them.

This means the next couple of settings in the '**Comment Moderation**' section are irrelevant, since ALL comments are now held for moderation. We can therefore ignore that section.

NOTE: Moderating comments might sound like a lot of work, but it is essential. If you have your site set up to auto-approve comments, you pages will end up full of spam remarks, and all kinds of gobbledegook. Needless to say that would take a lot more time cleaning up than moderating comments.

The '**Comment Blacklist**' is a good way to fight spam. You can include email addresses, IP addresses, and certain words in the box. If a comment matches any of those lines, it is automatically marked as spam. If I end up getting a lot of spam comments from a particular IP address, I usually add that to this list as well.

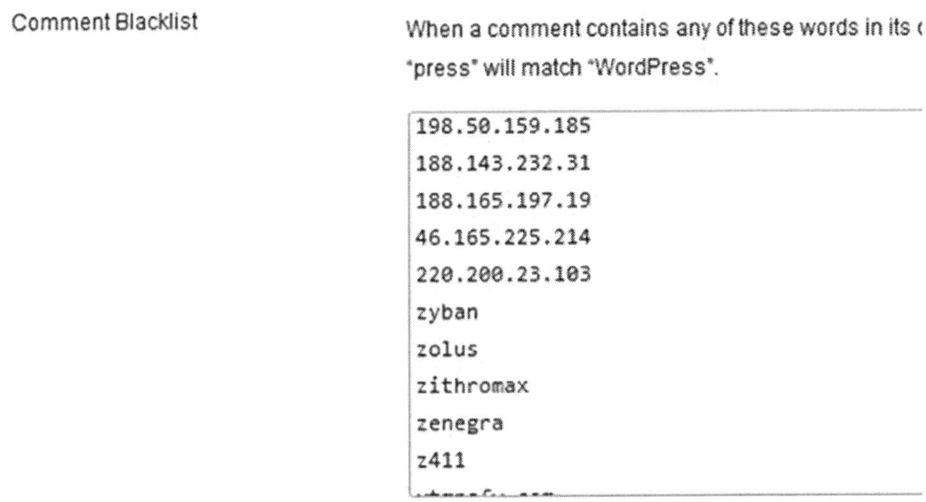

You can also search Google for a “WordPress comment blacklist” which will get you started. Just add one item per line, and save your changes when done.

The final section on the Discussion Settings relates to the use of “Avatars”.

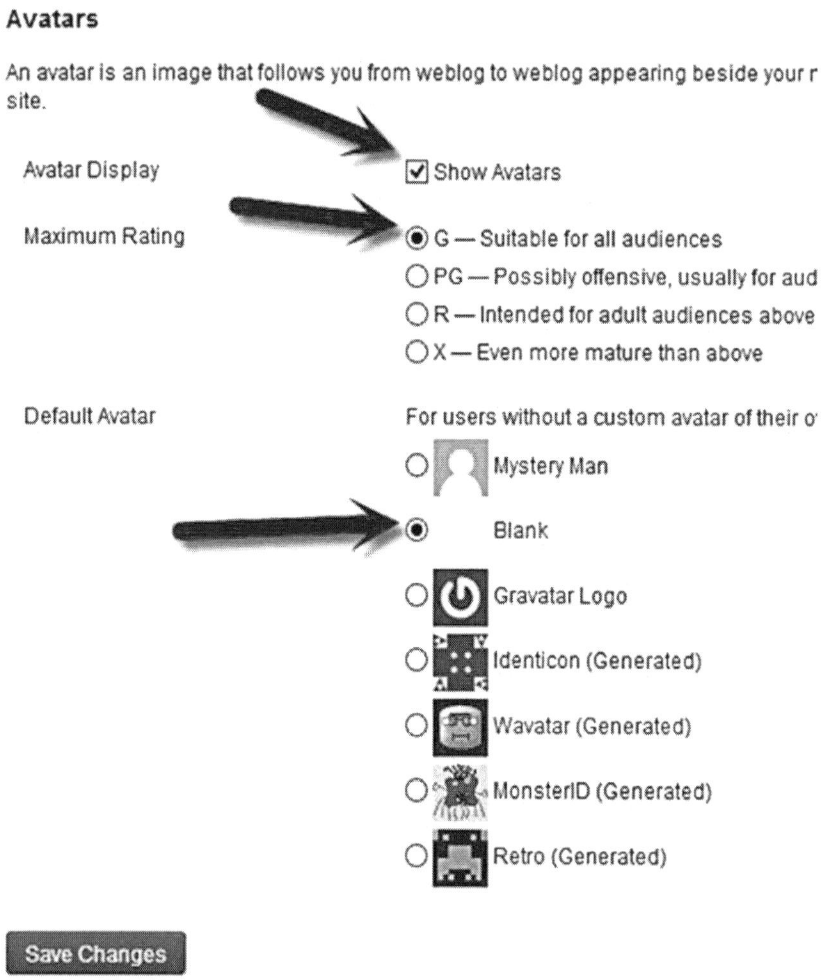

An Avatar is a small image of the author. If the author of a comment has a Gravatar (http://gravatar.com/) assigned to the email address, and they use that same email to leave a comment, then that Gravatar is shown as their avatar.

I recommend you check '**Show Avatars**'. I think this helps the comment section become more active, since visitors to your site can see little photos of real people leaving remarks. Site visitors like to know who they are dealing with, a face behind the name as it were, so these images help instil confidence and help gain site credibility.

I would recommend you check the 'G' rating, so the avatars on your site should be suitable viewing for all ages.

Also, select '**Blank**' for the default avatar. Avatars take time to load, thus increasing the page load time. With blank selected, if a person does not have a Gravatar setup, no image is loaded for that person.

6.5. Media Settings

While the settings here allow us to determine the maximum sizes of images in posts, I recommend you do that manually on a post by post basis at the time you create them. Therefore, there are no specific settings in the Media Settings section that we need to change for SEO purposes.

6.6 Permalinks Settings

The Permalink settings are important, because whatever you enter here will influence the way the URLs are displayed for the pages on your website.

The default WordPress setting will produce URLs like this:

Mydomain.com/?p=123

The '**?p=123**' parameter in this URL is simply a call for the page with Page ID = 123. This is not very useful for visitors, it looks ugly, and it's certainly not helpful to search engines.

A lot of people will use the 'post name' option, which uses the post title in the URL. Actually it uses the post 'slug' which is the portion of the URL that represents the post. But by default that will be the post title unless you change it. For example, if you had a post called 'Liverpool win in Istanbul', then the URL for that post would look like this:

Mydomain.com/Liverpool-win-in-istanbul

Note that capitals are stripped out, as well as some other characters like apostrophes.

There is a problem that I read about with this permalink structure. Basically, as the site gets larger, WordPress struggles to locate the post if it only has the post 'slug' (filename), to go on. It therefore takes longer to load pages. In order to fix this problem, you need to add in either the page ID, or the category into the permalink. I actually recommend you use a permalink that contains the category anyway, so even if this wasn't an issue with the latest WordPress, I'd still recommend you choose '**Custom Structure**' and enter the following as your permalink structure:

/%category%/%postname%/

Here it is in my settings:

Now the URL of any page will include the category and filename of the post. A typical URL for a post might look like this:

Mydomain.com/dog-breeds/alsatians

So in this case, the post filename is 'Alsatians', and the post is in the 'dog breeds' category.

IMPORTANT:

With Google's Panda and Penguin looking for what Google calls 'webspam', we need to be very careful about choosing the correct category names for our site, especially if we are including the category in the URL.

For example, if your site is called mydietreviews.com, and you had a category called 'diets', then a URL might look like this:

my**diet**reviews.com/**diets**/hollywood-**diet**/

This URL has the word 'diet' in it three times. That could well be seen as keyword stuffing and should be avoided. If you think that this type of situation will arise on your site with the categories you have chosen, then play it safe and use this alternative permalink:

/%post_id%/%postname%/

Post_id is replaced with the ID of the post (basically an integer number that is assigned to a post at the time you publish it). Your URL may then look like:

my**diet**reviews.com/1045/hollywood-**diet**/

A URL like this appears is a little less spammy, yet includes the page_id which helps WordPress locate the page faster.

At the bottom of the common settings, there are some optional choices:

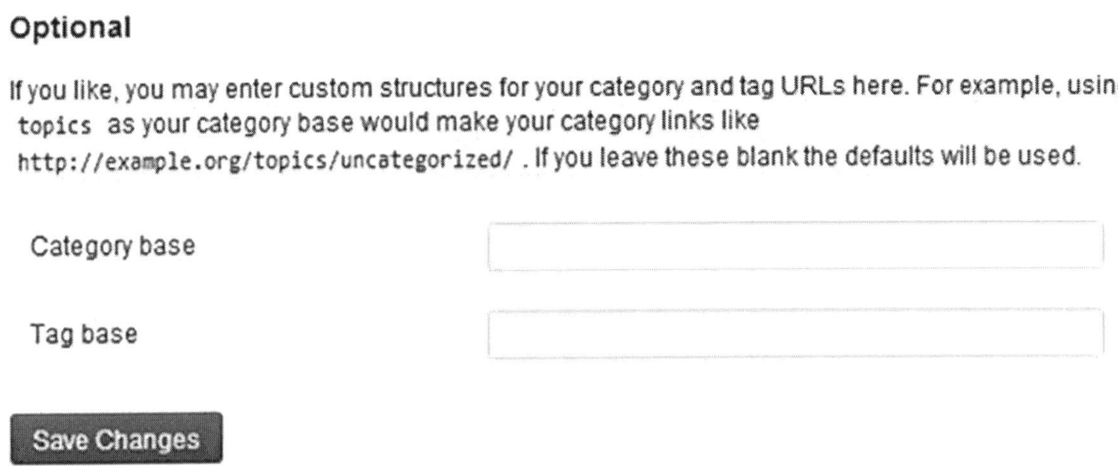

To understand what these options do, I need to tell you how WordPress assigns the URL for category pages and tag pages. Essentially, every category page will have the word 'category' in the URL, and every tag page will have the word 'tag' in the URL. Therefore, using the examples above, the category page URL would look like this:

mydietreviews.com/**category**/diets/

This category page will then show all the posts in the diets category.

Similarly, a tag page URL would look something like this:

mydietreviews.com/tag/fat-loss/

Any posts on your site that were tagged with the term 'fat loss' would be listed on this page.

OK, back to category base and tag base settings. These will replace the word 'category' or 'tag' in these URLs, with whatever you specify here.

If you set the category base to be 'abracadabra', then the category URL would become:

mydietreviews.com/**abracadabra**/diets/

Before Panda and Penguin, category and tag bases were used to keyword stuff the URLs. Today, leave them blank as they will only get your site into trouble.

7. Plugins

Before we look at the plugins, I need to mention that many are updated frequently and their appearance can change a little as a consequence. That means the screenshots in this book may not be identical to what you are seeing in your Dashboard. Most changes are minor though, so you should still be able to set everything up properly, even if your plugin is a different version to the one that I am showing in this book.

What I am going to do in this section is get you to install certain plugins. We won't go through the configuration of each one just yet; we'll do that later in the book when we need to achieve certain SEO goals.

There are a few essential plugins to get your WordPress site ready for the search engines. I'll cover these first, and I recommend you install ALL three of them. I'll then list a few other plugins that you may find useful, and explain what they do. You can hold off installing these until you know whether you will need them or not.

To install the plugins, login to the Dashboard, and from the left side column, go to Plugins -> Add New. You will see a search box & button. Enter the plugin names in the search box as I state them below, and then install and activate each one.

7.1. Essential Plugins

1. WordPress SEO

This is a comprehensive SEO plugin that will create a self-updating sitemap and allow us fine control over the SEO of the site.

Search for "WordPress SEO".

This is the one you are looking for, by Joost de Valk:

Click the Install now link, and once installed, activate the plugin.

2. W3 Total Cache

This plugin is essential because it speeds up your website. Page load speed, as mentioned previously, is an important part of SEO. Google like fast loading pages, and once we have this plugin configured, your site should load several times faster than before.

Search for "W3 Total Cache".

This is the one you are looking for, by Frederick Townes:

W3 Total Cache Details | Install Now	0.9.2.11	★★★★☆	The only WordPress Performance Optimization (WPO) framework; designed to improve user experience and page speed. Recommended by web hosts like: Page.ly, Synthesis, DreamHost, MediaTemple, Go Daddy, Host Gator and countless more. Trusted by countless companies like: AT&T, stevesouders.com, mattcutts.com, mashable.com, smashingmagazine.com, makeuseof.com, yoast.com, kiss925.com, pearsonified.c... By Frederick Townes.

Install and activate the plugin.

3. Dynamic Widgets

The final essential plugin is called Dynamic Widgets, and this allows us to create dynamic, context-sensitive sidebars (and other elements), on our web site.

Search for "dynamic widgets", and look for this one by Qurl:

Dynamic Widgets Details | Installed	1.5.4	★★★★★	Dynamic Widgets gives you full control on which pages your widgets will appear. It lets you dynamically show or hide widgets on WordPress pages by setting conditional logic rules with just a few mouse clicks. No knowledge of PHP required. No fiddling around with conditional tags. You can set conditional rules by Role, Dates, Browser, Theme Template, Language (WPML or QTranslate), URL, for the Home... By Qurl.

Install and activate the plugin.

That's it. Those are the three essential plugins we need to setup for SEO purposes.

7.2 Non-essential Plugins

I won't be going into details on installing and configuring these plugins. I will just tell you what they do, and if you want to add them to your site, you can use the help documents that come with them should you need assistance setting them up.

Remember this though; the more plugins you install on your site, the slower it will potentially load. Therefore keep plugins to a minimum, and only use ones that you actually need.

1. WP Policies

This plugin will create a default set of 'legal' documents for your site. Things like disclaimers, terms of service, privacy page, etc. I am no lawyer, so cannot comment on how good these documents are, but they are the types of documents you need to have on your site, so I think they're better than having none.

Search for "wp policies"

2. Google XML Sitemaps for Video

If you have a lot of videos on your site, even YouTube videos, then this plugin will create a separate sitemap for them that you can submit to Google Webmaster Tools; hopefully getting better indexing rates for them. As a bonus, Google likes to rank video highly in its search engine results pages (SERPs), especially YouTube, so if you have YouTube videos embed into your pages, you can get them indexed with this plugin.

Search for "video sitemap"

Google XML Sitemap for Videos Details | Install Now	2.6.1	★★★★☆	Sitemaps are a way to tell Google, Bing and other search engines about web pages, images and video content on your site that they may otherwise not discover. The Video Sitemap plugin will generate an XML Sitemap for your WordPress blog using all YouTube videos that you may have embedded in your blog posts. Your Video Sitemap will includes web pages which embed videos from YouTube or which links ... By Amit Agarwal.

3. YARPP

This one stands for 'Yet Another Related Posts Plugin'. It basically creates a list of related posts, dynamically, for each post on your site. These posts can be automatically inserted after a post's content, or you can insert related posts as a widget, meaning you can place them into any widgetized area of your template, for example, a sidebar.

Search for "yet another related post"

Yet Another Related Posts Plugin Details | Install Now	4.0.6	★★★★☆	Yet Another Related Posts Plugin (YARPP) gives you a list of posts and/or pages related to the current entry, introducing the reader to other relevant content on your site. Thumbnails: a beautiful new thumbnail display, for themes which use post thumbnails (featured images) New in YARPP 4! Related posts, pages, and custom post types: Learn about CPT support. Templating: The YARPP templating syst... By mitcho (Michael Yoshitaka Erlewine).

4. Contact form 7

This plugin makes it easy to setup a contact form on your site. A contact form is an essential part of any website. Whether or not you expect your visitors to contact you, the search engines expect good sites to have this option.

Search for "contact form 7"

Contact Form 7 Details | Install Now	3.4.2		Contact Form 7 can manage multiple contact forms, plus you can customize the form and the mail contents flexibly with simple markup. The form supports Ajax-powered submitting, CAPTCHA, Akismet spam filtering and so on. Docs & Support You can find docs, FAQ and more detailed information about Contact Form 7 on contactform7.com. If you were unable to find the answer to your question on the FAQ... By Takayuki Miyoshi.

5. WP-DBManager

This plugin is one I install on all of my sites. It looks after your WordPress database, optimizing it regularly, and sends you periodic backups via email (crucial in case you ever have a server crash, or your site gets hacked).

Search for "WP DB Manager"

WP-DBManager Details | Install Now	2.63		Allows you to optimize database, repair database, backup database, restore database, delete backup database , drop/empty tables and run selected queries. Supports automatic scheduling of backing up, optimizing and repairing of database. Previous Versions WP-DBManager 2.40 For WordPress 2.7.x WP-DBManager 2.31 For WordPress 2.1.x To 2.6.x WP-DBManager 2.05 For WordPress 2.0.x WP-DBManager 1.00 F... By Lester 'GaMerZ' Chan.

6. Automatic Updater

Keeping your WordPress install (and plugins), up to date is a good idea to prevent security holes in your site. This plugin will do just that, checking for updates periodically and then automatically updating WordPress and/or your plugins. I personally use this, but only have it set to update WordPress, not the plugins. Plugins can take a while to catch up once a new version of WordPress is released, so I prefer to manually update those once the authors tell us they are compatible. Later in the book, I'll show you how to manually update WordPress and the plugins.

Search for "automatic updater"

Automatic Updater Details | Install Now	0.8.5		Automatic Updater keeps your WordPress install up to date with the latest releases automatically, as soon as the update is available. It supports updating stable releases, nightly releases, or even regular SVN checkouts! If you're working on a WordPress Multisite install, it will properly restrict the options page to your Network Admin. While this will be useful for the vast majority of sites, p... By pento.

7. Broken Link Checker

If your site has a lot out outbound links to other websites (by the way, linking to authority sites within your niche is a good idea), then this plugin can check your outbound links and tell you if any are broken. Google don't like broken links on a site, and may punish you if you have a lot of them. Therefore, this plugin can help ensure this does not become a problem.

Search for "broken link checker"

Broken Link Checker Details | Install Now	1.8		This plugin will monitor your blog looking for broken links and let you know if any are found. Features Monitors links in your posts, pages, comments, the blogroll, and custom fields (optional). Detects links that don't work, missing images and redirects. Notifies you either via the Dashboard or by email. Makes broken links display differently in posts (optional). Prevents search engines from f... By Janis Elsts.

8. Social Essentials

Social Essentials adds social media sharing to your site. That is, buttons for your visitors to share your content on Twitter, Facebook, Google +, Pinterest, and Stumbleupon. It is a great idea to add this feature to your site, as Google are taking notice of social signals and using them in their ranking algorithm. Encourage your visitors to share your content!

To be honest, there are a lot of plugins with similar functionality, so if you already know of one that you like, use it instead of social essentials.

Search for "social essentials"

Social Essentials - Social Stats and Sharing Buttons Details | Install Now	1.3.1		Social Essentials provides you with: A simple way to add social sharing buttons to your posts and pages. A simple way to add a call-to action to your buttons, to increase social engagement. Stats that show you how much your content is being shared, in detail. The following social networks are supported for both stats and buttons: Twitter Facebook (like/share button) Google+ StumbleUpon Pinte... By Shane Melaugh.

9. Growmap or Akismet

These are two anti-comment spam plugins, i.e., they block spam in comments automatically. Install either of these and you'll get far fewer spam comments. Of the two, Akismet (which comes pre-installed with WordPress), is the better option in my opinion, however, it is also commercial. Growmap is a free alternative.

Search for "Growmap"

Growmap Anti Spambot Plugin Details | Install Now	1.2		This plugin will add a client side generated checkbox to your comment form asking users to confirm that they are not a spammer. It is a lot less trouble to click a box than it is to enter a captcha and because the box is genereated via client side javascript that bots cannot see, it should stop 99% of all automated spam bots. A check is made that the checkbox has been checked before the comment i... By Andy Bailey.

10. Pretty Link

Pretty Link Lite is a free plugin (there is a commercial version too, but the free version is all most people need). What this plugin does, is allow you to setup redirects on your site. Therefore, if you want to use an affiliate link on your page(s), you could set up a link like mydomain.com/affproduct, and this would redirect to the affiliate site. Why bother? If you don't know why you would want to do this, then you most probably don't need this plugin. One other nice feature of it though, is that it tracks clicks on all of the pretty links you set up, which can be very useful.

Search for "pretty link lite"

Pretty Link Lite Details | Install Now	1.6.4		Pretty Link Pro Upgrade to Pretty Link Pro Pretty Link Pro is a significant upgrade to Pretty Link Lite that adds many tools and redirection types that will allow you to create pretty links automatically, cloak links, auto-tweet links, replace keywords thoughout your blog with pretty links and much more. You can learn more about Pretty Link Pro here: About | Features | Pricing Prett... By Caseproof.

11. Social Stickers

Social Stickers is a neat way of adding social follow buttons to your site. Do you want your visitors to follow you on Twitter? Facebook? Google +? Pinterst? Quora? Social Stickers will add these buttons to your site.

Search for "social stickers"

Social Stickers Details | Install Now	2.1		This is a simple plugin that shows the various social networks you use in the form of "stickers" (see screenshots). It is also fully themable and you can make your own theme in a minute. What this plugin offers: Themes (fully themable, you can easily create your own theme) You can customize the order of the icons (each theme has its own order) Add your own social networks Widget mode Supports s... By Bostjan Cigan.

Finally there are a few commercial plugins that might interest you. One in particular helps with on-site SEO.

12. CI Backlinks

This plugin allows you automate the internal linking of content across your site. It is a plugin I use on all of my websites, because internal linking done manually is an almost impossible task. For example, when you add a new post to your website, you'd need to go and find all other posts that mention that topic so an internal link can be created. With this plugin, you setup the rules and internal links are updated automatically as you add new content.

More details from: http://ezseonews.com/wpseo

13. VIA Curation

Getting you visitors to contribute content to your site is a great idea as it gets people involved with your project. VIA Curation does this by way of submission forms. From these forms, your visitors can submit articles, images and videos to your website.

Obviously you get to moderate all submissions.

More details from: http://ezseonews.com/wpseo

14. WP Secure

This plugin helps to keep your WordPress install secure against hackers. When this plugin is installed, even if a hacker gets hold of your username and password, they'll still not be able to login. How's that possible? It's magic! No, not really, but it is clever!

More details from: http://ezseonews.com/wpseo

15. WP Sticky

The next plugin is WP Sticky. It allows us to 'stick' posts at the top of archive pages:

This comes in handy for non-Genesis themes if you want to create introductions to category and tag pages (see later in the book for details on this).

OK, that brings an end to my list of essential, and not so essential, plugins. Make sure you get the essentials installed before moving on. We'll be starting to configure them very soon.

8. Keeping WordPress Up to Date - WordPress & Plugins

It is important that you always keep WordPress and plugins up to date. Hackers typically look for exploits in WordPress, so updates fix any known problems, thus keeping your website protected.

Fortunately, WordPress makes it easy to know if there are any updates to the core program itself, or any plugins and themes that you have installed.

If a WordPress update is available, you'll see the notification in the Dashboard at the top & center.

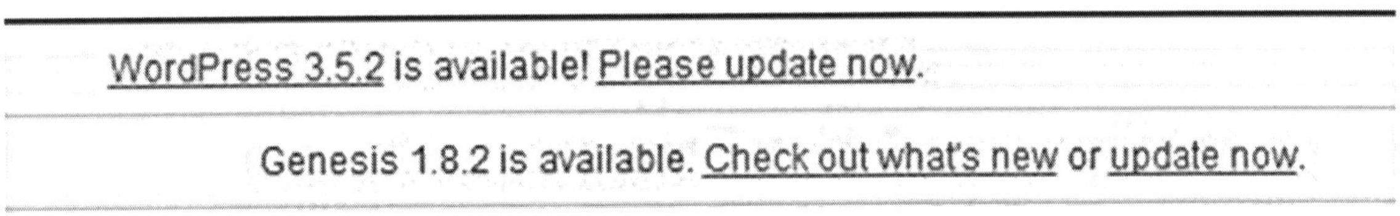

As you can see from the screenshot, some themes, like Genesis, also show its update notifications at the top of the Dashboard too, directly under the WordPress announcement.

To update WordPress, you can just click the '**Please update now**' link and follow the simple instructions.

There are other visual cues in the dashboard that also notify you of various updates.

If a plugin update is available, you'll see a number appear next to Plugins in the left sidebar. The number tells you how many plugin updates are available.

Finally, there is a quick way to see all updates in one area of the Dashboard. Click on the word 'Dashboard', at the top of the left sidebar, and the menu opens. Directly under the 'Home' link is a menu item called '**Updates**'. Again, you'll see a number next to it if there are any updates available.

Click on '**Updates**' to be taken to the updates screen. This can have up to three sections. At the very top, if a WordPress update is available, you'll see an option to install it. Under that, if plugins are available for update, you'll see them here. Simply check the plugins you want to update, and then click the '**Update Plugin**' button.

At the bottom of the page, if a theme has an update, you should see it listed here too (though that will depend on the theme and where you got it from). Again, check the theme(s) you want to update, and click the '**Update Themes**' button.

If you prefer to have the updates done for you automatically, check back in the plugins section of this book, where I mention a plugin called Automatic Updater that can do this for you.

9. Duplication on Category, Tag & Other Archive Pages

As mentioned at the beginning of this book, these pages are the root of many SEO problems. Let me show you an example of this.

I've created a dummy post for a fictitious gift website. The post is called 'Gift ideas for children', and it's in a category called 'children'.

After posting the article, here is my homepage:

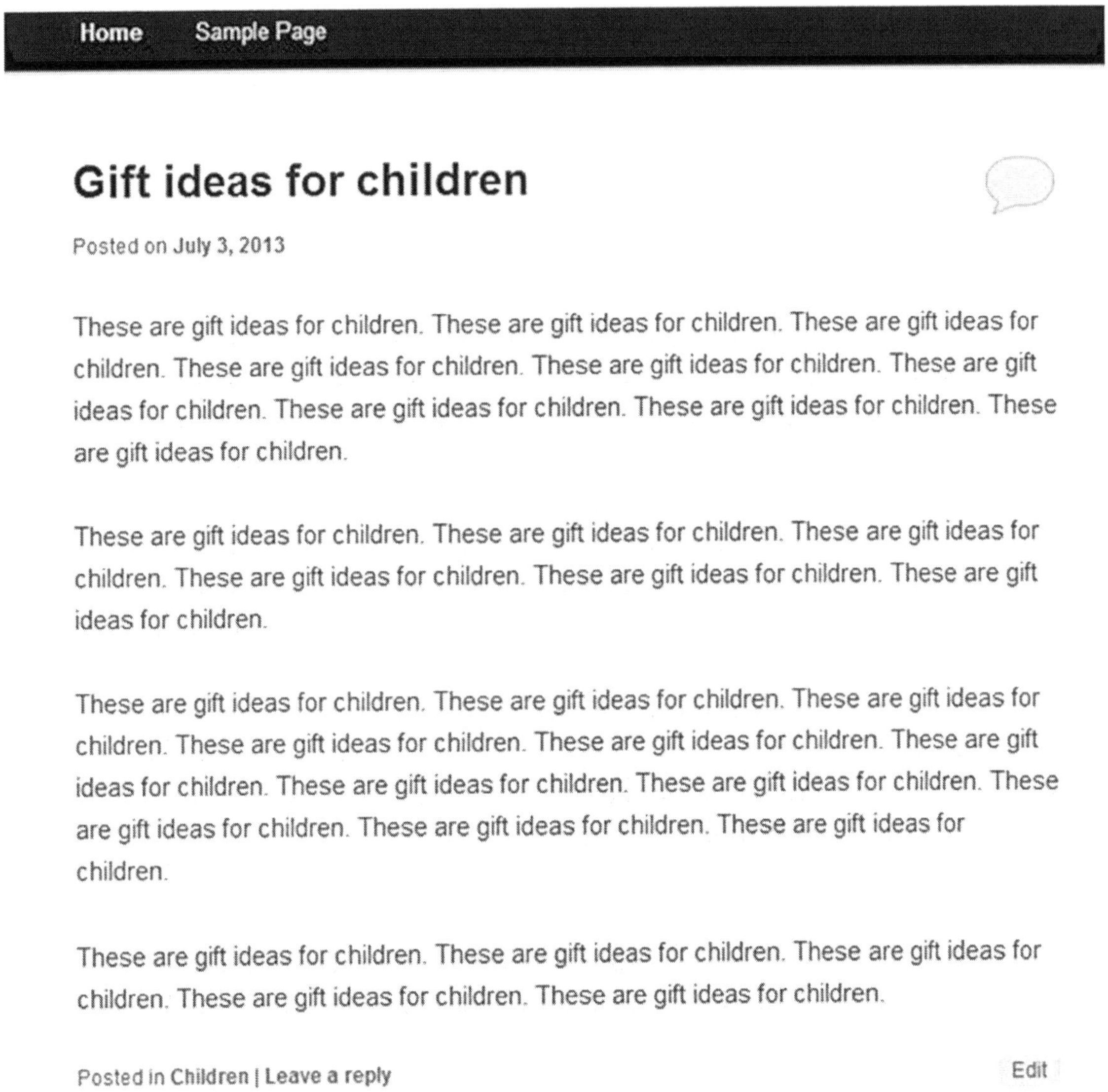

The title of the post is actually a hyperlink that will open a page which contains an exact copy of the article. That means we now have two identical copies of the same post, but that's only the tip of the iceberg.

Look at the screenshot above under the title where it says 'Posted on July 3, 2013'.

That date is a hyperlink to the date archive. Clicking on it takes me to a page that shows all posts that were published on that date. Here it is:

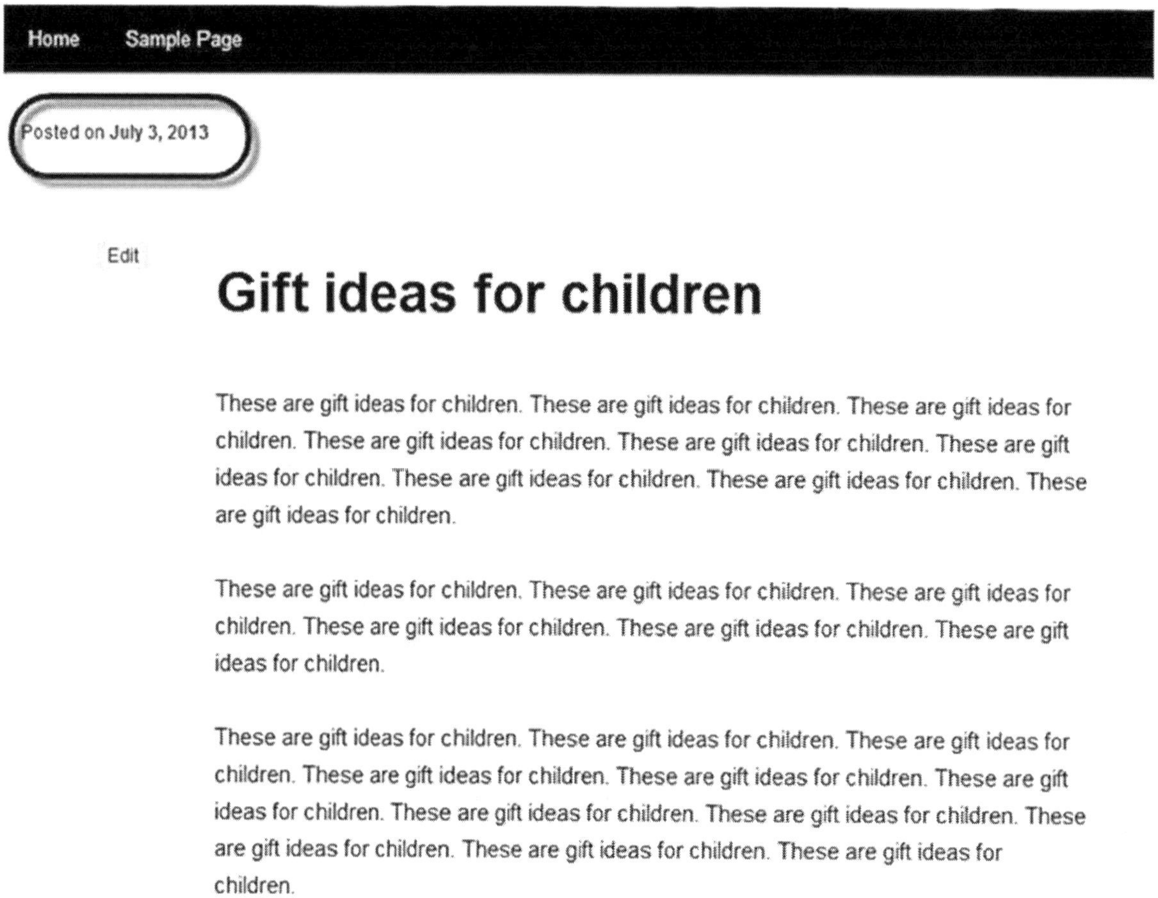

The same full post again.

Go back to the homepage screenshot. See at the bottom of the post where it says 'Posted in children'. '**Children**' is the category, and the word 'children' is a hyperlink. If I click that, it takes me to the children category page:

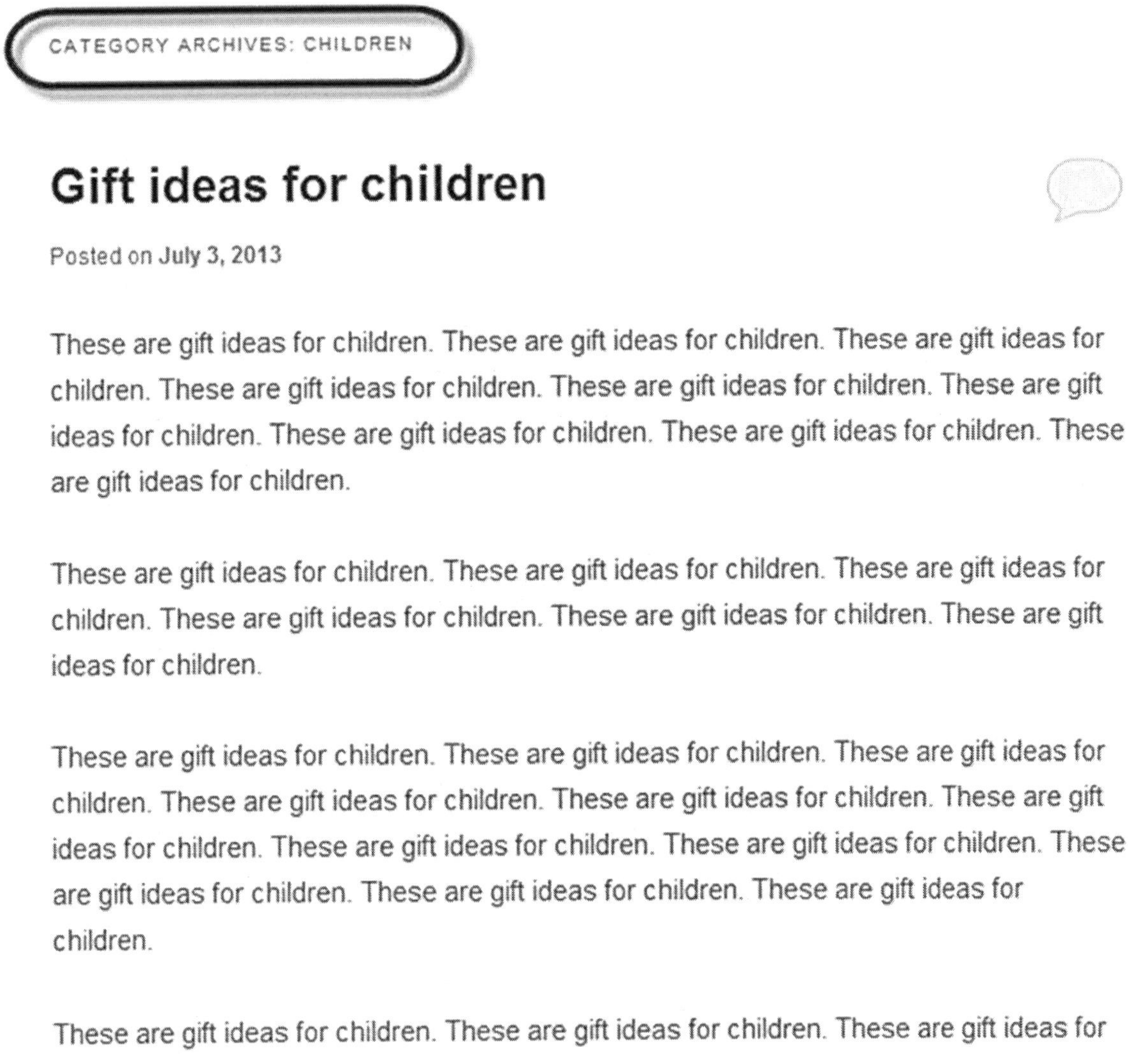

CATEGORY ARCHIVES: CHILDREN

Gift ideas for children

Posted on July 3, 2013

These are gift ideas for children. These are gift ideas for children. These are gift ideas for children. These are gift ideas for children. These are gift ideas for children. These are gift ideas for children. These are gift ideas for children. These are gift ideas for children. These are gift ideas for children.

These are gift ideas for children. These are gift ideas for children. These are gift ideas for children. These are gift ideas for children. These are gift ideas for children. These are gift ideas for children.

These are gift ideas for children. These are gift ideas for children. These are gift ideas for children. These are gift ideas for children. These are gift ideas for children. These are gift ideas for children. These are gift ideas for children. These are gift ideas for children. These are gift ideas for children. These are gift ideas for children. These are gift ideas for children.

These are gift ideas for children. These are gift ideas for children. These are gift ideas for

That page also contains the full post.

The duplication doesn't stop there. WordPress has also created an author page. If I go to the author page:

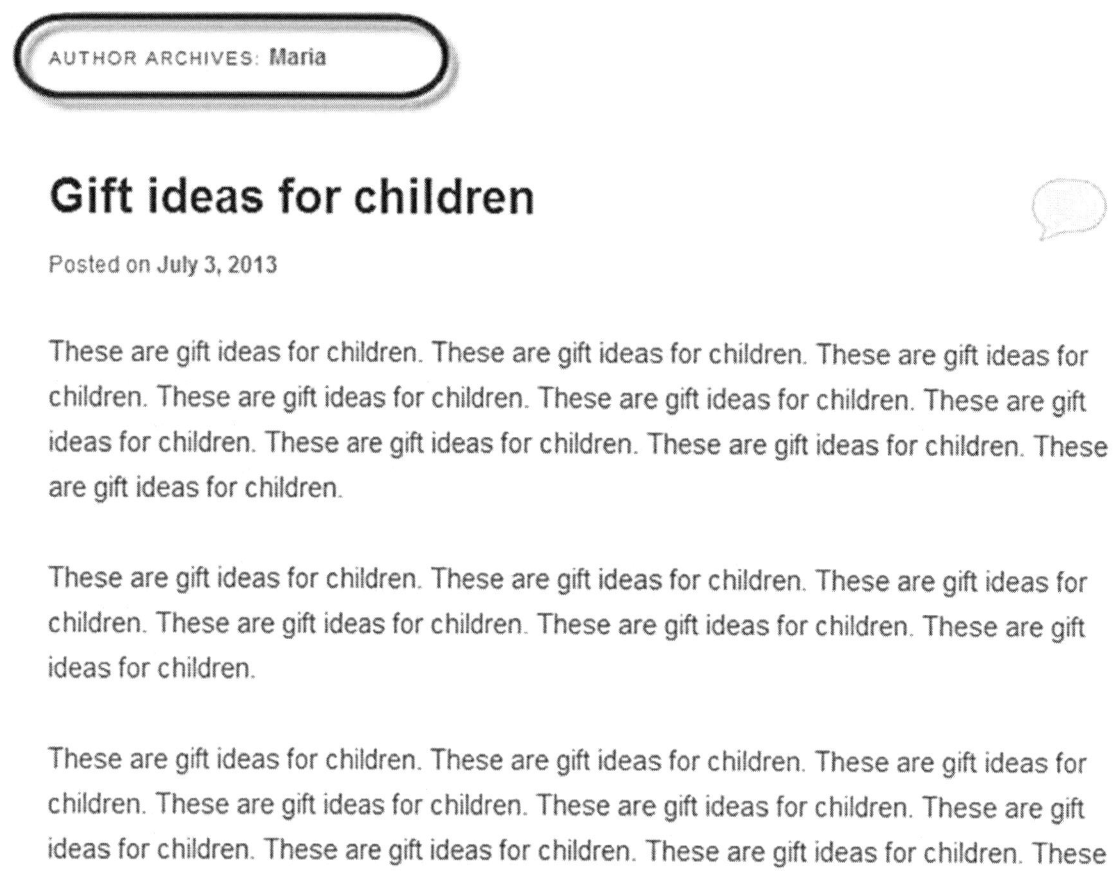

Once again, we have yet another duplicated copy of the same article.

But wait, there's more! What if I added a few tags to the post? Here I've added four tags to this demo article:

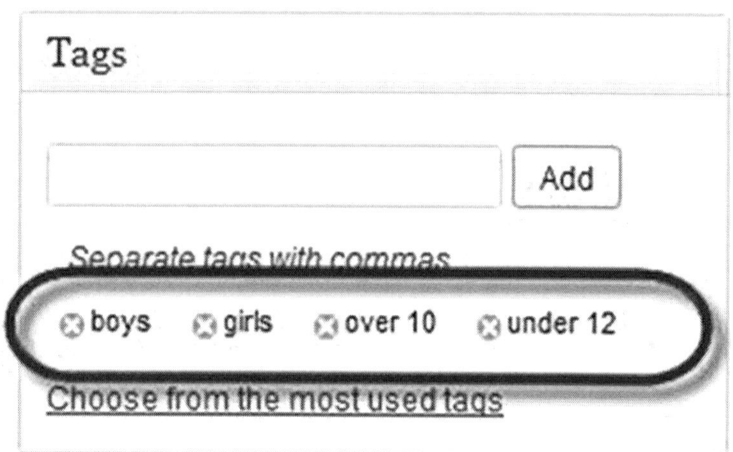

The tags are boys, girls, over 10 & under 12. These are supposed to help classify the gift ideas. However, WordPress creates a page for each of these tags, and guess what?

I'll give you a clue by showing you one of the four tag pages:

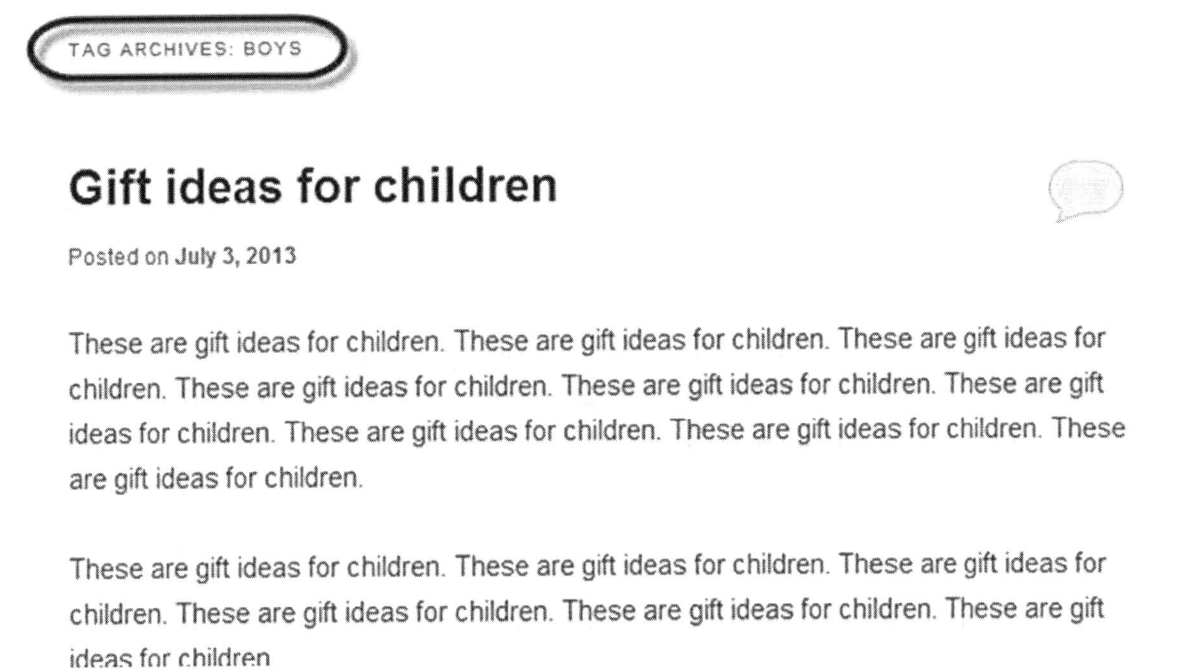

TAG ARCHIVES: BOYS

Gift ideas for children

Posted on July 3, 2013

These are gift ideas for children. These are gift ideas for children. These are gift ideas for children. These are gift ideas for children. These are gift ideas for children. These are gift ideas for children. These are gift ideas for children. These are gift ideas for children. These are gift ideas for children.

These are gift ideas for children. These are gift ideas for children. These are gift ideas for children. These are gift ideas for children. These are gift ideas for children. These are gift ideas for children

Yes, that's right. The full article is published on each of the four tag pages too.

So how many times does this one post appear on the site? Well assuming I haven't missed one or two copies (something which is quite possible), we have the following:

Homepage, post page, category page, date archive, author page, and four tag pages. That's nine copies of the exact same article. And that happens with every article you publish on your site.

Now do you see why WordPress desperately needs to be SEO'd? This type of duplication can kill your rankings in Google.

If you are starting to have palpitations, thinking you have made the wrong decision choosing WordPress, relax. I'll walk you through it step by step. It really isn't so difficult to solve these problems once you know how.

10. Menus & Site Navigation

Visitors like a site with good navigation and Google likes a site that keeps its visitors happy. Of course, there is more to it than that. Good navigation on a site will help the search engines find, and even categorize your content.

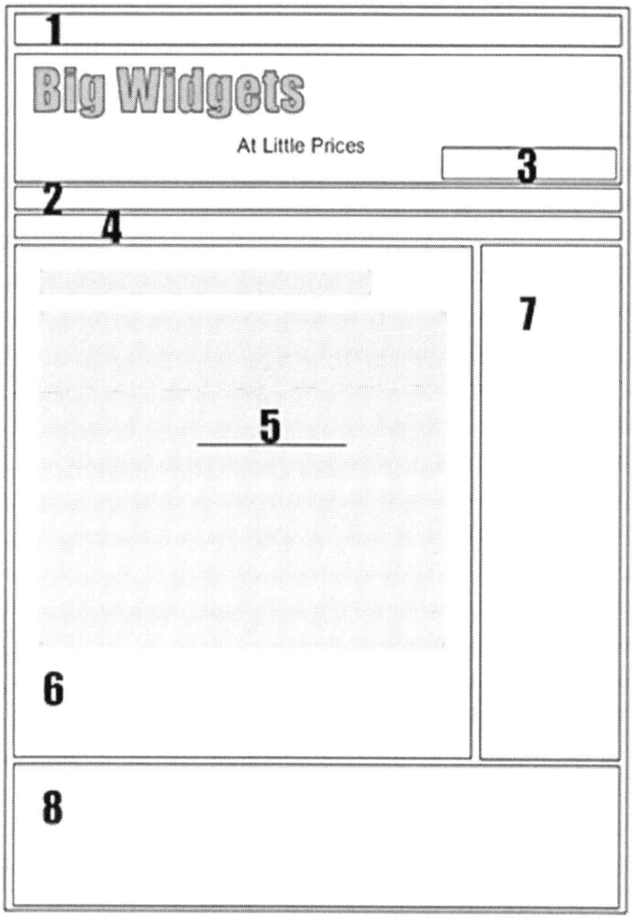

On a website, there are various places where navigation can appear. These typically include:

1. A menu above the site logo.
2. A menu below the site logo.
3. A search box in the same area as the site logo, often off to the right.
4. Breadcrumb navigation underneath the page header, but above the webpage opening header.
5. Links to other pages within the body of the content, as in-context links.
6. After the content of the page, maybe as a 'related articles' or 'You may also be interested in these' types of link lists.
7. A menu in the left and/or right sidebar.
8. A menu in the page footer.

Where you put your navigation may be determined by your choice of WordPress template. For example, some templates offer positions 1 or 2, but not both. Others offer both positions. And some may offer two navigation menus in position 2, but none in position 1.

As for the search box, this can appear in the logo area, or in the sidebar. I've even seen them in page footers. Therefore this diagram is only a rough guide.

Before we look at how to create the various forms of navigation in WordPress, let me mention one thing. Create your navigation for human visitors, not search engines. That means using the most logical and aesthetically pleasing links in the menu. Do not, under any circumstances, stuff keywords into your navigation menus and links.

For example, if you had a website about prom dresses, and had sections on your site to various brands of prom dress, you might be tempted to use something like:

- PacificPlex Prom Dresses
- Ever-Pretty Prom Dresses
- Moonar Prom Dresses
- Hot from Hollywood Prom Dresses
- US Fairytailes Prom Dresses

Notice the repetition of the words 'Prom Dresses'. Why do you think some webmasters do this? Is it to help their visitors? Well, considering the whole site is about prom dresses, I'd assume not. This is done purely for the search engines for two reasons:

1. In this menu, the phrase 'prom dresses' appears five times in the hope that the page would rank better for that term. In the good old days of pre-2011 SEO, this would have worked. Today it's more likely to get you a Penguin penalty.
2. Each item in the menu will link to a page on the site. That link uses anchor text (the text you as the visitor see for any given link). In this type of menu, the keyword-stuffed anchor text is there as an attempt to boost the rankings of the page the link points to for its anchor text phrase. Say if this site had 100 pages, each using the same prom dress menu. This means each of the five pages in the menu would have 100 links pointing to them. That's 100 of the exact same anchor texts. Again, pre-2011, this worked. Today it does not, and this tactic will come back to bite you (or do Penguins nip?).

TIP: Look at the 'SEO' on your site. If you cannot say with 100% that you have done it in your visitor's best interests, then get rid of it. This goes for site navigation, content, and internal linking between pages, etc.

OK, with that said, how do you implement navigation into WordPress?

Well, there are a number of different ways.

You can use plugins. You can also use the menu system built into WordPress.

In many cases you will know exactly which links you want in a navigation area. These links are usually fixed and rarely change. In this instance, I recommend you use the menu system built into WordPress.

On other occasions, you might want a list of the most recent posts, or posts related specifically to the current one. These menus are constantly changing as new content gets added to the site, and are therefore best handled with plugins.

10.1. Recommended Navigation

Let me make the recommendations first, and then I'll show you how to implement them.

To start off (you can add or change this later), I suggest that you have the following four navigation features:

1. **One menu:** Either above or below the site logo, or in the footer, where there are links to your 'legal pages'. That's the Contact, Privacy, Disclaimers, About Us, and so forth. These links should be 'nofollowed', and the actual legal pages should be set to 'noindex', 'Follow' and 'No Archive'.
2. **A search box**: If your theme supports a search box in the header area, you might want it there. However, I personally prefer a search box at the top of the sidebar (right or left, whichever I use).
3. **A main navigation menu:** Either in or below the logo or in the sidebar (right or left), that links to the main sections of your website (the main categories).
4. **Sidebar dynamic menus:** Each category (or main section), of your site should have a different navigation menu in the sidebar. Google likes dynamic menus which change depending where on a site a visitor is. For example, if you are in the mountain bike section of a site, the main navigation menu should be related to mountain bikes. If you are in the road bike section, the main navigation menu relates to road bikes.

Personally, the type of sites I build also benefit from a 'related posts' section, either after the main content of a post, or in the sidebar (done using the 'Yet Another Related Posts' plugin). However, it depends on the type of site you build, so this may not suite your particular project. I also implement internal linking between the posts on the site using context-sensitive links (this is done using the 'C.I. Backlinks' plugin). The internal linking of posts on a site is something that most of the big players do (see Wikipedia for example), and it really does help your pages get indexed and rank better.

10.2. Implementing the Four Main Navigation Features

Let's look at the 'legal menu' first.

10.2.1. Implementing Legal Menus

If you login to the Dashboard and go to Appearance -> Menus, you'll be able to create a menu that contains links to your legal pages.

I won't go through the details of creating individual menus here, as that is covered in my WordPress for Beginners book (http://www.amazon.com/dp/B009ZVO3H6). However, I will show you how to make the links in the navigation menu 'nofollow'.

Pull down the Screen Options (top right of the Dashboard), and make sure that '**Link Relationship (XFN)**' is checked.

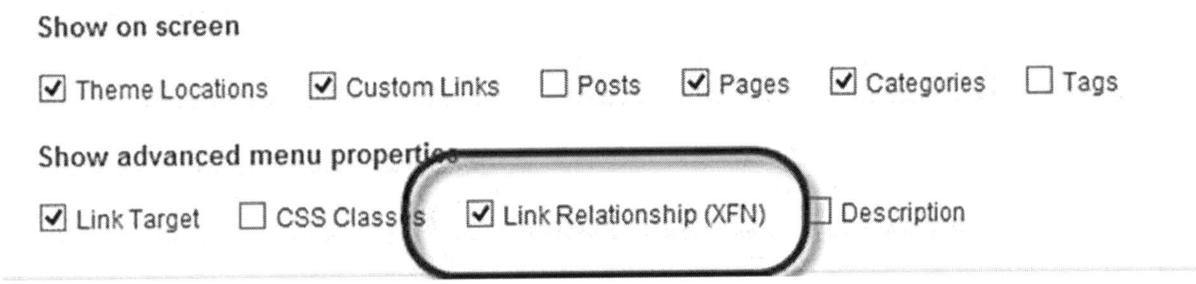

You can now expand the items in your menu:

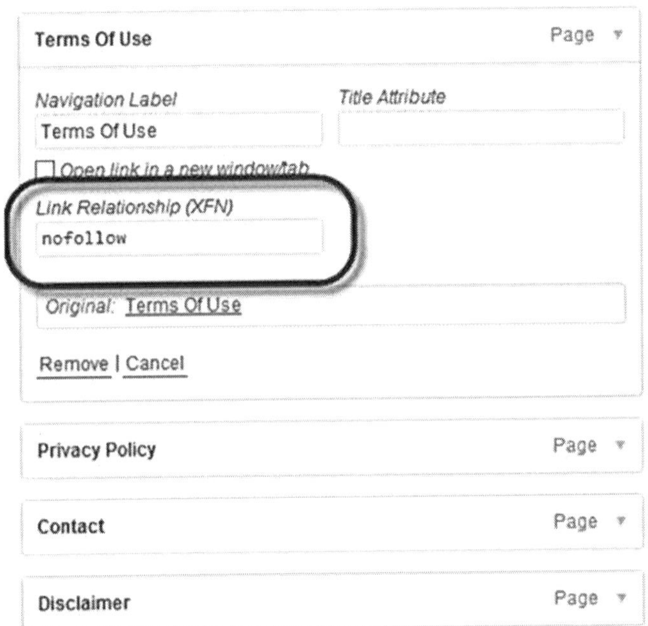

Type the word **nofollow** into the link relationship box.

Repeat this for all your legal pages; and don't forget to save your menu.

Once you have the menu saved, you can then insert it into the header area, or the sidebar. To do this, look to top left of the 'Menus' screen and you'll see a section called '**Theme Locations**'.

These are defined by your theme, and you'll see one or two locations available. For most themes, these theme locations are above and below the logo, which is exactly what we want.

The theme I am using in the screenshot above is the Genesis Lifestyle theme. Primary Navigation Menu is above the Logo, and the Secondary Navigation Menu is below it.

To place the legal menu in the header area of the page, simply select the menu you created from the dropdown box, in the position you want it to appear i.e., Primary or Secondary Navigation.

OK, so how do you add the menu to the footer?

Well, with Genesis themes, this is easy.

Go to the Appearance -> Widgets screen. You should see a '**Custom Menu**' widget available. You'll also see a footer area (or three), on the right hand side. Simply drag the Custom Menu Widget into the Footer Widget area, and then select the legal menu:

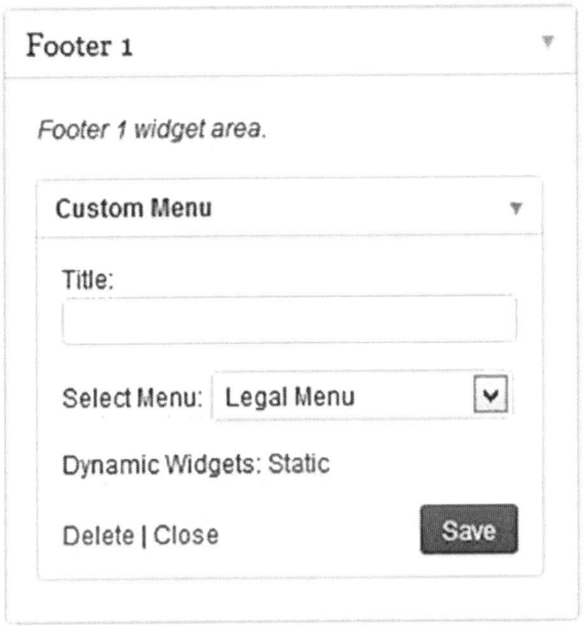

This will then display the legal menu in your site's footer:

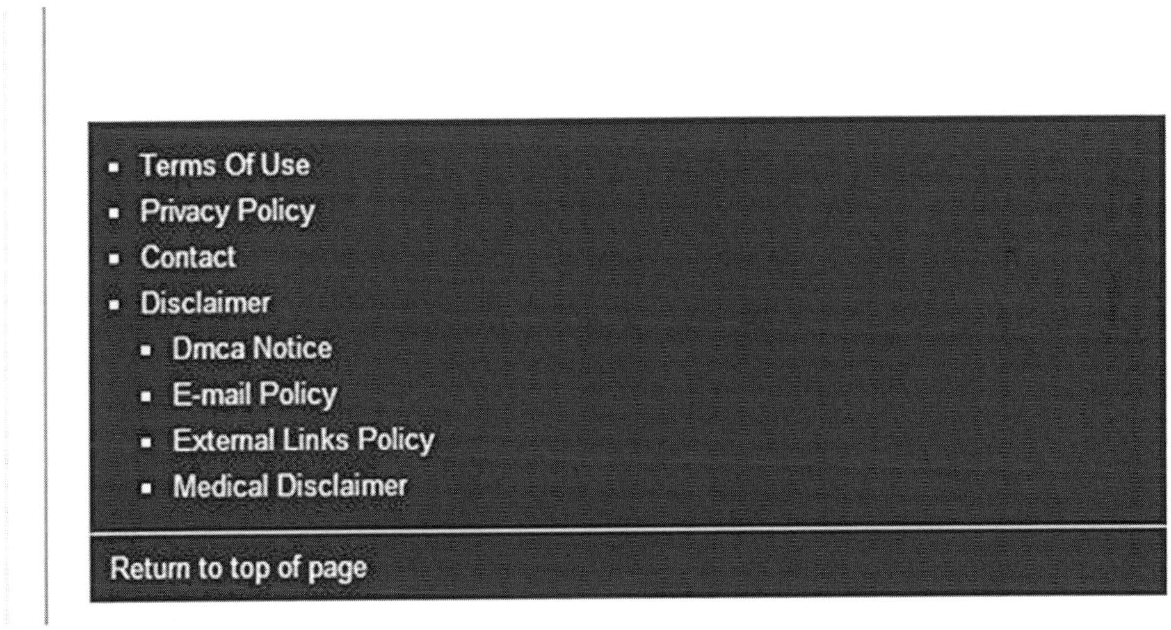

Again, all links will be nofollow because we set that up in the actual menu.

However, there is one other task we need to do. That is to make sure our legal pages are setup so that they are 'noindex', 'Follow', and 'No Archive'. Fortunately, this is easy with the WordPress SEO plugin we installed earlier.

Go to each of your legal pages in turn and open them in the editor (Pages -> All Pages, then click on the title of the page in the list).

The WordPress SEO plugin has added a section to all post/page edit screens. It's labelled as **WordPress SEO by Yoast** and it has three tabs. We want to select the '**Advanced**' tab:

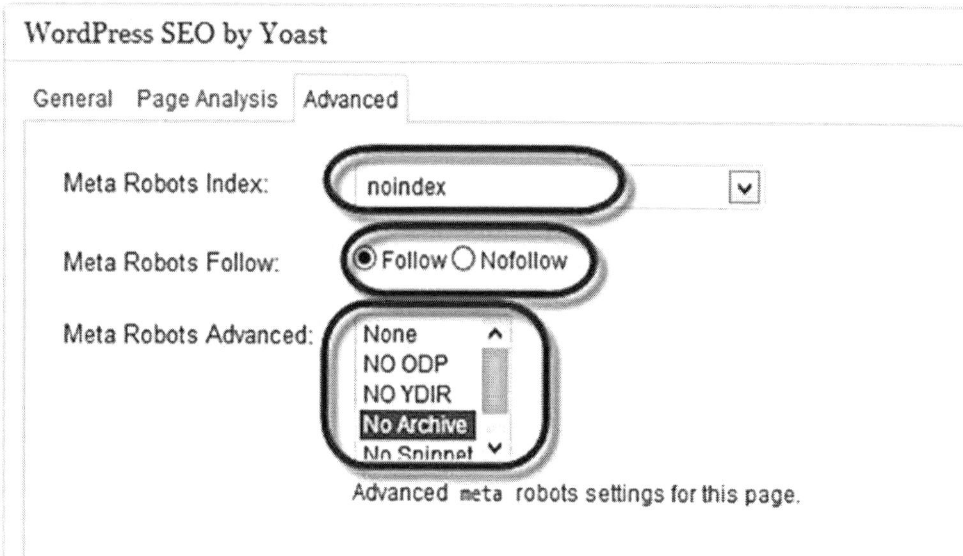

Select '**noindex**' from the dropdown box at the top, '**Follow**' from the radio button, and '**No Archive**' from the list box.

Now click the '**Update**' button to save the changes.

Repeat this procedure for all other legal pages (and pages/posts that you don't want to appear in the search engines).

OK, now you have a legal menu on your site, with links set as nofollow, and the pages themselves set as noindex. These two settings will prevent Google from indexing pages that are not important to your site, and thus stop valuable Page Rank from flowing to these pages, meaning more link juice for your important content.

10.2.2. Implementing a Search Box

WordPress comes with a search widget, so you can start off by using that. They aren't actually very good, so I recommend you eventually switch to using a Google custom search (search Google for instructions when you are ready), but the WordPress search feature will do to get you started.

Simply drag the '**Search**' widget to the widgetized area where you want it to appear. In some themes you'll get a '**Header Right**' option. This is to insert a widget into the right hand side of the logo area. You can drag the search box widget there if you want to. Alternatively, drag it to the top of the main or primary sidebar.

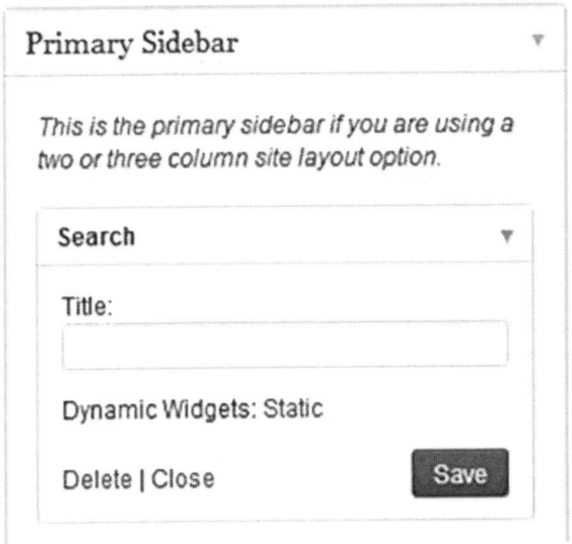

You can enter a title for the widget if you like. The title will then appear right above the search box. However, since most people are used to seeing a box with a search button, the title isn't strictly necessary, it's personal preference.

10.2.3. Main Site Navigation Menu

The main site navigation is inserted into the sidebar in exactly the same way we saw the legal menu inserted into the site. Drag and drop a '**Custom Menu**' widget into the area you want your main navigation to appear. I nearly always put it in the main sidebar. Now, the last type of navigation I suggested you use is dynamic navigation. That means the navigation that points to the main sections (categories), on your site, and will probably only appear on the homepage. Once you are in other areas of the site, you'll use a different navigation menu. Let's look and see how we do that.

10.2.4. Dynamic Navigation Menus

To achieve dynamic menus, we need the '**Dynamic Widgets**' plugin that we installed earlier. When this is installed, EVERY widget you add in the Appearance -> Widgets section of the dashboard has a new feature:

See the **Dynamic Widgets: Static**?

That word 'Static' is a hyperlink that takes you to the settings for the widget. From there you get to specify exactly where on the site you want the widget to appear.

The default setting is 'Static', which means the widget appears on every page & post of the entire site, but you can change the default. Say you only want the widget to appear on the homepage, then the word 'Static' changes to 'Dynamic', and you'll get a few other details in the widget area showing you what 'Dynamic' settings you are using.

Assuming you have already created a main navigation menu that links to the main categories of the site, let's set it to only appear on the homepage.

Open the '**Custom Menu**' in the widget area:

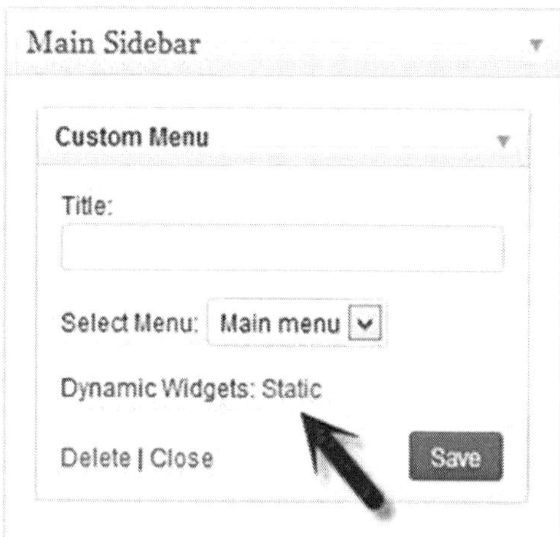

Click the '**Static**' link.

This opens up a large page of options.

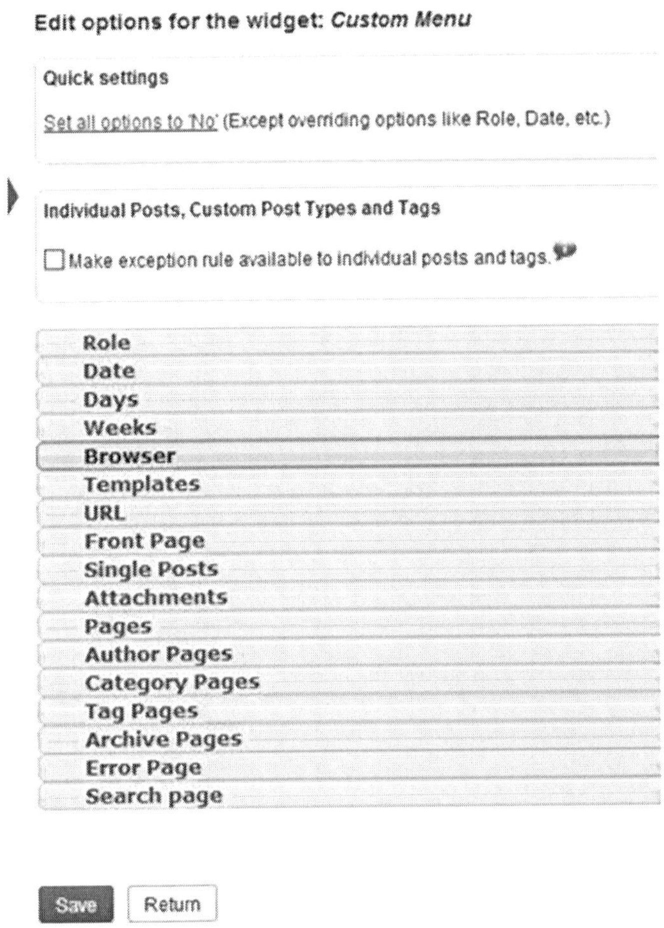

Each of these 'horizontal bars' will open up if you click on them.

Since we only want the menu to appear on the homepage, the first thing we need to do is click the link at the top of these options: **Set all options to 'No'**.

If we now click on any one of these bars, it will expand, showing us that it is set to 'No'.

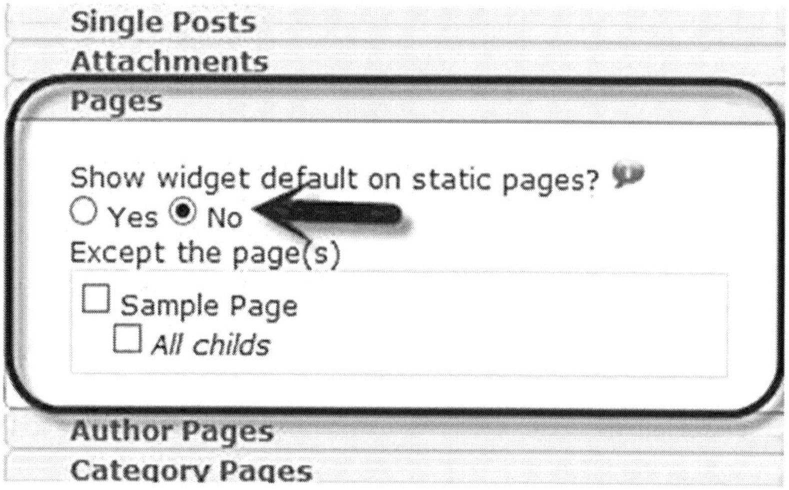

This means the widget will not appear anywhere on the site. We need to fix this by opening up the homepage options (called 'Front Page' in this plugin), and select '**Yes**'.

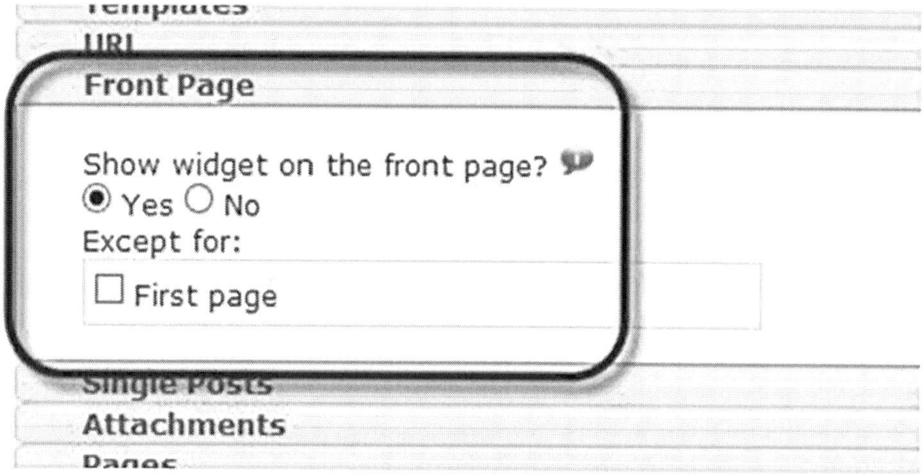

Now, don't forget to save the settings by clicking the '**Save**' button at the bottom. This will then return you to the widgets area of the Dashboard.

If you look at the Custom Menu widget, you'll see that additional information I told you about:

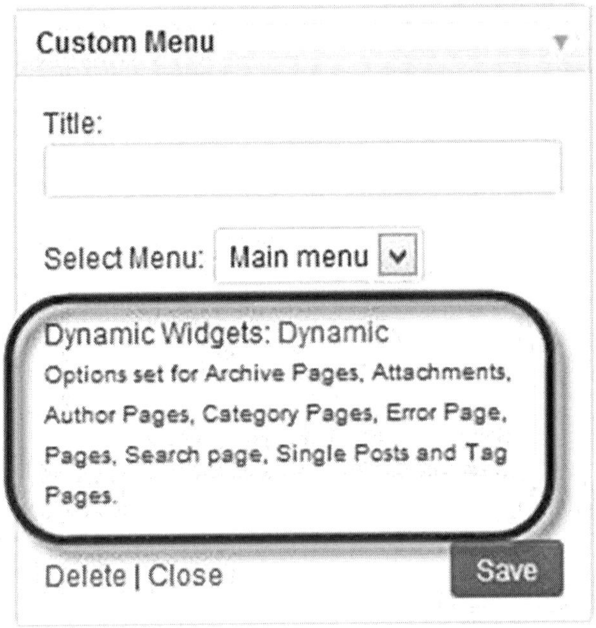

The word 'Static' now reads 'Dynamic', and we can see that the options have been set for various pages on the site.

If you check your site, you will find the main navigation menu only appears on the homepage.

To get dynamic menus for each specific area of our site, we need to setup the menu in the Appearance -> Menu section. For example, if you have five categories on your site, set up five Custom Menus, and include the most relevant menu items for each category.

Next, add all of these custom menus to the sidebar, and then go into them, one by one, and change the settings for where they should appear on your site.

For this example, let's assume I want the custom menu to appear only in the '**Hot from Hollywood**' category (that's the category page plus any posts in that category).

Step one will be to click the link to set all options to 'No', just as we did for the homepage. Next we need to change two settings.

The first is in the '**Category Pages**' settings:

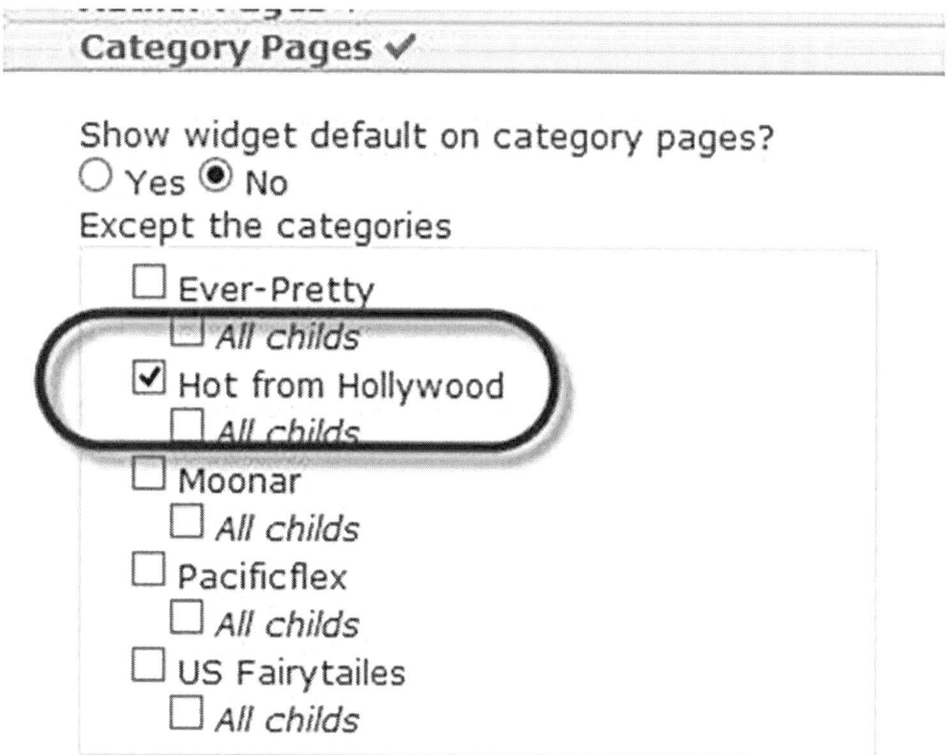

Select '**No**' at the top, and then check the '**Hot from Hollywood'** checkbox. This may sound counter-intuitive, but read the information on the plugin settings screen. We are checking the Hot from Hollywood category so that it will be the exception. We don't want the widget to appear on category pages EXCEPT the one(s) that are checked.

OK, once saved, that will show the menu on the 'Hot from Hollywood' category page. We also need to make it appear on the posts within that category, so we have to set the '**Single Posts**' options.

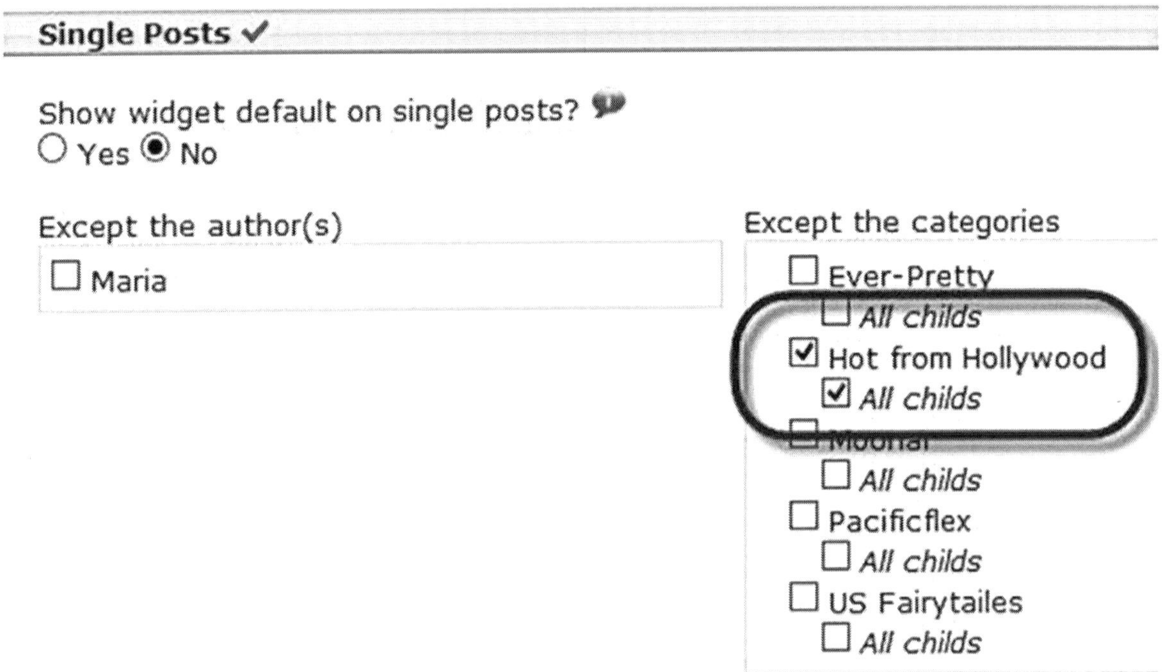

Again, we select '**No**' at the top because we don't want this widget appearing on posts, except the ones we check

The 'Hot from Hollywood' category is selected, but you also have the option to check '***All childs***', which will mean any 'Hot from Hollywood' sub-categories will also have this menu.

OK, once done, save your changes.

The menu will only appear on the 'Hot from Hollywood' category page AND all the posts within that category.

You can explore the other settings for the dynamic widgets plugin. You will see an enormous level of control over which pages your widgets appear on.

Using the techniques shown in this chapter, you can easily create custom sidebars, and custom footers, etc, with any type of widget in any area that is widgetized.

This is the easiest way to create dynamic navigation systems on your website. Don't forget, besides navigation systems, you can also serve up custom adverts, custom subscription boxes, custom videos, etc., and all on different sections of the site.

11. A Custom Logo for Your Header?

By default, WordPress displays your site name and tagline (configured in the Settings -> General Settings menu), as the logo for the site.

While the default site name and tagline may be OK for most projects, they often don't give the best impression to your visitors. And since a lot of modern SEO is all about keeping the visitor happy, you may want to create (or have created for you), a professional image logo and use that instead. Remember, you never get a second chance to make that first impression!

While it's beyond the scope of this book to show you how to create a logo, I can show you how to use a custom logo image on your site, but how you achieve this will vary somewhat between themes.

Go to the Appearance -> Themes menu:

You will see your selected theme active at the top (I'm using the default Twenty Twelve theme for this demonstration). There is more than likely a 'Header' link here. This will take you to your site's header options, so click on it.

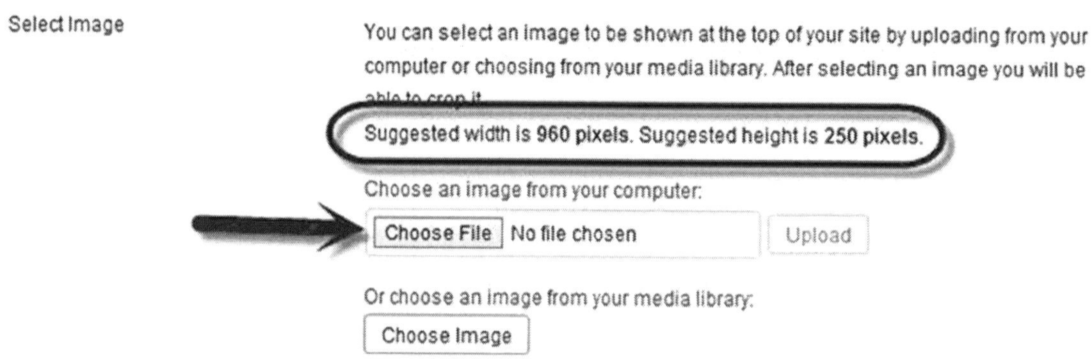

You should be given a suggested logo dimension. The dimensions for the Twenty Twelve theme are 960 pixels by 250 pixels. Make sure you create your logo using the *exact dimensions* as recommended by your theme, or you may have to crop it once it's uploaded.

You can select the logo from your computer or from your WordPress Media Library, if you uploaded it there. If you select an image logo from your computer, make sure you click the '**Upload**' button after selecting the file.

The only other thing you need to do is remove the default logo text. There is a check box that you simply need to uncheck:

Make sure you save changes when done. Your new logo should now be active site-wide.

12. Comment System

The comment systems and how to integrate them into your site, is an important, yet often over-looked piece of the on-site SEO puzzle.

The comments on your site are VERY important. A lot of comments tell visitors that your site is busy. If it's busy, then it's likely to be trusted by more people. If it's trusted, it will do better in Google too.

However, all of this is dependent on having good quality comments. Comments need to add to the 'conversation' that has gone before them. Put more specifically, do the comments add to the original article, either by way of an opinion, additional information, or a question? Another good type of comment is when a visitor replies to someone else's remarks, but again, only if those replies are adding to the conversation. These are the types of comments you need to try and get on your site.

When a website is new, it's all too easy to approve poor comments just to make the site look visited. Don't do it! Never approve a comment *unless* it actually adds something to the post topic and conversation already on-going, that's if there are other comments of course.

Typical comments you should NOT approve include the congratulatory comments, like "Well done!", or "Great post". Even "Thanks for writing about this topic in a way I can understand". Although the latter might sound sincere, it adds absolutely nothing to the conversation because there is no reference to the topic in question.

Get used to approving only the best comments. Even if you don't get very many to begin with (which is quite possible), great comments add value to the overall visitor experience of your website. Or to put it another way, a website full of poor & spammy comments will put your visitors off and they won't have much confidence in you or the credibility of your site.

13. RSS Feeds

WordPress automatically creates several RSS feeds for your site.

You can access the main feed for your site by adding **/feed** to the end of your domain URL.

The feed for my SEO website is: **ezSEONews.com/feed**.

We setup the RSS feed earlier to show just 10 posts, and only the title and excerpts of those. Therefore, the main feed will show the last 10 posts you published on your site.

WordPress also creates six other feeds:

1. Comments - this feed shows the last 10 comments made on your site.
2. Post-specific feeds - which show the last 10 comments made on a particular post.
3. Category feeds - which show the last 10 posts made in a particular category.
4. Tag feeds - which show the last 10 posts using a particular tag.
5. Author feeds - showing the last 10 posts made by a particular author.
6. Search feeds - showing the search results for a particular keyword phrase.

I won't go into details showing you how to find all of these feeds. If you are interested, you can read the WordPress codex article on this topic:

http://codex.wordpress.org/WordPress_Feeds

From an SEO point of view, feeds are interesting. For example, there are a number of RSS feed submission services where you can get backlinks to your site by submitting your feed(s). Whenever you add fresh content, these feeds get updated, linking back to the new page. In terms of helping pages rank higher, these types of links won't do much good, but they can get your new content indexed a lot quicker. What I would suggest here is not to overdo this type of submission. Pick maybe three or four of the top RSS feed sites, and submit a feed to each (you can choose different feeds for each if you want).

One thing I like to use feeds for is adding a recent posts section to my site's sidebar, or footer. WordPress comes with a feed widget, and all you need to do is supply the feed URL for it to work.

For example, on my SEO site, I have a category on Kindle Publishing. I can grab the feed URL for that category:

http://ezseonews.com/seo/kindle-publishing/feed/

I then add it to an RSS widget by using the Dynamic Widget plugin we saw earlier. This will only show that RSS feed on other posts in the Kindle Publishing category.

Here is the widget set up:

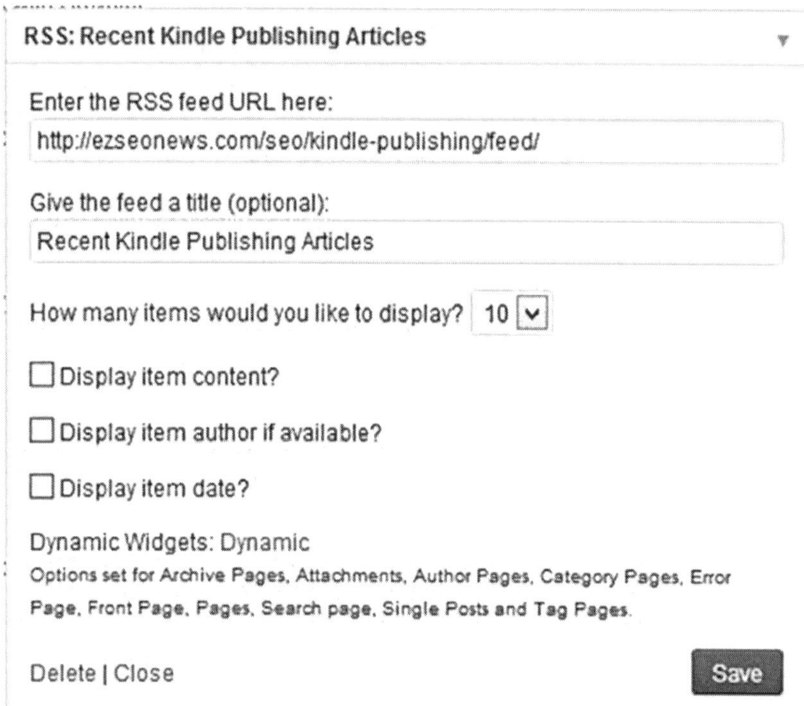

Here is the widget in action on the 'Kindle Publishing' articles (and category), pages.

This has a couple of benefits:

1. You can highlight other recent articles in a given category. If someone is reading an article about one aspect of Kindle publishing, the chances are these other articles will be of interest too.
2. From an SEO perspective, this is good because you have inter-linking of the Kindle publishing articles, each reinforcing the theme of your pages and providing spiderable links to the other articles in the 'silo'.

14. Google Authorship & WordPress User Profiles

Google is always updating its algorithm. There are hundreds of minor updates every year, with some major ones sprinkled in between. In the last couple of years, we've had to contend with Panda, Penguin and then Penguin 2.0 (which was a major upgrade to the original). All of these updates have been necessary, because Google has faced a constant battle with webmasters trying to game the system; that is webmasters who want their content to rank #1 in the Google search results pages.

We all want to be ranked #1 for various search phrases - obviously - but we don't all deserve these top slot(s). Google has a problem with webmasters that try to force their content to the top of the first page. Google wants total control. They need to be able to decide which content deserves to be at the top, and not leave that up to webmasters, who can, and do, try all manner of techniques to get these valuable positions.

One of the most abused SEO techniques over the years has been link building. The general principle has always been more is better. Webmasters have always considered link building to be a safe practice because you cannot control who links to your site. Google themselves even told us once that links could not hurt a site's rankings.

I guess the search giant finally snapped, because today, bad links can cause you ranking problems. To help webmasters fix link problems, Google introduced the disavow tool. You can use this to list those links pointing at your site which you do not approve of. This now means that site owners have full control over the links to their pages, signifying Google have shifted the responsibility of bad links away from their algorithm, and onto the webmaster. In other words, if you have bad links pointing at your site, it is *your* fault as far as Google is concerned.

While the Google vs. Webmasters battle has raged on all these years, Google has been constantly looking for other 'signals' they could use to help them better rank web pages. The holy grail of 'signals' would be one that webmasters could not manipulate to their advantage, and they may have just come up with the answer.

14.1. Google Authorship

Google introduced 'Google Authorship' as a way to connect a piece of content with its true author. By setting up Google authorship, and using it properly, you can tell Google about all of the content you have scattered around the internet.

So you might be asking how this could be used as a ranking factor. Well, let's consider a couple of scenarios.

Peter is an expert in alternative medicine. He has his own website, but also contributes to several industry leading websites with regular articles. His writings are excellent, they get good traffic, and there is a lot of social interaction with visitors. With Google authorship, Peter can tell Google about all of his content, and Google can do the rest. They will be monitoring the 'feedback' from visitors to Peter's pages around the web, and be able to assign him an 'author rank'. Now, what if Google decided that any new article written by Peter deserved to rank higher, simply because he had become a trusted author?

OK, let's now take the example of Sean. He's a marketer and has his hands in lots of pies. He has multiple websites based in health 'niches', and submits content around the web to various other websites and blogs which accept guest posts. But because Sean is not an expert, his articles don't appear on the top industry websites, so he had to settle with making his presence known on lower quality ones.

Google knows all about Sean's websites, which have low traffic and high bounce rates. In addition, the guest posts Sean has been making are on sites that have a lot of ads. In fact, those sites are setup specifically to make money with AdSense, and the owner accepts just about any article from anyone, which is why they accept Sean's pieces. Because of this, visitors also don't spend long reading his articles on any of these sites either. Sean's 'author rank' is not great, so when Google notices another one of his articles, they don't give him a boost in rankings, in fact they push his new content even further down the SERPs.

Is Author Rank Real?

Right now? Probably not. In the near future? Probably so. We need to remember that Google authorship is still a relatively new concept, and there are a lot of problems Google needs to sort out before they'd trust author rank as a major part of their algorithm.

What we do know is that in 2011, shortly after Google Authorship was released, Google engineer, Othar Hansson, mentioned that they may use data collected from Google authorship to help rank content. In addition to this, at the Edinburgh International TV Festival, Eric Schmidt (who, at the time was CEO of Google), suggested that Google+ could be used as an 'identity rank' (http://bit.ly/vPmvAp), which ultimately could sort out the good authors from the bad.

Whether it exists now or not, I believe it will be an important ranking factor at some point in the future, so I encourage you to establish your authorship for the content that you create.

There are several other advantages for implementing Google Authorship, even if author rank isn't one of them - yet!

- See your photo next to your entries in the SERPs. This not only builds your brand, but it also catches the eye of the web searcher, so...
- An image in the SERPs, next to a listing, can increase click through rates.
- People searching Google will be able to add you to their Google circles, or find out more about you by visiting your Google profile, all from within the search result listing.

Often there will be a 'more...' link next to the entry in the SERPs, which opens up a custom search showing more of that author's content.

14.2. Setting up Google Authorship

There are a couple of ways to do this, depending on whether you have control of the site your content is appearing on or not. You can read instructions from Google to learn more:

https://plus.google.com/authorship

14.2.1. The Process, Step-by-step If You Own the Domain

Step 1: You first need to have a Google plus account. If you have a Gmail address, then you just need to claim your Google plus profile. To do this, go to:

https://plus.google.com/

Login with your Gmail login details and follow the instructions to get set up with Google Plus.

IMPORTANT: Please note that you should only have ONE Google plus account, so use your main Gmail address. Although discussing the use of Google plus is beyond the scope of this book, I can tell you that you can setup Google Pages for each site you own. What this means is that you can effectively manage multiple sites from within a single Google profile.

Step 2: Upload a profile picture, making sure your face is clear. If you don't have a clear headshot, Google will not show your image in the SERPs.

If you want a short primer on Google+, read this post here:

(http://www.orbitmedia.com/blog/google-plus-guide).

Step 3: Login to Google+, and go to your profile page (click your image top right and select '**View Profile**'). Now go to the '**About**' page. There is a section labelled '**Contact Information**' on the 'About' page. Click the edit link and add your email address.

Step 4: While this step should be unnecessary, I recommend you do it nonetheless.

On the '**About**' page of your profile ('About' link located top left), there is a section labelled '**Links**'. Click the edit button and add your website's homepage URL to the '**Contributor to**' section.

Before you leave your Google Plus profile, grab the URL in the browser address bar.

Step 5: Now login to your WordPress Dashboard, and go to Users -> Your Profile.

Scroll down and you'll see a box for your Google + profile URL:

You will notice that the Google plus URL has some parameters at the end.

You can delete everything after the final '/', so in my screenshot, I'd delete from **about?hl=......** to the end of that line.

You also need to make sure that the field '**Display name publicly as**' is set to the exact same name as your Google+ profile:

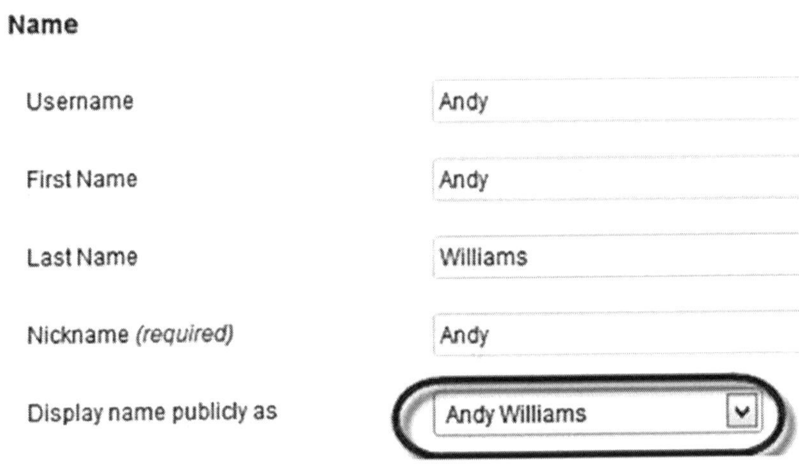

Now go to the SEO menu, and click on '**Social**'.

This takes you to the WordPress SEO settings for social features. Click on the Google+

tab, and select your author name from the top drop down box:

You do not need to enter your Google + profile URL here. By selecting your name, the plugin adds a rel=author tag to your homepage, so Google plus knows it's yours.

The pages on your website now link to your Google + profile, and your profile links to your site. Authorship should now be established, so let's go and check it using the Google Rich Snippet testing tool:

http://www.google.com/webmasters/tools/richsnippets

Enter your homepage URL, and click the preview button:

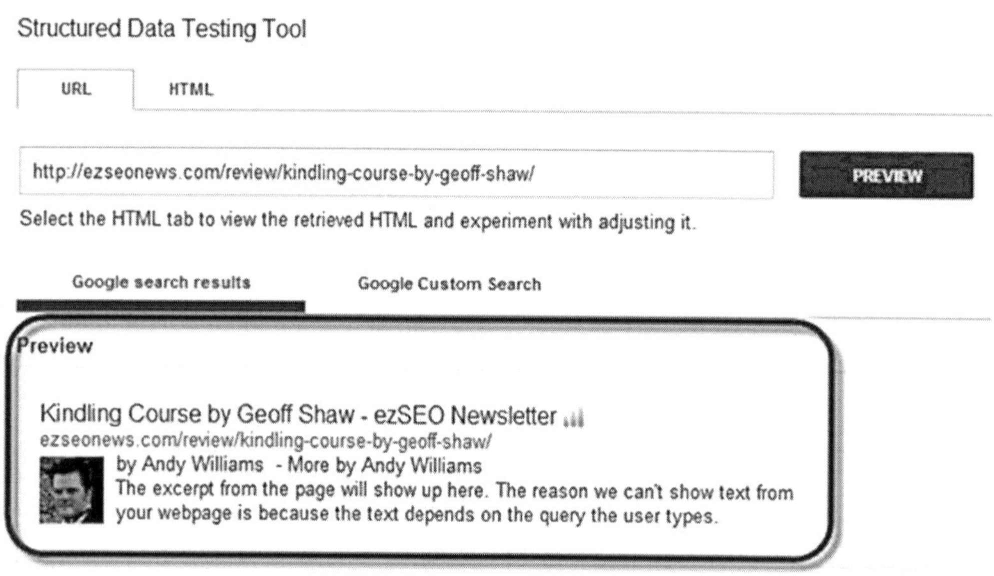

Your Google plus profile image should now show up next to your entry preview.

14.2.2. What About Guest Posts?

If you are likely to have content on websites you don't actually own, how can you tell Google you wrote those articles?

Well, this is quite easy, providing the site that hosts your content allows you to enter HTML into your articles.

Step 1: Add the guest post site to your Google Plus '**contributor to**' section (See step 4 of the previous section if you need a recap).

If it's a one-off post on the site, you can link directly to the post itself. If you have (or intend to have), several posts on a particular site, you can link to its homepage URL.

Step 2: Link your guest post to your Google profile using the following code:

<a href="**GOOGLEPLUSURL**?rel=author">Google+</a>

Just swap the **GOOGLEPLUSURL** part with your actual profile URL.

Now go and check your guest post in the Rich Snippet Testing tool.

14.3. Gravatars & the Author Bio on Your Site

Since you've bothered to add your profile image next to your pages in the SERPs, doesn't it also make sense to add that profile image to the pages on your site? This also helps build brand, but not only that. People like to know who they are dealing with, and a face behind the name adds trust and credibility to your site(s) too.

The first step in adding a photo to your posts is to sign up for a Gravatar:

(https://en.gravatar.com/).

When you get there, you'll see a box where you can add your email address. You need to enter the *exact* same one that you used for your WordPress site.

You will then be asked to '**Sign in with WordPress.com**'. If you don't have an account with WordPress.com, then you can sign up for one there first.

OK, now all you have to do is just follow the on-screen instructions.

Once your account has been setup, you can upload an image and connect your email address to that photo. Be sure to use the same image that you have in your Google Plus profile. It's better for branding to use the same image on our site as the one that shows up in the SERPs.

You can add multiple email addresses to your Gravatar account, so if you control lots of sites, or have many email addresses, you can assign the same (or different), image to every email you'd like a Gravatar for.

Once this is setup, if you leave comments on blogs that have Gravatars enabled (btw, most of them do), then your image will show up next to your comments (assuming you entered the same email address when submitting them). Some forums also use Gravatars for images, so as you can see, we have multiple ways to brand ourselves and build trust around the web.

14.3.1. Genesis Users

To setup the author bio on your posts, login to the dashboard and go to the Users -> Your profile page.

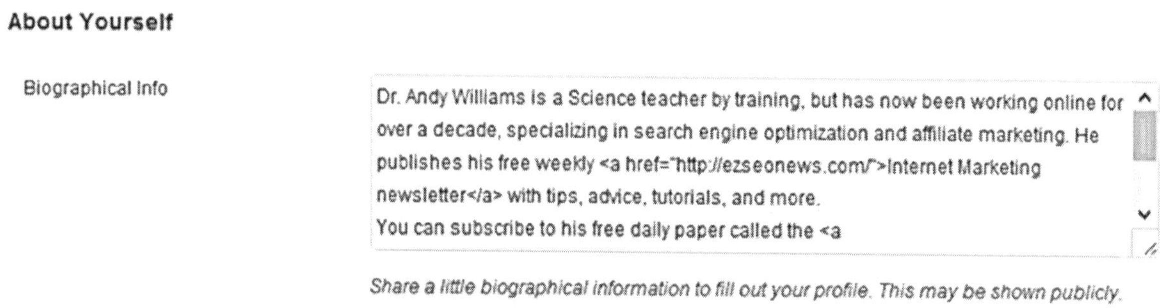

In the '**Biographical info**' box, enter the bio that you want to appear for each post on your site.

Now scroll down a little to the '**Author box**' section.

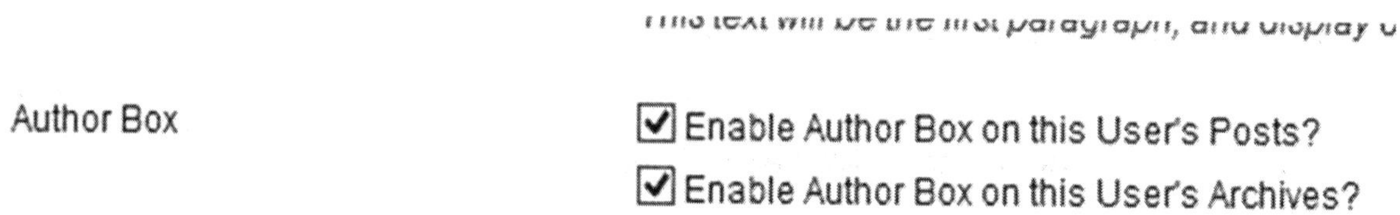

Enable both check boxes.

This adds the author box to individual posts, and also the author archive page.

Here is the author box after one of my posts:

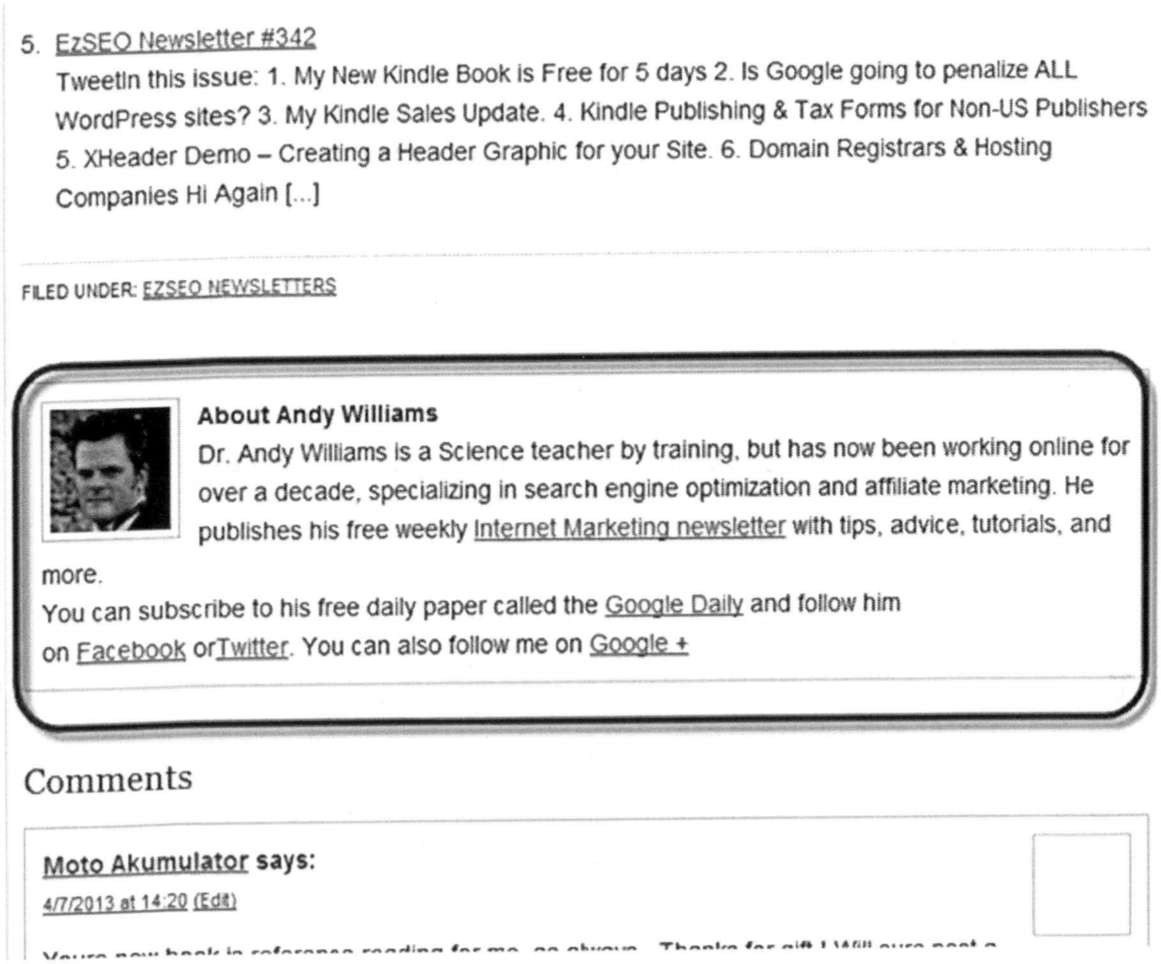
5. EzSEO Newsletter #342

TweetIn this issue: 1. My New Kindle Book is Free for 5 days 2. Is Google going to penalize ALL WordPress sites? 3. My Kindle Sales Update. 4. Kindle Publishing & Tax Forms for Non-US Publishers 5. XHeader Demo – Creating a Header Graphic for your Site. 6. Domain Registrars & Hosting Companies Hi Again [...]

FILED UNDER: EZSEO NEWSLETTERS

About Andy Williams

Dr. Andy Williams is a Science teacher by training, but has now been working online for over a decade, specializing in search engine optimization and affiliate marketing. He publishes his free weekly Internet Marketing newsletter with tips, advice, tutorials, and more.

You can subscribe to his free daily paper called the Google Daily and follow him on Facebook orTwitter. You can also follow me on Google +

Comments

Moto Akumulator says:

4/7/2013 at 14:20 (Edit)

14.3.2. Non-Genesis Users

For non-Genesis users, you'll need to see whether or not your template has an author bio box feature. If it does, you can use that. If it doesn't, there are some plugins that add this functionality to any WordPress site. I cannot recommend any particular plugin as I don't use one. You should be able to find some by searching the WordPress plugin directory (http://wordpress.org/plugins/).

15. Robots.txt File

The robots.txt file is a plain text file that contains various instructions for the search engines. It includes details on specific folders and files that the search engines should, or should not spider.

For example, you can tell the search engines to ignore all files within a specific folder on your server. A good example of a folder that search engines should keep out of is the WordPress plugin folder. The files there are not content pages on your site, so why would you want the search engines sniffing around in there? If you allow them to, they'll index the PHP files in those folders, and so list them in the SERPS as content on your site. Not really what we want is it?

Using a robots.txt file is easy enough. Just create a text file in any text editor, and add in the commands. Once done, simply upload it to the root folder of your WordPress site.

On the WordPress website, they show a suggested example robots.txt file. You can find it here:

http://codex.wordpress.org/Search_Engine_Optimization_for_WordPress

However, since we are using Yoast's WordPress plugin, a lot of what we need to do in terms of excluding search engine spiders, is done for us. In a post on the subject (http://yoast.com/example-robots-txt-wordpress/), Joost de Valk (the author of the WordPress SEO plugin), goes through the WordPress example and explains why most of it is not really necessary.

In Yoast's article, he suggests a much simplified robots.txt file, and it's similar to the one he currently uses on Yoast.com. Here it is:

User-Agent: *
Disallow: /wp-content/plugins/

I personally add a couple of extra lines to mine. The first one is to disallow spiders from going into the cgi-bin folder:

Disallow: /cgi-bin

The majority of site owners never have any files and sub-directories in this folder anyway, so it's not critical for most. The other line I add to my robots.txt file is one that tells the spiders where my sitemap is located.

You can find the location of your sitemap by going into the XML Sitemap settings found in the SEO menu in the left sidebar.

Click the '**XML Sitemap**' button and your sitemap will open in the browser:

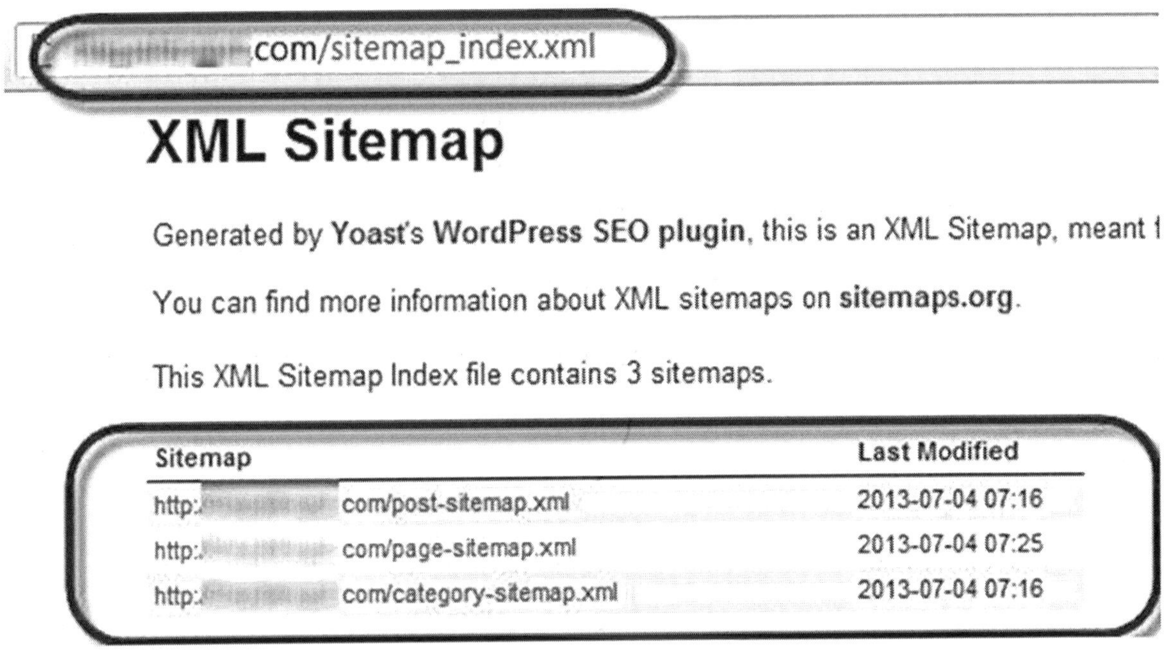

You now have a choice. You can copy the URL from the address bar of your internet browser and use that as your sitemap URL. Alternatively, you can grab the URLs of the individual sitemaps listed below, and add each one separately to your robots.txt file.

I like to add all three (you could have more or less), sitemaps to my robots.txt file.

Those lines look like this:

Sitemap: http://mydomain.com/post-sitemap.xml

Obviously I've switched my real domain in that URL.

My complete robots.txt file therefore looks like this:

User-Agent: *

Disallow: /wp-content/plugins/

Disallow: /cgi-bin

Allow: /wp-content/uploads

Sitemap: http://mydomain.com/post-sitemap.xml

Sitemap: http://mydomain.com/page-sitemap.xml

Sitemap: http://mydomain.com/category-sitemap.xml

After saving this as a plain text file called **robots.txt**, just upload it to your site's root folder (this is where WordPress is installed).

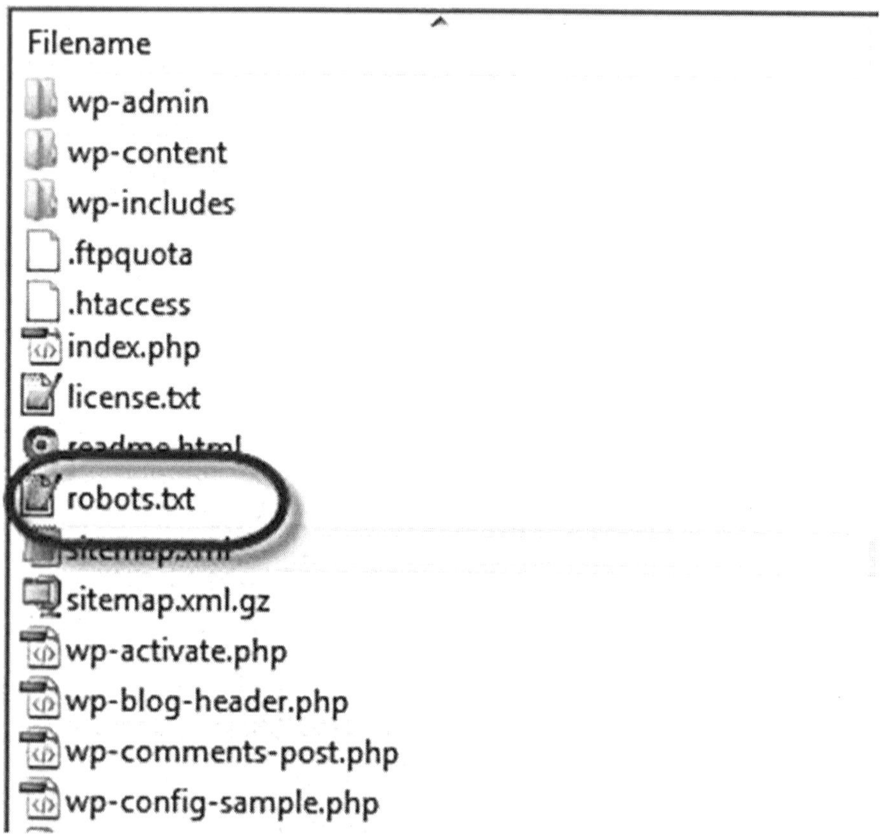

In the screenshot above, you can see the robots.txt file in the same folder as the wp-admin, wp-content & wp-includes folder. Seeing these folders simply confirms I have uploaded it to the correct place.

16. WWW or No WWW?

You see some websites with the 'www.' prefix, and others without. Google actually treats these as different URLs. When you have links pointing to your site, you need them to all show the same, either with the www. or without it.

You therefore need to decide which way you want your site's URL to be displayed.

Once WordPress is installed, visit your homepage by typing in the www. version of the domain. See what WordPress does by default. More often than not, it will be the non-www version and you will be automatically redirected there. So even if you type in the www. of the URL, it won't show once the page loads.

My advice is to use whatever WordPress shows you by default, unless you have a good reason to want the other version.

Once decided on your preferred version, login to your WordPress Dashboard and go to the Settings -> General screen

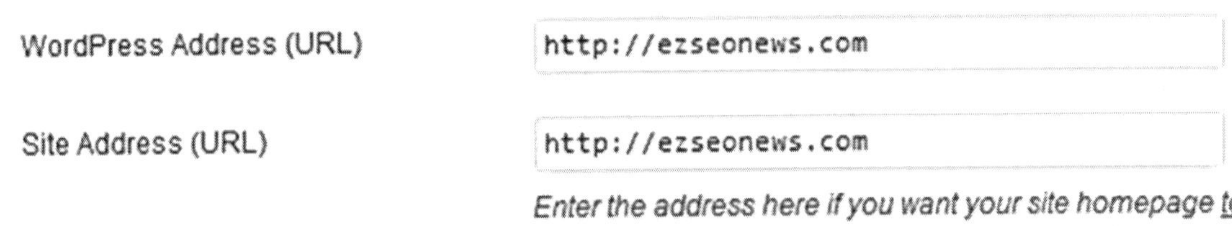

Now you need to tell Google which version you want to use. You can do this in Google Webmaster Tools, so login to your GWT account, and click on the site you are working on.

Now click on the cog icon located in the top right, and select '**Site Settings**'.

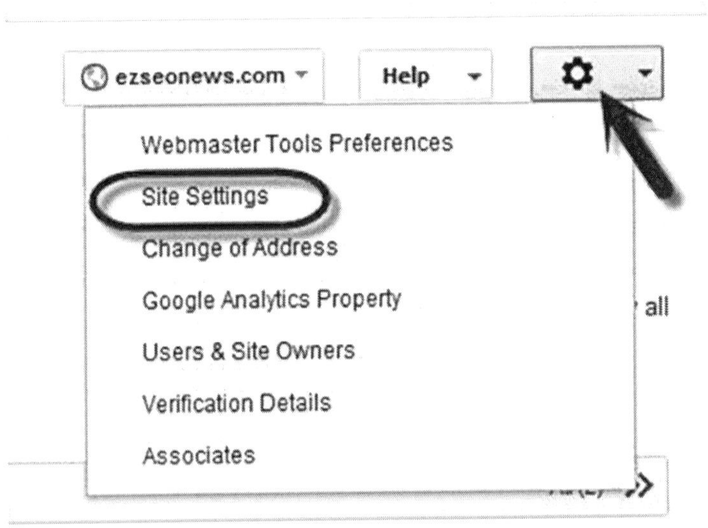

In the screen that loads, you can select the correct version of your site by selecting the '**Preferred domain**' radio button:

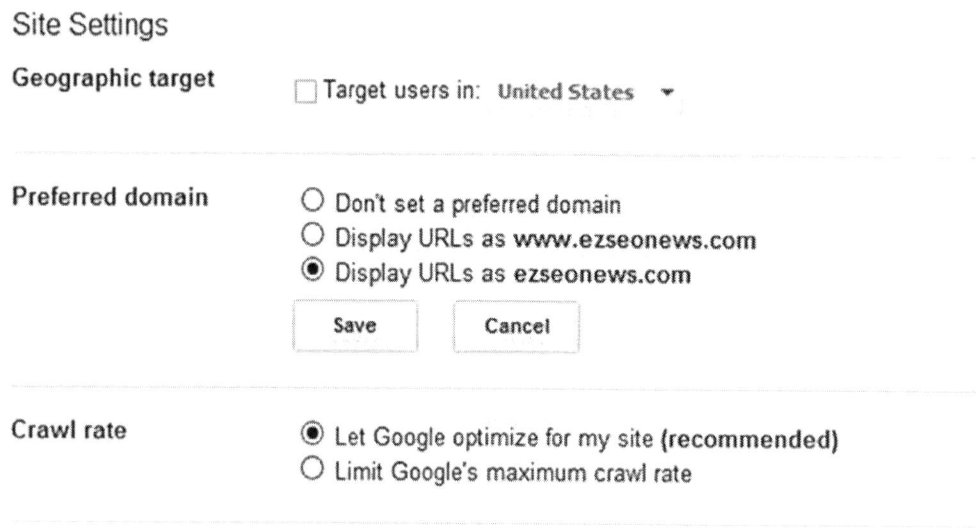

Note, that you can also select the '**Geographic target**' for your site on this screen. Just check the box and select your preferred target location.

If your site is for a worldwide audience, then leave this box unchecked. However, if your site is really only for the UK, as one example, then check the box and select the United Kingdom from the drop down. This asks Google to give your site preferential treatment on the UK Google. However, that doesn't automatically mean you'll rank better there.

17. Pages Versus Posts

While I covered this in my WordPress for Beginners book, it is important you understand the basics, so I'll go over fundamentals again here.

One of the things that many WordPress beginners get confused about is the difference between WordPress Pages and WordPress Posts. What makes things even more confusing is the tendency to call any web page a 'page', even if it is actually a 'post'.

To try to make things clearer, when I am referring to a web page loaded in your browser, whether it's been created as a WordPress post or a WordPress page, I'll call it a web page. If I am specifically talking about a WordPress post or a WordPress page, then I'll make sure I prefix the words post and page with 'WordPress'.

Here is a quick key:

Web page: Any web page that's loaded in your internet browser.

WordPress Page: Content created as a WordPress 'Page'.

WordPress Post: Content created as a WordPress 'Post'.

Got it? OK, let's carry on.

With WordPress, we need to make the distinction between WordPress pages and WordPress posts, as they are both different and have distinctive purposes.

Let's look at the features of these two:

17.1. Posts

- Can be displayed chronologically or in reverse chronological order in a number of places on your site, including author pages, category pages, most recent posts, and RSS feeds.
- They are assigned to categories.
- They can be tagged.
- Posts can allow visitor comments.
- Posts appear in your site's RSS feeds and can therefore be syndicated to email subscribers if using a service like FeedBurner.
- Posts can have excerpts, which is basically a short summary of the written piece. These can be used by WordPress and plugins to supply a Meta Description tag, and short descriptions of posts in related posts features, etc.
- Posts do not have a custom template feature. There was a feature introduced in WordPress 3.1 called 'Post Formats'. Not all themes support these, but they are available to all theme developers if they wish to use them. Basically, this

feature allows posts to be classified as: *standard, aside, audio, chat, gallery, link, quote, status* or *video*, and their appearance changes depending on the post format. You can read more about post format here: http://codex.wordpress.org/Post_Formats

17.2. Pages

- These are 'static' and not listed or sorted by date order. They are, however, hierarchical, so you can have a parent page with several child pages.
- Pages are not put into categories.
- Pages do not have tags.
- Although it is possible to enable comments on pages, this isn't typically something you want to do.
- Pages do not appear in your site's RSS feed and are therefore not syndicated to email subscribers when using FeedBurner.
- Pages do not have excerpts.
- Pages can use a 'custom template' feature making it possible to vary the appearance of them (read your template documentation to see what is available).
- You can setup a WordPress page to be used as your homepage.

17.3. When to Use WordPress Pages, and WordPress Posts

As you can see, there are several distinct differences between the two.

In terms of SEO, Google doesn't care whether a web page is created as a WordPress page or a WordPress post. However, the features we have available with WordPress posts make them the obvious choice for content that we hope to rank well for in the SERPs. Because of this, I recommend you use WordPress pages and WordPress posts as follows:

Use WordPress pages for the 'legal pages' (disclaimers, privacy statement, contact, about us, etc), and use WordPress posts for everything else.

When I say everything else, I am referring to all content that is written to engage the visitor. If it's something you want a visitor to read, and maybe comment on or share to their own social circles, definitely use a post.

By sticking to this simple rule, you can take advantage of the way WordPress was designed to work, and thus get maximum SEO benefits out of it. The only exception I make to this rule is when I want to setup my homepage using a WordPress page, rather than one which displays the last 10 WordPress posts (more on this in the next chapter).

18. Setting up the Homepage

There are two main ways of setting up a homepage in WordPress. You can either create a WordPress page for it, or you can base your homepage to display the latest WordPress posts.

You make that decision in the **Settings -> Reading** options.

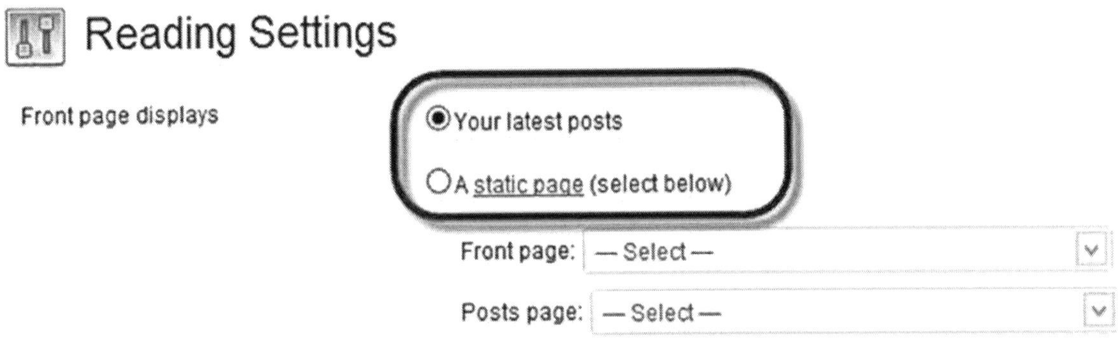

Essentially, using a WordPress pages for your homepage means you can have a more 'static' front page, i.e., one that doesn't change too much.

If you choose to go with the 'latest posts' option for your homepage (as is typical for blogs), then it will always be changing, showing your very latest post at the top of it.

WordPress themes have evolved, and one of my favourite features of the Genesis theme is the way it handles the homepage. The Genesis framework was the first template system I found that allowed us to create a homepage using widgets. You should be familiar with widgets by now, but if not, just think of them as user-definable areas where you can insert whatever you want.

The Genesis child themes do differ in the number and location of widgetized areas on the homepage, so you would need to check them out before buying one.

For example, the Genesis Lifestyle theme gives you three widgetized areas in addition to the usual header, sidebars and footers. You have 'Home', 'Home left' and 'Home right' and these are positioned directly where the main content of the homepage will go.

Here are those three widget areas:

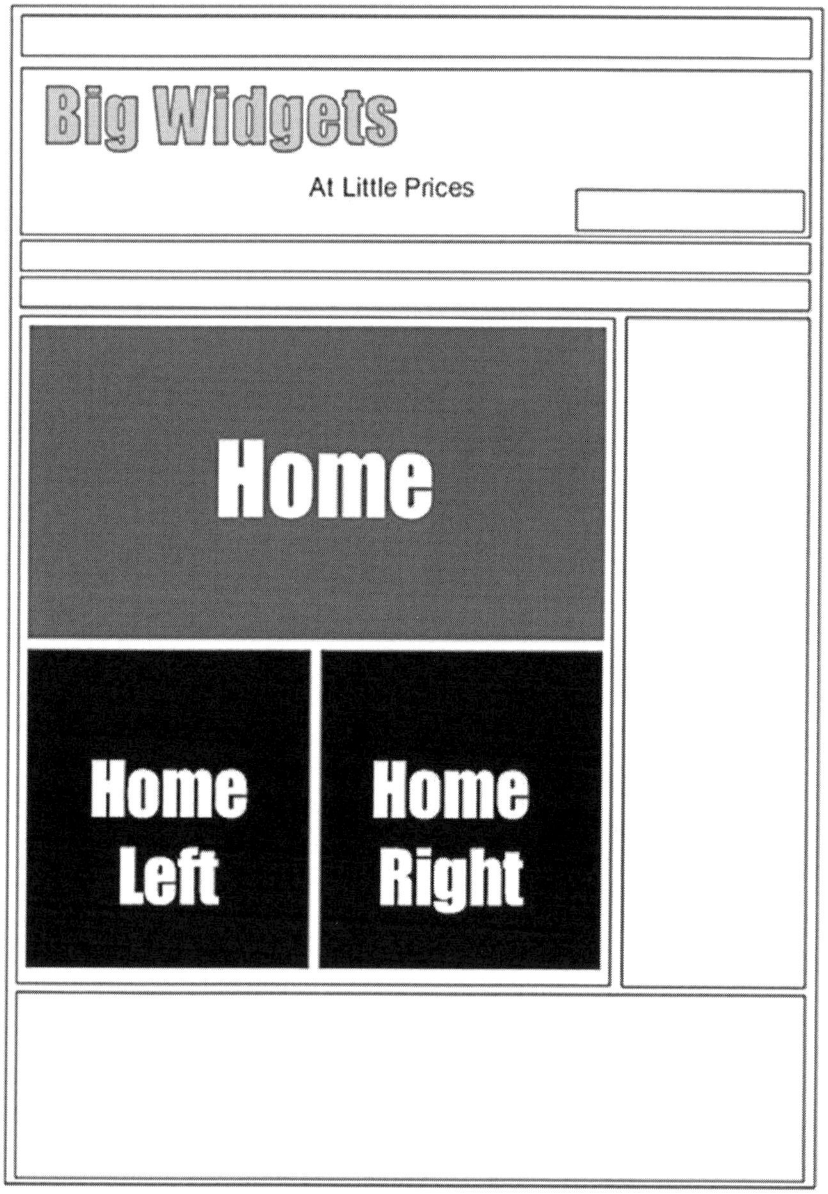

Those three widget areas can contain posts, pages, or just about anything else.

You can see this theme in action on the Lifestyle demo theme site:

http://demo.studiopress.com/lifestyle/

By contrast, the Genesis Balance theme has two homepage widget areas called 'Home Featured Left' and 'Home Featured Right'.

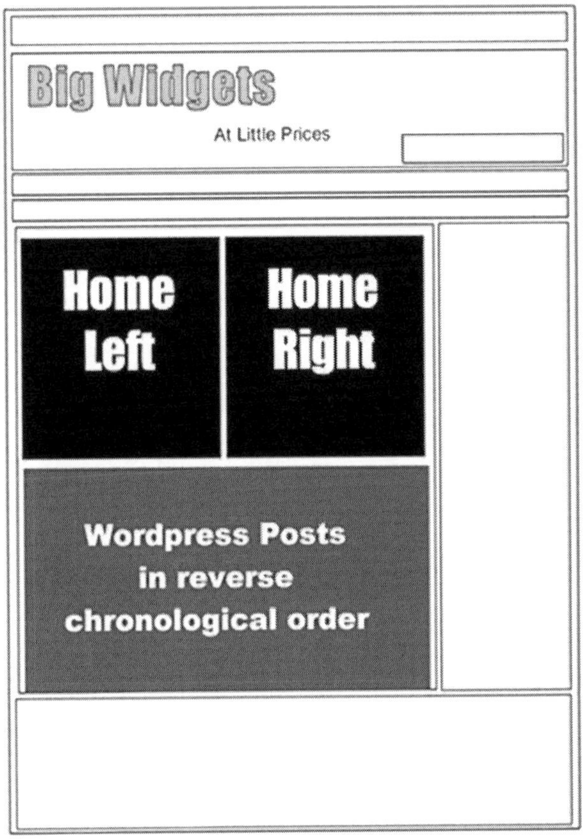

Under the 'home featured left' and 'home featured right' areas of the homepage, the normal WordPress loop is used to show the latest posts in reverse chronological order. You can also check out the Balance theme demo site to see how these widgetized areas were designed to work:

http://demo.studiopress.com/balance/

The two boxes at the top of that demo site are controlled by these two widgets.

I love the Genesis child themes because they give me so much scope for designing a homepage the way I want it to appear. The idea of using widgets for the homepage, wherever it came from, is pure genius.

18.1. Genesis Homepage Widgets

Genesis Framework comes with some really nice widgets that can help you create a great looking homepage (although these widgets can be used in any widgetized area, not just the homepage). Here are the ones that come pre-installed with Genesis:

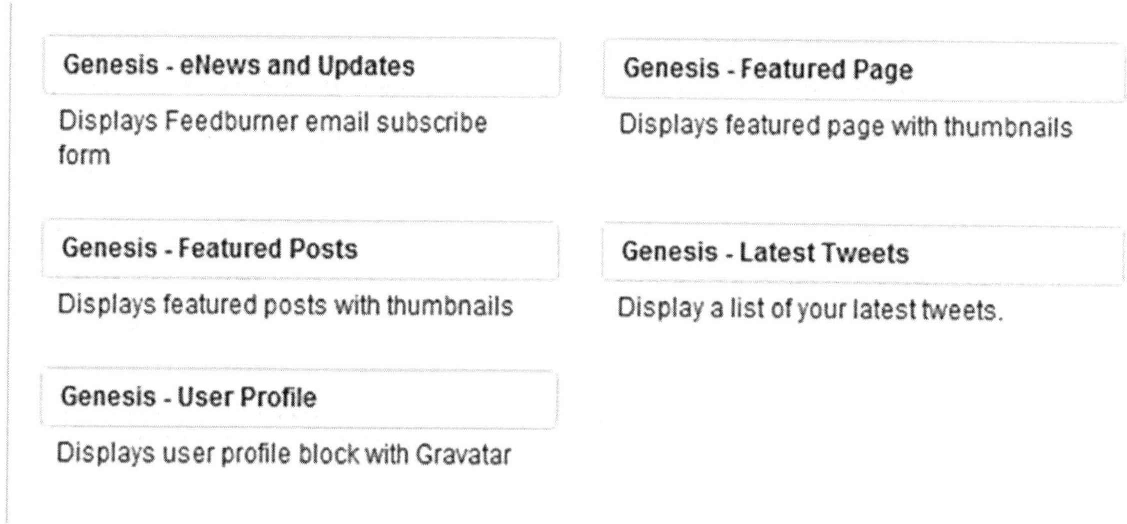

For some reason, two of those widgets have been depreciated, and when you try to install them, you are told to download and install different ones. I'll show you which they are as we go through them.

18.1.1. Genesis - eNews and Updates

This is one that has been depreciated. When you add it to a widgetized area, you'll see a link in the widget setup to download the 'Genesis eNews Extended' widget.

One of the important aspects of modern SEO is the need to keep visitors happy, and keep them coming back. This plugin allows you to insert an email-capture form on your site.

A good place to add this is at the top of the sidebar. If you are using a template like the Genesis Balance child theme, then this would go nicely in the top widgetized area of the homepage. Having your sign-up form as one of the first things a visitor sees on arriving at your site is a smart move, providing that page makes a good first impression of course.

When the plugin is installed, you'll find the new widget in the widgets area of the Dashboard. On adding the widget, you can enter a FeedBurner ID to get the form to link to a FeedBurner account (this is so that people are notified when new content is added to your site), or you can set it up to work with your mailing list provider.

If you want to set this up, see the instructions that come with the plugin/widget.

18.1.2. Genesis - Featured Page

This is one of my favourite widgets for the homepage. It allows you to add a featured post to it. I typically add a featured page to the top of my homepage and then use other widgets below it that to fill out the page.

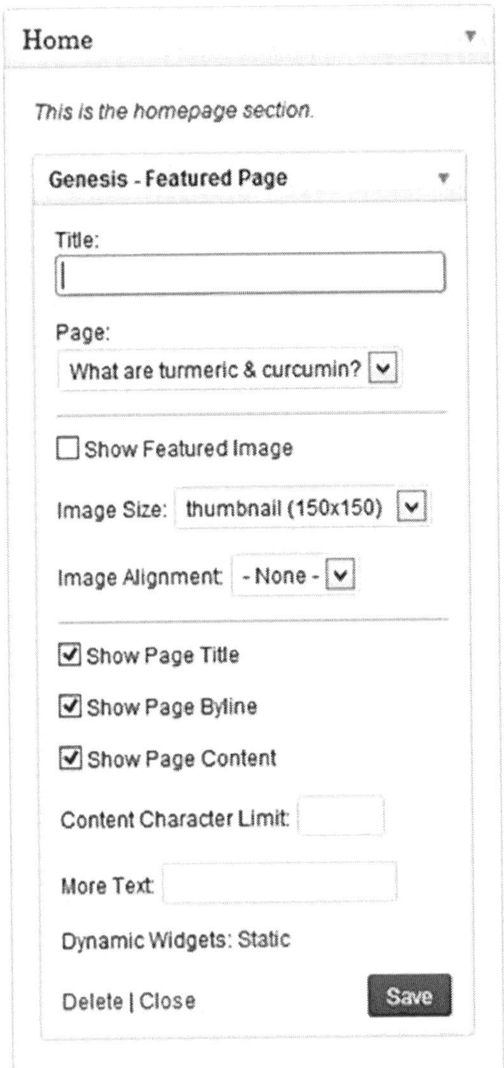

From an SEO perspective, if you add a complete featured post to the homepage, then you will not want the same post indexed on the post's own page (remember how WordPress duplicates the content?). There are two options that I have used on my sites.

1. Go in and set the page to noindex, follow (done from the 'Advance' tab of the WordPress SEO by Yoast plugin), so that the only copy of that article Google will know about, and therefore index, is the one on the homepage.
2. Use the <!—more--> tag to limit how much of the page is shown on the homepage. I cover this in the next section of the book. I typically just show the first paragraph, which is usually a good introduction to the content.

If I use a featured page at the top of my homepage, it will be a page I setup which basically introduces the whole site and the concept of the project. When I first construct the site, I'll set that page as my homepage (see above). As I begin to add posts, I'll switch to showing only the first paragraph of the page (using the more quicktag), in one of these widgets, and then display post excerpts underneath.

In the screenshot above, you see that the widget can be configured to show the featured image, page title, byline & content. You can also limit the number of characters of the content that are displayed. However, I recommend you use the more quicktag for that, as you'll be able to display *exactly* what you want, whereas the former option might cut off the excerpt mid-sentence.

18.1.3. Genesis - Featured Posts

This widget is similar to the 'Featured Page' widget, except this one displays a number of posts instead. On the Genesis themes, where you have 'home left' and 'home right' widget areas, I typically add featured posts widgets to these underneath my featured post widget (in the Home widget area). That way I have the following layout on the homepage:

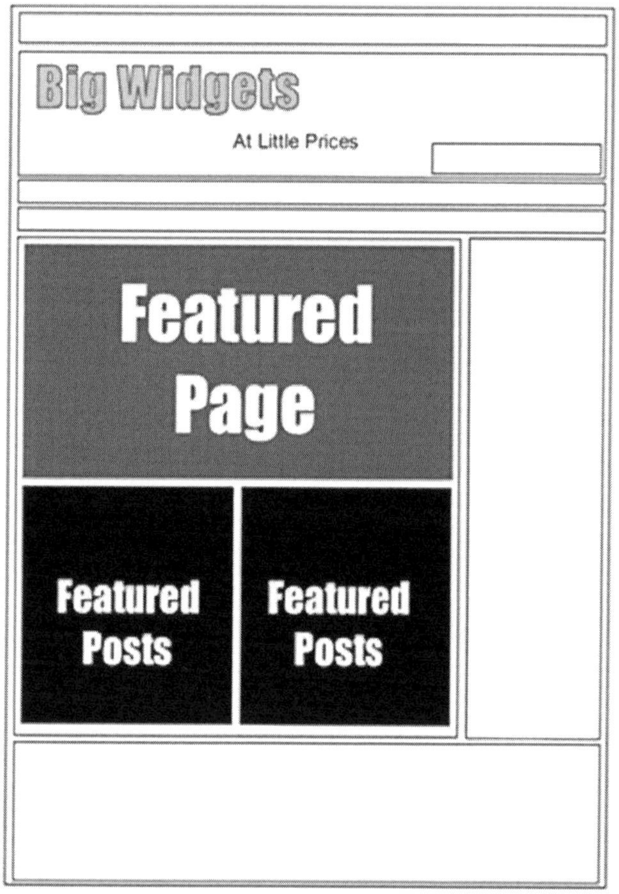

Using the featured posts widget is easy. Simply drag and drop it into the widgetized area and you'll get a stack of options:

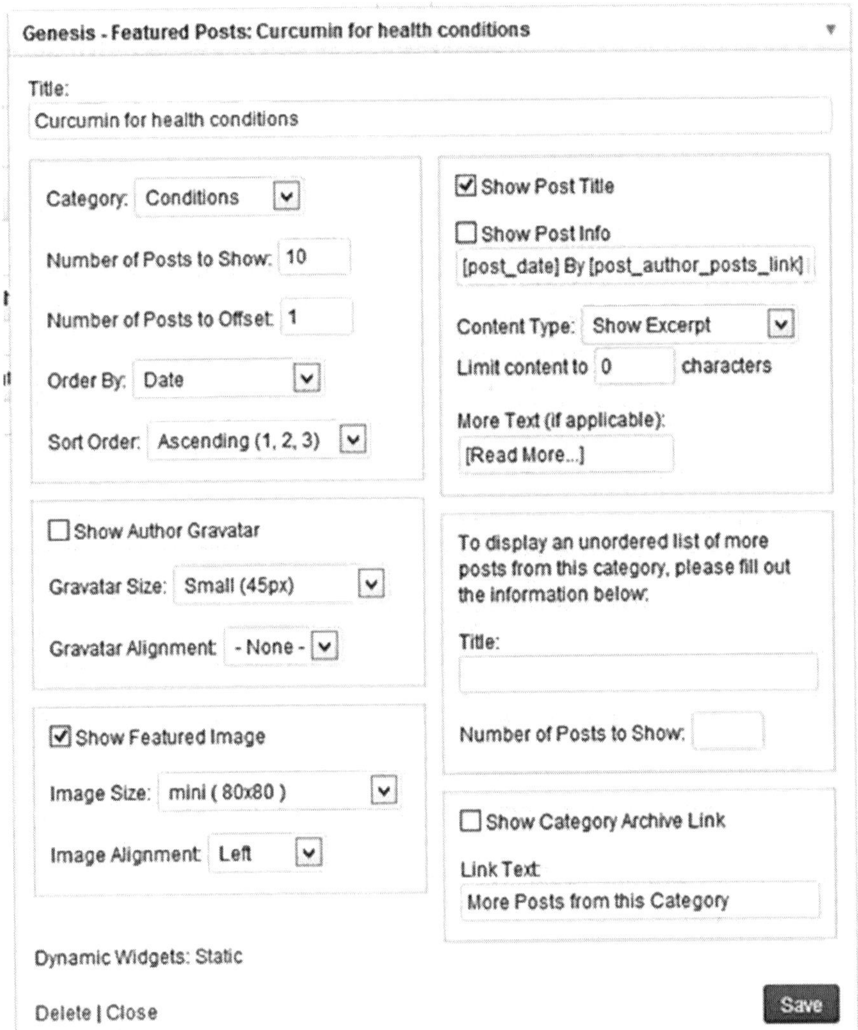

You can select which category you want to pull posts from, how many posts to show, and you can even offset the posts, for example, to skip the first X number of posts.

There are a number of reasons why you might want to offset the posts. One is if you are using two of these widgets to display posts from the same category. You might show the first five in one widget, and then in the second widget, you need to offset it by '5' so that the same five don't show up.

I often have mine offset by '1' if I am using a non-Genesis theme. This is because the first post in all of my categories is an 'announcement' post, created by the WP-Sticky WordPress plugin. You'll see why later in the book, when I show you how to set up category pages.

Other possibilities with the featured posts widget include how you order the posts, whether a featured image is shown next to them, plus other options. This plugin is highly customizable, and one of the most useful I've seen for constructing a homepage.

For SEO purposes, I recommend you set the widget to '**Show Excerpts**' for each post. We'll look at how to add excerpts to a post later in the book. If you forget to add an excerpt to a post, the plugin will use the opening text in the article as its description.

18.1.4. Genesis - Latest Tweets

This is another widget that is depreciated. When you add it to a widgetized area, you will be asked to install a different plugin. The widget allows you to add an element to your site that shows your recent tweets on Twitter. If you make use of Twitter, that can be a good feature as it will encourage people to follow you (that's assuming they like what they see in the stream displayed on your site).

I will just mention that this plugin does seem to stop working at times, so do make sure it is functional if add it to your site.

18.1.5. Genesis - User Profile

As I've mentioned previously, people like to deal with 'real' people. This widget allows you to add your photo and short bio to your website. I usually add mine in the footer area:

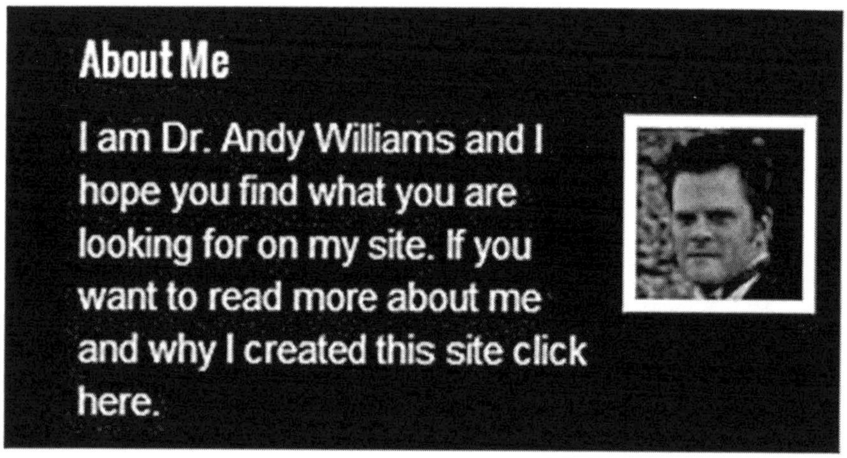

You have a few options with this widget:

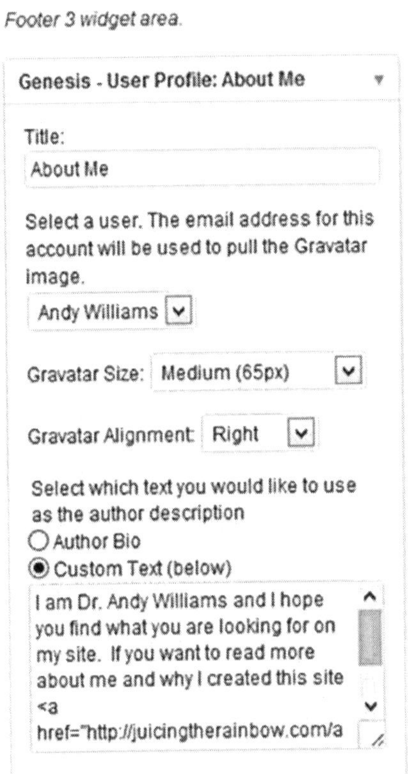

Give the widget a title, select your user profile, and choose the preferred alignment and size of the image. You can then use the bio you setup earlier in your user profile, or you can add custom text if you want (which is what I have done in my screenshot).

There are a couple of other options with this widget:

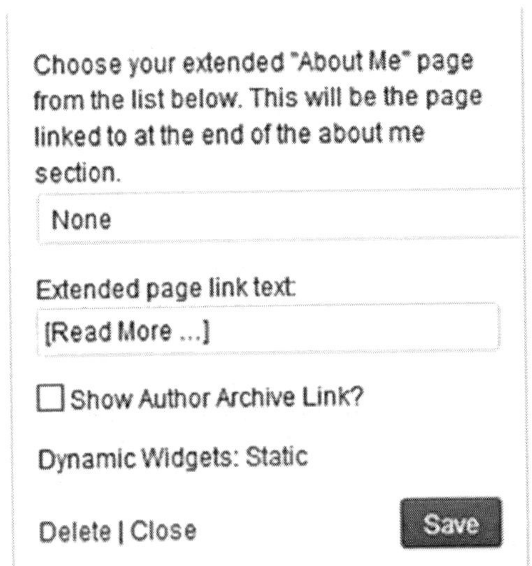

For example, you can specify a page on your site with a more complete bio. This will then be linked to at the end of the 'About Me' section.

You can also include a link to your author archive on the site (which I don't really recommend as the author archive page is not very user friendly to be honest).

By using these widgets, you can create a homepage that links to the most important pages on your site, and that's good for both SEO and your visitors.

18.2. The <!--more--> Quicktag

When you insert the <!--more--> quicktag into the text of a post, it will break the post at that exact point, and only display the text above the tag. There will be a 'read more' link at the point of the break, so people can click on that and be taken to the full article.

While this quicktag can be used for any post on your site, I like to use it on posts appearing on the homepage in order to stop full piece from being displayed. This helps to reduce duplication on the site.

Here is an example on my ezSEONews.com website.

See where it says 'Read More'? That is the position of the 'more tag' in my article. Here it is in the post editor:

NOTE: Add the more tag in the 'Text' tab of the editor.

When using this 'more' quicktag, we have another method of adding an introduction to an article, and a link to read the whole piece on its own 'post' page. We just select the first paragraph of the post, add a more tag after it, and it's done.

Note that when you use this 'more tag', and have an excerpt created for a particular post, the more tag will be used on the homepage, author page, category page and tag page, while the excerpt will be used on the search page, plus some areas controlled by plugins, such as the related post, recent posts, and so on.

18.3. "Nofollow" Links

This isn't just an attribute to be used on homepages; it is a concern for all posts and pages on your entire site.

The nofollow tag can be added to any link to stop the search engines from following it.

Here is an example link with the nofollow attribute assigned to it:

<a href="http://google.com" **rel="nofollow"**>Google</a>

It's a good idea to nofollow links on your site that you don't want to waste link juice on. These include the legal pages (contact, privacy, etc). We've already seen this earlier in the book when we setup the legal menu to automatically nofollow the links.

I'd also recommend you nofollow *all* affiliate links.

When you are writing content that links to another authority website, do NOT add nofollow. We want Google to know we endorse these other credible sites by leaving the nofollow off the link.

These guidelines go for all pages on your site, and not just the homepage.

18.4. Getting Social on Your Site

It is a good idea to include ways for your visitors to follow you on various social channels that you use, e.g. Twitter, Facebook & Google plus, to name but three. A great widget that can add this to your site is the '**Social Sticker**' that I mentioned in the plugin section. This will add buttons to your posts that visitors can click on to follow you on social media. Here is an example:

The plugin can easily add buttons like this to your site's sidebar, included on *every* web page of your site, and not just the homepage.

Google are certainly paying a lot more attention to social shares as ranking signals, so you will also want to have a social sharing plugin installed for adding buttons to every post on the site like the one below:

KD Suite review

17/6/2013 BY ANDY WILLIAMS • 21 COMMENTS (EDIT)

Back in July 2012, I started publishing on Amazon Kindle using Geoff Shaw's excellent Kindle publishing course as my guide. That journey has resulted in a substantial monthly income from my books. I have been so impressed with the potential of Kindle publishing that I intend to devote a bigger chunk of my own time to this market. I had even considered writing a piece of software to help me decide on the best books to write (i.e. those with big markets that are selling well in Kindle). However, last week I saw an email promotion for something called the KD Suite. I went to watch the video on the sales page and immediately bought it. I've been playing with it ever since and I love it.

19. SEO When Writing Content

In this section, I just want to highlight a few points about writing content and SEO, plus mention the specific features you can use to help with the Search Engine Optimisation on your WordPress pages and WordPress posts.

With any type of content, posts or pages, it is important to follow a few general rules to ensure you do not fall foul of Google's Panda or Penguin algorithm. In the old days of SEO (pre-2011), webmasters tried to rank specifically for a keyword phrase or two, and would insert the exact phrase in a number of places like the title, filename, H1 header, opening paragraph, closing paragraph, ALT tags, and also worked into various other paragraphs within the article body too. Today that is just asking for trouble. The era of targeting specific words and phrases are just about over.

The best approach to writing good quality content is to write for your visitor, and not the search engines. If you right naturally, and with a sound knowledge of the topic, you will automatically include relevant words and phrases into your content anyway, which will help it rank for a whole host of search phrases. By all means include a specific phrase somewhere, such as the title or H1 header, but don't, whatever you do, start stuffing the same phrase in as many places as possible. Google are clever enough now to know what the page is about, even without strategic keyword placements by the webmaster. Concentrate on providing great quality content that will please your visitors, and that Google will want to rank highly because it deserves to.

With that in mind, create a compelling headline for your post, and don't try to stuff it with individual keywords or keyword phrases either. Just aim to create quality content, and forget about trying to optimise it for any specific words or phrases.

Tip: If you read your content out loud, and it sounds unnatural because of keywords that have been forced into the text, then it's not great content.

Another thing to think about is the 'slug' of your post or page. The slug is the filename, and it is automatically generated by WordPress when you publish content. WordPress takes your content's title, replaces spaces with dashes, removes any non-alphanumeric characters, and uses that (see below):

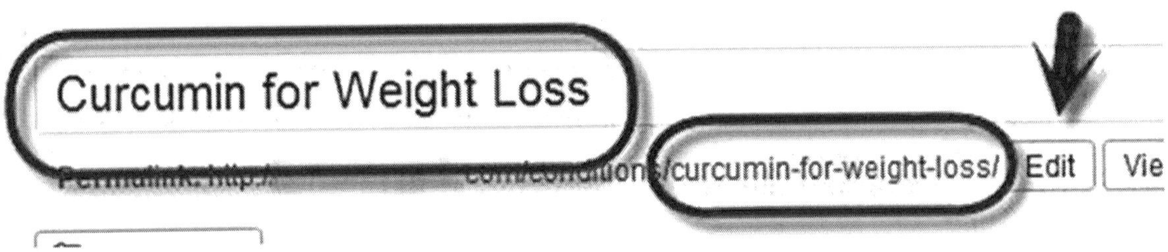

In the screenshot above, the title of the article is 'curcumin for weight loss'. The slug that WordPress created is **curcumin-for-weight-loss.**

You can change the slug if you want to; perhaps if there's a better way of naming it, or maybe the title of your article is long (it's a good idea to keep your URLs short). To edit the slug, click the '**Edit**' button next to the permalink URL at the top of your post/page, and then modify it to what you want. Finally, make sure you Publish/Update your page to save the changes.

19.1. SEO for WordPress Pages

The first thing I should mention about WordPress pages is that they can now have comments. This wasn't always the case, but I guess WordPress caved in to popular demand (of those that used pages for content when they should have perhaps used posts!).

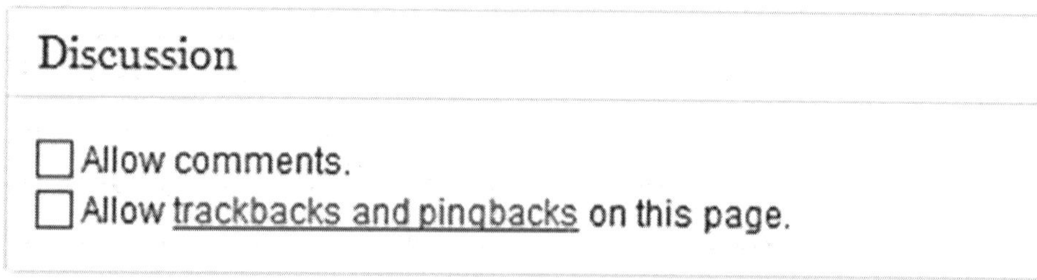

The way we are using WordPress pages (for legal pages), it's unlikely you'll want to enable that option. We don't particularly want people commenting on our privacy policy or contact pages! However, if you do have a page that you would like to enable comments on, this is where you do it on a page-by-page basis (the Discussion box is located below the text editor). If you don't see it, check the screen options (top right of the Dashboard).

Fortunately, a lot of the SEO we control on pages (and posts), is supplied to us by the Yoast WordPress SEO plugin. You'll find a section created by this plugin as you scroll down the page edit screen. It's typically located just under the text editor:

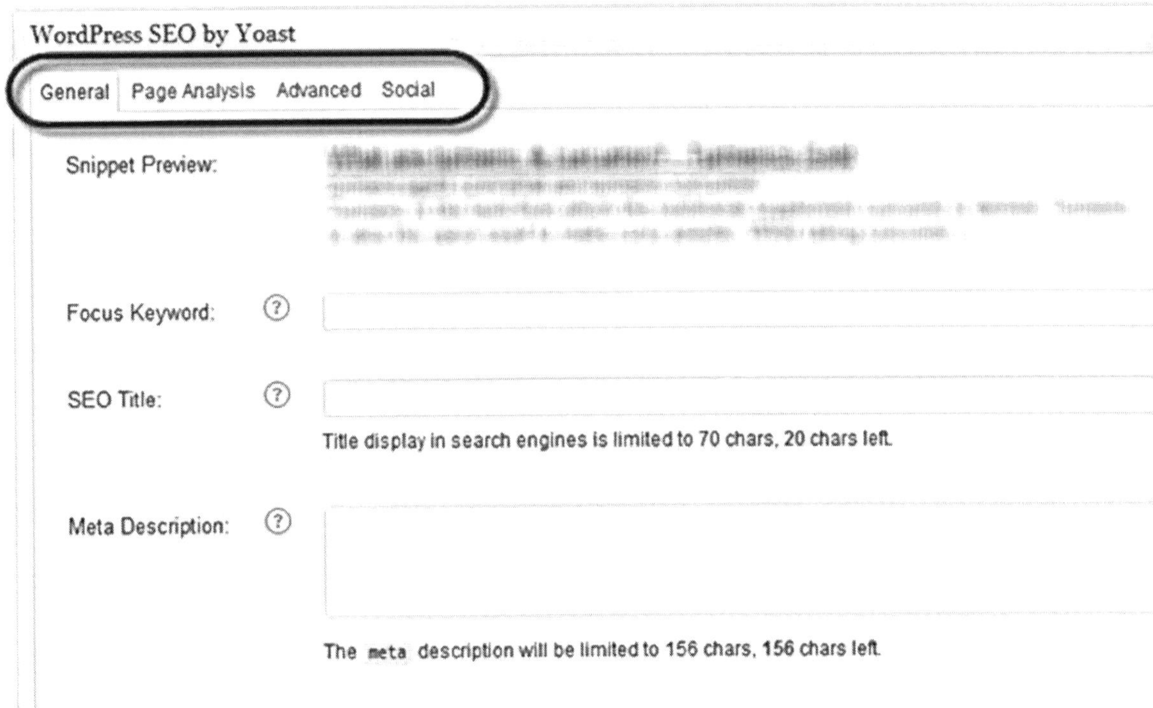

There are 4 tabs across the top of this plugin. The first is the '**General**' tab. This shows a preview of what your listing is likely to look like in Google, with Title, URL and Description.

Below the '**Snippet Preview:**' there is a box labelled '**Focus Keyword**'. I would leave this empty and not use this feature of the plugin. When on-page SEO was all about optimizing for a specific keyword phrase, this plugin helped to make sure that phrase was found in all of the important parts of the page (title, header, article, etc). This is a dangerous procedure these days, so I recommend you do NOT use this plugin's on-page optimisation features.

There are also boxes for an SEO Title and Meta Description. If you are unhappy with the title WordPress created for you (possibly with the help of the Yoast WordPress SEO plugin, as you'll see later in the book), you can create your own title that will be used when the page is rendered.

The Meta Description box allows you to create a unique Meta Description tag for your page. If the page is one that you hope people will visit through the search engines, then add a good description here; otherwise leave it blank and Google will create a description for your page from its content.

The '**Page Analysis**' tab of this plugin is used to help optimize the page around your focus keyword. We aren't using this, so ignore this tab altogether.

On the '**Advanced**' tab, there are some really useful features:

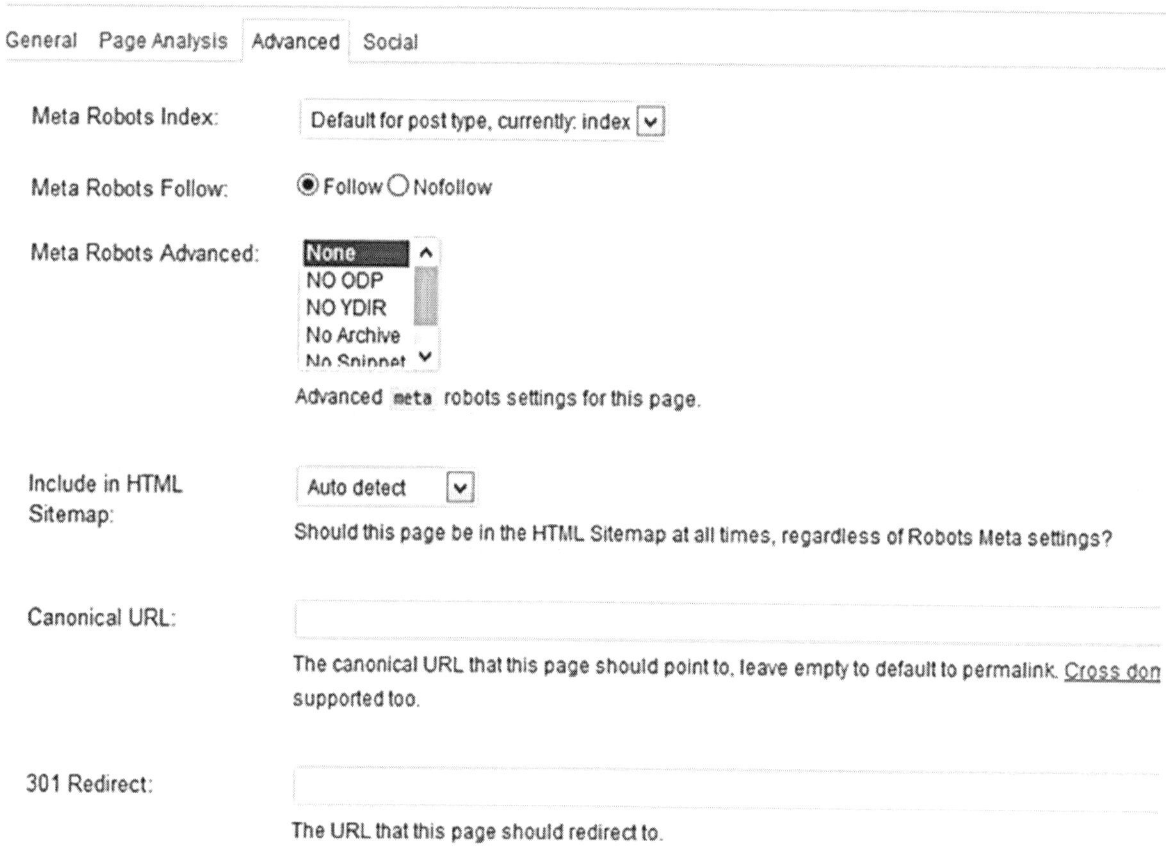

At the top, you have the option of controlling search engine robot commands for the page.

The '**Meta Robots Index:**' dropdown box is set to allow spiders to index the page by default. You can, however, set this to 'noindex' if it is a page you don't want the search engines to include in their search results.

I recommend you set *all* your legal pages to 'noindex'.

Under this box is the '**Meta Robots Follow:**' from where you can specify whether you want links on the page followed or nofollowed. I recommend you leave this to follow for *all* pages, since we want links on the page to be followed in order to help the site's indexing.

Next we have the '**Meta Robots Advanced:**' options. You can set a few preferences here. The only time you really need to change this from the default of 'None', is when you don't want a page archived in the search engines. Again, I recommend this for *all* legal pages as this will prevent Google from retaining a cached version of them.

Now we have the '**Include in HTML Sitemap:**' option. Here we can specify whether or not we want the page to appear in the sitemap that Yoast's WordPress SEO plugin creates. For legal pages, I would select '**Never include**'. For everything else, leave it at the default setting of '**Auto Detect**'.

The next box allows you to specify a '**Canonical URL:**' for the page. You should not have to bother with this option as WordPress looks after it for us.

The '**301 Redirect:**' option allows you to enter a URL that this page should automatically redirect to. That is, when someone loads the page, it redirects to the URL you enter here. 301 redirects are typically used to notify the search engines that a page or post has permanently moved to a new URL. For example, if you had a page that had a lot of links pointing to it, but you wanted to move that page to a new URL - for whatever reason - you could 301 the original to the new, and all those links would still count to towards the ranking of the new page URL.

On the '**Social**' tab, you can enter a custom description for the page so that if someone shares it on Facebook or Google+, this description will be used instead of the default one.

OK, that's the Yoast WordPress settings for WordPress pages. Let's now look at SEO on WordPress posts.

19.2. SEO for WordPress Posts

WordPress posts have a few more SEO options than WordPress pages. We still have the Yoast WordPress SEO plugin options that we saw in the previous section on 'WordPress Pages', and they are used in exactly the same way. If you need to noindex, follow a post (as we will do later when we look at setting up category pages), then you do it using the '**Advanced**' tab of that plugin's options.

Also, you will notice that if you go to **Posts -> All Posts**, in the WordPress Dashboard, there are a few extra columns tacked on to the end of the table:

I would suggest you ignore these columns, as they are part of the keyword optimisation features in the plugin. Remember I advised you earlier not to use those features as they are likely to hurt, rather than help, your site's rankings).

19.2.1. Post Categories

One of the benefits of using posts for publishing your main, visitor-orientated content is that you can group them into categories. These act as organised 'silos' of content, all related to the core topic. When you add a post, you can select the category from a list of those which you have already set up.

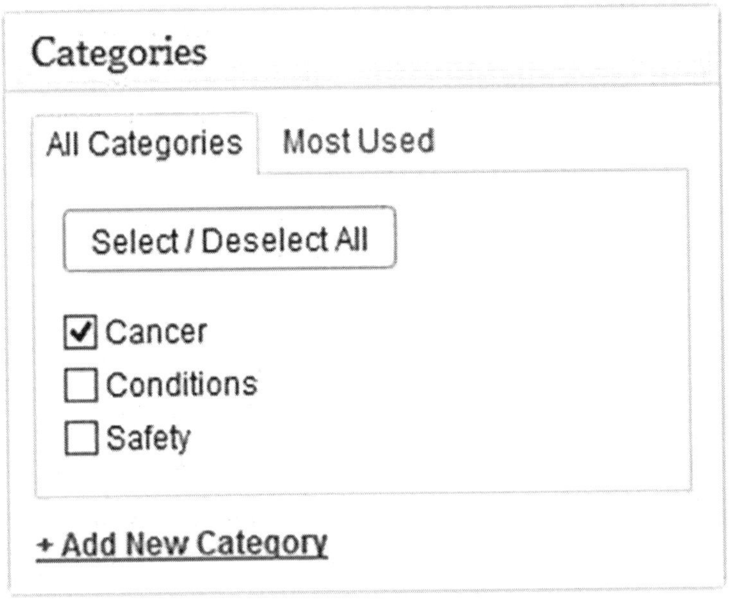

From an SEO point of view, it is better to only have posts in ONE category. If you find that you need to categorise a post into multiple categories, then you probably don't have the correct categories in the first place. Categories should be broad enough so that there isn't much, or any, overlap. If you find that you want to further classify your posts, look at using tags instead. We'll be looking more into tags later in the book.

There are a few reasons why one post for one category is a good idea.

Firstly, if you put a post in three categories, then three copies of that post will be created (one on each category page), though we will largely overcome this problem later when setting up the category pages. A more important reason for the one post one category rule is the SEO benefit. We want categories to contain tightly focused groups of content. Using a plugin like YARPP (see the plugins section of this book for details), we can setup a 'Related Posts' section for every post on the site. These related links (or excerpts with links to the related posts), show other posts within the same category. Therefore related posts are interlinking with each other, and that will help boost your rankings. This is because Google likes it when a post has links from related content. Another SEO benefit comes from the category pages. These pages link out to highly related articles on the site, so once again, the relevancy factors of links to-and-from related content is a big on-page SEO advantage.

19.2.2. Post Tags

Tags are an additional way to categorize your content. When you add a post, you can enter one or more tags for it:

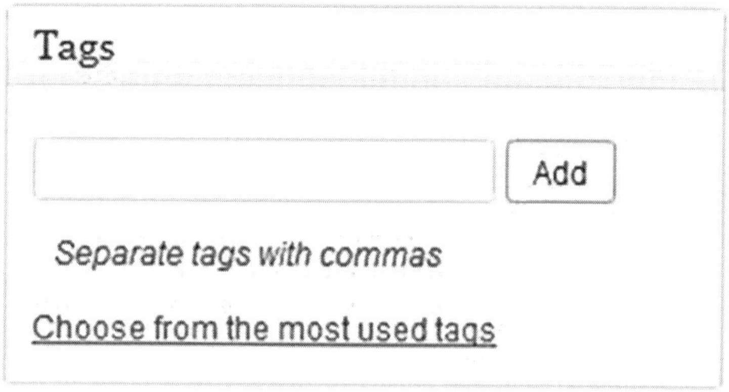

You simply enter them, with each tag separated by a comma.

For every tag you enter, WordPress creates a separate webpage that lists all posts using that tag. As you can imagine, duplicate content is an issue again. When a site uses tags incorrectly, major SEO problems arise. For example, I've seen websites that have dozens of tags per post. In many cases, a tag might only be used ONCE on the entire site. That means the tag page will contain one article. What is the point of that tag page, since the article already appears on its own post webpage?

The purpose of tags is similar to the purpose of categories. It's used to assemble related content into related groups so that visitors (and search engines), can find information more easily.

For example, suppose you had a website about Huskies with lots of content, videos, and photos. You could setup categories like grooming, feed, training, etc. You might also like to categorise your posts according to whether they were articles, photos or videos. You might then use the tags: articles, photos, videos. Some pieces of content would include two, or even all three of these tags, and that is fine. We do still end up with duplication issues because the same article may then be posted on two or three tag pages. However, we'll look later at how we can minimise this duplication issue and add more value to tag pages.

The benefit of the tag pages is that it adds an extra level of categorisation which the visitor will find useful (if done properly). So, someone looking for images of Huskies can visit the 'photo' tag page, and find all the pictures listed together on there. It's the same principle for those looking for videos or content, etc.

From a search engine point of view, tag pages do tend to rank well because multiple posts typically point at each tag page. Later in the book, we'll look at how we can modify these tag pages to offer our visitors, and the search engines, even more worth.

My two suggestions for using tags is to only use those that appear (or will appear), on multiple posts of the site, and that you limit the number of tags per post to a maximum of four or five.

19.2.3. Post Formatting

At the top of the WYSIWYG (What-You-See-Is-What-You-Get), editor on the edit post screen is the toolbar.

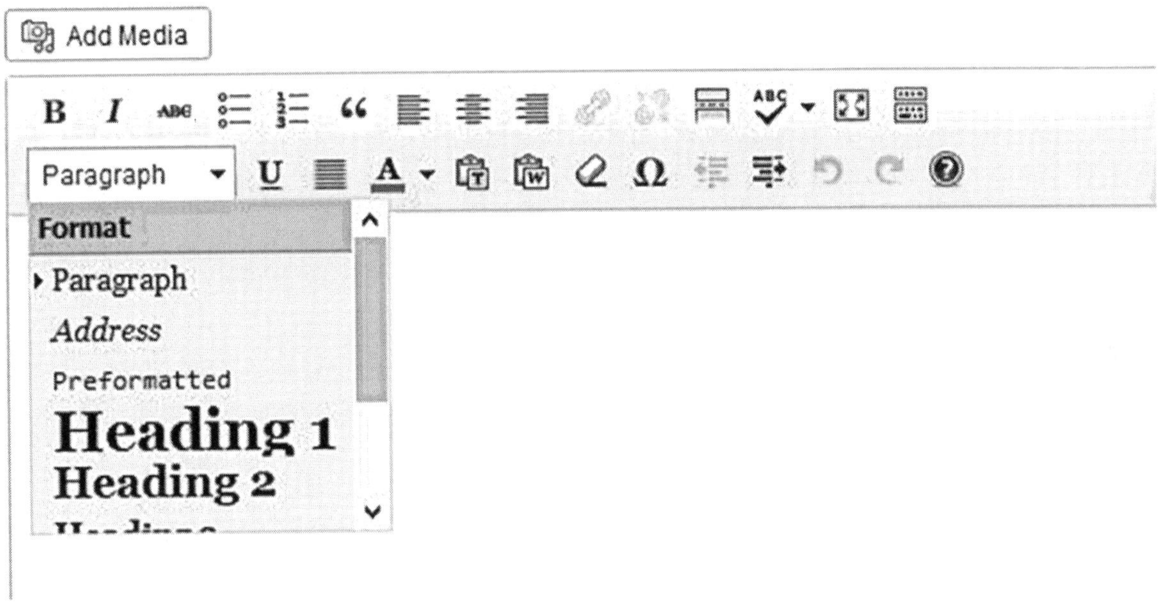

By default, the toolbar only contains the top row of buttons. To show the bottom row of tool buttons (which includes the important text formatting dropdown box), you have to click the button on the far right of the top toolbar. That button toggles between top only, and both toolbars.

Note: With formatting comes great responsibility.

With formatting options, like bold, underline & italics, only use them where you would if search engines did not exist. What I mean by that is do not be tempted to put bold or italics on the words and phrases you want to rank for. This might have worked a few years ago, but today it's a signal to Google that you are trying to over-optimise your page for those words and phrases. SEO on your page should be 'invisible', meaning it should not be obvious what you are trying to rank for when reading the content.

For headers, only include one 'Heading 1' headline per page (this uses the H1 HTML tag). Your template is likely to use an H1 for the title of the post, so you shouldn't add a second H1 header. Use headlines in hierarchies, with an H2 being the start of a new section, and H3 as sub-sections of the H2. If you then start a new section, use another H2.

Again, as with all areas of your content, do not stuff keyword phrases into headlines because they'll do you NO favours.

We've already discussed the extra features that the Yoast WordPress SEO plugin adds to post and page edit screens, and how you can use them to change the Title or Meta Description of your page or post. Therefore we won't go into that again. Instead, let's move on to excerpts.

19.3. Optimizing Images Used in Posts

The '**Add Media**' button above the toolbar, allows you to insert images and other media into your posts and pages. For images used in posts, I would recommend you optimize them as follows:

- Try to compress the image to as small a size as possible before uploading. Remember that when someone visits your page, the images have to download to their computers, thus slowing page load times.
- Keep image file size small, and resize images to the correct size (dimensions) before uploading. For example, if your theme content area is 600 pixels, and you want the image to take up half the width of the content, resize the image so that it is 300 pixels wide.
- Give your image a name that best describes it. Once again, remember not to keyword stuff here, and don't use words and phrases that are irrelevant to the image.
- Use ALT tags for all your images, and I say again, don't keyword stuff. Describe the image appropriately so that blind or partially sighted users can understand your content.

19.4. Internal Linking Between Posts

The YARPP plugin we mentioned in the plugins section of this book will create 'related posts' sections on each of your posts if you want them there. That helps to interlink your related content and spread link juice around your site. One of the more powerful 'on-page techniques' is to link words and phrases in one post to another 'related post', though you shouldn't do this just for the sake of internal linking.

Let me give you an example of how this is used for maximum SEO benefit.

Suppose you had an article called 'World's Best Hot Dog Recipe', and in that article you mention a special tomato sauce that you make for your hot dogs. On your site somewhere you have shared that recipe. Therefore, in the hot dog article, when you mention the special sauce, you link to that post on your site. Internal linking like this is natural, helps visitors, and is a powerful SEO tool to help our pages rank better.

I did an experiment with internal linking on one of my sites. I described the experiment and results here:

http://ezseonews.com/backlinks/internal-linking-seo/

19.5. Featured Images for Posts

Posts can be assigned a featured image, which is used to show up next to the post wherever it is listed on your site. Whether you use them or not depends on how you want your site to look. Personally I think they help break up blocks of text on a webpage, therefore helping the visitor to navigate to stuff easier.

If you do use them, make sure you follow the image optimization tips above for these as well. Remember, if you have a list of say 20 posts on a page, with 20 featured images, they are going to slow the page load time considerably. Optimizing these images as best you can, both in size (KB), and dimensions (pixels), will help to improve page load speeds.

19.6. Post Excerpts

Excerpts are short summaries of your post. Think of them in the same way as you think of a Meta Description. It should be something short and enticing to the visitor. Remember, these extracts will be displayed on various areas of your website serving as descriptions for the posts.

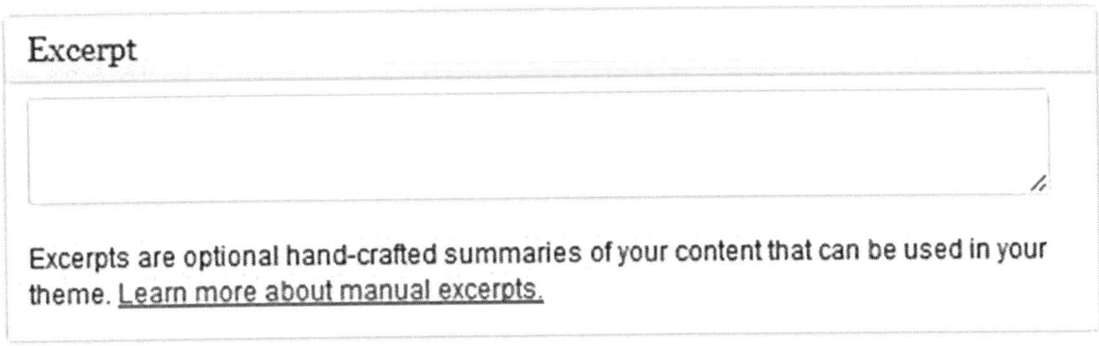

If you don't see this section, check the Screen Options (top right of the WordPress Dashboard).

Excerpts have to main purposes:

1. To add a description to the posts in your RSS feeds.
2. To supply summaries to posts in various areas of your site, like search results, tag & category pages, author pages, etc. (depending on the theme you are using).

Excerpts may also be used as the Meta Description tag with some themes.

A good reason to use excerpts is that they provide complete descriptions for any post. If you don't have excerpts written for a post, then WordPress will create a description based on the content of your page, and that will usually stop mid-word or mid-sentence.

I therefore recommend writing an excerpt for *all* posts on your site.

19.7. Allow Comments & Trackbacks on Posts?

You can enable or disable comments and trackbacks on posts if you want to, either globally or on a post -by-post basis. I recommend you keep comments enabled on all posts, because social interaction is an important aspect of our SEO efforts.

Trackbacks are a little more difficult to give a hard and fast rule about. Essentially, a trackback is like a comment sent to your site from another site, when that other site links to yours. While it is nice to know who is linking to us, this feature has been heavily abused by spammers. This means that 99% of the time, a trackback is bogus and no link exists. The reason the spammers do this is to try to get you to approve their 'trackback', which then goes live on your site with a link back to theirs. I tend to turn trackbacks off on all posts by default because spammers were taking up too much of my time; constantly checking to see if a site had really linked to mine or not. Don't forget, you can choose whether to enable or disable globally, or on a post by post basis.

19.8. Scheduling Posts

There may be times when you want to schedule posts into the future. For example, if I am adding 10-20 posts to my site (let's say I just got a bunch of content from my ghost writer), I would schedule those posts to be released over 2-3 weeks. Doing this encourages the search engine spiders to come back more regularly. It can also incite visitors to return more often when they see that fresh content is being added frequently.

To schedule posts, look to the 'Publish' section located on the right of the post edit screen:

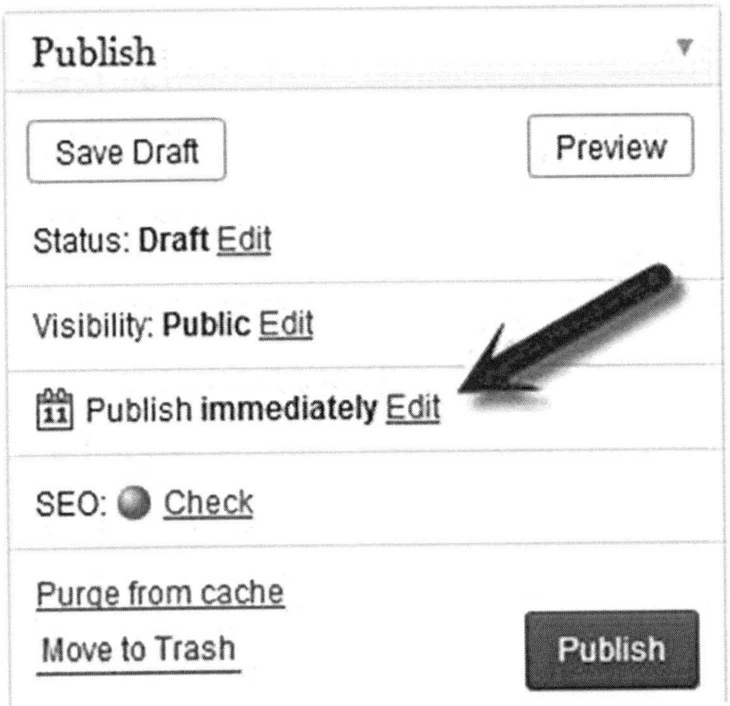

Where it says '**Publish immediately**', there is an '**Edit**' link that allows you to change the date and time of publication. The edit link expands the area:

Now you can select a date, and even a time, for when the article will be published. When that date and time arrives, WordPress automatically publishes the article for you. You do not have to login or do anything else once this is set up.

20. Setting up Category Pages

Categories are used to classify posts, and WordPress will create 'category pages' which list all posts within that category. This helps visitors and search engines alike.

When you setup a category on your site, I highly recommend you give your new category a description.

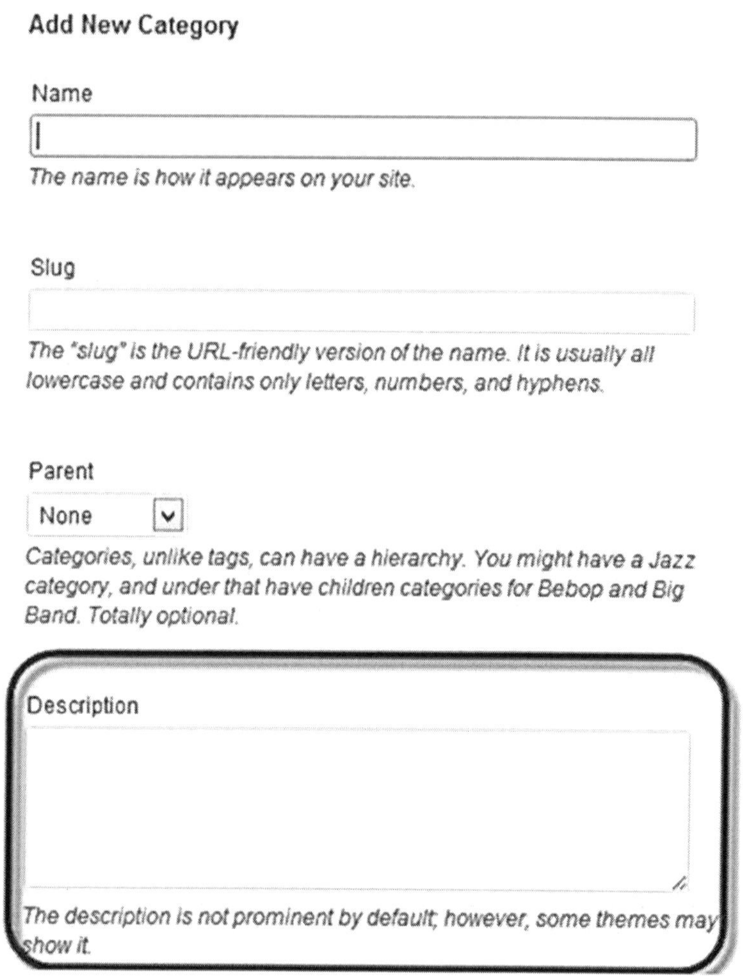

These descriptions are used as mouse-over hints if you are using a category widget in your sidebar.

It's the little things that make the biggest difference, and small details like this help guide your visitors, and therefore make your site stand out from the vast majority that don't bother with such features. It is also worth mentioning that the text you enter for the description will appear in the code of your web page (as a Title Tag in the URL of the category link), and Google obviously sees that.

OK, let's leave the setting up of categories, and turn our attention to category pages.

This is where I do things a little differently from most others.

20.1. A Typical Category Page

A typical WordPress category page will just list all of the posts in that category. It will look something like this:

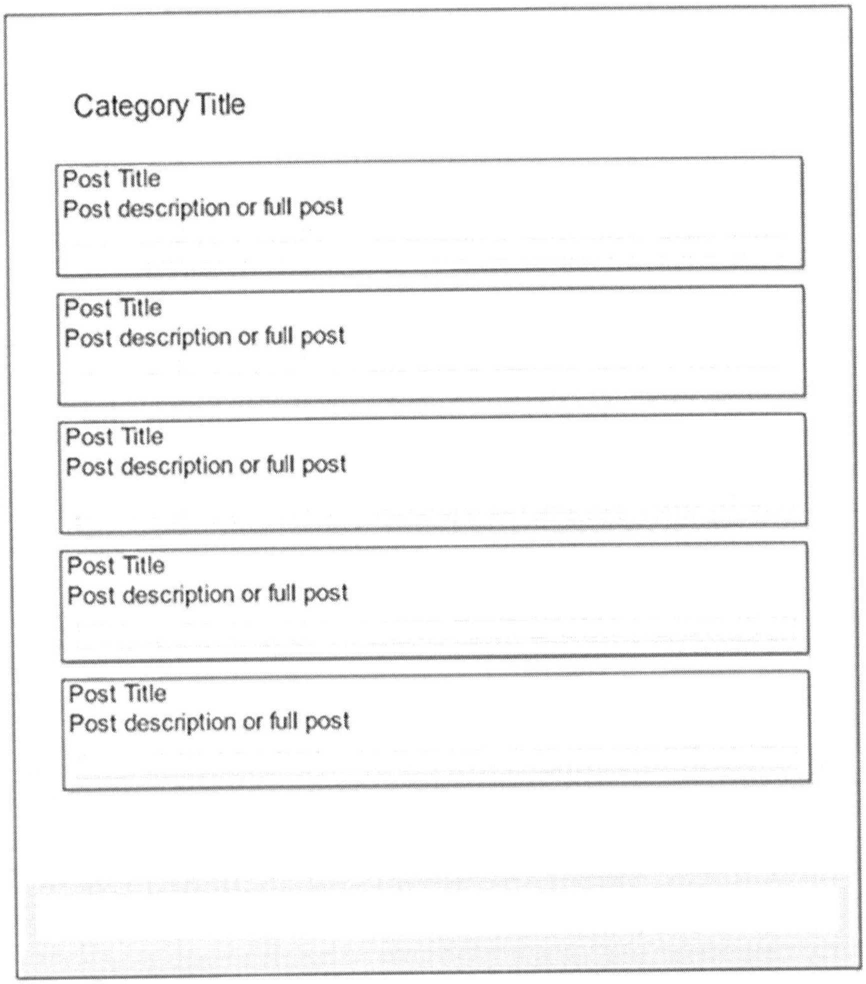

Depending on the theme you are using, those posts may be showing as title with excerpt, or title with full post. Obviously the latter would cause huge duplication problems since these category pages would contain the complete text of all posts within the category.

If this is what your category pages look like, then you should *noindex, follow* the category pages. We can easily do this thanks to the WordPress SEO plugin (located under the text editor in the WordPress Dashboard).

NOTE: The SEO plugin allows you to treat entities globally, or on a one-by-one basis.

Therefore you can globally set all category pages to *noindex, follow*, or you can set just one or two category pages to *noindex, follow*. The same goes for tag pages, posts, pages, etc.

20.1.1. Globally Set All Category Pages to Noindex, Follow

To make *all* category page *noindex, follow*, go to the **SEO -> Titles & Metas** section, and click on the '**Taxonomies**' tab.

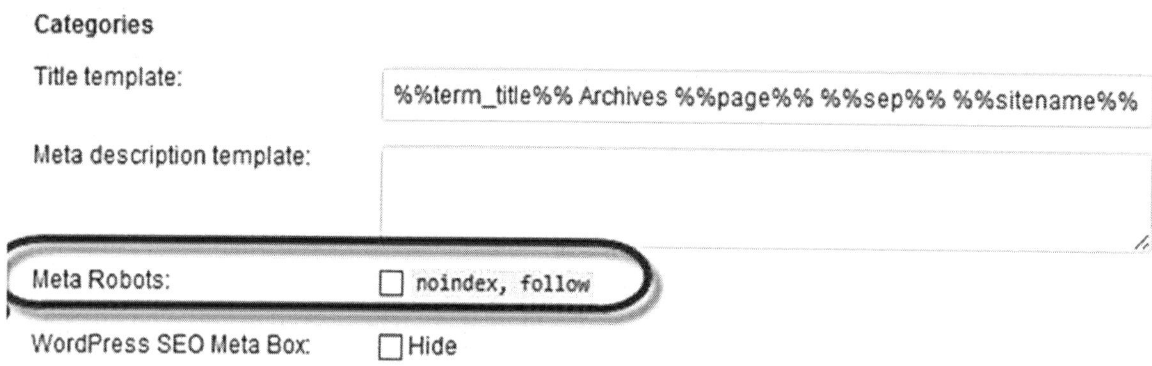

Simply check the '**Meta Robots**' check box, and all category pages will become *noindex, follow*. This means search engine robots can find the category pages and follow links on them, but it won't index and include them in the search results.

20.1.2. Setting Individual Category Pages to Noindex, Follow

To make category pages *noindex, follow* on a one-by-one basis, you need to go to the **Posts -> Categories** section of the Dashboard, and click on a category's '**Edit**' link for the one you want to modify.

Note: You need to create the category first, and then go in and edit it, because these extra options are not found on the main screen from where you create new categories.

When you go into the category edit screen, there are a number of new options available to you thanks to Yoast's WordPress SEO plugin.

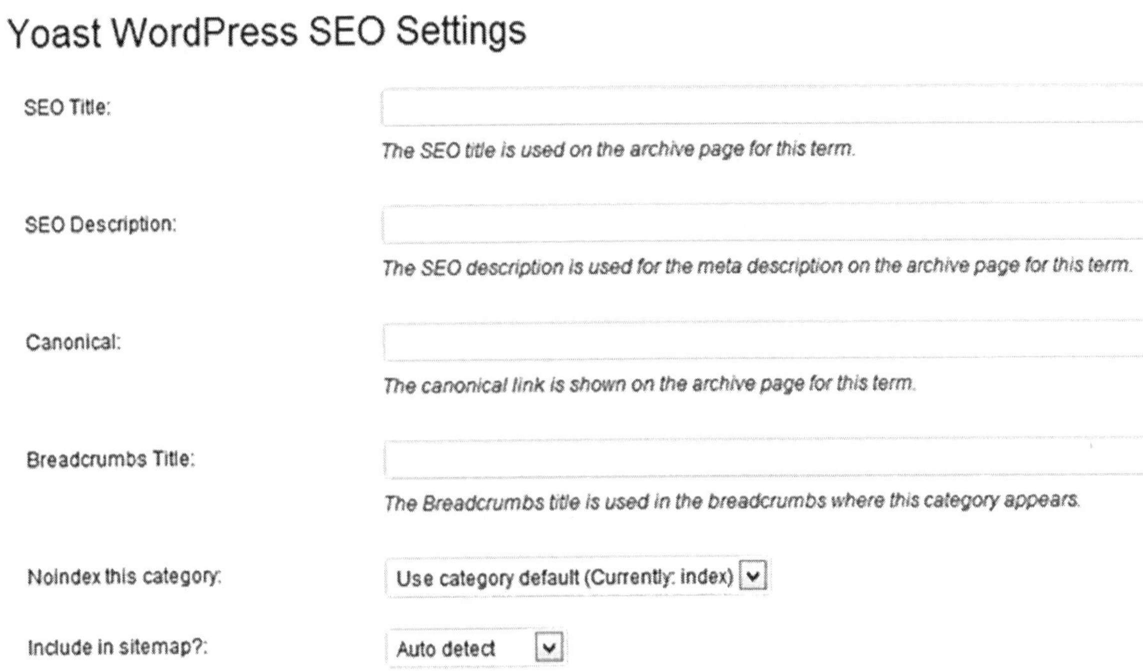

These options allow us override any or all of the global category settings. On a one-by-one basis, we can define a custom Title and Description, make the category page *noindex, follow*, and exclude it from the sitemap.

NOTE: If you *noindex, follow*, your category pages, I don't recommend excluding the category pages from the sitemap. Google will find the category pages in the sitemap and then spider them to find all of your content. But Google won't index and rank these pages, which is what we want.

20.2. A Better Category Page?

Instead of just listing posts within a category, wouldn't it be better if our category pages looked like this:

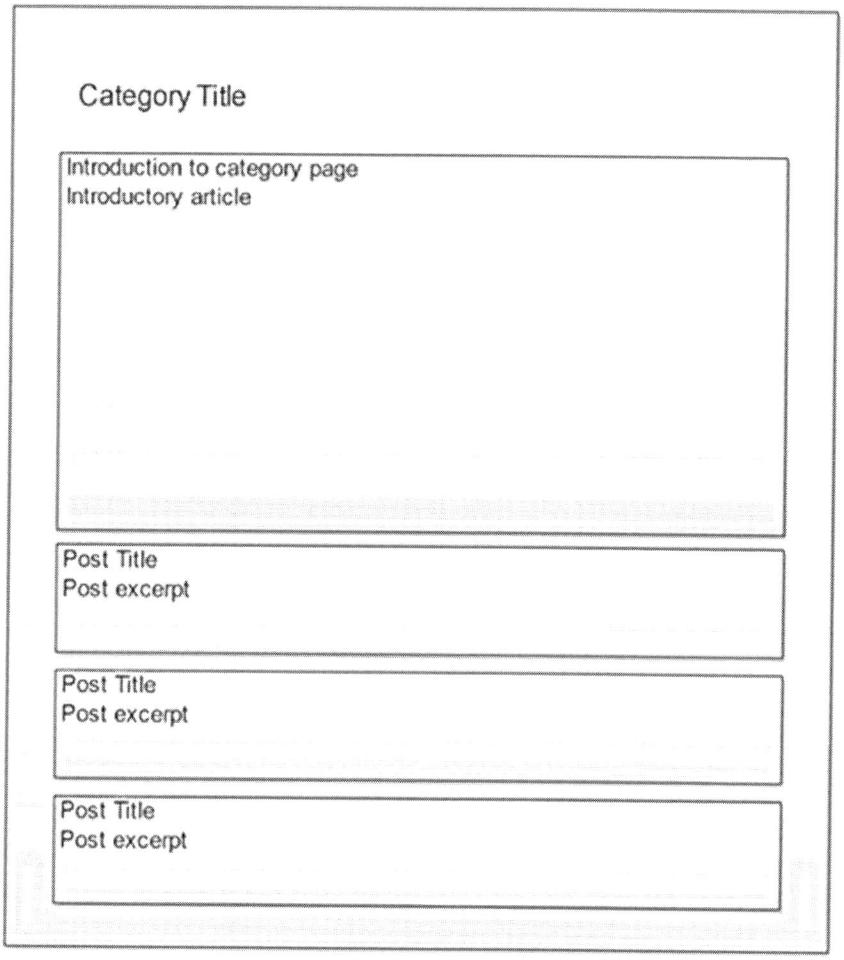

In this category page, there is a text introduction to the category, followed by post Titles and post Excerpts of all the articles within the category.

The written introduction adds SEO benefits, in that this page now has some unique content on it, and introduces the posts in the category to both my visitors and the search engines. I typically add this type of introduction to *all* of my category pages, and then leave them as *index, follow*. This is because I want the search engines to index and rank my category pages when they're set up in this way.

20.2.1. For Genesis Users

The Genesis theme has some features built in that allow you to add this type of introduction to both category pages, and tag pages. I love the fact that Genesis has built this into their theme because it makes things that much easier.

Early Genesis versions were a little buggy with formatting and line-spacing issues.

However, with the latest versions of Genesis, this feature seems to work well. And while you cannot create formatted text with a WYSIWYG editor, if you know some basic HTML, you can use it in the descriptions without any problems.

If you are using Genesis, and you want to check out these features, go back to the Posts -> Categories edit page, and you'll see the following (underneath the Yoast category settings):

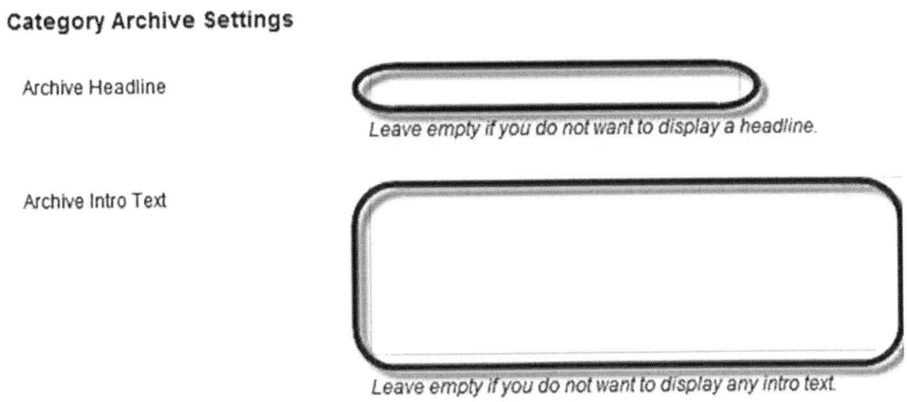

Here you can add both a headline and introductory text.

This will then be fixed at the top of the category page before the posts are shown. You then need to make sure that only the title and excerpts of posts are displayed, and you can do that in the **Genesis -> Theme Settings**.

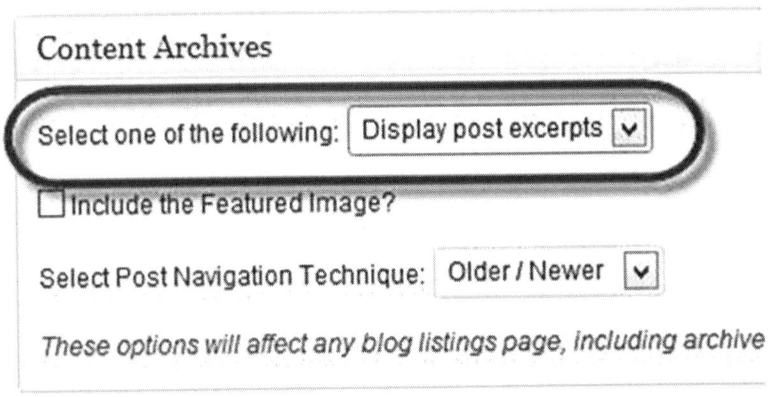

Change that drop down box in the '**Content Archives**' section to 'Display post excerpts'.

That's all there is to it. Genesis users can use this built in feature to easily add unique introductory content to their category pages.

But what if you don't use Genesis? Well, you can use WP-Sticky, a plugin to help achieve a similar result.

20.2.2. Using WP-Sticky

While this method is not needed by Genesis users, I still use it on a lot of my sites because of the flexibility it offers.

The process is not perfect (see the note about hierarchical categories at the end), but it does allow you to use WordPress posts as introductions on category pages.

Since WordPress posts can include images, videos, text formatting, email capture forms, calls to action, and so on and so forth, your introductions can be anything you want them to be.

To use this feature, we need the plugin called WP Sticky. We mentioned it in the plugins section of the book, so go and install that if you haven't already done so.

Once installed, head on over to **Settings -> WP-Sticky**, and change the top option to yes:

Note: WP-Sticky allows us to permanently fix an article to the top of a category page. It works in a different way to the 'sticky' feature built into WordPress, so don't try to do this technique without the WP-Sticky plugin.

This is what we are going to do:

- Create a WordPress post to be used as an introduction to a category.
- Stick it to the top of that category page.
- Setup the category page to show one full post, followed by excerpts of all other posts. If you are using Genesis themes, I'll give you the instructions to set this up. If you are using a different theme, you'll need to contact their support desk to find out how and if this is possible. If it is not possible, simply revert to plan A, and *noindex, follow,* all category pages.
- Now *Noindex, follow,* the introduction post (no archive it too, and also remove it from the sitemap), so that the search engines do not index it. This is because we only want the full post displayed and indexed on the category page.

1 & 2. Creating the Post and sticking it to the top of the category

Once you have written the post that you'll be using for the introduction of a category, select the category for the post, that is, the one you want the post to introduce. Now look for the WP-Sticky options on the right hand side of the edit screen.

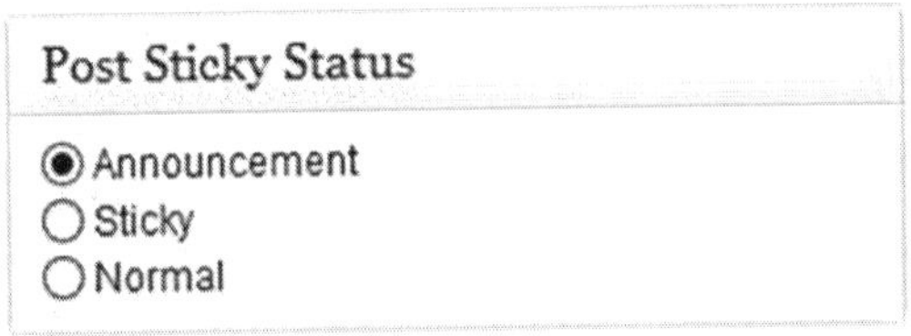

You want to save this post as an '**Announcement**'. This will permanently stick it to the top of the category page.

3. Setup WordPress to show one full post, then excerpts for *all* category pages

Genesis Users:

In order to get Genesis to do what we want, we need to create a new template file and upload it to the child theme folder.

In a text editor, type out the following code:

```
<?php
remove_action('genesis_post_content', 'genesis_do_post_content');
add_action('genesis_post_content', 'custom_post_content');
function custom_post_content() {
   global $loop_counter;
   if( $loop_counter < 1 ) {
      the_content();
   }
   else {
      the_excerpt();
   }
}
require_once(PARENT_DIR . '/index.php');
?>
```

Now save the file as **archive.php** and upload it to the child theme folder.

Here it is in my Lifestyle child theme folder:

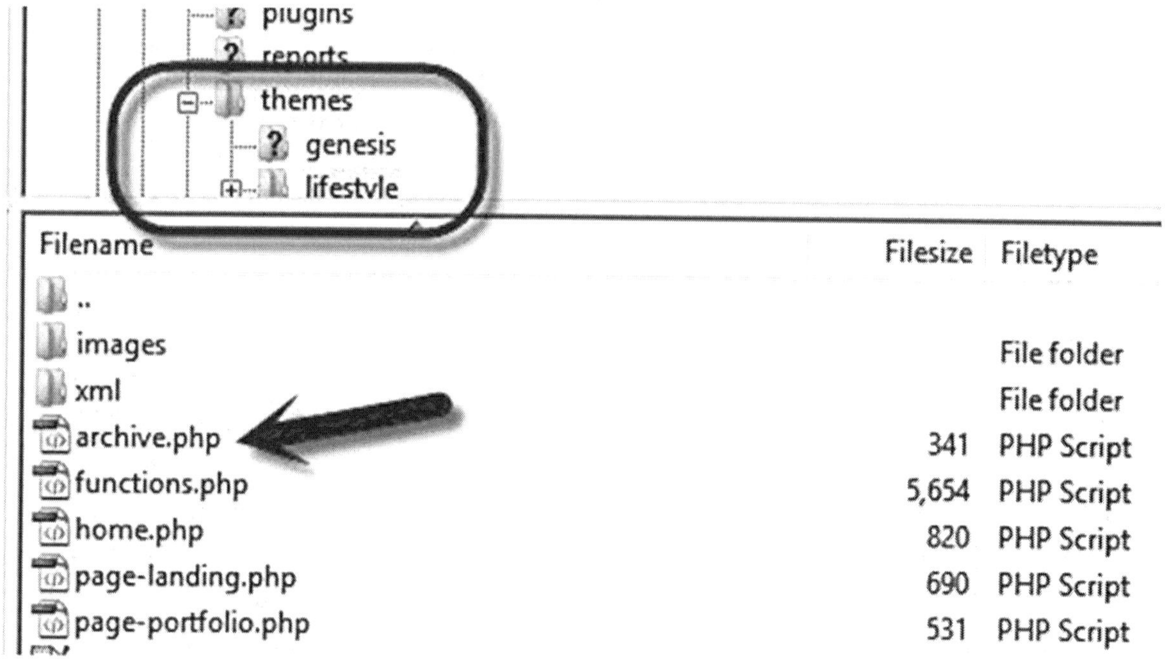

That's it! Your category pages should now show the first post as a full introductory post, followed by just the titles and excerpts of the remaining posts within those categories.

Non-Genesis Users

If you want to try to get this to work with a different theme, you may need to contact the theme's support and ask for help. Just tell them that you want the category pages on your site to show one full post, then the titles and excerpts of all remaining posts. They should be able to tell you if it's possible, and if yes, how to go about doing it.

4. Robot settings and sitemap exclusion

The final stage of this setup is to *'noindex', 'follow',* the introductory post.

Just go in to edit the post as normal and use the Yoast WordPress SEO settings there to *noindex, and follow* it:

Set the **Meta Robots Index** value to **noindex.**

Set the **Meta Robots Follow** value to **Follow.**

Set the **Meta Robots Advanced** to **No Archive.**

Set **Include in HTML Sitemap** to **Never include.**

That's all there is to it. Your category page is now set up to show a full post first, then the titles and excerpts of all other posts in the category below that fixed intro.

A note about hierarchical categories

If you have categories with sub-categories, this technique won't work quite so well. It does work, but it's a little less controlled. You see, on the 'parent' category pages, after the fixed introduction post, the first few posts will always display the announcement posts created for the sub-categories, and then you'll get your remaining titles and excerpts.

This isn't an issue with Genesis users that opt for the built-in 'Intro Text' feature mentioned earlier.

21. Extending the SEO Value of Tag Pages

Tag pages can rank remarkably well because they tend to have a lot of internal links pointing at them (from all posts that use that tag). For this reason, I like to have these pages set as *index, follow*, but to be able to do this, we need to first modify the tag pages.

As we saw with the category setup in the previous chapter, Yoast's WordPress SEO plugin adds some extra features that allow us to better handle Category & Tag pages.

If you go and edit an existing tag (**Posts -> Tags**), you'll get the same Yoast settings we saw with the category pages, allowing you to create a custom Title and Description as well as being able to *noindex* a tag page and exclude it from the sitemap if you need to.

Inside the main **SEO -> Titles & Metas** settings, you can set the global rules for *all* tag pages, noindexing the lot if you want to.

NOTE: Like category pages, I don't recommend you exclude tag pages from the sitemap because they are useful to search engines for finding content on your site.

21.1. A Typical Tag Page

Again, just like the category pages, a typical WordPress tag page is just a list of all the posts on a site that have been tagged with a particular word or phrase. If this is what your tag pages are like, I recommend you **noindex,** and **follow** them in the global settings for tag pages.

21.2. A Better Kind of Tag Page

What I like to do is add an introduction to the tag pages in the same way that we handled the category pages.

Genesis Users

Fortunately for Genesis users, this is built into the theme like it is for the category pages.

Just login to your dashboard and go to **Posts -> Tags**. Click on the tag you want to add the introduction for, and you can then write the introductory text (just as we did for category pages).

Non-Genesis Users

For non-Genesis themes, you will need to ask your theme's support team if it is possible to add a fixed introduction to tag pages and then have all other posts display as titles and excerpts.

21.3. Tag Pages Summary

If you *can* set up your tag pages with introductions, then I recommend you globally set tag pages as *index, follow*, and add introductions to all tag pages.

If you cannot setup your tag pages to include an introduction, and then show all other posts as titles and excerpts, then I recommend you *noindex*, and *follow* all your tag pages. This is to prevent any potential duplicate content issues.

For those of you who want to implement intro text on tag and category pages, but don't use Genesis, you might be interested in this article on Yoast.com:

http://yoast.com/wordpress-archive-pages/

Just a word of warning though; you will need to play around with PHP code.

22. WordPress for SEO Plugin Setup

Yoast's WordPress plugin provides a massive amount of SEO control over your WordPress site. When you install it, you'll find SEO options popping up in several areas of your Dashboard. These areas can be divided into two main parts; those that control settings globally, and those that control settings on a one-by-one basis.

The 'Global' settings are found in the SEO menu of the WP Dashboard:

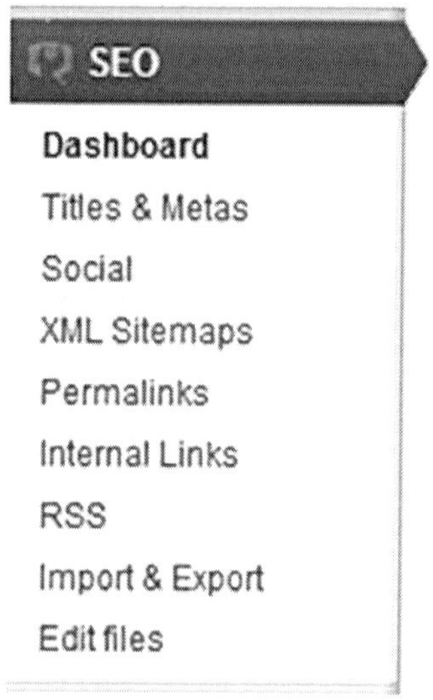

Changes made in here will affect all posts, all pages, all categories, and all tag pages, etc. However, we can override these settings on individual posts, pages, and categories etc.

For posts and pages, you'll find the override settings on the '**Edit Post**' and '**Edit Page**' screens.

They look like this:

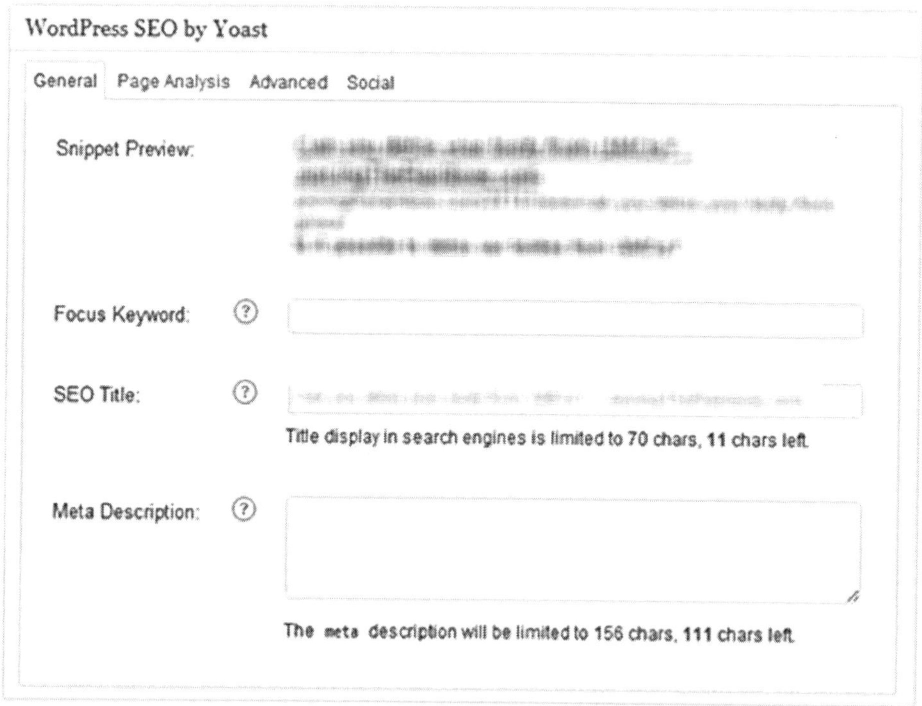

For Category and Tag page override settings, you go to the Posts -> Categories, or Posts -> Tags, respectively, and click on an item you want to edit. You'll then see the override settings for the individual category or tag page. Here are the override settings for a category:

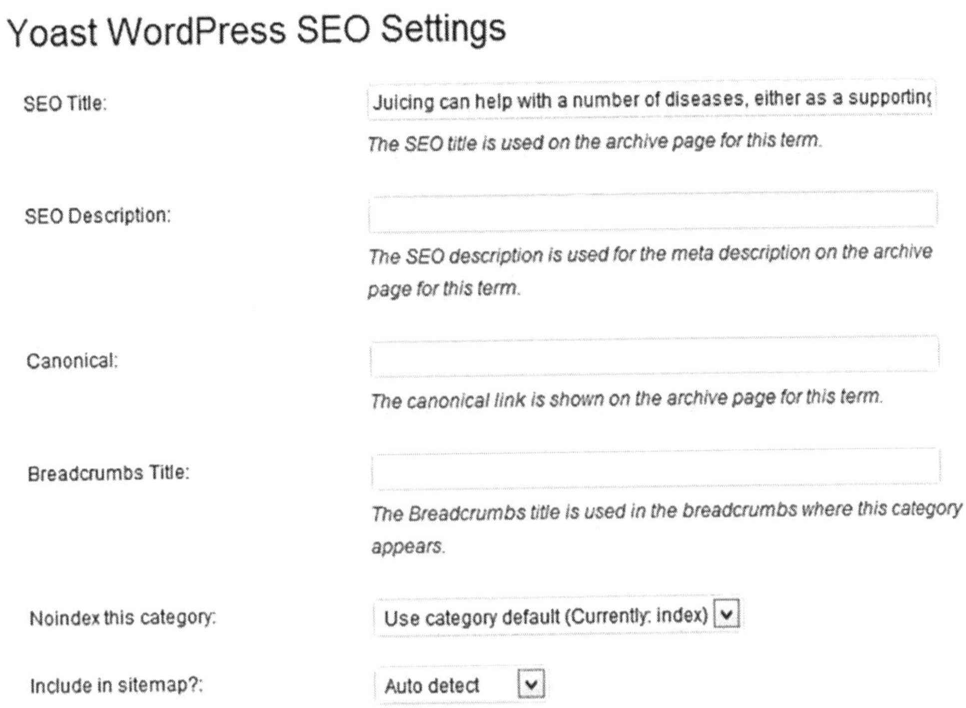

As you can see, you are able to set a different Title & Description, make the category index or noindex, and exclude from the sitemap if required. The Tag Page overrides are very similar to the Category ones.

OK, let's look at the '**Global Settings**'.

On the SEO -> Dashboard settings, you can click on the '**Start Tour**' button to learn more about the WordPress SEO plugin, and how it works. It will take you through the tabs of the plugin and show you basic information about the settings on each of those tabs.

There is nothing you need to set on this page of the plugin settings.

22.1. Title & Metas

The General tab

The '**Titles**' and '**Metas**' section has a lot of options, spread over several tabs.

On the '**General**' tab, you should not need to change the 'Title Settings' checkbox at the top. The plugin has auto-detected whether this box should be checked or not and set it for you.

The only setting on this tab that I suggest you check is the '**Noindex subpages of archives**'. As archive pages fill up with posts, WordPress will create new pages to hold additional posts. This option prevents these additional pages from being indexed. The first page will still be indexed, and this is the important one for us.

There is a section on this settings page called '**Clean up the <head>**'. Basically WordPress has added a lot of code to the head section of your pages. These options allow you to remove them. However, I don't recommend you change any of these unless you understand *exactly* what they do. Just leave them all unchecked.

The Home tab

The Home tab allows you to specify '**templates**' for the homepage Title, homepage Meta Description and homepage Meta Keywords tags.

Note: If you do want to use the Meta Keywords tags but don't see the option, then go to the 'General Tab' and check the box that says: 'Use meta keywords tag?'

So what is a template? Well, if you click over to the '**Help**' tab of the '**Titles & Metas**' section, you can see a number of variables. These variables can be used to setup a template. So, for example, if we wanted the homepage title to include the site name, we could use the variable **%%sitename%%** in the template for the homepage.

The plugin would then pull the site's name from the WordPress settings and insert it wherever it sees the **%%sitename%%** variable.

So we could use a homepage Title like this:

%%sitename%% :: Making your dog happier

If your site name (in the WordPress General settings), was '**Doggy Treats**', then when the homepage was loaded in a browser, the homepage title would display as:

Doggy Treats :: Making your dog happier

We could of course use a variable to insert the tagline of the site into the title. This would do it:

%%sitename%% :: %%sitesdesc%%

The title would then pull the site name and tagline from the '**General Settings**' tab of your WP Dashboard, and create the title from those.

Now, you might ask why bother using variables for the homepage title when you can just type in the *exact title* you want. The main reason is in case you ever update the site title or tagline in your settings. By using variables, our titles will automatically get updated, without us having to remember to go in and manually change them.

The plugin sets the default homepage title as follows:

%%sitename%% %%page%% %%sep%% %%sitedesc%%

By looking at the variable list on the '**Help**' tab, you can decode this to see that the homepage title would be the site name, followed by a separator (**%%sep%%** - this is usually a dash, but that depends on the theme you are using), and then the site description (tagline). The **%%page%%** variable is not relevant to the homepage so it will be blank (I personally remove that variable from the homepage title template). Using our previous example, the title could therefore be:

Doggy Treats - Making your dog happier.

The default homepage title is OK and I would leave it as it is if I were you. For the description, you can use variables if you want, but I generally just type in my own description for the homepage.

The Post Types tab

The '**Post Types**' tab allows you to setup the default Title, Description, Keywords, and index status, etc., for posts, pages & media.

Since I like my websites to be '**branded**' by the site's name, I always include the **%%sitename%%** variable in the title of my posts, usually at the end of the title template. The one that is installed by default is actually quite good, because it uses the posts title and the site name. It also includes the **%%page%%** variable, which I would remove.

So my preferred title template for posts is.

%%title%% - %%sitename%%

For the post description, I use **%%excerpt%%**. This will then use whatever excerpt I have entered for a post as the Meta Description tag.

Here is my completed posts section:

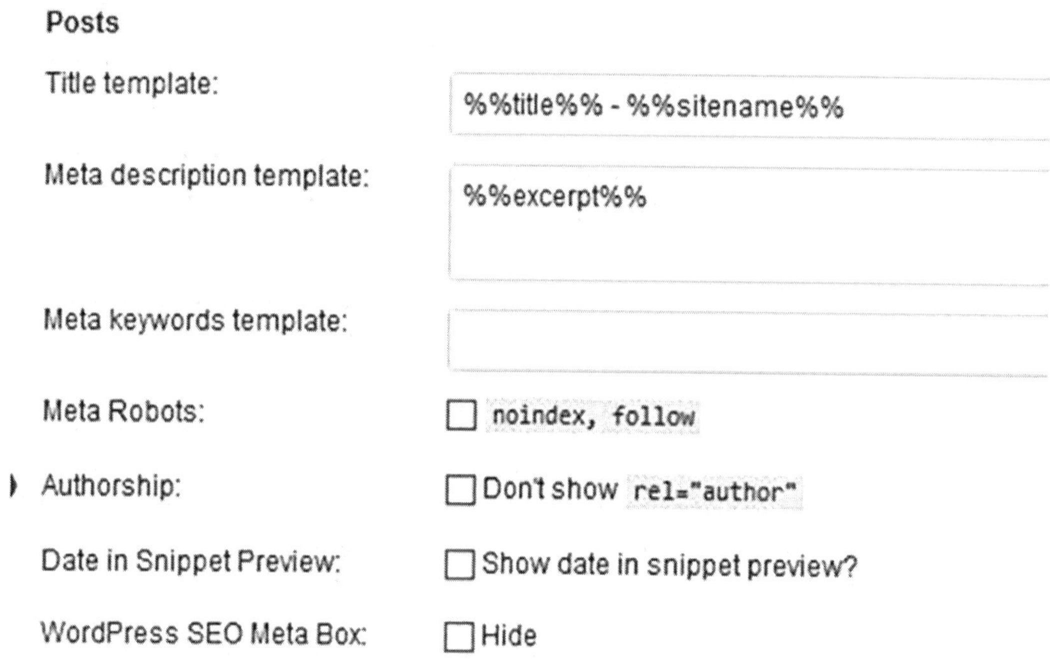

By default, I have the '**Meta Robots**' disabled so that all of my posts are index, follow. All four of these boxes can be left unchecked.

For pages, I use the same title template as for posts. I leave the description box empty, since the pages on my site are the less important 'legal pages', that I noindex, and follow anyway. If I happen to want a page to specifically have a description, I can do that as I am creating it (and make that one page index, follow if I want to), using the Yoast SEO settings on the edit post screen to override these global settings. Here are my page settings:

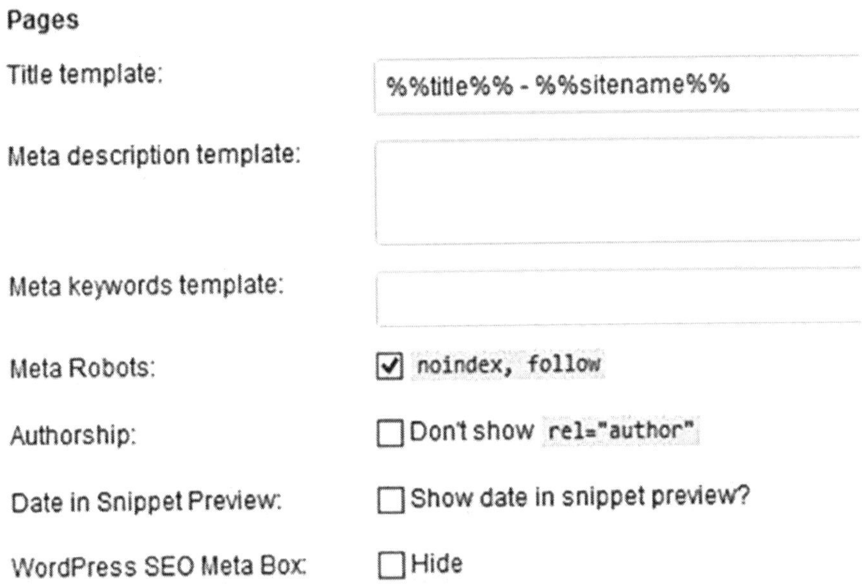

Notice that I have checked the noindex, follow box. This means that by default, all pages will be noindex, follow. Because of the way I use pages, I don't want them showing up in the search engines.

For media, these are special posts created by WordPress to hold information about the media you upload. I don't want mine indexed as separate pages, so here are the settings I use:

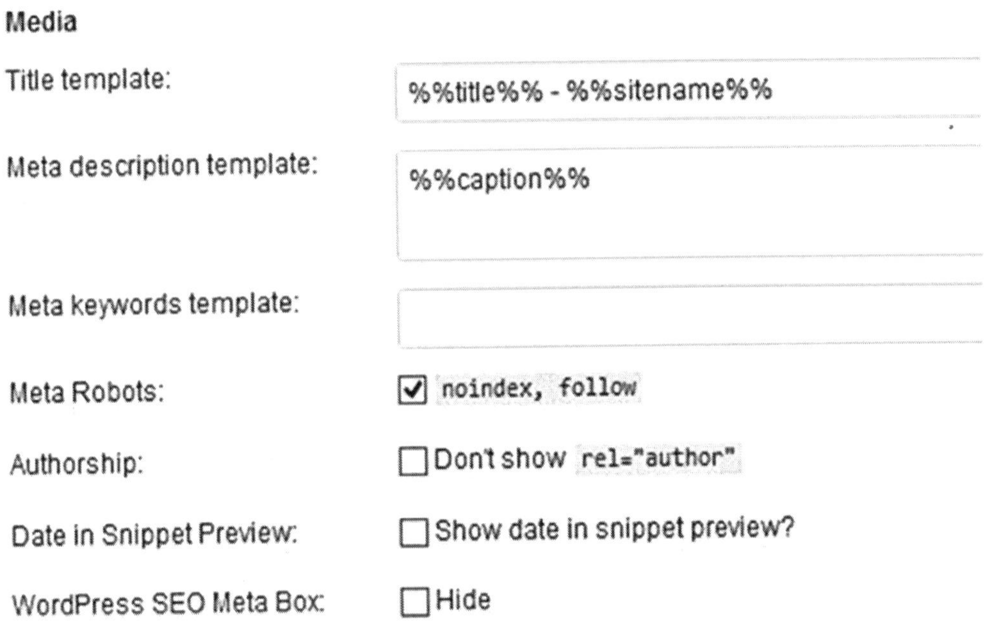

Again, the media settings use noindex, follow, because I don't want these files ending up in the search engines (I only want the posts that use these files to be indexed).

The Taxonomies tab

Under the 'Taxonomies tab', we can setup the global options for Categories, Tags, and Format.

Here are my settings for Categories:

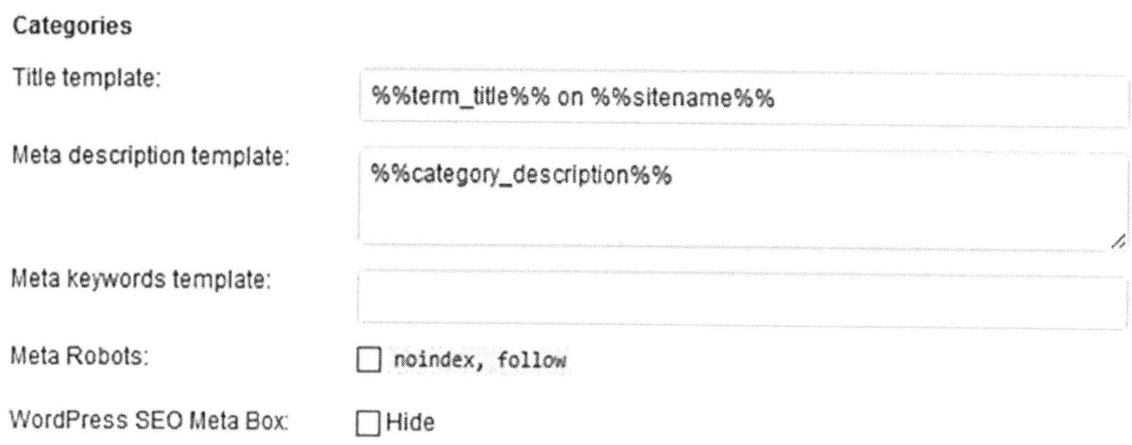

The **%%term_title%%** variable will be replaced by the category title and the **%%category_description%%** will be replaced by the description we entered for the category.

IMPORTANT: I have my category pages set globally to be indexed. That is because I set them up to include an introduction at the top, followed by post excerpts (See the category setup section of this book if you need to recap). If you do not use an introduction on your category pages, set the 'Meta Robots:' to noindex, follow.

Here are my Tags settings:

Again, I have my tag pages set to be indexed. That is only because I have an introduction on all of my tag pages, followed by excerpts of the posts using that tag (see the tag page setup section of this book if you need to recap). If you do not have introductory text on your tag pages, set the 'Meta Robots:' to noindex, follow.

The Format options under the 'Taxonomies' tab can be left unchanged.

The Other tab

This tab allows us to set the global settings for author and date archives, search pages, and 404 pages.

Here are my settings for author archives:

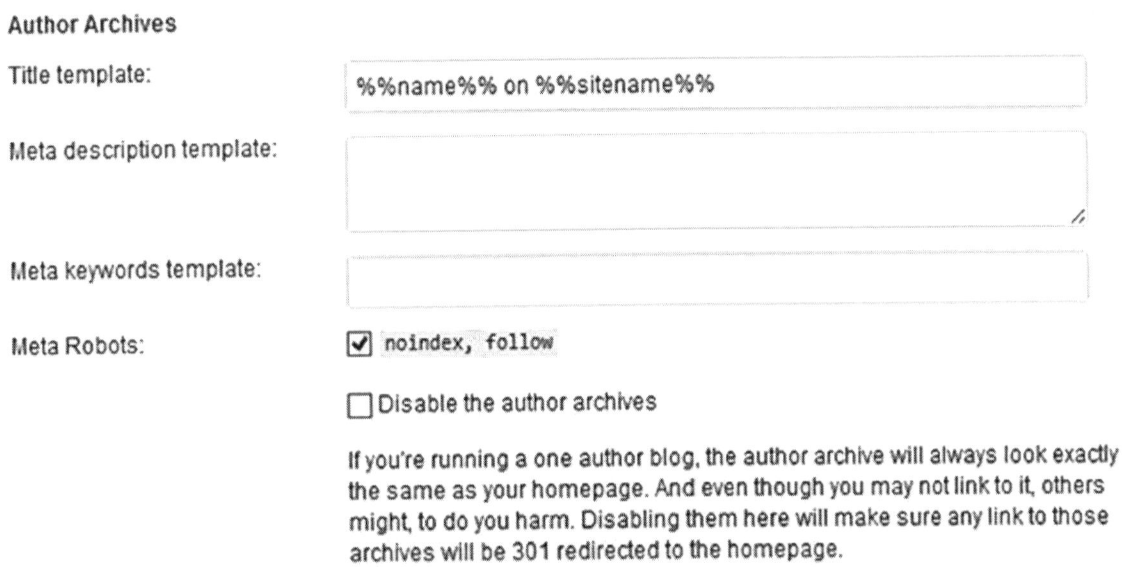

Note that for the 'Meta Robots:' I have noindex, follow checked. That is because I don't want the author archive pages to get into the search engines, as it would only add to the duplicate content problem. However, with this setting, Google can still follow the links on the page to help with the spidering of the site.

Since I have this set as noindex, there is no need to enter a Meta Description here.

For 'Date Archives', I use these settings:

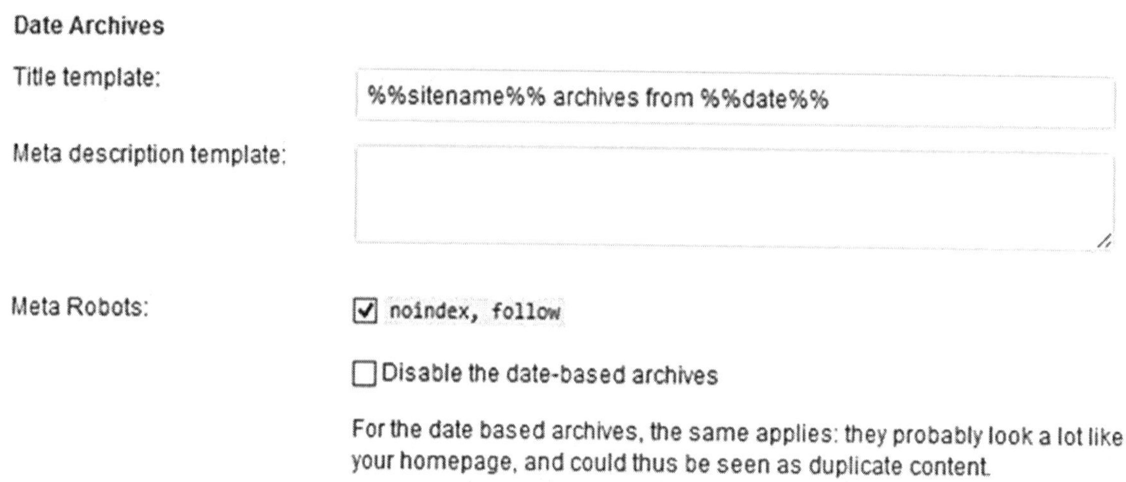

Again, this is noindex, follow to reduce duplicate content in Google.

The last couple of options are for the 'Special Pages'. I use these settings:

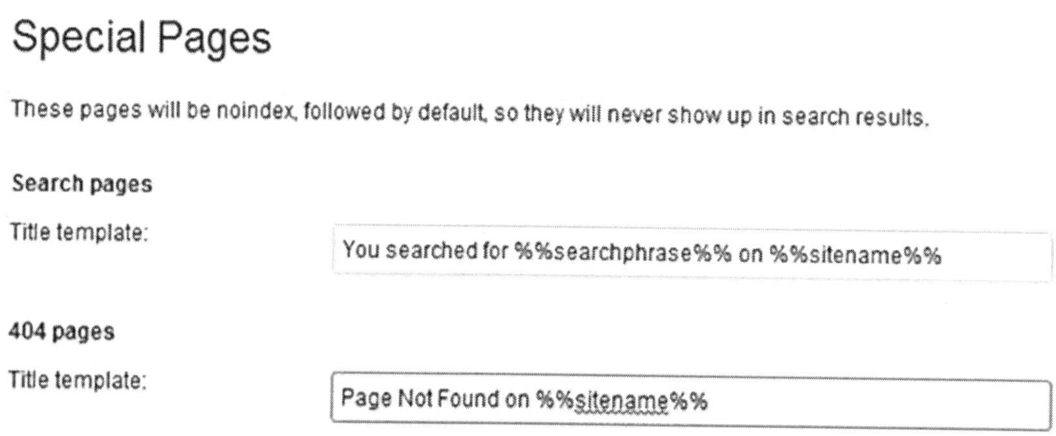

OK, that's the Titles & Metas sorted out. Let's look at the next set of options.

22.2. Social Settings

To access the 'Social Settings' tabs, click on the '**Social**' link in the SEO menu located left of the WP Dashboard.

These tabs help you to connect your site to Facebook, Twitter & Google+.

Facebook's Open Graph is used by a lot of search engines and social websites to tell them information about your site and about the pages they are visiting.

On the Facebook tab, check the box at the top to '**Add Open Graph Data**'.

With this checked, the plugin will add Facebook Open Graph Meta Tags to your pages:

```
<!-- This site is optimized with the Yoast WordPress SEO plugin v1.4.13 -
http://yoast.com/wordpress/seo/ -->
<link rel="canonical" href="http://[redacted]" />
<meta property='og:locale' content='en_US'/>
<meta property='og:type' content='website'/>
<meta property='og:title' content=[redacted]'/>
<meta property='og:url' content='[redacted]'/>
<meta property='og:site_name' content=[redacted] />
<!-- / Yoast WordPress SEO plugin. -->
```

What you do next depends on how you have your Facebook set up. Personally, I have a Facebook 'page' for each of my websites, and I recommend you do the same. You can then '**Add a Facebook Admin**' by clicking the button, and following the instructions on screen. Once you have connected your site to your Facebook profile, you can then add the Facebook Page URL in the settings. This will link the content on your site to your Facebook page.

In the code on your site, you will now see some extra Meta Data added if you check the source code:

```
<meta property='og:locale' content='en_US'/>
<meta property='og:type' content='article'/>
<meta property='og:title' content='[redacted]
<meta property='og:description' content=[redacted]
[redacted]'/>
<meta property='og:url' content='http://[redacted] '/>
<meta property='og:site_name' content='[redacted]'/>
<meta property='article:author' content='https://www.facebook.com/[redacted]' />
<meta property='article:publisher' content='https://www.facebook.com/[redacted]'/>
<meta property='fb:admins' content='[redacted]2'/>
<meta property='og:image' content='http://[redacted].com/wp-content/uploads/2012/05/beer-yeast-xs.jpg'/>
<meta property='og:image' content='http://[redacted].com/images/a80e02dee816_9E41/beer-yeast-xs.jpg'/>
<meta property='og:image' content='http://[redacted].com/images/a80e02dee816_9E41/peanuts-xs.jpg'/>
<meta property='og:image' content='http://[redacted].com/images/a80e02dee816_9E41/rice-xs.jpg'/>
```

Notice that there are article:author and article:publisher properties that connects the author to the Facebook page. There are also OpenGraph data elements that specify the images on your page. Now if someone shares your posts on Facebook, these images become available to that person to include next to their post.

OK, that's all we are doing on the Facebook tab. Let's move over to the Twitter tab.

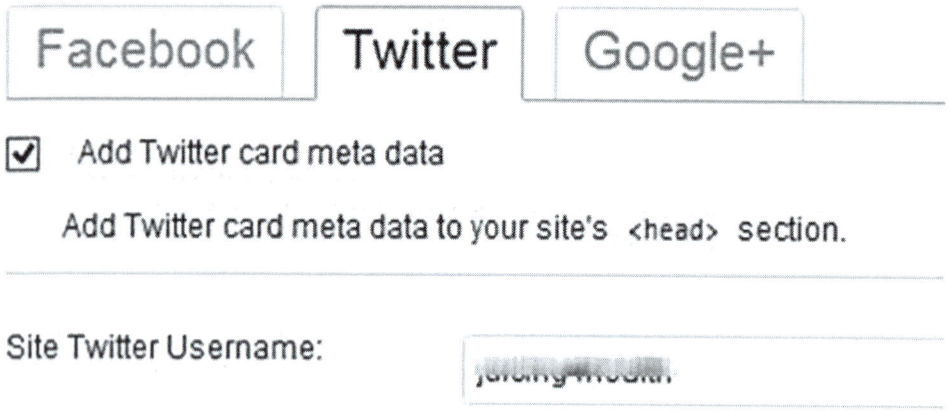

Check the box to add the Twitter card Meta Data to your posts, and enter your Twitter username below.

This will add the following Twitter card data to the source code of your site:

```
<meta name="twitter:card" content="summary"/>
<meta name="twitter:site" content="@j[illegible]
<meta name="twitter:domain" content="[illegible]"/>
<meta name="twitter:creator" content="@[illegible]"/>
<meta name="twitter:image:src" content="http://[illegible].com/wp-content/uploads/2012/05/beer-yeast-xs.jpg"/>
<meta name="twitter:image:src" content="http://[illegible].com/images/a80e02dee816_9E41/beer-yeast-xs.jpg"/>
<meta name="twitter:image:src" content="http://[illegible].com/images/a80e02dee816_9E41/peanuts-xs.jpg"/>
<meta name="twitter:image:src" content="http://[illegible].com/images/a80e02dee816_9E41/rice-xs.jpg"/>
```

When anyone tweets with a link to your site, the tweet will contain the usual stuff, but Twitter also scrapes the card data. When viewing the Tweet, the default view is the summary of the tweet (140 characters), but that can now be expanded to show the full Twitter card data.

For more information on Twitter cards, I suggest you read this post on the Twitter website:

https://dev.twitter.com/docs/cards

Finally we have the Google + settings.

First of all, select the author of the homepage (usually yourself), from the dropdown box at the top. This ensures that you will be assigned the author in the source code, using the all-important rel="author" property.

The box underneath is only to be used if you have setup a business page on Google Plus for your website. If you have one, add the URL of the page here, and that page will be assigned as the publisher of the content on the site.

22.3. XML Sitemap Settings

From the SEO menu on the left of the WP Dashboard, select '**XML Sitemaps**'. Having an XML sitemap for your site is really important. While it's not much use to visitors, it's a big help to search engines, as they use it to find your site's content.

Incidentally, with good navigation on your site, a search box, and a well-designed homepage, your visitors should not need a sitemap in order to find your content!

On the SEO -> XML sitemaps settings, check the box at the top to enable XML sitemaps. The screen will then expand to show more options.

Under the '**User sitemap**' section, check the box for '**Disable author/user sitemap**'.

Under '**General settings**', I enable the pings to Yahoo and Ask.com, so that these search engines are also informed (Google is automatically informed), when new content is posted on the site.

Under the '**Exclude post types**', I have pages and media checked, so no sitemaps are generated for these types. The only post types I want included in my sitemap are the post articles, and if you setup your site the way I do in this book, you will too.

Under the '**Exclude taxonomies**', I check the Format box only. However, I setup my 'Category pages' and 'Tag pages', to show an introduction, followed by excerpts of all posts in that group. If you set up your category and tag pages the way I do, leave those boxes unchecked. If you have your category & tag pages set as default (without an introduction), then check those boxes too.

Under the '**Entries per page**', you have the option of limiting a sitemap to a certain number of entries. If you leave this blank, the plugin defaults to 1000. Since Google can read sitemaps with 10s of thousands of entries, I leave this box blank, and suggest you do too.

When you have finished, click the '**Save Settings**' button.

You can now grab the URL(s) of your sitemap(s), and submit them to Google. You can find the sitemap by clicking the button at the top:

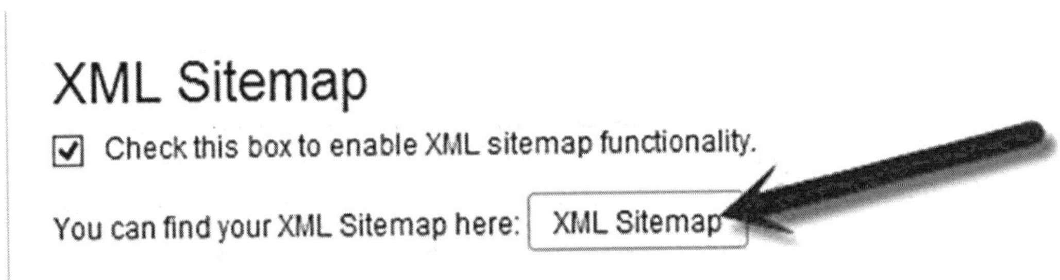

This opens the sitemap in your default web browser.

22.3.1. Submitting Your Sitemap(s) to Google

Earlier in the book, I recommended you sign up for Google Webmaster Tools (GWT). One of the reasons was to submit your sitemap(s) to Google, so that your site would be spidered and indexed quicker. By submitting your sitemap to Google, you are telling them directly that these are the important URLs for them to consider.

The first step is to login to GWT, and select the site you are working on. Then, in the side menu, go to **Crawl -> Sitemaps**.

In the top right of the sitemaps screen, you'll see a button to **Add/Test Sitemap**. Click it now.

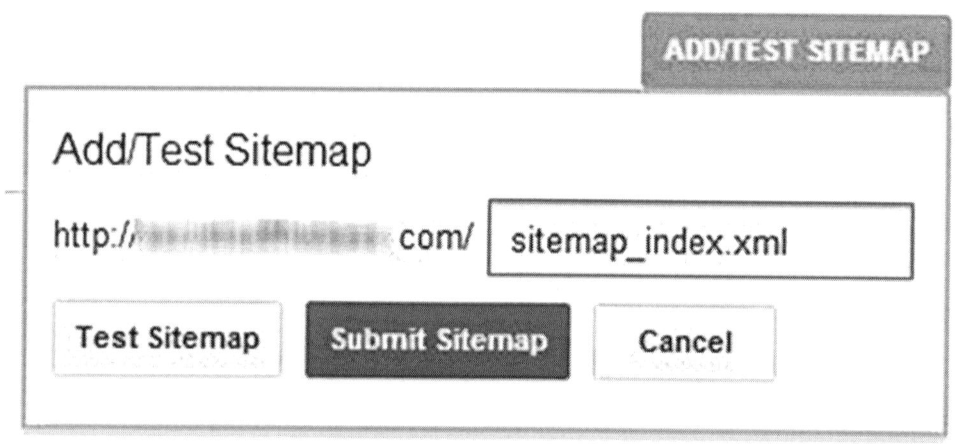

Complete the URL of your sitemap, and then click on the '**Submit Sitemap**' button.

NOTE: If you prefer, you can click the '**Test Sitemap**' button first to make sure you are using the correct URL, and that Google can crawl the sitemap properly. If you do that, just repeat the steps above to submit it once you are sure your sitemap status is okay.

Your newly submitted sitemap will be shown as pending. It usually takes a minute or two for Google to visit the sitemap and report back, so just wait a couple of minutes, and then refresh your browser. You should then see confirmation that Google spidered your sitemap and found the pages/images:

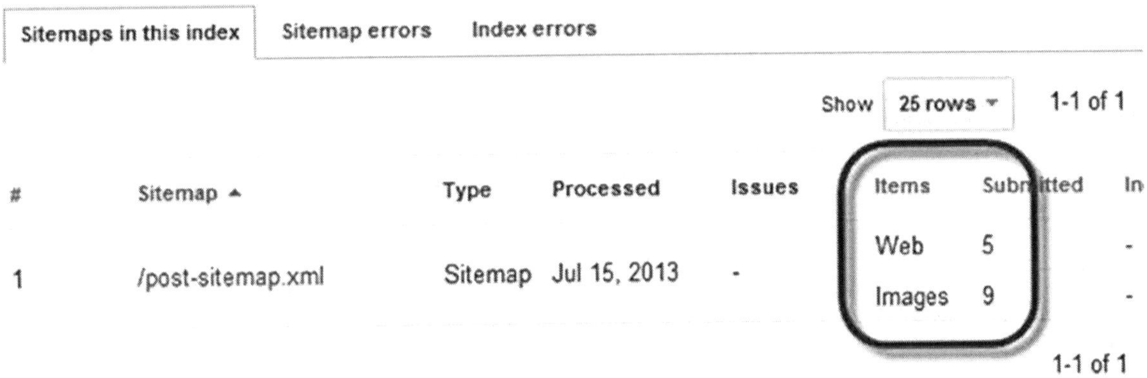

NOTE: If you have the '**Google XML Sitemap for Videos**' plugin installed, you can also submit your video sitemap in the same way.

22.4. Permalinks Settings

From the SEO menu on the left of the WP Dashboard, select '**Permalinks**'. These are basically the URLs of your pages as defined in the Settings -> Permalinks section of the Dashboard. We set those up earlier. However, the Yoast plugin gives us a few more options.

Remember when we setup the permalinks, I told you that category page URLs included the word 'category' in them? We had the opportunity to change that word to anything we chose, by entering a 'category base word'. Well Yoast's plugin allows you to remove the word 'category' altogether from all the category pages.

This is the first option on the '**Permalink Settings**' screen.

Personally, I leave it unchecked because I think the word 'category' helps both the search engines and site visitors, to know exactly where they are.

The second option of adding a trailing slash is also not needed, so leave that unchecked too.

The next option, '**Redirect attachment URLs to parent post URL**' is a good idea, so check that. When you upload a media file, WordPress creates an attachment file for the media, which can appear in the search engines. This option redirects these attachment files to the post the media was attached to instead.

The next two options, '**Remove the ?replytocom variables**', and '**Redirect ugly URLs..**' can both be left unchecked.

The final option on the permalinks screen is the '**Canonical Settings**'. This can be left as '**Leave default**'.

22.5. Internal Links Settings

From the SEO menu on the left of the WP Dashboard, select '**Internal Links**'. These options allow you to use breadcrumbs on your site. This is the navigation at the top of the post which shows a link to the home page, one to the category of the post, and the post name. They are designed to help visitors understand exactly where they are on your site.

I actually recommend you leave these settings blank, and just use the breadcrumb navigation that your theme is likely to have built into it.

22.6. RSS Settings

From the SEO menu on the left of the WP Dashboard, select '**RSS**'. The settings of the RSS screen are very useful and can help us combat spammers (the people who scrape our content using our RSS feeds, and then post it on their own sites). We can insert special text into the RSS feed, before, and/or after each item in the feed.

Yoast has set the default message as:

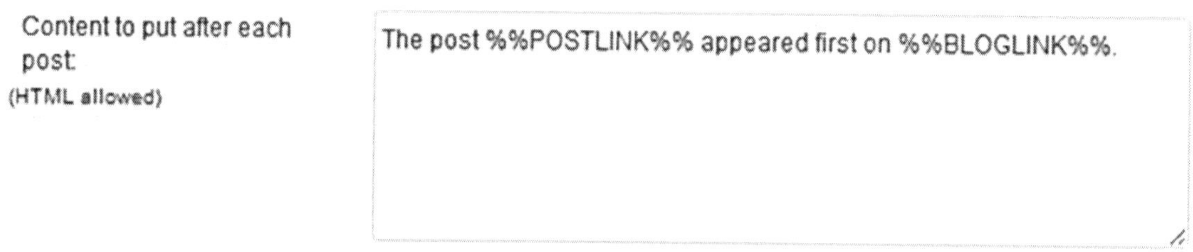

This text will be inserted after each item in the feed, with the variable **%%POSTLINK%%** replaced by a hyperlink to the post, using the post title as anchor text, and **%%BLOGLINK%%** replaced by a hyperlink using the name of our site as the anchor text.

Now, if any internet bot scrapes an article from the site and posts it on another site, this code will be inserted into that post, providing links to the original site. This can potentially help Google identify the original author (along with the Google authorship which we set up), so I would leave these settings at their default, with this code inserted into the '**Content to put after each post**' box.

22.7. Import & Export Settings

We can ignore these as they are used to import SEO settings from other popular SEO plugins.

22.8. Edit Files Settings

If you ever need to quickly edit your .htaccess file, you can do so here, as long as it is writable on your server. This is not something we need to do now though.

OK, those are the SEO settings for Yoast's excellent WordPress SEO plugin. This plugin gives us tremendous power and control over the 'SEO settings' for our site, and the content it hosts.

The final part of this book shows how to setup another very important SEO plugin called '**W3 Total Cache**'. It helps to speed up the load times of your website, so is very useful. Let's take a closer look.

23. W3 Total Cache Setup

W3 Total Cache is one of two very good WordPress caching plugins. The other is WP Super Cache. If you are a WordPress veteran, and have always used, and are happy with WP Super Cache, then I suggest you continue to use it.

If you have used W3 Total Cache before and know how to set it up for your server, then simply ignore this section.

Setting up W3 Total cache can be a little hit and miss sometimes, with some servers (or scripts on pages), disliking specific things you try to enable. It is therefore imperative that you make a backup of your database before you start to set up this plugin. For free, efficient backups, I recommend the '**WP-DB Manager**' plugin, mentioned earlier in the plugins section of this book.

I won't be covering all of the settings of this plugin. I will set you up with a good basic configuration though, and one which should be compatible with most servers, templates, plugins and scripts. However, if you find your site has any problem loading, simply reverse the changes you made, or deactivate the plugin altogether.

OK, so before we look at how to setup this plugin, let's just cover the why again. Here are a couple of reasons *why* a caching plugin is a good idea.

1. In terms of SEO, the faster the site loads the better.
2. In terms of your visitor, no one likes to hang around waiting for your web page loads. If it takes too long (we're talking in seconds here), then they'll be hitting the back button and checking out your competitor sites instead.

23.1. Setting up W3 Total Cache

I will assume you have already installed and activated the plugin, since we covered that earlier.

In your WordPress Dashboard (left side column), you have a new set of items under the '**Performance**' menu.

NOTE: I won't cover all of these settings, so just change the ones I do mention to the appropriate values. Assume that all other settings can be left at their default values.

23.1.1. General Settings

Click on the '**General Settings**' menu item.

This is where we can toggle the various caches on or off. Once they are toggled on, we go to another area of the settings to configure each of the caches.

Page Cache:

1. Enable page cache.
2. Page cache method - Disk enhanced.

Minify:

1. Enable minify.
2. Minify mode set to auto.
3. Minify cache method - Disk.
4. HTML minifier - Default
5. JS Minifier - JSMin (default)
6. CSS minifier - Default

Database Cache:

1. Enable database cache.
2. Database Cache Method - Disk

Object Cache:

1. Enable object cache.
2. Object cache method - Disk.

Browser cache:

1. Enable browser cache.

CDN:

Leave disabled for now. This is something you can activate and setup later, but you should contact your host support first, as some hosts, like StableHost, have easy integration with CDN, and it made a big difference to the stability of my site.

All other settings on the General Settings menu can be left at their default values.

Make sure you click the '**Save all settings**' button before moving on.

Return now to the '**Performance**' menu on the left of the WP Dashboard. You need to select each of the following items it in turn, and configure their settings as follows:

23.1.2. Page Cache

General:

1. Enable 'Cache front page'.
2. Enable 'Cache feeds: site, categories, tags, comments'.
3. Enable 'Cache requests only for mydomain.com site address'.
4. Enable 'Don't cache pages for logged in users'.

Leave all other settings in the Page Cache at their default settings.

23.1.3. Minify

General:

1. Enable 'Rewrite URL structure'.
2. Set 'Minify error notification' to Admin Notification.

HTML & XML:

1. Enable HTML minify settings.
2. Check Inline CSS minification.
3. Check inline JS minification.
4. Check line break removal.

23.1.4. Browser Cache

General:

1. Enable 'Set last-modified header'.
2. Enable 'Set expires header'.
3. Enable 'Set cache control header'.
4. Set 'Entity tag (eTag)'.
5. Set 'W3 Total Cache header'.
6. Enable 'HTTP (gzip compression)'.

That's it! Your W3 Total Cache is now configured with conservative settings.

Now go back to the '**Performance**' menu on the left of the WP Dashboard, and click on the button at the top to '**empty all caches**'.

Now head on over to GTMetrix.com and check your homepage speed. After the first check, hit the back button and check it a second time. The first time will take longer, but now the page is cached, so the second run will give you a better idea of your true page load time.

Here is one of my pages **BEFORE** installing W3 Total Cache:

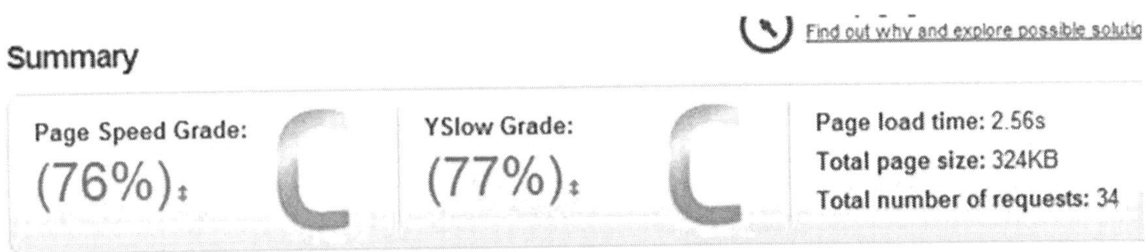

And here is the same page **AFTER** W3 cache was installed and configured (these are the results on the second run after clearing the cache):

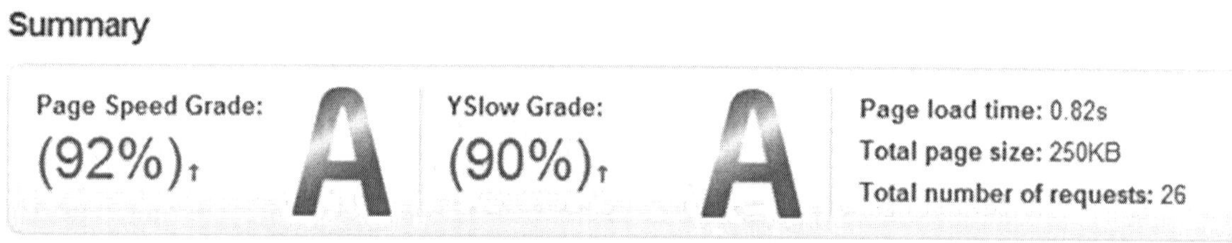

NOTE: I found a problem running '**VIA Curation**' plugin on one of my sites with W3 Total cache activated. The submission form would fail to render sometimes. The solution was to exclude the submission form page from W3 Total Cache.

You'll see a box in the Page Cache section. To find it go to Performance -> Page Cache -> Advanced -> Never cache the following pages:

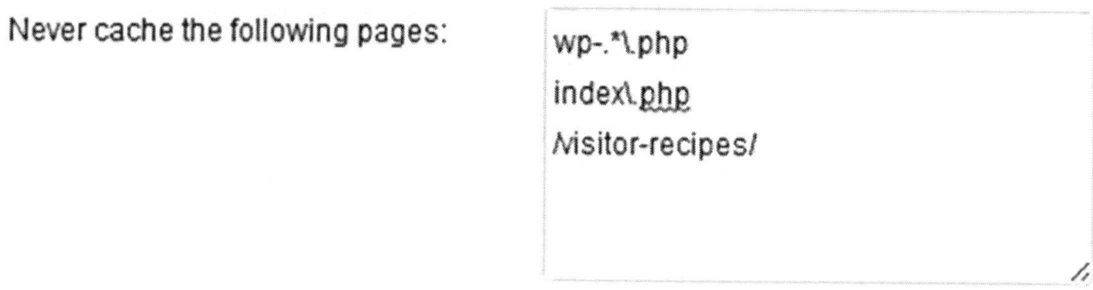

Just enter the slug of the page (page filename), into the box. There may already be items in there, so just add your page(s) at the end.

Useful resources

All resources mentioned in this book can be found here:

http://ezseonews.com/wpseo

Please leave a review on Amazon

If you enjoyed this book, or even if you didn't, I'd love to hear your comments about it. You can leave your thoughts on the Amazon website.

Search Amazon for **B00ECF70HU**

My other Kindle books

NOTE: All of these books are available in Kindle & paperback format. They are all available on Amazon.

SEO 2013 & Beyond

Search Engine Optimization will Never be the Same Again!

On February 11th, 2011, Google dropped a bombshell on the SEO community when they released the Panda update. Panda was designed to remove low quality content from the search engine results pages. The surprise to many webmasters were some of the big name casualties that got taken out by the update.

On 24th April 2012, Google went in for the kill when they released the Penguin update. Few SEOs that had been in the business for any length of time could believe the carnage that this update caused. If Google's Panda was a 1 on the Richter scale of updates, Penguin was surely a 10. It completely changed the way we needed to think about SEO.

On September 28th 2012, Google released a new algorithm update targeting exact match domains (EMDs). I have updated this book to let you know the consequences of owning EMDs, and added my own advice on choosing domain names. While I have never been a huge fan of exact match domains anyway, many other SEO books and courses teach you to use them. I'll tell you why I think those other courses and books are wrong. The EMD update was sandwiched in between another Panda update (on the 27th September) and another Penguin update (5th October).

Whereas Panda seems to penalize low quality content, Penguin is more concerned about overly aggressive SEO tactics. The stuff that SEOs had been doing for years, not only didn't work anymore, but could now actually cause your site to be penalized and drop out of the rankings. That's right, just about everything you have been taught about Search Engine Optimization in the last 10 years can be thrown out the Window. Google have moved the goal posts.

I have been working in SEO for around 10 years at the time of writing, and have always tried to stay within the guidelines laid down by Google. This has not always been easy because to compete with other sites, it often meant using techniques that Google frowned upon. Now, if you use those techniques, Google is likely to catch up with you and demote your rankings. In this book, I want to share with you the new

SEO. **The SEO for 2013 and Beyond.**

Search Amazon for **B0099RKXE8**

An SEO Checklist

A step-by-step plan for fixing SEO problems with your web site

A step-by-step plan for fixing SEO problems with your web site

Pre-Panda and pre-Penguin, Google tolerated certain activities. Post-Panda and post-Penguin, they don't. As a result, they are now enforcing their Webmaster Guidelines which is something that SEOs never really believed Google would do! Essentially, Google have become far less tolerant of activities that they see as rank manipulation.

As webmasters, we have been given a choice. Stick to Google's rules, or lose out on free traffic from the world's biggest search engine.

Those that had abused the rules in the past got a massive shock. Their website(s), which may have been at the top of Google for several years, dropped like a stone. Rankings gone, literally overnight!

To have any chance of recovery, you MUST clean up that site. However, for most people, trying to untangle the SEO mess that was built up over several years is not always easy. Where do you start?

That's why this book was written. It provides a step-by-step plan to fix a broken site. This book contains detailed checklists plus an explanation of why those things are so important.

The checklists in this book are based on the SEO that I use on a daily basis. It's the SEO I teach my students, and it's the SEO that I know works. For those that embrace the recent changes, SEO has actually become easier as we no longer have to battle against other sites whose SEO was done 24/7 by an automated tool or an army of cheap labor. Those sites have largely been removed, and that has leveled the playing field.

If you have a site that lost its rankings, this book gives you a step-by-step plan and checklist to fix problems that are common causes of ranking penalties.

Search Amazon for **BOOBXFAULK**

Kindle Publishing

Format, Publish & Promote your books on Kindle

Why Publish on Amazon Kindle?

Kindle publishing has captured the imagination of aspiring writers. Now, more than at any other time in our history, an opportunity is knocking. Getting your books published no longer means sending out hundreds of letters to publishers and agents. It no longer means getting hundreds of rejection letters back. Today, you can write and publish your own books on Amazon Kindle without an agent or publisher.

Is it Really Possible to Make a Good Income as an Indie Author?

The fact that you are reading this book description tells me you are interested in publishing your own material on Kindle. You may have been lured here by promises of quick riches. Well, I have good news and bad. The bad news is that publishing and profiting from Kindle takes work and dedication. Don't just expect to throw up sub-par material and make a killing in sales. You need to produce good stuff to be successful at this. The good news is that you can make a very decent living from writing and publishing on Kindle.

My own success with Kindle Publishing

As I explain at the beginning of this book, I published my first Kindle book in August 2012, yet by December 2012, just 5 months later, I was making what many people consider being a full time income. As part of my own learning experience, I setup a Facebook page in July 2012 to share my Kindle publishing journey (there is a link to the Facebook page inside this book). On that Facebook page, I shared the details of what I did, and problems I needed to overcome. I also shared my growing income reports, and most of all, I offered help to those who asked for it. What I found was a huge and growing audience for this type of education, and ultimately, that's why I wrote this book.

What's in this Book?

This book covers what I have learned on my journey and what has worked for me. I have included sections to answer the questions I myself asked, as well as those questions people asked me. This book is a complete reference manual for successfully formatting, publishing & promoting your books on Amazon Kindle. There is even a section for non-US publishers because there is stuff there you specifically need to know. I see enormous potential in Kindle Publishing, and in 2013 I intend to grow this side of my own business. Kindle publishing has been liberating for me and I am sure it will be for you too.

Search Amazon for **BOOBEIX34C**

CSS for Beginners

Learn CSS with detailed instructions, step-by-step screenshots and video tutorials showing CSS in action on real sites

Most websites and blogs you visit use cascading style sheets (CSS) for everything from fonts selection & formatting, to layout & design. Whether you are building WordPress sites or traditional HTML websites, this book aims to take the complete beginner to a level where they are comfortable digging into the CSS code and making changes to their own site. This book will show you how to make formatting & layout changes to your own projects quickly and easily.

The book covers the following topics:

- Why CSS is important
- Classes, Pseudo Classes, Pseudo Elements & IDs
- The Float property
- Units of Length
- Using DIVs
- Tableless Layouts, including how to create 2-column and 3-column layouts
- The Box Model
- Creating Menus with CSS
- Images & background images

The hands on approach of this book will get YOU building your own Style Sheets from scratch. Also included in this book:

- Over 160 screenshots and 20,000 words detailing ever step you need to take.
- Full source code for all examples shown.
- Video Tutorials.

The video tutorials accompanying this book show you:

- How to investigate the HTML & CSS behind any website.
- How to experiment with your own design in real time, and only make the changes permanent on your site when you are ready.

A basic knowledge of HTML is recommended, although all source code from the book can be downloaded and used as you work through the book.

Search Amazon for **B00AFV44NS**

Migrating to Windows 8

For computer users without a touch screen, coming from XP, Vista or Windows 7

Review: "What Microsoft should buy and give away now to drive sales"

New PCs are coming pre-installed with Windows 8, Microsoft's new incarnation of the popular operating system. The problem is, the PCs it is installed on are not usually equipped with the piece of hardware that Windows 8 revolves around - a touch screen.

Windows 8 is probably the least user-friendly version of the operating system ever released. It's almost like two different operating systems merged together. From the lack of a start menu, to features that only really make sense on a tablet or phone, Windows 8 has a lot of veteran Windows users scratching their heads. If you are one of them, then this book is for you.

After a quick tour of the new user interface, the book digs deeper into the features of Windows 8, showing you what everything does, and more importantly, how to do the things you used to do on older versions of Windows. The comprehensive "How to" section answers a lot of the questions new users have, and there's also a complete keyboard shortcut list for reference.

If you are migrating to Windows 8 from XP, Vista or Windows 7, then this book may just let you keep your hair as you learn how to get the most out of your computer. Who knows, you may even get to like Windows 8.

Search Amazon for **B00CJ8AD9E**

More information from Dr. Andy Williams

If you would like more information, tips, tutorials or advice, there are two resources you might like to consider.

The first is my free weekly newsletter over at ezSEONews.com offering tips, tutorials and advice to online marketers and webmasters. Just sign up and my newsletter, plus SEO articles, will be delivered to your inbox. I cannot always promise a weekly schedule, but I do try ;)

I also run a course over at CreatingFatContent.com, where I build real websites in front of members in "real-time" using my system of SEO.

9646266R00226

Printed in Great Britain
by Amazon.co.uk, Ltd.,
Marston Gate.